Logic, Thought and Language

ROYAL INSTITUTE OF PHILOSOPHY SUPPLEMENT: 51

EDITED BY

Anthony O'Hear

CAMBRIDGE
UNIVERSITY PRESS

PUBLISHED BY THE PRESS SYNDICATE OF THE UNIVERSITY OF CAMBRIDGE
The Pitt Building, Trumpington Street, Cambridge, CB2 1RP,
United Kingdom

CAMBRIDGE UNIVERSITY PRESS
The Edinburgh Building, Cambridge CB2 2RU, United Kingdom
40 West 20th Street, New York, NY 10011–4211, USA
477 Williamstown Road, Port Melbourne, VIC 3207, Australia

Printed in the United Kingdom at the University Press, Cambridge
Typeset by Michael Heath Ltd, Reigate, Surrey

*A catalogue record for this book is available
from the British Library*

Library of Congress Cataloguing-in-Publication Data applied for

ISBN 0 521 52966 2 paperback
ISSN 1358-2461

Contents

Contents

Preface

The essays collected in this book are based on the lectures given in London as part of the Royal Institute of Philosophy's annual lecture series for 2000–2001. In the essays the contributors each took an important theme in current philosophical debate and developed it in his or her own way. I think that the collection as a whole will be seen as an important contribution to the contemporary philosophical discussion of mind and language.

On behalf of the Royal Institute of Philosophy, I would like to thank the contributors for their lectures and essays. I have, though sadly to record that Gregory McCulloch died prematurely, shortly after giving his lecture. An original and wide-ranging thinker, he will be sorely missed.

I would also like to thank Sophie Allen for her painstaking editorial work and for compiling the index.

Anthony O'Hear

Notes on Contributors

R. M. Sainsbury
Professor of Philosophy at King's College London.

Gregory McCulloch
Formerly Professor of Philosophy at the University of Birmingham.

Julia Tanney
Lecturer in Philosophy in the School of European Culture and Languages at the University of Kent.

Alan Millar
Professor of Philosophy at the University of Stirling.

Gabriel M. A. Segal
Professor of Philosophy at King's College London.

Crispin Wright
Professor of Logic and Metaphysics and Wardlaw Professor at the University of St Andrews.

Christopher Peacocke
Professor of Philosophy at New York University.

A. W. Moore
Tutor and lecturer in Philosophy at St Hugh's College, Oxford.

M. G. F. Martin
Professor of Philosophy at University College London.

Scott Sturgeon
Lecturer in Philosophy at Birkbeck College London.

Timothy Williamson
Wykeham Professor of Logic at New College, Oxford.

S. G. Williams
Lecturer in Philosophy at Worcester College, Oxford.

Bob Hale
Professor of Philosophy at the University of Glasgow.

Charles Travis
Professor of Philosophy at Northwestern University.

What logic should we think with?

R. M. SAINSBURY

Logic ought to guide our thinking. It is better, more rational, more intelligent to think logically than to think illogically. Illogical thought leads to bad judgment and error. In any case, if logic had no role to play as a guide to thought, why should we bother with it?

The somewhat naïve opinions of the previous paragraph are subject to attack from many sides. It may be objected that an activity does not count as thinking at all unless it is at least minimally logical, so logic is constitutive of thought rather than a guide to it. Or it may be objected that whereas logic describes a system of timeless relations between propositions, thinking is a dynamic process involving revisions, and so could not use a merely static guide. Or again the objection may be that there is no such thing as logic, only a whole variety of different logics, not all of which could possibly be good guides.

I aim to disarm the last two objections to the initial idea that logic should be a guide to thought.

1. Logic and belief revision

How could logic guide our thought? Anything we can believe has an infinite number of logical consequences, but no sensible guide would tell us to take steps to believe all the logical consequences of anything we believe, for there is not enough time to obey and most of the added beliefs would be trivial.

There is something to the idea that we should consider our beliefs not just one by one but in larger groups, to see if we can logically extract some useful further information. We might try to implement this idea by the following prescription:

1. If some set of propositions X logically entails a proposition A and one believes each member of X then one should also believe A.

One problem has already been noted: (1) would require us to believe too much useless stuff (we would, for example, be endlessly forming conjunctions of our beliefs, to no good purpose). So an account of how logic might guide thought must somehow concern only

1

some subset of logical space, and must balance processing costs against cognitive gains.

The problem with (1) is not confined to the excessive number of propositions it would have us believe. A speedy being who, unlike us, could form one new belief in one second, another in half a second, a third in a quarter of a second, and so on, could form an infinity of beliefs in a couple of seconds. Prescription (1) does not give good advice even to such a speedy creature, for it takes no account of dynamic updating. Suppose such a creature set out to Gordon Square on Thursday 12th October 2000 believing that a logic lecture is to be held there on that day. Finding on his arrival that there is no lecture, he is not required, by logic or anything else, to believe that there both is and is not a lecture, despite the fact that A, B ⊢ A & B; that is, despite the fact that the contradiction is entailed by things he believes. Prescription (1) makes it sound as if all a rational creature does is add beliefs; there is no account of how they are taken away.

Logical entailment is one crucial logical relation, and its natural application as a guide is additive. But (1) provides nothing to control increase. We do better, I think, to concentrate on the closely related logical relation of inconsistency. In its immediate application, it decreases rather than increases beliefs: discovery of an inconsistency in our beliefs should make us abandon a belief. A first attempt to exploit inconsistency in finding a role for logic as a guide might be this:

2. One whose logical commitments are logically inconsistent should revise his beliefs in such a way that the commitments are consistent.

The main problem is that the inconsistency might be unrecognized, in which case the thinker would have no good reason to revise one of his commitments. Here is an example which illustrates this:

On Monday, James tells you that Jane was at the party and you believe him. On Wednesday, George tells you that Jane was not at the party and you believe him. You do not revise your previously formed belief, because it does not come to mind. If you were asked on Friday whether or not Jane was at the party, it's a toss up whether you would say Yes or No or something else. Under these circumstances, you've done nothing irrational. The irrational thing would have been to engage in belief revision with no reason before your mind.

It may be objected that we have a standing reason to scan all the time for inconsistency. But this is not a reason we recognize. Constant scanning would take up time and energy; we need a specific reason to use up these resources, and the mere abstract possibility of an inconsistency is not enough. Moreover, the prescription is too general: it does not give any clue about where to look for inconsistency, and this increases the probability that the effort would be wasted.

At least part of the problem is addressed by the following:

3. One who realizes that his logical commitments are logically inconsistent should revise his beliefs in such a way that the commitments are consistent.

But suppose the inconsistency is completely unimportant to you? Reverting to the displayed example, suppose you have no interest in whether or not Jane was at the party? Why should you invest effort in adjusting your beliefs, even if you recognize their inconsistency? That you should not becomes plainer when we consider the options in more detail:

(a) Resolve the contradiction by seeking out further information.

This may be impossible or absurdly costly. James and George may both now be dead, you may have no access to any other Jane-related informants, and so on. It would be crazy to say that logic requires you to hire a private detective to help gather evidence which might resolve this trivial matter.

(b) Abandon one or other of the beliefs without seeking further information.

But how to choose? As James and George are equally reliable, there is no reason for either choice.

(c) Abandon both beliefs.

This sounds appealing, but it may be a bad strategy. Suppose you learn that if Jane was at the party something terrible will happen to you unless you take a low-cost preventative measure, P. If you have simply abandoned your belief that Jane was at the party, this new information gives you no reason to do P. But intuitively you do have a reason.

The problem with (3) was that it paid no attention to the relation between the costs and the benefits of revision. We can at least gesture towards the needed comparison as follows:

3

4. One who realizes that his logical commitments are logically inconsistent has a defeasible reason to try to revise his beliefs in such a way that the commitments are consistent.

I do not hold this up as a final statement of a way in which logic could act as a guide. (For one thing, a more finished account should talk in terms of degrees of belief and commitment.) However, it should encourage optimism about the prospects for a substantive and intuitively satisfactory relationship between the static relations of logic and the dynamics of thought. A defeasible reason is one that can be overridden by others, and the range of potentially defeating reasons are intended to include the ratio of the importance of the topic to the amount of effort that would be required to arrive at a well grounded resolution. (Whether 'ratio' is to be taken literally as a number is one of the many issues that would arise in a detailed study of this issue.)

Prescription (4) is not intended to exhaust the possible ways in which logic could properly guide thought. It is consistent with the opinion that a logical principle should also serve as a guide in the sense of something we (perhaps implicitly, thanks to good training) consult when we think.

2. Which logic should we choose as our guide?

When people speak of logic without qualification, they probably mean classical logic: the logic of first order quantification with identity. This is a recent phenomenon, and we should not forget the enormous variety of alternatives to classical logic that have been proposed, of which the following list gives a sample of points of divergence from classical logic:

* Double negation:
    Classical logic accepts the inference from 'not not A' to 'A'; intuitionist logic does not.
* Existential import
    Classical logic rejects the inference from 'All Fs are G' to 'Some Fs are G'; Aristotelian logic accepts it.
* Disjunctive syllogism:
    Classical logic accepts the inference from 'A or B' together with 'not A' to 'B'; relevance and paraconsistent logics do not.
* Modus ponens:
    Classical logic accepts the inference from 'if A then B' together with 'A' to 'B'; some fuzzy logics do not.

* Ex Contradictione Quodlibet:
  Classical logic accepts the inference from 'A and not A' to 'B', where 'B' is an arbitrary proposition; paraconsistent logic does not.
* De Morgan
  Quantum logic rejects de Morgan's laws.
* Instantiation:
  Classical logic accepts the inference from 'Everything is F' to 'α is F'; free logic does not.
* Negation
  Classical logic holds that negation toggles between truth and falsehood; option negation denies this.
* Conditionalizing disjunctions:
  Classical logic accepts the inference from 'A or B' to 'if not A then B'; probabilistic logic does not.

Logics can differ about what they count as an inconsistency. For example, within some free logics the beliefs that *everything is self-identical* and *Vulcan is not self-identical* are consistent, but they are classically inconsistent. So the objection that we cannot simply hold that 'logic' should be our guide is correct. We have to choose the right logic. But how could this choice be made? Will not making it inevitably involve reasoning, in which case some logic is already presupposed? The remainder of this paper addresses this methodological issue. I introduce it by considering how one might argue for or against the last three non-classical logics on my sample list.

Instantiation:

Classical logic adopts the following rule of instantiation:

If $X \vdash \forall v \varphi v$ then $X \vdash \varphi \alpha$

If some set of sentences entails a universal generalization, then that same set of sentences entails what results by deleting the quantifier in the generalization and putting a name in place of every occurrence of the quantifier's variable. A natural application to English suggests we should regard the following as valid:

5. Everything is perishable, therefore Socrates is perishable.

But intuitively this is not valid: it could be that everything is perishable and Socrates is not (if he did not exist).

This is straightforwardly accommodated by the free logical instantiation rule:

If $X \vdash \forall v \varphi v$ then $\{X, \exists v(v = \alpha)\} \vdash \varphi \alpha$

R. M. Sainsbury

We have to supplement the premises which sustain the generalization with one which affirms the existence of the object we will use in the instantiation. This supplementation does not occur in (5), so (5) is not validated by the free logical instantiation rule.

We have here an argument, eminently defeasible of course, for preferring some version of free logic to classical logic: free logic respects intuitions about validity which classical logic does not.[1]

The argument is defeasible because it provides no reason for thinking that only free logic can deliver appropriate judgments of validity. Perhaps other adjustments to classical logic can conform to the alleged datum (the invalidity of (5)), and this shows that the argument, even if good against classical logic, does not point specifically towards free logic.

It is also defeasible because the claim on which it rests, the invalidity of (5), can itself be challenged. Perhaps when we assess validity we should hold the domain constant. When we ask after the validity of an argument we start with the objects actually involved in the premises, whether as objects quantified over or objects referred to; the worlds relevant to validity are those containing just these objects. On this ruling, only worlds containing Socrates are relevant to the validity of (5), and the case envisaged, in which Socrates does not exist, is irrelevant. So we should reject the alleged datum.

This suggestion does not accord with classical semantics, so it would in any case involve moving away from classical logic, even if not in the direction of free logic. But the suggestion about validity does not accord with our intuitions or our best judgments. Consider the following argument:

6. Everything is a duck; so everything flies.

Suppose that all actual ducks are essentially fliers, but that if evolution in New Zealand had taken a slightly different course its range of flightless birds would have included flightless ducks. Holding the domain constant would rule that (6) is valid: every world containing just the ducks our world contains verifies the conclusion if it verifies the premise. But intuitively the possibility of flightless ducks shows that it could be that everything is a duck without everything flying, and this intuitively establishes the invalidity of the argument.

Classical logic could accommodate the validity of (5) by resisting the formalization of the premise as no more complex than '$\forall x F x$'.

---

[1] I first heard the argument from Yannis Stephanou, though he does does not himself endorse it.

Why not treat 'Everything is physical' as having the same form as 'Every ring is circular'? Then (5) would be formalized by the invalid

$$\forall x \ (Fx \rightarrow Gx) \vdash G\alpha$$

which shows that the original argument was wrong not in its datum (the invalidity of (5)) but in its assumption that this could not be accounted for classically: (5) is invalid because it lacks the premise 'Socrates is a thing' ($F\alpha$). (A similar result would be attained within an essentially classical framework by formalizing with binary quantifiers.)

In this discussion free use has been made of intuitions (beliefs held with justification but without ground) and of principles of reasoning. There was no sense that we could not start reasoning until we had resolved the question of which logic to use as our guide.

Option negation:

The capacity for deliberative choice is at least no less developmentally basic than the capacity for language. Any language user must be capable of deliberative choice, and arguably some non-language-users (for example, apes) have the latter capacity. It is therefore not crazy to look to the preconditions for deliberative choice for guidance about the character of language. The suggestion I wish to consider is that the exercise of choice requires a concept of negation which has had a hand in moulding the behaviour of current words for negation.

A chooser must take herself to be confronted with a range of options. We think of the options as exclusive, and the suggestion is that this exclusivity generates the distinctive concept of option negation. I see my options for action as A and B. To select A is to deselect B: NOT-B expresses this deselection. In the context, A and NOT-B are equivalent, and so are NOT-A and B. If we think of the options as marking the truth or falsity of some statement, option negation will behave classically: deselecting truth amounts to selecting falsehood, that is, NOT-true amounts to false; and NOT-false amounts to true.

Within the structure of options, option negation is a more general notion than classical negation, and can explain otherwise puzzling features of negation. For example, not only are the following never normally heard as inconsistent, it is impossible to hear them as inconsistent:

7. It's not a car, it's a Volkswagen.

R. M. Sainsbury

8. No, I have not *pak edd zee soo eet cass ez*. I have packed the
suitcases.[2]

Presumably the advertising agency thought there would be something striking about (7), but they certainly did not suppose the audience would infer that a Volkswagen is not a car, which would be a
classical consequence. One could imagine (8) uttered with some irritation as a response to 'Af you pak edd zee soo eet cass ez?' by one
who has tried to help the speaker with her pronunciation. Again, it
is classically inconsistent, but it is impossible to hear it thus. This is
hard to explain classically, since any 'pragmatic' account should presumably start with perceived literal inconsistency, and that is just
what, I think, cannot be perceived.

Within the option negation framework, all is straightforward. In
(7) the options are to call it a car or to call it a Volkswagen, and the
former is deselected. In the (8) the options are to say 'I af pak edd
zee soo eet cass ez' or to say 'I have packed the suitcases' and the
former is deselected. All interpretation involves bringing to bear
something more than what is usually counted as semantic knowledge, for example a hearer must at a minimum know what language
the speaker is speaking. In the case of option negation the hearer
must latch on to the relevant options, and an account must be given
of how this is possible. The problem seems much more tractable
within this framework, however, for a basic notion in dialogue is
what the right thing to say is, where the right thing does not equate
to a true thing, and applying this notion to both (7) and (8) gives an
appropriate result: the right thing to say is that it's a Volkswagen,
not that it's a car, and the right thing to say is 'I have packed the
suitcases', not 'I af pak edd zee soo eet cass ez'. This seems much
more straightforward, and amenable to systematic theory, than an
account which begins by attributing to the hearer a realization of
the literal inconsistency of (7) and (8).

It is a striking feature of our conception of options for action that
the discovery that two options we have been considering can be
combined is represented as a third option: A, or B, or both. (The
discovery of this third option seems often to be made by the more
intelligent of parties to a discussion of what to do.) Option negation
now manifestly differs radically from classical negation, for NOT-
both amounts to A or B; and NOT-A amounts to B or both. 'Both'

[2] Examples of this kind abound in Horn, L. R. (1989) *A Natural History
of Negation* (Chicago: University of Chicago Press), who uses them to
ground a distinct notion of negation which he calls 'metalinguistic
negation'.

differs from 'and', for 'both(A,B)' entails 'NOT-A' and also 'NOT-B'. Likewise 'neither' is a further option, so a common choice situation is A, B, both or neither. Such a four way partition could be used to model a system of truth values allowing for both gluts and gaps, as well as plain truth and falsehood, so the options for a statement are: true, false, both or neither. 'Both' entails 'NOT-true' and also 'NOT-false'.

This may seem mere idling: anyone can invent a strange particle which behaves in odd ways. In defence of option negation, I plead its basis in the notion of choice, and its capacity to explain oddities about our actual uses of negative particles. Here is a further oddity. Berkeley accused Locke of 'manifest contradiction' when, in speaking of the abstract idea of a triangle, he said that

> it must be neither oblique nor rectangle, neither equilateral, equicrural, nor scalenon; but all and none of these at once. (*Essay* 4.7.9)

I suspect I am not alone in thinking that there is a natural and consistent interpretation of Locke's words 'all and none of these at once'. We cannot consistently apply both 'equicrural' and 'scalenon', but I wish to focus just on whether 'all and none' is automatically inconsistent. Within the option negation framework, it is not. Taking 'all' as an extension of 'both', it actually entails NOT-o, for each other option o, and 'none' could be seen as summarizing these entailments.[3]

What counts as inconsistent within an option negation framework differs from what counts as inconsistent within the classical framework, so if logic is to be a guide in anything like the envisaged way we have to make a choice. The point of the present discussion is not to make that choice, but only to point out that one cannot rule out in advance the possible relevance of empirical data about how we have developed as agents. It is supposed to be an empirical and historical fact that our actual use of negation grew out of option negation. This is in principle susceptible of aposteriori confirmation or disconfirmation. This suggests that it is possible to have evidence of an aposteriori kind for or against a logical principle, and that this evidence can be what Field has

---

[3] At a conference on the history of logic at King's College London in November 2000, Graham Priest cited Plotinus as an example of an early dialetheist: 'The One is all things and no one of them.' If Plotinus was operating in the option negation framework, we need not see him as affirming anything inconsistent.

called primary: it is evidence which in principle could outweigh non-empirical evidence.[4]

Conditionalizing disjunctions:

Classical logic accepts the inference from 'A or B' to 'if not A then B'; probabilistic logic does not. So classically, but not probabilistically, the combination '(A or B) but not: (if not A then B)' is inconsistent. We need to choose between these logics.

The discussion is not (and could not be) supposed to impugn the validity of the pattern:

$$A \lor B; \text{ so } \neg A \rightarrow B.$$

But if a logic is to apply to our thought, it must do so via our natural expression of thought, our natural language. Strictly speaking, then, the first paragraph of this section should claim that, as most obviously applied to natural language, classical logic accepts the inference from 'A or B' to 'if not A then B'.

A much discussed instance of the principle is the following:

9. Either the gardener did it or the butler did it; so if the gardener didn't do it, the butler did.[5]

The following seems a reasonable system of belief.

The most likely hypothesis is that the gardener did it and got the butler to act as his accomplice, but the butler would never have acted alone: he is too decent a chap, just suffers from weak will, and the gardener can be very persuasive.

One who has these beliefs is committed to thinking it highly likely that either the gardener did it or the butler did it. But it seems that he could hardly think it at all likely that if the gardener didn't do it, then the butler did. On the contrary, he must think that if the gardener didn't do it, it's very unlikely that the butler did: the butler would not have acted alone. So it seems to be reasonable to assign a high probability to the premise and a low probability to the conclusion. Yet if an argument is valid in the classical sense, the conclusion has to be true if the premise is, and so it would not be reasonable to assign the premise a much higher probability than the conclusion.

[4] Field, Hartry (1996), 'The aprioricity of logic', *Proceedings of the Aristotelian Society* **96**, 359–79.

[5] Cf. Stalnaker, Robert (1975), 'Indicative conditionals', *Philosophia* **5**, 269–86. Reprinted in Jackson, Frank (ed.), *Conditionals*, (Oxford: Oxford University Press), pp. 136–54.

The same point can be illustrated with numerical assignments. A probability function which makes the following assignments seems perfectly reasonable:

Pr(The gardener did it) = 0.9; hence
Pr(The gardener did it or the butler did it) $\geq$ 0.9
Pr(If the gardener did not do it, the butler did) = 0.1.

The last probability is a consequence of one's supposition that it is highly unlikely that the butler acted alone. An argument with a premise to which it is reasonable to assign high probability and a conclusion to which it is reasonable (in the same informational state) to assign low probability is not valid.

Some other examples of the same pattern of argument are more likely to strike one intuitively as invalid:

Either I'll catch my train or I'll be on time for work; so if I miss my train I'll be on time for work.[6]
Either he'll throw an even number or he'll throw a 6; so if he doesn't thrown an even number, he'll throw a 6.

It may be objected that the argument proves too much. Suppose *modus ponens* is valid. Even so, one could reasonably assign high probability to A and to if A then B without automatically assigning high probability to B. For example, I believe that there are some unsold tickets and that if there are some unsold tickets I will be able to buy one at the door. I am highly confident in both beliefs, which entail that I will be able to buy one at the door. Yet when I arrive I find that I cannot buy one at the door: they have all been sold in an unexpected late afternoon rush. I then assign zero probability to the proposition that I will be able to buy one at the door. Should we conclude that *modus ponens* is not valid? Obviously not. But this case differs from the one relating to the gardener and the butler (9), for in the present case the high probability assigned to the premises does or should change when the new information revises the probability of the conclusion down to zero. In (9), by contrast, the probability assignments are rationally cotenable in a single informational state.

I conclude that (9) is indeed invalid and hence that either classical logic must be revised or it must not profess to be able to formalize English conditionals as material conditionals. As in the previous cases in which an alternative to classical logic has been considered, the point has been not to demonstrate that the alternative is or is not

---

[6] Cf. Edgington, Dorothy (1995), 'On conditionals', *Mind* **104**, 235–329.

correct, but to prepare for methodological reflections on how a logic could be chosen (without some logic having already been chosen in order that there is a logic to guide the choice). In the present case, intuitions about reasonable degrees of belief were used to evaluate a logical principle. The intuitions are subject to empirically or apriori based disconfirmation, for example Dutch Book arguments.

3. Methodological conclusion

The arguments sketched for or against the three non-classical logics (free logic, option negation logic, and probabilistic logic) did not appeal to some unchallengeable core of logic that must be taken for granted in all thought or discourse. The arguments appealed to considerations of completely different kinds. In the case of free logic, an allegedly invalid argument was produced, and was said to be a counterexample to classical logic. The only support offered was intuition. The proposed verdict on the argument did not depend upon challenging the intuition of invalidity, but rather on challenging its status as a counterexample: with appropriate formalization, its invalidity could be accommodated within the classical framework. In this discussion, everything was *apriori*. By contrast, historical and psychological considerations were supposed to be available to support option negation. *Apriori* reasoning would be involved as well, if the resulting logic were to be developed, but an essential empirical component would remain. In the final case, of conditionalizing disjunctions, logical validity was tested by its impact on subjective probabilities. What was drawn from the area, for example the general principle that a rational person could not, relative to a single state of information, assign greater uncertainty to the conclusion of a valid argument than to the sum of its premises, was largely *apriori*, but in contrast to the first case the considerations were indirect. We were not asked to intuit the validity status of some argument: rather, reasons were provided for making a possibly counterintuitive judgment of its status. The probability theory which was relied upon, though *apriori*, is not merely intuitive, for it is well known that intuitions about probabilities are often demonstrably defective.

The mere fact that the considerations were different in each case undermines the thought that there is an unchallengeable core from which we should work outwards in trying to determine which is the correct logic. This diversity is apparent with other alternatives to classical logic. For example, the case for intuitionistic logic is typically grounded on general considerations about the nature of meaning; the fate of bivalence has been linked with that of metaphysical realism; quantum phenomena have been said to undermine de Morgan's Laws; and various revisions of classical logic have been suggested in order to accommodate specific problems (for example, sorites reasoning).

We ought to have encountered an is/ought problem. In this kind of context, we can adduce how or what we in fact think, but how can we simply *adduce* how or what we ought to think, for that is the very question at issue? Will we not have found ourselves moving invalidly from facts about what we take to be so to facts about what we ought to take to be so? This did not appear to be a pressing issue in the examples sketched, and this fact requires some explanation.

An appealing general view in epistemology is that our beliefs are 'innocent unless proved guilty'. Less metaphorically, the 'innocence principle' is that we are justified in our beliefs, unless we have reasons for suspicion. (So *'proved* guilty' is too strong: any decent criticism needs to be examined, and if left unexamined defeats justification.) To say that we are justified is not to say that we have further beliefs that provide justifying reasons, but is only to say that we are justified. Holding the beliefs which the innocence principle says are justified is not subject to coherent specific criticisms (as things stand right now) for any such criticism would automatically count as a suspicion, and criticized or suspect beliefs are not held by the principle to be justified.

We could extend this to our logic: our inferences, likewise, are innocent unless proved guilty, or, more accurately, unless there is some ground for suspecting them. We are justified in reasoning as we do, unless we discover some reason for thinking that these ways are not good. If correct, this would explain why we have encountered no is/ought problem.

Those of our actual inferential practices which we have no reason to suspect are ones in which we are justified in engaging. This means that in appealing to some inferential practice, even in the course of throwing doubt upon another, we are appealing to an inferential pattern we are justified in using, and this takes us straight over the supposed gap between 'is' and 'ought': if this is in fact how we reason, and we have no ground for suspicion of this reasoning, then this is how we should reason. The general idea is the same as in non-foundationalism about empirical justification: nothing is sacrosanct, but we have to start somewhere and there is no thinkable alternative to starting with the beliefs we actually have at some particular moment and which (at that moment) we have nothing

R. M. Sainsbury

against. The logical boat, as much as the empirical one, must be reconstructed at sea, plank by plank, with no plank privileged and with no pre-ordained right starting-point. On this picture, any logical principle can in theory be criticized, and we need not first establish the correctness of the logical principles lying behind the criticism, though these themselves may be targets of criticisms in due course.

The innocence principle has been criticized. One must certainly accept that it does not tell the whole story about justification: it does not say how it is transmitted or defeated or how revisions should occur. But it has also been claimed that the principle does not state a sufficient condition for justification: a justified belief needs to have a suitable aetiology.[7] There are at least four ways in which this could be absent:

10. The belief is reached on the basis of bad reasons (ones which do not genuinely support the belief).
11. The belief is of a kind which requires other beliefs as reasons if it is to be justifiably believed, and no such reasons are held.
12. The belief is a product of a cognitive mechanism which is operating defectively.
13. The belief is a product of a cognitive mechanism which is operating under conditions for which it is not fitted.

Illustrations:

Of (10): One person believes that there is a £50 note in his pocket through a combination of perception and memory: he has just looked to check. His belief is justified. By contrast, someone who reaches the same belief merely through wishful thinking is not justified, even if she has no other belief which would cast suspicion on this one.

Of (11): A complex mathematical statement is properly believed only on the basis of a proof. This assertion is potentially directly inconsistent with innocence, but could be supported by the following contrast. Two people get to a certain point in a proof of some complex mathematical claim, C, from which C follows immediately. One person sees this immediate inference and on the strength of it comes to believe C. The other does not see the inference, but believes C anyway, saying to himself 'Well, this simply has to be true'. It seems that although the first person is

[7] Pollock, John L. (1986), *Contemporary Theories of Knowledge,* (Savage, Maryland: Rowman and Littlefield); second edition 1999, with Joseph Cruz.

justified the second is not, even if he has no grounds to suspect the conclusion.[8]

Of (12): Jaundice is supposed to make white things look yellow. Someone suffering from this disease who believes that something is yellow is arguably not justified in that belief. Although cognitive mechanisms sometimes make manifest that they are not working properly (e.g. if some part of the body goes numb, the sense of touch is manifestly lost in that part), this is not always so. Of (13): If one's head is under water, sounds are distorted. A belief formed on the basis of hearing in this circumstance is arguably not justified. Although cognitive mechanisms sometimes make it manifest that they are in an environment for which they are not fitted (e.g. if it is dark, our visual system manifestly does not work) this is not always so; we might not appreciate the distorting influence on hearing of being under water.

On this view, innocence is an oversimplified version of the following truth: a belief with a satisfactory aetiology is justified, provided there is no ground for suspicion.

For present purposes, we can allow these illustrations of the alleged failure of innocence to pass unchallenged, for, I shall suggest, the justification of inferential practices, including tendencies to regard certain collections of propositions as inconsistent, has special features which give a different slant to these kinds of criticism.

The contents of some beliefs, like the one about the £50 note in the illustration of (10), demand a specific kind of aetiology, one which is ultimately perceptual. This helps us to envisage a possible alternative justification-defeating aetiology. It is not clear that the same goes for inferential practices, considered as dispositions to move from beliefs to beliefs. Clearly there are good and bad such dispositions, but their character as good or bad is not a function of their aetiology. A good disposition might have become internalized in a 'bad' way, thanks to a hectoring and dogmatic teacher, for example, and a bad disposition can be acquired on the basis of the highest authority. This does not preclude the use of empirical material in casting suspicion on, or contributing justification to, an inferential practice. We have seen such a role in the case of option negation, and there are many others. It remains the case that our inferential practices, unlike beliefs about the whereabouts of £50 notes, do not *demand* this.

[8] Cf. Pollock and Cruz (op. cit. 1999: 83) for this example and for some of the ideas in this section.

R. M. Sainsbury

Does not the admission that there are bad inferential practices mean that the attack on innocence succeeds? This would require that one would be unjustified in exercising a bad disposition, even if one has no ground to suspect it. This opinion is not supported by the illustrations, nor, as far as I am aware, by anything else. If the disposition is 'bad' then it will not transmit justification, or will not result in a correct judgment of consistency or inconsistency; but that is not the same as saying that the agent was not justified in exercising the disposition. Just as one can be justified in believing a falsehood, treating as true what is in fact false, one can in principle be justified in behaving as follows: exercising a disposition which does not in fact transmit justification as though it were one which did, or exercising a disposition which does not in fact lead to a correct verdict about the consistency status of some propositions as though it did.

Turning to the kind of case envisaged in (11), the present discussion relates to primitive inferential practices, ones which are not justified in terms of others. This means that no parallel example can be forthcoming for the inferential practices at issue here.

Perception provides clear examples of 'cognitive mechanisms', like the visual and auditory systems, so we can make good sense of their failing to function properly. Moreover, various kinds of failure can be manifest. Cases of manifest failure are no threat to innocence, for the manifest failure constitutes a ground for suspicion. In the case of non-manifest failures, we can be drawn by one of two analogies: since non-manifest failure is failure, it is justification-defeating; alternatively, since it is not manifest, it leaves justification intact. Defenders of unqualified innocence will take the second analogy, and opponents the first. But in the case of inferential practices, the scene is different. We have no, or very little idea, about the cognitive processes which underlie inferential practices. There are no analogues of sense-organs or appropriate operating conditions or appropriate subject matters (for logic is topic neutral). There are no cases in which failure of a mechanism underlying good reasoning is manifest independently of bad upshots: nothing corresponding to a numb bodily part or, for vision, the absence of light. To suppose that the mechanism responsible for some inferential practice is malfunctioning is no different from supposing that the practice is a bad one. In this case, we can judge only by ends and not by means. But I have already said that I see no reason for thinking that to engage in a bad practice is eo ipso to reason in an unjustified way, any more than any party to this discussion would think that a false belief is eo ipso unjustified.

I suggest, therefore, that innocence needs no qualification in its application to logic, that is, to our inferential practices: whatever one may think about beliefs of the kind which should stem from memory or perception, aetiology does not figure as a condition for the justification of our primitive inferential practices. For these, innocence is a correct principle: we are justified in engaging in the practices we in fact engage in, provided that we have no ground to suspect them. In considering alternative logics, we do typically provide grounds for suspecting some inferences in which we engage: if those suspicions are not laid to rest, our justification is undermined. In providing 'grounds' for suspicion of some inferential practice, we thereby engage in others. Following this route, we cannot cast suspicion on all of them at once, so we are not engaged in a self-defeating enterprise.

King's College London

Further Reading

On logic and reasoning:
Harman, Gilbert (1986), *Change in View*. Cambridge, Mass: MIT Press.

On free logic:
Burge, Tyler (1974), 'Truth and singular terms,' *Nous* **8**, 309–25. Reprinted in Lambert, Karel *Philosophical Applications of Free Logic*, Oxford, New York, 1991, pp. 189–204.

On conditionalizing disjunctions:
Edgington, Dorothy (1995), 'On conditionals,' *Mind* **104.414**, 235–329.

On non-classical logics:
Haack, Susan (1974), *Deviant Logic: Some Philosophical Issues*. Cambridge: Cambridge University Press.

On justification:
Dummett, Michael (1978), 'The justification of deduction'. In his *Truth and Other Enigmas*. London: Duckworth.
Field, Hartry (1996) 'The aprioricity of logic.' *Proceedings of the Aristotelian Society* **96**, 359–79.
Pollock, John L. and Joseph Cruz (1999) *Contemporary Theories of Knowledge*. Lanham: Rowman and Littlefield. Second edition; first edition with Pollock as sole author 1985.

Mental Representation and Mental Presentation

Reflections on some definitions in *The Oxford Concise Dictionary*

GREGORY McCULLOCH

To the memory of Alan White

The idea of *mental representation* occupies a rather prominent place in much contemporary discussion, both in philosophy and cognitive science, and not as a particularly controversial idea either. My reflections here, however, are intended to douse much of that discussion with some cold water. I should emphasize at the outset that I have no problems at all with the very idea of mental representation. What I find quite unsatisfactory is the philosophical or doctrinal underpinning of much current theorising about it. Anyway, I shall suggest that talk of mental representation needs at least to be supplemented with, if not actually replaced by, a distinct notion of *mental presentation,* which cannot be reduced to it. But I start with the notion of an impression.

1. An IMPRESSION is either *the act of impressing a mark* on something, or it is *the mark impressed*.[1] So there are two impressions involved when I use a seal on a piece of wax: my act of using the seal (the *impression-act*), and the pattern that sets in the wax (the *impression-object*). Equally, though, an impression is *an effect produced (esp. on the mind or feelings)*. Thus I make such an impression-object on the minds of people at the cocktail party by going to it dressed as a yellow walrus. Harmlessly I shall also speak here of another impression, my impression-act of producing the effect at the party. And I'll say that the party-going case involves examples of *folk-psychological impressions*.

John McDowell speaks of impressions in another way, as episodes of a fact's impressing itself on a subject.[2] These episodes

---

[1] Words in capitals have material from their dictionary definition displayed between asterisk quotes.
[2] See John McDowell, *Mind and World* (Cambridge, MA: MIT Press, 1994 and 1996), 9–10, 139–46.

fall into the same overall category as impression-acts, except that in their case the 'agent' is a fact which brings itself to the notice of a subject. Anyway, call them *impression-episodes*.

When speaking of impressions in connection with pieces of wax, the intention is quite unproblematically mechanistic. But it is, of course, somewhat controversial whether talk of the folk-psychological impressions in the cocktail party case is equally mechanistic (and parallel remarks apply to the words 'effect' and 'produced' in the dictionary definition). The controversy I have in mind is not the same as whether the impressions at the party are (a) physical or at least (b) real. Suppose we allow for the sake of argument that these folk-psychological impressions are there to be named (rather than, say, explained away adverbially) and that everything nameable is physical. That settles issues (b) and (a), but it leaves open the issue I want to focus on.

We can approach my issue thus. Imagine an etymological investigation which established that the wax-related use of 'impression' came first and that the word later came to be applied in folk-psychology metaphorically or by analogy. Or imagine an etymology that established the opposite. Either would leave to be addressed the strength of the analogy, or the matter of how literally and in what respects one should compare wax-impressions with folk-psychological impressions. And I hope now that it is quite clear that such issues can be raised regardless of etymology. Someone I shall call The Wittgensteinian would warn very strongly against pressing the analogy in a certain direction. And in doing so she would have in mind someone else—a character I'll call The Cartesian—who has a tendency to do just that. According to The Cartesian, the way the seal informs the wax is a good model on which to construe the way in which things mechanically produce an effect on the mind. And what taking The Cartesian's line adds up to, in part anyway, is the idea that folk-psychological impression-objects are produced not just when one does something particularly dashing or remarkable, such as going to a party dressed as a yellow walrus, but whenever some worldly thing has a certain kind of effect on a subject. The effects in question occur during *perceptual episodes*.

There is at least overlap between impression-episodes (as introduced by McDowell) and perceptual episodes, since at least some cases of facts' impressing themselves on subjects are perceptual episodes (e.g. as in X sees that this nettle has withered). The Cartesian would say that in such a case individual items such as the nettle produce impression-objects in the mind of the subject in question. Perception, according to The Cartesian, embraces impression-episodes which involve the production of folk-psychological impression-objects in perceiving subjects.

2. Now PERCEPTION is *the ability of the mind to refer sensory information to an external object as its cause*, and perceptual episodes thus involve the exercise of this ability. My character The Cartesian interprets part of this as follows. Just as in the mechanical case we have (a) the seal, (b) the piece of wax, (c) the impression-object mechanically made on (b) by (a); so, in a case such as perceiving a nettle, we have (a') the nettle, (b') the mind, (c') the impression-object mechanically made on (b') by (a') during the impression-episode. Seventeenth-century work on such things as optics and physiology certainly encouraged The Cartesian to take this model very seriously indeed. And going back to the definition of perception, all of this is supposed to take care of *sensory information* (= the impression-object) and *external object* (= the nettle). That leaves the residual matter of *the ability of the mind to refer ... to ... as its cause*. Here I shall allow The Cartesian to construe this as the demand to explain or describe what it means to say that our impression-episodes purport to disclose to us a world of objects that exist independently of these episodes. And the concept of mental representation, my ultimate concern, is embroiled with a certain way of trying to meet this demand.

There are various ways, of course, for The Cartesian to proceed. One way—taken by someone called The Empiricist—involves so construing impression-objects that they somehow in themselves bring in the required reference to episode-independent objects, either by the way they cluster together, or because they have the reference built into their nature as individuals. One version of this second approach, taken perhaps by The Straw Man, is to say that impression-objects are *mental pictures* which by their nature take the mind out beyond itself to what they depict. Of course, they have to be able to do this to the mind without calling upon any prior or independent ability of it to interpret them as depicting such-and-such, since such an ability presupposes the very capacity-to-represent-or-make-reference-to which is being addressed. But—as The Wittgensteinian will forcibly point out—neither pictures, nor any other obviously conceivable item, can plausibly be said to do this job. Moreover, how they cluster together seems very much to be in the eye of the beholder. So—pending a completely different approach to the issue (see below §4)—The Empiricist looks to have failed, and is generally taken to have done so.

Gregory McCulloch

To come at the matter from another direction: The Cartesian is anyway fond enough of pointing out that effects do not in general resemble or otherwise in themselves signify their causes, so that this can hardly be taken for granted in the case of impression-objects. Of course, to repeat, effects can be *taken* to signify their causes, or interpreted as so doing—as when I see that the letter was franked by your seal, or notice the wet ground and retrodict rain—but this is based on something other than intrinsic features of the effects (e.g. in this case certain of my mental capacities). So if impression-objects do not have dubious intrinsic features such as those posited by The Straw Man, yet still get themselves involved, in the way described by The Empiricist, in perceptual episodes as defined above, something else has to be called upon to explain how they come to be referred by the mind to external objects. According to another of my characters—The Rationalist—the *intellect* has to be brought in to do this job somehow. But I shall for the time being neutrally construe the issue as yielding a demand for an account of *mental representation* which draws on resources beyond those invoked by The Empiricist.

3. REPRESENTATION is either *the act of representing* or *the thing that represents*. But there are different kinds of representation-act, as when I serve as your lawyer in court or as my leader's ambassador to Costa Rica. And there are different kinds of thing that represent: words, pictures. Anyway, what The Cartesian needs in giving an account of *mental* representation is something closer to *call up in the mind by description or portrayal or imagination; place a likeness of before the mind...* (and this involves what I shall mean henceforth by '*folk-psychological representation-act*'). What The Empiricist wanted was for folk-psychological impression-objects to be such *likenesses*, ones which were capable, moreover, of doing the *calling up* themselves. The Rationalist, on the other hand, takes it that the *calling up* is done by the intellect. Either way, I am taking it that an account of mental representation is an account of *calling up*, and that The Empiricist's own proposal looks bankrupt.

Even The Wittgensteinian would allow that there are folk-psychological representation-acts, because one can in the normal run of life *call things to mind*. I am prepared to go further and allow that *every* episode of thinking about something is a folk-psychological representation-act in that sense: so in thinking Venice is beautiful I call Venice (inter alia) to mind. Here I would be joined by The Cartesian. In addition, neither I nor The Wittgensteinian need deny that such folk-psychological representation-acts can involve representation-objects. Quite harmlessly, when I perform a representation-act I am a *thing that represents*, and hence *I* am a representation-object. In addition, if I utter the words 'Venice is beautiful' in giving expression to my thought that Venice is beautiful, then my act incorporates the production of (linguistic) representation-objects. Hence I take it that there is no real controversy over the very idea of a representation-object. But The Cartesian will go much further than all this, and assert that every folk-psychological representation-act (a) involves representation-objects which are (b) in the mind of the subject (just like folk-psychological impression-objects). These are what I shall call *mental representation-objects*, and I think that this idea certainly does raise real controversy. In fact, I think it is pretty hopeless.

If this sort of appeal to mental representations is not to collapse into The Empiricist's view, these mental representation-objects have to be very special indeed. They can't be impression-objects (for that just is Empiricism). Yet they have to do the *calling up* job The Empiricist wanted impression-objects to do. But the problem with impression-objects seemed to be that they could only do the *calling up* if they had what were above referred to as 'dubious features', such as intrinsically depicting. How can such features be any less dubious when had by mental representation-objects? Or: if mental representation-objects can have them, why can't impression-objects? Clearly it will not take us further forward here merely to say, with The Rationalist, that representation-objects stand in a favoured relation to the intellect, which explains how they can have the sorts of features denied to impression-objects. This just pushes the problems back one stage. How can involving the intellect help, and why couldn't it have the same function with respect to impression-objects?

Pending an answer to that question, it is tempting to conclude straight away that The Cartesian's appeal to mental representation-objects is quite hopeless. But no doubt that seems impossibly quick, and this probably for one of two reasons: either

(a) because you take it to involve more than it need, or
(b) because you think that The Cartesian need not assert that mental representation-objects represent intrinsically.

As regards (a), one needs to be very clear that in rejecting mental representation-objects one would not, for example, be denying that there is a language encoded in the brain which comprises words of Mentalese which refer to, among other things, nettles. This is an empirical matter, after all. What one would be denying is that such representation-objects, if they exist, are *in the mind*.[3] And one would be denying that they intrinsically represent nettles etc. This brings us to (b). Here one might think that it is open to The Cartesian to offer, for example, the view that they represent by *causally covarying with*. So I turn now to *causal covariance accounts of representing*.

4. Causal covariance between A and B cannot be necessary and sufficient for A to represent B unless representation is more or less everywhere, including in the B-to-A direction, and there is no representation of the acausal. Nor will it help to restrict oneself to cases where A is mental and B causal, since non-mental things (words, pictures) can represent. But I shall suppose all of that can be dealt with, along with the provision of any further constraints required (e.g. of a biological type), and focus on putatively mental items which causally covary with distinct non-mental items.

Still, taking this line—call it the *covariance+* account—leaves all the big matters outstanding.[4]

Note for a start that The Empiricist could easily have offered such a covariance+ view as the required account of how folk-psychological impression-objects themselves serve as mental representation-objects. And to see what is wrong with that suggestion, let us consider an example which in fact can plausibly be modelled quite closely on the seal + wax case with which I began: the example of a sting on the leg caused by nettles. Just as we have (a) the seal, (b) the piece of wax, (c) the impression-object mechanically made on (b) by (a) so, very arguably, we have (a˝) the nettle, (b˝) the mind, (c˝) the sting mechanically produced in (b˝) by (a˝). If we were being ultra-cautious, we might insist on '(b‴) the leg' rather than '(b˝) the mind', but stings are not just in the leg (like a bone) but are also, by

[3] See Gregory McCulloch, 'Let the vat-brains speak for themselves', *Ratio* (forthcoming).

[4] It may seem that once 'external' matters such as the causes of representations are invoked to explain their representality, the view ceases to be Cartesian. After all, isn't the classical Cartesian idea that my representations have whatever representational properties they have regardless of whether they hit their targets (rather than a demon)? Well, in a straightforward sense, my cat-representations *don't* represent cats in the demon scenario: although, of course, they (are supposed to) purport to. Presumably, once traditional notions of mental representation-object have been dropped (intrinsicaly meaningful pictures and the like), the idea of *purported* representation is meant to be carried by talk of *narrow* content or aspects.

their nature, in the mind (unlike the bone): and we can anyway afford not to be ultra-cautious.

There is a perfectly innocuous sense in which these stings represent nettles or call them to mind. They do this in a way that closely matches the way in which the impression in the wax represents or calls to mind the seal (and, beyond that, the seal's owner). But the seal's mark's capacity to do this is very clearly parasitic on our abilities to take things in a certain way, as signs or symbols. And if the analogy is as close as it otherwise looks (and as The Cartesian after all wants it to be), we should say the same thing about the sting: *given* our ability to think about nettles, and *given* the observed causal covariance between stings like that and nettles, we can treat the stings as indicating that nettles are nearby. But, of course, that story presupposes the mind's ability to think about, mentally represent, nettles; something which is not being explained by saying that the stings represent nettles: just as saying that the impression-object in the wax represents the seal does not explain how we can interpret it as doing so, how it can call the seal to mind for us. Note again how natural (but in itself fruitless) it is to appeal at this point to the intellect, in the manner of The Rationalist: just as we interpret the wax impression, the intellect interprets the stings. To underscore the main point, note too how unnatural it would be to call the stings 'true' when they are caused by nettles and 'false' when they are not. Of course any associated *belief* to the effect that nettles are nearby would be true or false as the case may be: but that's another matter, still to be addressed, since believing presupposes the ability to *call up in the mind by description or portrayal or imagination; place a likeness of before the mind...*

What all this shows is that if there are any mental representation-objects of the kind posited by The Cartesian, they cannot be modelled very closely on impression-objects like our sting (or *the mark made in the wax*, for that matter). And see now how irrelevant or at least premature the suggestion to offer a causal covariance+ account of representing has become in this context. What we really need to know is what, if anything, makes a mental representation-object a mental representation-object. Until we can answer that question, talk of causal covariance+ is not even addressing the right issue, and cannot distinguish impression-objects such as stings from mental representation-objects.

I suppose the obvious reply is that mental representation-objects, unlike stings, will be a certain kind of syntactic unit in a computational language (or something analogous in something analogous— I mean here to leave room for as many possibilities as The Cartesian can coherently come up with), and *that* is what makes them what they are. There's no obvious analogy of this in the case of the seal and wax, but perhaps that is neither here nor there, since we are leaving that model behind anyway. What we should focus on instead is The Cartesian's claim that these mental representation-objects, just like the stings, are *in the mind*, as they have to be if they are to explain the mind's ability to make reference to independent things (and as 'mental' implies). After all, even if being the appropriate kind of syntactic unit is sufficient for being a representation, it clearly is not sufficient for being a *mental* representation. The question is, then: what is it for a syntactic unit to be *in the mind*?

5. So: 'in the mind'. Stings are in the mind in the sense that they figure as part of the furniture of consciousness: they are *phenomenological objects*. A PHENOMENON is *the object of a person's perception; what the senses or the mind notice*. And the PHENOMENOLOGICAL is thus whatever pertains to objects of perception, to what *the senses or the mind notice*. Phenomenological items like stings make a mark on the mind reminiscent of the way the seal makes a mark on the wax because they are *noticed*. So would be the mental images posited by The Straw Man to serve as things for *calling up* the world. And although the idea of consciousness *per se* is puzzling and highly resistant to systematic theorising of a certain kind, mention of it in this connection at least gives some proper substance to the idea that the mind has a mark made on it which is in some way analogous to the seal's mark on the wax: there's an alteration in a certain medium.

The real problem hereabouts is how to construe the corresponding point in the case of mental representation-objects. While they are very literally in the brain, in what sense are they in the mind? Not in the way that stings are, that's for sure. No amount of embarrassment could lead The Cartesian nowadays to hold that the syntactic items which she believes mental representation-objects to be are phenomenological items rather like stings: that would be far too close either to what The Empiricist says, or to what The Straw Man says, and is patently ludicrous. Or to be more cautious: if mental representation-objects do figure as phenomenological items, they do not figure so *as such*; that is, as syntactic units in a computational language. So a natural (and common) option here is for The Cartesian to deny, perhaps implicitly, that mental representation-objects are phenomenological in any sense, and claim that they make a mark on the mind simply in virtue of their *causal role in the brain*, a role which is not supposed to be independent of their syntactic nature or 'shape'. This gives The Cartesian what I shall call a *causal/syntactic account of being a mental representation-object*, to add to the causal covariance+ account of representing introduced above. And overall this gives a causal account of mental representation-objects in two dimensions: one to do with what it is to be such an object, the mark it makes on the mind—that's the causal/syntactic bit—and one to do with what such an object represents—that's the covariance+ bit.

Well, I don't think that this two-dimensional causal approach is any use at all, for all kinds of reason.[5] Here I want to try to cut a long story short by focusing first on the similarities and differences between *being stung by a nettle* and *seeing a nettle*. These are both phenomenological episodes, and we can stipulate that the ones we are focussing on involve a subject who knows quite a lot about, can think about, nettles, can recognise them in the ordinary run of things etc. Now if a phenomenon is *the object of a person's perception; what the senses or the mind notice*, then nettles are at least candidate phenomena: when the kind of subject we have stipulated sees a nettle, her senses notice it.[6] Perhaps we can say the same thing about when she is stung: arguably her senses notice the nettle. But now we need to enforce some crucial distinctions.

If we consider these phenomenological episodes just as they (phenomenologically) are in themselves, then nettles do not, strictly speaking, figure in the stinging *qua* experience. What figures in the stinging is the sting, and this is experienced not as a part or property of the nettles, but as an effect, an impression-object, in the body. Even if being stung puts one in mind of nettles, makes one think Nettles!, still the sting itself is experienced as a bodily effect, a state of part of the leg, a state-of-the-leg which is internal to, not independent of, the episode in question. Things are quite otherwise where the seeing is concerned. The impression- or perceptual

---

[5] Two hugely influential examples of such broadly Cartesian two-dimensionalism are the (structurally almost identical, though in detail quite different) positions developed by Jerry Fodor (e.g. in *Psychosemantics* (Cambridge MA: MIT Press, 1987)) and Colin McGinn (in *Mental Content* (Oxford: Blackwell, 1989)). For further detailed criticisms of this approach see Gregory McCulloch, 'Bipartism and the phenomenology of content' in (*Philosophical Quarterly* **49**, 18–32) and 'Phenomenological Externalism' in N Smith (ed.) *Reading McDowell: On Mind and World* (Routledge, forthcoming)

[6] See Gregory McCulloch, 'The very idea of the phenomenological', *Proceedings of the Aristotelian Society* **93** (1993, 39–57).

episode of seeing a nettle purports to disclose to us, to use the phrase introduced earlier, something—namely the nettle—which exists independently of the episode. And then on the one hand: seen aspects of the nettle, such as its shape and colour, are experienced not as impression-objects or bodily effects, not as something internal to the episode, but as features of the (independent) nettle. And on the other hand: *nothing* is experienced as a bodily effect, in a normal case of seeing a nettle. If anything makes a (phenomenological) mark on the mind in such a case, it is *the nettle* purportedly disclosed. There is no further phenomenological item analogous to a sting: no 'visual sensation' or impression-object.

To say all this is not to deny

(a) that in the seeing, the nettle also makes a *causal* mark at least on the brain;

nor is it to deny

(b) that such a mark can be called a *visual representation-object* of the nettle. In fact, I'll just assume that it can.

It is not even to deny

(c) that this visual representation-object is itself a phenomenological item.

But it is to deny

(d) that it is phenomenological *as such*:

even if we do experience such visual representation-objects, we do not experience them as visual representation-objects, but (in this case) *as nettles*. So we should still require an account of how it is that a visual representation-object can be such as to be experienced as a nettle. Note the temptation here to posit mental pictures which the mind 'looks through'. Note too that even if there were a 'visual sensation', a (phenomenological) item analogous to a sting, this would still not make it intelligible how the nettle is presented in the visual experience. Being an impression-object, the 'visual sensation' could at best be interpreted or taken by the mind/intellect to be of a nettle (just as both the sting and the impression-object in the wax can be interpreted or taken to be of their causes). Still *the ability of the mind to refer sensory information to an external object as its cause* has been left unexplained in its visual manifestation: whether or not there are 'visual sensations', whether or not there are visual representation-objects, even ones which play a phenomenological role (though certainly not as such, recall). This to-be-addressed matter is what I call the phenomenological issue of *mental presentation*.[7]

6. A PRESENTATION is either *the act or an instance of presenting; the process of being presented* or it is *the thing presented*, where to present can be to *exhibit (an appearance etc)*, *esp. for public attention or consideration*. In the case of seeing a nettle, what we have seen is that The Cartesian's notion of visual representation-object is itself silent on the visual presentation of nettles, since it just does not address the fact that the nettles are presented or exhibited. Let's say that this presenting is actually done by our visual representation-objects: they are the presenters. Then: either these visual representation-objects make a phenomenological mark or they do not. If they do, then it still needs to be explained how they make a mark by presenting nettles, rather than appearing as themselves. If they do not make a phenomenological mark, then the matter of the presentation of nettles in the phenomenology is still to be addressed. Either way, then, the matter of the presentation of the nettles is still to be addressed. It needs to be explained what it means to say that, in seeings, the nettles are (visual) presentation-objects.

Of course, The Cartesian can here go through the motions of appealing to causal considerations, conceiving of visual representation-objects as things with a certain kind of causal/syntactic role. This role would of course be some ways different from that of the

---

[7] The notion is easily to be found in Frege:

> It is natural ... to think of there being connected with a sign (name, combination of words, written mark), besides that which the sign designates, which may be called the *Bedeutung* of the sign, also what I should like to call the *Sinn* of the sign, wherein the mode of presentation is contained. (p. 152)
> The *Bedeutung* ... is the object itself ...; the idea which we have in that case is wholly subjective; in between lies the *Sinn*, which is indeed no longer subjective like the idea, but is yet not the object itself. The following analogy will perhaps clarify these relationships. Somebody observes the Moon through a telescope. I compare the Moon itself to the *Bedeutung*; it is the object of the observation, mediated by the real image projected by the object glass in the interior of the telescope, and by the retinal image of the observer. The former I compare to the *Sinn*, the latter is like the idea or intuition. (p. 155).

Both quotes are from Gottlob Frege, 'On *Sinn* and *Bedeutung*', in M. Beaney (ed.) *The Frege Reader* (Oxford: Blackwell, 1997).

corresponding mental representation-object, and would be taken to account for what kind of mark these visual representation-objects make. Then The Cartesian might further advert to their causal covariance+ with nettles to explain how the nettles get into the visual story. In sum: as with mental representation-objects, this sort of story would be offered as an account in two dimensions, of mark made and thing represented. The very obvious problem, however, is that the big point is simply unaddressed, and the parallel with impression-objects has been lost. That is, there is nothing here that addresses the fact that a phenomenological mark is made in the visual case, just as it is in the case of impression-objects such as stings. The suggestion just made is that The Cartesian could try to rest content with the idea of a causal mark only. But while that may look satisfactory where mental representation-objects are concerned—though I shall suggest below that it is not altogether—it is quite clearly unsatisfactory when we consider perceptual episodes such as seeing a nettle. Such episodes are themselves phenomenological episodes, aspects of consciousness. Simply adverting to the fact that these supposed visual representation-objects are *of nettles* is insufficient, since the same is true of mental representation-objects, which are supposed not to make a phenomenological mark. Indeed, being *of nettles* is true even of some non-mental representation-objects. We are thus two steps away from what is required: non-mental things can be *of nettles*, and mental things can be *of nettles* without presenting nettles. Moreover, simply to emphasise that we are concerned here with *visual* representation objects is to advert to what needs to be addressed, rather than to address it. Or perhaps better: that just seems to get us as far as saying that visual representation-objects have a different causal role—eye-involving etc.—from that of ordinary mental representation-objects. That still leaves the issue of presentation outstanding.

7. Recall now that stings make a mark on the mind by being phenomenological items, and a PHENOMENON is *the object of a person's perception; what the senses or the mind notice*. NOTICE, moreover, is either one's *attention or observation (it escaped my notice)*, or it is to *perceive, observe*. Running round these circles, we at least get the message that stings are objects of a kind of perception, what has been called inner sense or introspection (INTROSPECTION: *the examination or observation of one's own mental and emotional processes*). What this offers, to The Cartesian anyway, is a way of trying to accommodate the idea that visual representation-objects figure as phenomenological items, or are at least implicated in the presentation of nettles. The thought here would be that the two-dimensional causal story accounts for the visual representation-objects' representationality, while the fact that they can also be objects of introspection, of one's *notice*, accounts for their making of a phenomenological mark, their powers to present. Otherwise put, it is our *noticing* our visual representation objects of nettles which, in the case of seeing, constitutes the nettles' being visual presentation-objects. The difference then with mental representation objects would be, as it were, we just don't *notice* them.

There are at least two ways of developing this. The first would amount to a form of indirect realism, according to which

(a) the visual representation-objects are directly perceived (*noticed*) whenever they are operative,

and

(b) such *notice* also amounts, in favourable circumstances, to indirect perception of the likes of nettles.

The second would involve the claim

(c) normally, visual representation-objects serve simply to present nettles to consciousness,

although

(d) they can come to play a different role, namely as the (direct) objects of introspection, which is how they can figure as phenomenological items.

But both ways of proceeding are quite hopeless. The first suggestion is too close for comfort to The Empiricist view rejected much earlier. If the visual representation objects are (directly) *noticed* whenever they are operative, and in favourable cases subserve (indirect) perception of the likes of nettles, then either:

(i) they are to be construed as having intrinsic *noticeable* properties which call-nettles-to-mind;

or

(ii) they are to be construed as impression-objects like stings which represent nettles in the way that the wax-impression represents the seal.

But (i) involves introducing the 'dubious features' derided by The

Wittgensteinian, while (ii) leaves the mind's capacity to interpret the impression-objects unexplained. And while it might seem open to appeal here to the independent capacity of the mind to represent—the fact that it hosts mental representation-objects—we should anyway note that (ii) has the decidedly unfavourable quality, especially in a phenomenological story, of not squaring with the phenomenological facts. As noted earlier, there are no 'visual sensations' to be *noticed*, and interpreted, anyway.

So much for the indirect realism comprising suggestions (a) and (b). The second suggestion ((c) and (d)) was that visual representation-objects normally serve to present what they represent (e.g. nettles), although they can come themselves to be the direct objects of introspection. The problems with this are as follows.

(i) Since being an object of introspection is in the present section being taken to explain what it is to make a (phenomenological) mark, the implication of (c) and (d) is that visual representation-objects normally make no phenomenological mark. But this misses the intended target: seeing itself, not just introspecting-when-seeing, is (at least usually)[8] a phenomenological episode.

(ii) In other words, the capacity of visual representation-objects to present nettles in ordinary perception is simply being taken for granted rather than in any way explained by this sort of appeal to introspection.

Think now of what introspection turns up when one is seeing a nettle. What it does not turn up is a 'visual sensation', as we have seen. What it does turn up is a nettle-being-presented. And now see that

(iii) the capacity even of *introspection* to have nettles presented to it is also simply being taken for granted.

I draw two morals from these failures to cope with examples of mental presentation. The *first* is that The Cartesian's two-dimensional causal approach to visual representation is hopelessly inadequate because it fails to address the fact that visual representation involves presentation, or making a phenomenological mark, as well as (or instead of) making a causal mark, on the mind. And the *second* is that construing *noticing* on the model of introspection is hopeless, at least in the case of visual perception. Even if the idea of

[8] The 'usually' is there to leave room for familiar examples such as driving to work 'on autopilot'; while the 'at least' covers the fact that the interpretation of such examples is controversial.

introspection as a perceptual capacity has some role to play, for example in an account of our awareness of impression-objects such as stings, it cannot deliver a general theory of the phenomenological. It cannot, in particular, shed *any light at all* on the notion of mental presentation of extramental things like nettles.

Given how prevalent it has become to urge that consciousness is to be conceived as representation of representation, I hereby claim that these two morals are quite significant.

8. I want to wind down now by suggesting how to extend these conclusions to apply to the two-dimensional account of mental representation-objects also. *Pace* The Cartesian as we have been allowing her to proceed, it is simply not true that mental representation-objects (if they exist) merely make a causal mark on the mind: sometimes, at least, they make, or are implicated in the making of, a phenomenological mark. I shall offer three examples, the first involving the first-person point of view, and the other two involving the third-person point of view.

So: *consciously thinking* that nettles are nearby is every bit as phenomenological as *seeing* that nettles are nearby. By this I just mean that thinking about nettles can be just as much a feature of one's conscious life as is seeing nettles.[9] According to The Cartesian's story, such episodes of thinking involve mental representation-objects, whose causal/syntactic role makes them representation-objects, and whose causal covariance+ with nettles makes them *of nettles*. But none of these causal matters figures as such in the phenomenology, so The Cartesian's story fails to address the phenomenological dimension here, just as it does in the case of seeing. So what does figure in the phenomenology? Well, just as in the visual case the seeing is *of nettles*, so in the thinking case, the thinking is *of nettles*. And—surely really undeniably—just as this is a matter of nettles being *presented* in the one case, so it is in the other. In both cases it is *nettles*, and not some other thing, to which my consciousness is directed (albeit in different ways). And I take it that it needs no explicit spelling out that there is no future here in talk of impression-objects ('cognitive sensations'), nor of the operations of introspection, in order to explain these phenomenological facts. If such talk cannot get a grip in the visual case, it certainly will not get a grip in the cognitive case. So a natural (and standard) avenue for The Cartesian to explore would be to deny, or try to finesse, the claim that

[9] See Gregory McCulloch, 'The very idea', 'Bipartism': cf. Galen Strawson, *Mental Reality* (Cambridge, MA: MIT Press, 1994) pp. 6–7.

conscious thinking is a phenomenological episode in the appropriate sense. But any tendency to see this as the beginning of satisfying way out ought to be strongly inhibited, to put it mildly, by the fact that The Cartesian's approach has already been seen to be barking up the wrong trees in the visual case. So she is not exactly launching from a firm platform where matters phenomenological are concerned. For the rest, just try a bit of conscious thinking about nettles now; and now try to deny that it is *nettles* that your consciousness is presented with. Or to say what it is presented with *instead*. Nettle-sensations? Oh, come on!

Before considering my other two examples, I should emphasise that this one does not give The Cartesian a way out. A point made earlier was that while a two-dimensional causal account of mental representation-objects might work, the same trick could not be turned in the case of *visual* representation-objects, since these involve the additional matter of mental presentation. But The Cartesian might claim that in the light of the present example of presentation in conscious thinking, all contrast between mental respresentation-objects and visual representation-objects has been lost. So why can't the two-dimensional causal account be the whole story in both cases after all?

The answer is that not all cognitive activity is conscious, that not all episodes which the Cartesian claims to involve mental representation-objects also result in a phenomenological mark being made on the mind. Not all mental representation involves mental presentation. So talk of mental representation-objects still needs to be supplemented if not replaced by talk of mental presentation in some cases.

I turn now to the two further examples of mental presentation announced earlier. This time they are third person ones, involving 'outer sense' like the visual case.

Consider: just as I can

(1) see that nettles are nearby

and

(2) (consciously) think that nettles are nearby;

so I can

(3) (a) see you signal or (b) hear you say that nettles are nearby.

Cases (3a) and (3b) are unquestionably phenomenological, so the material matter to address is what I am presented with in them. The easy bit here is: in (3a) I am presented with *you*, and I am also presented with certain of your gestures; while in (3b) I am at least presented with your words, however that unpacks.

In case (3a), where I see you signal that nettles are nearby, we could say that your gestures, with which I am presented, are themselves representation-objects to the effect that nettles are nearby. Then there are at least two candidate models for what all this amounts to. On the one hand, what I am literally presented with are gestures which I interpret in a further contribution. On the other hand, what I am literally presented with are, as one might say, ready-interpreted gestures: gestures-of-nettles. The choice between these candidates is actually rather less crucial than it may seem. For there is no excluding possible cases where my entertaining of the thought you signal is a fully conscious act on my part, analogous to the case where I just think to myself that nettles are nearby. Since, as we have seen, in such cases of conscious thinking, nettles are presented to my consciousness, so we can conclude that in case (3a), likewise, nettles are presented. In other words, nettles are already in the phenomenology in case (3a), and the question we have raised is really to do with, as one might say, the medium of this phenomenological appearance of nettles. Is it to be my conscious thinking or your gestures? In fact I don't see why it can't be both: my seeing the message in your gestures just is (or incorporates), in the circumstances, my entertaining of the thought that nettles are nearby. However this may be, the crucial point is that the heat is anyway taken out of the putative choice since the option of introducing the idea that I interpret your gestures is not a *rival* to the suggestion that a case like (3a) involves a presentation of nettles. Nettles are presented anyway. And if that is so, it makes it all the easier for us to give unprejudiced room to the thought that we would ordinarily contrast cases which involve interpretation—as when, for example, your gestures are ambiguous, indistinct, unexpected or unfamiliar—with cases where I easily and effortlessly *see what you mean*, without more ado. On this relaxed approach for which we have given unprejudiced room, it would be a *phenomenological fact about your gestures that they present nettles to my consciousness*.

Case (3b), my hearing you say that nettles are nearby, is different in a number of ways. If I have no other perceptual access to you, it is at least to be discussed whether *you* are presented to me. But in addition, or rather prior, to that, there is anyway a mass of issues to deal with concerning whether I am presented with your words, or with the noises you make, or with impression-objects ('auditory sensations'), and if so whether I interpret them or find them ready-interpreted. Even so, it again seems to me that there is less heat to be generated here than may initially seem. For once again, there is no ruling out the fact that a possible such case could involve my fully conscious entertaining of the thought that nettles are nearby as a integral accompaniment of your saying so. And since the nettles are thus already in the phenomenology in such a case, nothing especially controversial in the present context hangs on the issue whether I have to do some interpreting of something in order to get your message. So, finally, it seems that we can give unprejudiced room to the idea that we would ordinarily contrast cases where I have to do some interpreting—as when, for example, your words are indistinct or I am not fully proficient in your language—with cases where I easily and effortlessly *hear what you mean*, without more ado. On this relaxed approach, it would be *a phenomenological fact about your words that they present nettles to my consciousness.*

Finally, then, I offer cases (3a) and (3b) as further examples, to sit beside *seeing a nettle* and *consciously thinking of nettles*, of situations where merely talking of mental representation of nettles is at best incomplete or insufficient, and is in need of supplementation if not replacement by further, different, talk of the mental presentation of nettles. The next thing for me to do, of course, is to offer you my thoughts on mental presentation. But that will have to wait for another time. Perhaps unsurprisingly, the true story according to me involves a proper account of *content*, which is therefore—if I'm anywhere near the right lines—not delivered or even properly addressed by all this talk of mental representation we keep hearing.[10]

University of Birmingham

---

[10] This paper originates from a conversation I was having with my friend and colleague Harold Noonan. We were talking (as often) about Frege and I said that dealers in the idea of mental representation who saw what they were doing as filling out Frege's notion of mode of presentation, without more ado, had simply not entitled themselves to Frege's metaphor. Harold replied that it's not clear what it is to be entitled to a metaphor. This is my attempt at clarification, in this particular case.

Self-knowledge, Normativity, and Construction

JULIA TANNEY

> *He tried to look into her face, to find out what she thought, but she*
> *was smelling the lilac and the lilies of the valley and did not know*
> *herself what she was thinking—what she ought to say or do.*
>
> Oblomov

1. Much of modern and contemporary philosophy of mind in the
'analytic' tradition has presupposed, since Descartes, what might be
called a realist view about the mind and the mental. According to
this view there are independently existing, determinate items
(states, events, dispositions or relations) that are the truth-conferrers of our ascriptions of mental predicates.[1] The view is also a cognitivist one insofar as it holds that when we correctly ascribe such a
predicate to an individual the correctness consists in the discovery
of a determinate fact of the matter about the state the individual is
in—a state which is somehow cognized by the ascriber. Disputes
have arisen about the nature of the truth-conferrers (e.g., whether
they are physical or not) and about the status and the nature of the
individual's own authority about the state he is in. A dissenting
position in philosophy of mind would have to be handled carefully.
It would, most importantly, need to allow for the objectivity of
ascriptions of mental predicates at least insofar as it made sense to
reject some and accept others on appropriate grounds. Perhaps such
a position in the philosophy of mind can be likened in at least one
way to what David Wiggins has characterized as a doctrine of 'cognitive underdetermination' about moral or practical judgments.[2] In
comparing his position of cognitive underdetermination about
moral or practical judgments to some things Wittgenstein has said
about the philosophy of mathematics, Wiggins suggests that, 'In the

---

[1] Henceforth, I shall speak of *states* or *events* for ease of exposition. By
'independently (or antecedently) existing', I mean states whose existence
does not depend on any epistemic interest the subject might take in them.

[2] See 'Truth, Invention and the Meaning of Life', 'A Sensible Subjectivism', and 'Truth, and Truth as Predicated of Moral Judgements',
reprinted as essays III, IV, and V in *Needs, Value and Truth* (Oxford: Basil
Blackwell, 1987).

assertibility (or truth) of mathematical statements we see what perhaps we can never see in the assertibility of empirical (such as geographical or historical) statements: the compossibility of objectivity, discovery, *and* invention.'[3]

In this paper I intend to develop the idea that the 'compossibility of objectivity, discovery and invention' is a part of our ordinary (i.e., non-scientific and non-theoretical) understanding of the mental.[4] If this is correct, it is important, since contemporary theories do not make sense of this compossibility: they fail, in particular, to leave room for the inventive aspects of self-ascription.[5]

My strategy involves appealing to intuitions about the acceptability or appropriateness of certain ascriptions of mental concepts. To generate these intuitions it will be helpful to rely on the description of a possible person and her thoughts made out both in a certain degree of detail and over a significant period of time. I shall be looking at selected details from Goncharov's *Oblomov* and asking my reader to consider some of the scenes concerning the character Olga.[6]

2. The so-called 'Cartesian' model of the mind is a model in which discovery plays a role *par excellence*. This model supposes that one's thoughts, feelings, concerns, needs, values and principles, are played out in an 'inner theatre' of the mind that is constitutively independent of any epistemic interest the subject might take in it. More problematically, it also supposes that these items are available completely and unmistakably as a result of introspection.

Consider carefully what this picture is committed to. Our experience of these events is thought to be unmediated in the sense that it would not be subject to norms or rules; these events would be

---

[3] 'Truth, Invention and the Meaning of Life', op. cit., p. 130.

[4] This paper develops some of the ideas I suggested in 'A Constructivist Picture of Self-Knowledge' *Philosophy*, **71**, no. 277 (July 1996), pp. 405–22.

[5] That they cannot make sense of it comes as no surprise, once it is noted that the goal of so-called 'naturalism'—to locate the mental within nature conceived as the realm of law—is *ipso facto* removing from the mental the first-personal point of view or participant perspective that seems so important for retaining the inventive aspect. For this reason it would seem as if any theory of mind that conceives its starting point as the recoil from dualism—(e.g. behaviourism, identity theories, functionalism, and even anomalous monism)—and attempts a full-bodied or modified physicalism, will be unable to account for the inventive or constructive aspect of the mental.

[6] All references are to the Penguin edition, translated by David Magarshack, 1954.

38

simply *given* as part of our immediate experience. If our ability to classify them and to recognize them, as classified, is to be infallible this means that our bringing them under concepts—and this would be a matter of applying rules—would not be subject to error. Introducing names for these experiences into our language would presumably involve simple association of the object or event with a name, or 'baptism' by ostensive definition. Such classifying or naming, however, would be a private activity, since the experiences classified and named are not accessible to others and the associations cannot be checked by anyone else.

There is a problem with this view. The Cartesian wants the inhabitants of the mind to have an existence that is independent of any epistemic interest taken in them; in this sense he is a realist. He must therefore allow a sufficient gap between what is grasped when the subject 'turns his mental eye inward' and his grasping it. One might reasonably require that in order to effect this gap and bring out the true independence of the nature of the objects of the mind it has to be *in some sense* possible for the subject to get it wrong. But the introduction of infallible access thwarts this possibility.

The Cartesian might attempt to dig in his heels and claim that the fallibility associated with our sense-perception of the external world simply fails to apply to the perception of our own minds. Whereas in sense perception the possibility of error is a mark of the independence of the object perceived, he might deny that a viable realism about the mental requires such a possibility. It just requires that there be a mental item or state that is constitutively independent of the subject's gaze. Success is assured, then, since on this view the 'mental eye' and its conceptual machinery functions perfectly.[7]

The opponent of this view must then turn his attention to the idea of perfectly functioning conceptual/perceptual equipment. And, indeed, he might plausibly maintain that the very idea of an explanation that posits perfectly functioning machinery is of dubious coherence. For if we posit a mechanism that functions perfectly and cannot go wrong, then we cannot appeal to this mechanism as an *explanation* of the ability. The reason is simply that there would be no way to distinguish any purported explanation using a mechanism that cannot go wrong from a mere description of what would constitute success. As long as it is explanatorily indistinguishable from such a description, there is no reason to posit the mechanism to begin with. And if there is no perfectly function-

[7] See Crispin Wright's discussion of the Cartesian view in 'Wittgenstein's Later Philosophy of Mind: Sensation, Privacy, Intention', *Meaning Scepticism*, K. Puhl (ed.) (Berlin: de Gruyter, 1991), pp. 126–47.

ing mechanism, then the whole idea of objects before the mind that are perceivable by this mechanism is threatened.

The Cartesian model invites us, in effect, to compare the referents of our mental concepts 'in their definiteness to objects which are already lying in a drawer and which we then take out.'[8] To give this realist aspect of the Cartesian view—the idea that mental items exist in their definiteness independently of any act of identification or endorsement—more chance of success, let us disentangle it from the Cartesian notion of infallibility. The idea that a person might not be aware of what he is thinking is an idea that many people nowadays will be happy to accept. (Many feel this was a discovery of Freud; an idea that along with the Freudian notion of the 'unconscious' has not only permeated our commonsense psychological practices but, in the kindred (though in aspects quite different) form of 'tacit' knowledge, has permeated contemporary theorizing about language and mind in the cognitive sciences. Some of the minority who remain sceptical about unconscious thoughts have even indicated that the fallibility of the first-person ascriptions stands or falls with Freud's technical notion of the unconscious. In my view, both ideas are wrong. Freud's examples of *parapraxes* in *The Psychopathology of Everyday Life* were convincing because he identified, and put a name to, patterns of action and speech that were candidates for motivated behaviour that could be recognized as such by anyone to whom the patterns were pointed out (including the agent himself). I am not familiar enough with literary texts to know when authors started exploring the idea that the intentions and motivations could be discerned without the agent's awareness. But the idea figures commonly in Russia in the works of Dostoyevsky and Goncharov (the latter began writing *Oblomov* in 1849). In France it is evidently to be found in the work of Diderot (*Jacques le Fataliste* (written in 1773)) and it is a major theme in Constant's *Adolphe* (1816), thereby predating the popularization of Freud's work at least in France by a century or more.)

Consider a scene from *Oblomov* in which the fallibility or, in this case, the incompleteness of the subject's own gaze is manifest. Here, the idea that the contents of Olga's mind are apt for 'discovery' is especially appropriate. The reader is made aware not only of Olga's

[8] The quotation is from §193 of Wittgenstein's *Philosophical Investigations*, trans. G. E. M. Anscombe (Oxford: Basil Blackwell, 1953). He uses the metaphor to illuminate the idea that a machine's action seems to be in it from the start (and the metaphor of a machine had been introduced in an attempt to make sense of the idea that an act of meaning can in some sense anticipate reality (§188)).

words but also of her own thoughts in the form of 'inner speech'. But some of her thoughts and feelings she is not yet able to recognize: that she is in love with Oblomov, that she was pleased (albeit flustered) by Oblomov's sudden declaration of love, and that she is horrified as he attempts to take it back. Oblomov speaks first, trying to make up with her after rashly declaring his love:

> 'Please believe me, the whole thing—I mean, I don't know what made me say it—I couldn't help it,' he began gradually growing bolder. 'I'd have said it if a thunderbolt had struck me or a stone had crashed on top of me. Nothing in the world could have stopped me. Please, please don't think that I wanted—I'd have given anything a moment later to take back the rash word. ...'

> She walked with her head bowed, sniffing the flowers.
> 'Please forget it,' he went on, 'forget it, particularly as it wasn't true....'
> 'Not true?' she suddenly repeated, drawing herself up and dropping the flowers.
> Her eyes opened wide and flashed with surprise.
> 'How do you mean—not true?' she repeated.
> 'I mean—well—for God's sake don't be angry with me and forget it. Please, believe me, I was just carried away for a moment—because of the music.'
> 'Only because of the music?'
> She turned pale and her eyes grew dim.
> 'Well,' she thought, 'everything's all right now. He took back his rash words and there's no need for me to be angry any more! That's excellent—now I needn't worry any more. ... We can talk and joke as before.'
> She broke off a twig from a tree absent-mindedly, bit off a leaf, and then at once threw down the twig and the leaf on the path. 'You're not angry with me, are you? You have forgotten, haven't you?' Oblomov said, bending forward to her.
> 'What was that? What did you ask?' she said nervously, almost with vexation, turning away from him. 'I've forgotten everything—I've such a bad memory!'
> He fell silent and did not know what to do. He saw her sudden vexation but did not see the cause of it.
> 'Goodness,' she thought, 'now everything is all right again. It's just as if that scene had never taken place, thank heaven! Well, all the better. ... Oh dear, what does it all mean? [...]
> I'm going home,' she said suddenly, quickening her steps and turning into another avenue.

Julia Tanney

> There was a lump in her throat. She was afraid she might cry. (pp. 207, 208)

Oblomov sees that his attempt to take his rash words back is more distressing to Olga than his original declaration of love but does not understand why. She is mollified when he is forced virtually to redeclare his love and he is left feeling confused. Only later, in reflecting on the moment when she breaks the lilac sprig, does he come to realize that she loves him. He approaches her again, carrying the lilac sprig, armed with this new knowledge.

> 'What have you got there?'
> 'A twig.'
> 'What sort of twig?'
> 'As you see: it's lilac.'
> 'Where did you get it? There is no lilac here. Which way did you come?'
> 'It's the same sprig you plucked and threw away.'
> 'Why did you pick it up?'
> 'Oh, I don't know. I suppose I was glad that—that you threw it away in vexation.'
> 'You're glad I was vexed! That's something new. Why?'
> 'I won't tell you!'
> 'Please, do, I beg you.'
> 'Never! Not for anything in the world!'
> 'I implore you!'
> He shook his head.
> [...]
> 'What's the matter? Is it something dreadful?' she said, her whole mind concentrated on the question, glancing searchingly at him.
> Then gradually realization came to her: the ray of thought and surmise spread to every feature of her face and, suddenly, her whole face lit up with the consciousness of the truth. ...Just like the sun which, emerging from behind a cloud, sometimes first lights up one bush, then another, then the roof of a house and, suddenly, floods a whole landscape with light. She knew what Oblomov's thought was.
> 'No, no,' Oblomov kept repeating. 'I could never say it. It's no use your asking.'
> 'I'm not asking you,' she replied indifferently.
> 'Aren't you? But just now —'
> 'Let's go home,' she said seriously, without listening to him. 'Auntie is waiting.' (pp. 216, 217)

After this scene, Olga goes home and immediately begins acting like a woman in love; I shall discuss this transformation shortly. For the present all we need notice is that these passages illustrate nicely the sense in which 'discovery' is an apt description of what sometimes happens in self- and other-ascriptions. It also illustrates nicely the sense in which these ascriptions might qualify as 'objective.' Whatever pattern of thought and behaviour is supposed to indicate a person's mental states, it is often identifiable by others. In this case Oblomov is the first to identify some of Olga's thoughts and feelings. When Olga finally comes to see them, her recognition results from inference or a chain of reasoning: in this case via her realization of Oblomov's thoughts about the significance of her behaviour.

3. One of the problems with the Cartesian model is its failure to leave room for a requisite sense of objectivity. Another is its failure to accommodate the intuition that at least for many mental states (paradigmatically ones involving 'propositional attitude' concepts) the criticism we incur when we misascribe results from a kind of explanatory failure. Indeed, what generally defeats a self-ascription is its failure to fit into a rationalizing story. According to the perceptual model, defeat is rather a matter of failing to track the private items that exist in the mind's eye. Of course, even on this Cartesian model what is tracked may be—contingently—(part of) an explanatory project. But later philosophy of mind has accorded mental concepts (especially those apt to play a role in reason-explanation) with more than a merely contingent explanatory role: the intuition—which forced those attracted to physicalism to withdraw to token physicalism—is that propositional attitude concepts in particular (and hence the emotional states that presuppose them) are — constitutively—explanatory concepts.

Functionalism—the dominant position in contemporary philosophy of mind—seems to avoid both objections to the Cartesian model and yet retain the sense in which self-knowledge is comfortably seen as a matter of discovery. This theory of the mental says that when we ascribe a mental concept to an individual, this concept refers to a state the person is in that has appropriate causal connections to sensory input, behavioural output, and other internal states.

According to this doctrine, success in ascription would fundamentally be a matter of tracking or homing in upon those states with the appropriate causal specification. Functionalists might still maintain that the point of mental-concept ascription is to render intelligible the one to whom the concepts are ascribed, as long as it is the causal role that is doing the explanatory work. This picture would seem to be consistent with ideas exemplified in the scenes from *Oblomov* at least insofar as ascription is tantamount to the discovery of a pattern. It is also consistent with the idea that a person might not be in the best position to notice this pattern (as causal role).

Problems arise, however, when one reflects on what exactly is doing the explanatory work. Although I will not argue for this here, I think it is doubtful whether functionalists can consistently maintain that the explanatory project is a *rationalizing* project or that mental concepts are explanatory in virtue of the way in which 'things are made intelligible by being revealed to be, or to approximate to being, as they rationally ought to be'.[9] They will not be able to do this, at least, if such a style of explanation is 'to be contrasted with a style of explanation in which one makes things intelligible by representing their coming into being as a particular instance of how things generally tend to happen.'[10]

If, as I believe, these styles of explanation are indeed different,[11] then a question arises about functionalism's relation to our ordinary, commonsense ascriptive practices where these are understood as making fundamental use of *rationalizing* explanations. Functionalism, as originally conceived, was a thesis about the meaning of mental predicates—presumably about the meaning of those predicates used within our ordinary, commonsense, psychological practices. As such, its viability as a theory of mind would depend upon whether the concepts ascribed within these practices do, in effect, track internal, functionally individuated (physically realized), causally efficacious states or events.

My suspicion is that they do not. I mention this difference in explanatory patterns—between causal-explanatory patterns on the one hand, and rationalizing patterns on the other—because I suspect it will be of utmost importance. For it is arguably the rationalizing pattern and not (or not merely) the causal-explanatory one that allows the reintroduction of an inventive aspect to the role of self-ascriptions.

4. I now intend to consider what is intuitively attractive about the idea that a person has some inventive or creative role to play in

[9] The phrase is John McDowell's in 'Functionalism and Anomalous Monism', *Actions and Events: Perspectives on the Philosophy of Donald Davidson*, Lepore and McLaughlin (eds) (Oxford: Basil Blackwell, 1985), p. 389.

[10] Ibid. p. 389

[11] See my 'Why Reasons May Not be Causes' *Mind & Language*, **10**, nos. 1/2, pp. 103–126.

respect to his mental life. I have discussed how it makes sense to say that Olga's realization of her love for Oblomov came as a discovery (one that Oblomov had made before her). But to call it a 'discovery' would only be partly correct. A few hours after Olga realizes her feeling for Oblomov, she becomes transformed.

> He waited nervously and with trepidation for Olga to come down to dinner, wondering what she would say, how she would speak, and how she would look at him. ...
>
> She came down—and he could not help admiring her; he hardly recognized her. Her face was different, even her voice was not the same. The young, naïve, almost childish smile not once appeared on her lips; she did not once look at him with wide-open eyes questioningly or puzzled or with good-natured curiosity, as though she had nothing more to ask, find out, or be surprised at. Her eyes did not follow him as before. She looked at him as though she had studied him thoroughly, and, finally, as though he were nothing to her, no more than the baron—in short, he felt as though he had not seen her for a whole year during which she had grown into a woman. (pp. 222, 223)

Olga is transformed from someone who was (arguably) in love into someone who now acts in self-conscious awareness of her love or in accordance with her own conception of how a woman in love should act. Might not this passage suggest that there is something right about the idea that the nature of the love she has 'discovered' is changed as a result of these subsequent actions, and hence as a result of this self-awareness? The idea would be not merely that her love for Oblomov causes her transformation into a 'woman' or even that her *awareness* of it does, but rather that her awareness and her endorsement of it somehow affect the love or the shape of the love itself. They play a role in a more complex 'rationalizing project' that involves her own conception of how a woman in love should act. This explanation of her behaviour (that she is in love with Oblomov), its endorsement by Olga, and its role in an ongoing rationalizing project give shape to, or articulate, a pattern or a possibility which in turn (retrospectively, as it were) supports the original explanation that Olga is in love.

Charles Taylor has, in a series of articles, attempted to argue for the idea (which he credits to Heidegger) that a person's self-conception partly constitutes the mental state he is in.[12] He argues that much of what we think, feel, and value is not the result of our being moved by forces like gravity or electro-magnetism. Our desires and aspirations are given formulation in words or images; they cannot but be articulated or interpreted by us somehow. But these articulations

> are not simply descriptions, if we mean by this characteriza-
> tions of a fully independent object, that is, an object which is
> altered neither in what it is, nor in the degree or manner of its
> evidence to us by the description. In this way my characteri-
> zation of this table as brown, or this line of mountains as
> jagged, is a simple description.
>
> On the contrary, articulations are attempts to formulate
> what is initially inchoate, or confused, or badly formulated.
> But this kind of formulation or reformulation does not leave
> its object unchanged. To give a certain articulation is to shape
> our sense of what we desire or what we hold important in a
> certain way.[13]

Taylor gives his own example of what he means but the point can be developed by staying with the character of Olga and by noting how Olga's endorsement of herself as a woman in love gives shape to, or articulates what—although it amounted to a 'discovery'—had been inchoate or confused before.

An analogy might be helpful. Think about a duck-rabbit design, which, although ambiguous between being either the head of a duck or a head of a rabbit, is arguably not the head of a cow or pig. Now, imagine that when the figure is drawn with more detail (a body is added) it becomes a duck and not a rabbit. The analogy would be that Olga's pattern of behaviour before her reflections was in cer-tain ways indeterminate (although certain interpretations of her behaviour could be ruled out) just as the duck-rabbit design is inde-terminate or ambiguous (though certain interpretations can be ruled out). After her reflections and her endorsement of one pattern (she recognizes it as a duck), she behaves in a way that is consistent with that recognition. Her endorsement of it (as a duck) and her subsequent behaviour allow the pattern to develop in such a way (say, it develops a beak, webbed feet, feathers, etc.) that renders the other interpretation no longer viable.

This idea can be spelled out in more detail when we consider what happens to Olga later in the novel. Her relation with Oblomov has

[12] See especially 'What is Human Agency?', 'Self-Interpreting Animals', and 'The Concept of a Person', reprinted as chapters 1, 2, and 4, respec-tively in *Human Agency and Language: Philosophical Papers* (Cambridge: Cambridge University Press, 1985).

[13] 'What is Human Agency', op. cit., p. 36.

come to a painful end and she has slowly started to enjoy, and depend more and more upon, the company of her old friend, Stolz. Stolz falls in love with Olga and she is confused about her feelings for him.

If she loved Stolz, then what was her first love? Flirtation, frivolity, or worse? She blushed with shame and turned hot at this thought. She would never accuse herself of that. But if that was her first pure love, what were her relations to Stolz? Again play, deception, subtle calculation, to entice him into marriage so as to cover up the frivolity of her conduct? She turned cold and pale at the very thought of it. But if it was not play, or deception or calculation—so ... was it love again? But such a supposition made her feel utterly at a loss: a second love—eight or seven months after the first! Who would believe her? How could she mention it without causing surprise, perhaps—contempt! She dared not think of it. She had no right. She ransacked her memory: there was nothing there about a second love. She recalled the authoritative opinions of her aunts, old maids, all sorts of clever people, and, finally, writers, 'philosophers of love'—and on all sides she heard the inescapable verdict: 'A woman loves truly only once.' [...] (pp. 400, 401)

Olga concludes that what she feels for Stolz must only be a sisterly love. Stolz confronts her about her baffling behaviour and she is eventually forced to confess that she had been in love with Oblomov and she tells him the whole story of their courtship. When she then shows Stolz a letter Oblomov had written to her very early in their relationship, Stolz uses it to interpret Olga's past feelings rather differently.

'Listen,' he said, and he read: ' "Your present *I love you* is not real love, but the love you will feel in the future [...] You have *made a mistake*" (Stolz read, emphasizing the words) "the man before you is not the one you have been expecting and dreaming of. Wait—he will come, and then you will come to your senses and you will feel vexed and ashamed of your mistake" ... You see how true it is,' he said. 'You were vexed and ashamed of—your mistake. There is nothing to add to this. He was right and you did not believe him—that is all your guilt amounts to.' [...]
'I did not believe him. I thought one's heart could not be mistaken.'
'Yes, it can, and sometimes very disastrously! But with you it never went as far as the heart,' he added. 'It was imagina-

Julia Tanney

tion and vanity on one side, and weakness on the other.' [...] (pp. 411, 412).[14]

When Olga comes to accept this new interpretation of her feelings for Oblomov (albeit mistakenly, I would judge), her love for Stolz becomes a possibility for her in a way that it could not have been without this change of self-conception. She could not rationally hold that she was in love with Oblomov, that a woman only loves once and that she now is in love with Stolz. With Stolz's encouragement she gives up the idea that she had been in love with Oblomov. Once her self-conception or 'practical identity'[15] has been made consistent, she is able to reinterpret her feelings for Stolz as more than mere sisterly love and thereafter allows herself to act freely upon this new conception. The romantic love for Stolz thus takes shape. It is presumably this sort of phenomenon that leads Taylor to claim that

> [w]e can say therefore that our self-interpretations are partly constitutive of our experience. For an altered description of our motivation can be inseparable from a change in this motivation. But to assert this connection is not to put forward a causal hypothesis: it is not to say that we alter our descriptions and then *as a result* our experience of our predicament alters. Rather it is that certain modes of experience of our predicament are not possible without certain self-descriptions.[16]

5. Richard Moran has recently argued, *pace* Taylor, that the sense in which a person's self-conception affects his emotions or other first-

---

[14] Oblomov wrote the letter that Stolz refers to out of a mixture of cowardice and vanity: partly in an attempt to derail the impending complication that such a relationship would bring to his life, and partly to witness Olga's distress as she reads the letter. His claim that Olga does not really love him is, I think, most implausible, but it is an interpretation with which Stolz can tempt Olga.

[15] The term is taken from Korsgaard, C., *The Sources of Normativity* (Cambridge: Cambridge University Press, 1996).

[16] Taylor, 'What is Human Agency?', op. cit., p. 37.
Compare:

> Our contingent practical identities are, to some extent, given to us— by our cultures, by our societies and their role structures, by the accidents of birth, and by our natural abilities—but it is also clear that we enter into their construction. And this means that the desires and impulses associated with them do not just *arise* in us. When we adopt (or come to wholeheartedly inhabit) a conception of practical identity, we also adopt a way of life and a set of projects, and the new desires which this brings in its wake (Korsgaard, op. cit., p. 239)

order mental states is not a logical, individuative, or constitutive one: it is causal.[17] If his argument is sound, then it might undermine the constructivist view I am attempting to defend and lend plausibility instead to the idea that our mental concepts refer to states that play a complex causal role.

There is a constant slide, Moran argues, between two different stances we might take toward our mental states. On the one hand, we might take what he calls a 'theoretical stance' towards our mental states *qua* independently existing objects and describe or track them. On the other, we might take a practical stance toward them and make a restricted, 'indirect' decision about what to believe or what to intend. This latter, practical question about what to believe is 'transparent to', or answered in the same way as, our theoretical questions about (what is true in) the world.

According to Moran, the rationality of agents has a dual aspect: it ensures that a person's beliefs will aim at the truth, and it ensures that a person's second-order beliefs about his own mental states will affect his first-order beliefs. For example, if the self-interpreter notices an inconsistency or a contradiction in his first-order beliefs his theoretical question about what he believes 'involves reasoning guided by the question of what is true about the object of belief'.[18] The idea, presumably, is that the theoretical question about what I believe will transform itself into a practical question about what *to* believe, since the observation that one's belief is false is, at least *prima facie*, sufficient to destroy the belief. Moran insists that this relationship between second-order and first-order beliefs is not to be construed as a constitutive or logical relationship. It is simply a matter of the tendency of theoretical questions to transform themselves into practical questions. He concludes that 'self-understanding and self-change *can* be understood in a way that maintains the logical independence of interpretation and its object.'[19]

But Moran avoids, I think, the crucial issue in characterizing one of the stances I might take toward my beliefs as *practical* instead of *normative*. On the latter conception, it will be much more difficult to make out a contrast between two different stances, since the normative cuts across the distinction between the theoretical and the practical. There would be some truth, for example, in saying that theoretical questions about what I believe can transform themselves into normative questions about what I should believe, in a way that is transparent to questions about what is true in the world. But

[17] 'Making Up Your Mind', *Ratio*, **1**, (1988), p. 148.
[18] Ibid. p. 148.
[19] Ibid. p. 149.

Julia Tanney

questions about what I believe also are influenced by questions about what would explain (rationalize) my actions (both past and anticipated present ones), what would best cohere with the other beliefs that I hold or that I have held, as well as my principles, my long term projects, and so forth.

In order to make out his case that beliefs are logically independent of the subject's gaze, Moran suggests that we focus on a person's *past* beliefs and his present interpretations of them, because practical questions do not apply to these and in such cases, the theoretical question about what I believed will not be influenced by practical questions about truth (and thus the question about what *to* believe). The idea is that the theoretical identification of a past belief will not transform itself into a practical question about what *to* believe, since the practical question is now out of date.

But questions about what would explain my actions, what would best cohere with the other beliefs, and so forth, might well influence my identification of a past belief as much as they will influence my identification of a present one. Indeed, because of the pervasiveness of these normative criteria on belief identification, it simply is not clear that there is a viable distinction between a theoretical and a normative stance I might adopt toward my own mental states. (Notice how this point is suggested in the passage from *Oblomov* cited as the epigram to this paper: Olga did not know herself what she thought—what she ought to say or do.) Moran might be right in saying that I can ascribe to myself a past but not a present belief that I know to be false. Nonetheless, because of the other normative constraints (besides the aim for truth) on belief identification, there is plenty of scope to re-introduce the idea that a person's self-conception plays a constitutive, and not merely causal, role in *shaping* (and not merely in describing) his first-order mental states.

In order to pursue this idea further, consider the obligations or entitlements that self-ascription, or indeed any epistemic claim, imposes. A particular ascription, for example, will commit the ascriber to a certain range of justifications he might give for it, if challenged. It will commit him to a range of considerations that would count against it or would follow from it, and included here, of course, would be a certain range of actions. Should a sufficient number of the further commitments fail to obtain or to be endorsed, this puts increased pressure on the self-ascriber to withdraw the original ascription. To take a simple example, suppose that my choice of restaurants might be explained by either the quality of the food or the location. My accepting the latter as a reason, then, ought to affect my attitude toward the suggestion that I might find equally good food elsewhere. I might, of course, be wrong about why I chose the restaurant (and the alacrity with which I agree to go elsewhere might suggest a reason to suspect that I was). In this case, I ought to re-evaluate my reason for choosing this restaurant. My continued acceptance of location as a reason even if I agree without hesitation to go elsewhere creates a tension which needs sorting either by introducing other reasons for acting into the picture (e.g., I recognize that my companion wants very badly to dine elsewhere) or by my construing my decision to go elsewhere as one that fails to reflect my preference. This is similar to the unstable position Olga found herself in when trying to sort out her feelings for Stolz. My own understanding of or take on my mental attitudes carries with it rational constraints on my future choices, decisions, actions, explanations, criticisms, and justifications. This is true for reasons or attitudes that I attribute to myself as a result of reflection or interpretation; it is also true for immediately ascribed expressions or avowals.

Intentional actions, propositional attitudes, and affective states that presuppose them are identified as such by their role in a pattern of other thoughts and actions. I would like to suggest that if the pattern is a rationalizing one, and thus explanatory in the sense that 'things are made intelligible by being revealed to be, or to approximate being, as they rationally ought to be', then at least many patterns will be 'open-ended' and lend themselves to further, and perhaps different interpretations. Consider how John Wisdom characterizes the idea:[20]

> Suppose two people are speaking of two characters in a story which both have read or of two friends which both have known, and one says 'Really she hated him', and the other says 'She didn't, she loved him'. Then the first may have noticed what the other has not although he knows no incident in the lives of the people they are talking about which the other doesn't know too, and the second speaker may say 'She didn't, she loved him' because he hasn't noticed what the first noticed, although he can remember every incident the first can remember.

Like an aesthetic dispute about, say, the beauty of an object, or a legal dispute about, for instance, whether reasonable care has been exercised, reasons for or against a certain judgment can be adduced. But in cases such as these,

> we notice that the process of argument is not a *chain* of demonstrative reasoning. It is a presenting and representing of those features of the case which *severally co-operate* in favour

[20] 'Gods', *Logic and Language* (Oxford: Basil Blackwell, 1963 (originally published 1951)), pp. 191–192.

of the conclusion, in favour of saying what the reasoner wishes said, in favour of calling the situation by the name by which he wishes to call it. The reasons are like the legs of a chair not the links of a chain.[21]

This is plausibly the case when we make evaluative judgments in matters of ethics or in practical deliberation about what it would be rational to do as well. Wiggins makes a similar point in a passage in which he is discussing an idea that can be salvaged from a naïve non-cognitivism in ethics and imported into a more sophisticated doctrine of cognitive underdetermination:

> ...not all the claims of all rational concerns or even of all moral concerns (that the world *be* thus or so) need be actually reconcilable. When we judge that this is what we must do now, or that that is what we'd better do, or that our life must now take one direction rather than another direction, we are not fitting truths (or even probabilities) into a pattern where a discrepancy proves that we have mistaken a falsehood for a truth. Often we have to make a practical choice that another rational agent might understand through and through, not fault or even disagree with, but ... make differently himself. ... [22]

It seems to me that the freedom alluded to here with respect to our practical choices figures as well as a feature of our interpretive practices. I suggest that it is arguably indeterminate at the time she broke the lilac whether Olga loved Oblomov just as it was arguably indeterminate whether, at the time she was confronted by Stolz, she had sisterly or romantic feelings for *him*. (I think it is indeterminate whether Constant's Adolphe, in seducing Ellénore, was really in love or was rather simply carried away by the intensity of what had been a game.) Their 'self-takes' play a role in 'articulating' what had been indeterminate before.[23]

[21] Ibid. p. 195.

[22] Wiggins, D. 'Truth, Invention and the Meaning of Life', op. cit., p. 126.

[23] Or, in cases of self-deception, confusing or muddling what had been inchoate before. In these cases there are at least two strands of thought/action patterns manifested. One is the pattern that belies the agent's self-conception and uncovers her ignorance about her own mind. The other is the pattern—often of denials, of protestations, of avoidance—that is a straightforwardly rationalizable outcome of this self-conception. Adolphe, who is self-deceived about the obstacles to his worldy success, is not merely wrong to blame his relationship with Ellénore. His false conception about their life together feeds into a whole pattern of behaviour leading to a tragedy that is itself only rendered comprehensible by this conception.

Self-knowledge, Normativity, and Construction

The case I am making works for states that are inchoate, confused, or multiply interpretable. Not all mental ascriptions or avowals fall into this category. This may be because the subsequent commitments to which an ascription or avowal is answerable have been largely fulfilled, or because it involves relatively little by way of such commitments, like my expression of the desire to have a glass of wine after I have finished work for the day. Other of my desires and intentions—to develop my singing voice, to complete an edging of Bucks Point lace, to expend no more and no less than a reasonable amount of effort doing philosophy—are more complex. They involve commitments extending well into the future that will come into contact and conflict with other intentions, short-term desires, and perhaps some principles or values too. It is true that in considering the application of a concept like love, I am considering complex and pivotal (or central) patterns of action, running from and to numerous other sub-patterns. But although philosophy of mind's discussions tend to take simple, discrete actions (like raising one's arm to signal) as its paradigm case, it is committed to explaining the mental states that figure in an explanation of the projects, plans, commitments, and so forth that constitute a person's life as well.

That it is a *person*'s life is important here. Patterns of animal behaviour can be identified in and rationalized by intentional psychological terms.[24] But although animals can act in accordance with

[24] And perhaps even the 'differential response dispositions' shown by thermometers. Charles Taylor ('What is Human Agency', op. cit., p. 28) suggests parenthetically that Camus's Mersault might an example of someone who fails one test of personhood insofar as he lacks the ability to 'deploy a language of evaluative contrasts ranging over desires' (p. 23). Consider another character from *Oblomov*. Agafya Matveyevna Pshenitzyn, the woman whose elbows entrance Oblomov and eventually capture his heart, is described by the narrator as someone barely capable of self-reflective awareness.

> Had she been asked if she loved him, she would again have smiled and said yes, but she would have given the same reply when Oblomov had lived no more than a week at her house. (p. 374)
> ...
> He was a gentleman: he dazzled, he scintillated! And, besides, he was so kind; he walked so softly, his movements were so exquisite; if he touched her hand, it was like velvet, and whenever her husband had touched her, it was like a blow! And he looked and talked so gently, with such kindness. ...She did not think all these things, nor was she consciously aware of it all, but if anyone had tried to analyse and explain the impression made on her mind by Oblomov's coming into her life, he would not be able to give any other explanation. (p. 375)

some rational norms (and this might suffice to ascribe intentional states to them) they cannot *follow* those norms. They lack, that is, the meta-ability to understand what the norms commit them to. This will involve an ability to see ways in which a pattern might continue consistently with certain identifications but inconsistently with others. And this ability to recognize patterns and to act in accordance with them because they have been endorsed will introduce a complexity to the patterns that would have been inconceivable for non self-reflective beings. If what I have been arguing here is correct, part of this complexity will involve a kind of self-construction or self-constitution. It is the role of the (whole) person in this construction—the understanding of the commitments and obligations of a rational agent—that seems ill accommodated by causal, reductionist accounts.

6. I have suggested elsewhere that a plausible constructivism about the mental will go some of the way toward explaining the authority of first-person applications of mental concepts and the asymmetry between first- and third-personal ascriptions.[25] A plausible constructivism about the mental will also grant that the choices available in interpretation are not free or unconstrained—anymore than the choices available in musical composition are unconstrained. W. C. Kneale has argued that the important contrast for the constructivist is one that emphasizes the difference between geographical or historical claims on the one hand, and mathematical, and some ethical, practical, and aesthetic claims that are likened to artistic creation on the other.[26] No plausible use of 'invention' in this

[25] 'A Constructivist Picture of Self-Knowledge', op. cit.
[26] 'The Idea of Invention', in *Proceedings of the British Academy* vol. 39, 1955; pp. 85–108.

...

Agafya Matveyevna herself was not only incapable of flirting with Oblomov and revealing to him by some sigh what was going on inside her, but, as has already been said, she was never aware of it or understood it herself ... Mrs Pshenitzyn's feeling, so normal, natural, disinterested, remained a mystery to Oblomov, to the people around her, and to herself. (p.376)

Her brother even characterises her as an animal:

'She can't be expected to look after her interests, can she? A cow—that's what she is, a blamed cow: hit her or hug her, she goes on grinning like a horse at a nosebagful of oats.' (p. 357)

context would suppose that it means being capable of creating possibilities from nothing as some—incoherently, he thinks—believe God capable of. 'An artist can do no more than select an interesting possibility'.[27] As long as the distinction between say, geographical and mathematical claims is kept in mind (e.g., that America existed before the first men landed there but the infinitesimal calculus did not exist before it was first formulated), then, Kneale argues, the terms 'invention' and 'finding' may both be apt, since there is no relevant difference between making-with-the-mind and finding-with-the-mind. The contrast between the cases is rather (partly) between what we find with the sense organs and what we find with the mind.

If it is conceded that both the Cartesian and the functionalist suppose that it is something on analogy with a sense organ that 'finds' or 'discovers' the denizens of the mind—the 'mind's eye' on the first model, and an internal scanner on the second—then the contrast is one I can adopt. I am arguing for a rejection of *this* mode of discovery, and am plumping instead for the discovery or selection of something akin to an 'interesting possibility'. This would allow us to begin making sense, then, of the 'compossibility' of objectivity, discovery, *and* invention in the area of psychological discourse.[28]

University of Kent at Canterbury

[27] Ibid. p. 101

[28] This paper was written during study leave made possible by an AHRB Research Award, for which I would like to record my gratitude. It was first presented in March 1999 at a colloquium on Subjectivity hosted by the Kent Institute for Advanced Studies in the Humanities at the University of Kent. Thanks to John Flower, Edward Harcourt and Richard Norman for their comments, and to David Wiggins and Crispin Wright for helpful criticism and suggestions on the penultimate draft.

The Normativity of Meaning

ALAN MILLAR

1. The topic

In a discussion of rule-following inspired by Wittgenstein, Kripke asks us to consider the relation which holds between meaning plus by '+' and answering questions like, 'What is the sum of 68 and 57?'. A dispositional theory has it that if you mean plus by '+' then you will probably answer, '125'. That is because, according to such a theory, to mean plus by '+' *is*, roughly speaking, to be disposed, by and large, and among other things, to answer such questions with the correct sum. Kripke wants to emphasize, by contrast, that if you mean plus by '+' then, faced with the question, 'What is 68 + 57?' you *ought* to answer, '125'.[1] One could sum up the assumption about meaning which appears to underpin this criticism of dispositional theories in terms of the slogan that meaning is normative. Allan Gibbard gives us a way of reading that slogan which is suggested by Kripke's brief remarks:

> The crux of the slogan that meaning is normative ... might be another slogan: that *means* implies *ought*. To use roughly Kripke's example, from statements saying what I mean by the plus sign and other arithmetic terms and constructions, it will follow that I *ought* to answer '7' when asked 'What's 5 + 2?'.[2]

If Gibbard is right then the following are true: (i) The issue about the normativity of meaning is whether statements to the effect that one means such-and-such by an expression have normative implications. (ii) The relevant normative implications are statements to the effect that the subject in question ought to use the term in this or that way. I agree with (i) and, further, think that it is an important claim. If it is true then ignoring it would be like ignoring the fact that claims to the effect that a certain action is morally wrong have normative implications. For reasons which will emerge, I disagree with (ii) and will argue that the relevant normative

---

[1] Saul Kripke *Wittgenstein on Rules and Private Language* (Oxford: Blackwell, 1982), 37. Cf. 11 and 23f.
[2] Allan Gibbard 'Meaning and Normativity', in Enrique Villanueva (ed.), *Philosophical Issues 5: Truth and Rationality* 1994, 95–115. The quoted passage occurs on p. 100.

implications express not claims about what the subject ought to do but rather claims about what the subject is committed to doing.

One problem with the current state of play in this area is that while some philosophers appear to take the thesis that meaning is normative to be bedrock, others are either baffled by it or think the appearance of normativity can be explained away. Another problem is that there are different, not obviously equivalent, ways of formulating the thesis. My aim here is to work towards a clear formulation and to highlight considerations which make the thesis at least plausible.

2. Normativity, correctness and use

The claim that meaning is normative is not always expressed in terms of what users of a word ought to do. Sometimes it is formulated in terms of the idea that the meanings of words are associated with conditions of correct use. In this section I highlight a crucial ambiguity in the notion of correct use. In the next I consider how correctness is linked to what users ought to do.

In an oft-cited survey of ideas about rule-following, bearing directly on Kripke's reflections, Paul Boghossian formulates the thesis of normativity as follows:

> The normativity of meaning turns out to be ... simply a new name for the familiar fact that, regardless of whether one thinks of meaning in truth-theoretic or assertion-theoretic terms, meaningful expressions possess conditions of *correct use*. (On the one construal, correctness consists in *true* use, on the other, in *warranted* use.)[3]

What interests me in this statement is the fact that 'use' is clearly being understood to mean something like *application*.[4] To apply the term 'oak' is to predicate it of some object and thus say of that

[3] Paul Boghossian, 'The Rule-Following Considerations', *Mind* **98**, 1989, 513.

[4] Even where correctness of use is not, as in the quotation from Boghossian, identified with truth or warrantedness of application, uses which are applications are commonly used at least to illustrate correctness of use. See, for example, Gregory McCulloch, *The Mind and Its World* (London and New York: Routledge, 1995), 100, Barry Loewer, 'A Guide to Naturalizing Semantics', in Bob Hale and Crispin Wright (eds), *A Companion to the Philosophy of Language* (Oxford: Blackwell, 1997), 108–26 and Paul Horwich, *Meaning*, (Oxford: Clarendon Press, 1998), 92ff.

object that it is, depending on the context, oak or an oak. With use understood to be application, correct use, naturally, is taken to be true or warranted application. But this is not the only way to characterize correct use. Another way is to say that a use of an expression is correct if and only if it is in accordance with (in keeping with, faithful to) the meaning of the expression. This notion of correctness figures in discussions of rule-following by Crispin Wright and by John McDowell.[5] It is interesting to note that while a recent explanation of the idea of the normativity of meaning, in the glossary to Bob Hale and Crispin Wright (eds) *A Companion to the Philosophy of Language*,[6] clearly invokes the notion of correct application, it seems also to allude to the idea that correct use is use in keeping with meaning:

> It is a central ingredient in understanding an expression to grasp that there are associated with it conditions for its correct application. Put another way, it is essential to any expression's possessing whatever meaning it does, that there are rules for its correct use. In this sense, meaning is normative.[7]

It is the notion of rules of correct use which is suggestive of the idea that correctness of use is use in keeping with meaning, since use in keeping with meaning would be use in conformity with the rules for correct use which are fixed by the relevant meaning. The passage invites reflection on (a) the relation between application and use, (b) the relation between the two characterizations of correctness, and (c) the relation between conditions of correct application and rules of correct use.

(a) *Use and application.* Evidently use is wider than application. You use the term 'oak' when you ask, 'Is that an oak?' or when you say, 'Had that been an oak we would not have cut it down', but in neither of these cases do you apply the term to an object in the sense

[5] See Crispin Wright, *Wittgenstein and the Foundations of Mathematics* (London: Duckworth, 1980), ch. 2 and John McDowell, 'Wittgenstein on Following a Rule', *Synthese* **58**, 1984, 325–63. The notion also seems to figure in Boghossian's discussion at the point at which he emphasizes that normativity has to do with a relation between meaning something by an expression at some time and the use of that expression at that time. ('The Rule-Following Considerations', 513). This suggests that the use may or may not be in keeping with the meaning and would be correct if it is and incorrect if it is not.

[6] For details, see note 4.

[7] Op. cit. 674.

explained earlier, for your use of the term does not consist in anything which amounts to saying of something that it is an oak. Further, it is convenient to think of one's uses of a word as encompassing not only one's utterances of that word but also one's dealings with the word when understanding, or trying to understand, utterances of it by others. You use the term 'oak' if you infer from someone's saying, 'The oak is in splendid condition' that he is referring to a tree. We can think of these as *interpretative*, as opposed to *expressive*, uses of the word. Interpretative uses are not applications.

(b) *The two characterizations of correctness.* Using a term in keeping with a meaning contrasts with misusing it, on a very natural conception of misuse, which may be illustrated with the help of an example from Tyler Burge. In the example, a patient—let us call him Fred—applies the term 'arthritis' to a painful condition of his limbs in the belief that it applies to any painful condition of the limbs or joints. In so doing he is aiming to give the doctor accurate information about his condition. Clearly, Fred *misapplies* the term since it stands for a condition which is due to inflammation of the joints. His use is therefore incorrect in the sense of being false. Fred also uses the term incorrectly in the sense which goes with *misuse*. We have a plausible explanation of what makes the misapplication a misuse. Though he is aiming to give the doctor accurate information, Fred applies the term without regard to whether the condition to which it is applied is due to inflammation of the joints. Anyone who knew the conditions for true application of the term would be committed by that knowledge to avoiding such an application in an utterance aimed at conveying accurate information. Suppose that Fred's doctor, who knows perfectly well what the term 'arthritis' means, mistakenly takes Fred to have pain due to inflamed joints and applies the term to his condition on that basis. The doctor has certainly misapplied the term, but he has not on that account misused it—failed to use it in keeping with its meaning. He is not committed by his knowledge of the relevant conditions of true application to avoiding applications of the term on the basis in question, in contexts in which he is aiming by these applications to convey accurate information. Maybe his use displays some kind of incompetence at determining whether a patient has inflamed joints, but that is a different matter.[8] This case shows that a false

[8] It might be suggested that it cannot be merely knowledge of the conditions for true application of 'arthritis' which commits one to avoiding the use Fred makes of the term. This might be said on the grounds that since Fred and the doctor both know that 'arthritis' is given true application to

application is not necessarily a misuse, on the present understanding of 'misuse'. A variant of Fred's case shows that a misuse is not necessarily a false application. On some occasion Fred may apply 'arthritis' to a condition which is arthritis. The application is correct (= true), but if made regardless of whether the person had inflamed joints, and in an utterance aimed at conveying accurate information, then it is a misuse—knowledge of the conditions for true application of the term commits one to avoiding such applications. An important point to emerge from these observations is that we have a test for whether a use is a misuse and indirectly a test for whether a use is in keeping with the relevant meaning. *A use of a term is a misuse if and only if knowledge of the conditions for true application of the term commits one to avoiding such a use.* To put it another way: a use is a misuse if it fails to respect the conditions for the true application of the term. A use is correct in the sense of being in keeping with the relevant meaning provided that it is not a misuse. An application which is correct, in the sense of being true, may or not be correct, in the sense of being in keeping with the relevant meaning, and an application which is correct, in the sense of being in keeping with the relevant meaning, may or may not be correct, in the sense of being true. Thus correctness of use, conceived as true application is not the same notion as correctness of use conceived as use in keeping with meaning. It is open to those who take correct application to be warranted, rather than true, application to adopt a modified version of the position just reached. Use in keeping with meaning would, on the modified theory, be use which respects the relevant conditions for warranted application. I shall not explore further in that direction but will work with the idea that use in keeping with meaning is use which respects the relevant conditions for true application. The theory of meaning can hardly avoid making conditions of true application central. I assume that any further refinements required by consideration of conditions of warranted

---

a condition if and only if the condition is arthritis, what the doctor has and Fred lacks cannot be accounted for in terms of knowledge of the conditions for true application of the term. The right response here, I think, is that while both Fred and the doctor have knowledge of the conditions of true application of the term, the doctor, unlike Fred, appreciates what this knowledge commits him to. This appreciation amounts to the fact that the doctor knows enough about arthritis to know that unless a condition is due to inflammation of the joints it is not arthritis. We should resist the tempting thought that Fred does not really know the conditions for the true application of the term, since that makes it hard to see how it can be that he has *some* grasp of the meaning of the term.

application would still leave in place a conception of use in keeping with meaning as use respecting conditions for true application.

(c) *Conditions for correct application and rules for correct use.* The passage quoted above from Hale and Wright's *Companion* speaks of both conditions of correct application and rules for correct use. Clearly, conditions are not the same as rules. Rules may be followed or flouted; conditions may or may not be satisfied. Conditions of correct application, I am now assuming, are just conditions necessary or sufficient for an application to be true. Still, conditions for the true application of a term surely bear upon all uses of the term since any use of a term, whether an application or not, can be assessed in terms of whether it respects or fails to respect the conditions of correct application. Suppose you say to me, 'Cut down the oak', referring to the one and only oak tree in the garden. I understand what you are saying and thus know to which tree you are referring. Though I use the term 'oak' in this context I do not apply it. Even so, my use respects the conditions for true application of the term. But if I take you to be referring to a tree which is in fact a lime then that may be because I fail to respect the relevant conditions of true application, thinking falsely that the term 'oak' applies to trees which, unknown to me, are limes. With these considerations in mind it is not hard to see why it is plausible that conditions for true application give rise to rules. There is a sense of the term 'oak' in which it is given true application to an object if and only if that object is an oak tree (as opposed to oak, the type of wood). So it is plausible that those who use the term in that sense are subject to the rule: when that sense is in play, use 'oak' only in ways which respect those conditions of true application, that is, only in ways which are in keeping with its meaning oak tree.

Talk of what users of a word *ought* to do with it has been conspicuously lacking in the discussion of this section but was central to the topic announced in section 1. In the section which follows I consider how oughts might be brought back into the picture or, perhaps more accurately, discerned within the picture already sketched.

3. Oughts and commitments

From the position reached in the previous section one might well suppose that it is a short step to the view that

(1) 'Oak' has a sense on which it means oak tree

implies

(2) When that sense is in play 'oak' ought to be used in conformity with the following rule: use it in ways which respect the
conditions for true application fixed by its meaning oak tree.

This position is not quite the same as that captured by the *means-
implies-ought* slogan proposed by Gibbard and featuring in section
1. Filling out the latter in line with the results of section 2, and
applying it to 'oak', we have the view that

(3) At least on some occasions of use, you mean oak tree by 'oak'

implies

(4) You ought to use 'oak', on those occasions, in accordance with
the rule: respect the conditions for true application fixed by its
meaning oak tree.

The first position outlined makes how a *term* ought to be used
dependent on what *it* means. The second makes how a *person* ought
to use the term dependent on what *that person* means by it. But a
very natural thought at this point is that the two positions amount
to the same thing. To clarify the first position we need to say to
whom the 'ought' applies when it said that a term ought to be used
in such-and-such a way. The two positions would amount to the
same thing if those to whom 'ought' applies are those who, on some
occasions of use, mean oak tree by 'oak'. So the question to consider now is whether there is plausible reading of 'you mean oak tree
by "oak"' on which the two positions come to the same thing. I
think there is.

First we need to consider what makes (1) true. A plausible view,
in line with an honourable tradition of thinking on these matters, is
that what makes it true that 'oak' has a sense on which it means oak
tree is that there is a practice of using 'oak' to refer to a certain kind
of tree, an oak tree. Now a practice, in the sense which matters here,
is an activity governed by rules. In this case the practice is governed
by the rule to the effect that one respect the following conditions for
true application of 'oak': 'oak' is given true application to an object
if and only if it is an oak tree. The effect of conforming to that rule
is that when the relevant sense is in play one respects the conditions
specified. Participating in the practice makes one subject to that
rule although, as with other practices, like playing a game of soccer,
one may participate in the practice and also flout the rules. Now if,
just in virtue of participating in a practice, one ought, when the
practice is in play, to act in accordance with the rules which govern

it, then we have an explanation for why (1) implies (2): (1) is true if and only if there is a practice of using 'oak' to refer to oak trees and that being so it follows (by this explanation) that those who participate in the practice ought, when that practice is in play, to use 'oak' in accordance with the relevant rule.

The next step is to relate what has just been said to the notion of a person's meaning oak tree by 'oak'. What makes (3) true is that you are a participant in a certain practice—of using 'oak' to refer to oak trees—and that practice is in play on the occasions in question. (Which practice is in play is determined by whatever contextual factors determine that a given sense of the term is in play.) (3) implies (4), according to the account we are working with, because, just in virtue of the facts (i) that you are a participant in the practice of using 'oak' to refer to oak trees and (ii) that that practice is in play on a given occasion, you ought to use 'oak' on that occasion in keeping with its meaning oak tree. The story about practices, it seems, can explain both the transition from (1) to (2) and the transition from (3) to (4). Sometimes, however, our talk of what we or others mean by a word seems to admit of a different interpretation.

In giving a talk I might say, 'By "convention" I shall mean convention in Lewis's sense'. (Alternatively I might just say, 'Conventions, in my sense of that term, are conventions in Lewis's sense.') To make such a declaration is, in effect, to express an intention to use the word in certain ways, in particular, in ways which are in keeping with its meaning convention in Lewis's sense and thus in ways which respect the conditions for true application which are fixed by that meaning. So one might think that meaning something by a word is just intending to use it in keeping with a certain meaning. There is some support for such a view from the fact that saying what we meant to do is just a way of saying what we intended to do. Now with this notion to hand it might seem that we have a distinct account of what makes it the case that one ought to use a word in such-and-such ways. This time the idea is that in virtue of meaning such-and-such by a word, and thus, on the present understanding, intending to use it in keeping with its meaning such-and-such, one ought to use it in those ways which are in keeping with that meaning. Further, one might think that this 'ought' needs little explanation on the grounds that one ought to do what is required to carry out one's intentions.

I shall respond to this line of thought shortly. It will help if we first consider the relation between participating in the practice of using 'oak' to refer to oak trees, and intending to use 'oak' in keeping with its meaning oak tree. It is not at all clear that those who participate in the practice are bound to have the corresponding intention. Indeed, one might wonder whether they are bound to have any intentions at all regarding 'oak'. Might not young children participate in the practice without having reached the stage of having intentions concerning their use of the word 'oak'? And might not even mature participants in the practice lack specific intentions concerning their use of the word? A weaker view would be that mature participants must, at least, have a more general intention— a standing intention to use words with their received meanings. Even that might be too strong a condition. What is true, I think, is that part of what it is to be a mature participant in a practice of using a word is that one is so disposed that were one to discover that one's use is not in keeping with the relevant meaning of the word one would be prepared to adjust one's use. The manifestation of this disposition is an intentional adjustment of one's use. This is what Fred does when learns that he is wrong about the meaning of 'arthritis'. Had he not been disposed so to adjust his use, there would no basis for regarding him as having all along meant by 'arthritis' what his doctor means by it. It does not follow that he must have had an intention regarding the word all along, even though when he does adjust his use he does so intentionally and with a view to keeping faith with its received meaning. Somewhat similarly, one might be disposed to assent to a claim if it were put to one, such as that La Paz is to the south of Chicago, without ever having previously acquired a belief to that effect.

We should then resist a position which requires that participating in a practice of using 'oak' in keeping with its meaning oak tree must involve a standing intention to use 'oak' in keeping with its meaning oak tree, when that sense is in play. Still, the existence of the practice depends on there being participants capable of intentionally adjusting their uses of the word in response to the discovery that their existing usage is not in keeping with the relevant meaning. Much use in keeping with meaning is both unstudied and non-accidental. It is non-accidental, since the use will have been honed by encounter with the practice. It is unstudied because falling in with the practice will not have sprung from reflection on its requirements. But if, as on the present hypothesis, there really are rule-governed practices of using words with certain meanings, rather than mere regularities more or less widely conformed to, then there must be individuals who appreciate, or could be brought to appreciate, the requirements of the practice. That I take to be a conceptual truth about practices and one which highlights an important difference between the existence of a practice and the existence of by-and-large conformity with some regularity in behaviour. Note however that a person's appreciation of the requirements might just be a matter of being able to recognize that certain uses of a word are wrong and give some account of why. That does not require having an ability to formulate the rules of the practice.[9]

In the light of the stance on practices and intentions just sketched let us go back to the idea, introduced three paragraphs ago, that meaning oak tree by 'oak' is intending to use it in keeping with its meaning oak tree. This was of interest to us because it seemed to provide an account which is different from that which states that your meaning oak tree by 'oak' is a matter of your participating in a practice of using 'oak' to refer to oak trees. If this latter idea is filled out as I have suggested, and participation in a practice of using a word does not require having intentions regarding the use of the word, then we have two competing accounts of meaning oak tree by 'oak'.

There are two directions in which we could go at this point. One would be to hold that 'meaning oak tree by "oak"' is ambiguous; in one sense it is a matter of having an intention concerning the word and in the other sense it is not. Even if that is right it cannot be that what using a word in keeping with a meaning requires depends solely on the intentions of individuals. When individuals resolve to use a word in a particular way there needs to be a background of practice and action which makes sense of that resolution and enables uses which carry out the resolution to be understood. The other way of responding to the idea that there is a sense of meaning something by a word on which it is a matter of having an intention would be to deny that there is such a sense. Recall my saying that by 'convention' I mean convention in Lewis' sense. It is true that by saying this I am, in effect, announcing an intention. But it may be that my *saying* what I mean by the word indicates how I intend to use it simply because the saying of it is an expression of a deliberate, thus intentional, policy regarding my use of the word and not because what makes the saying true is my having that intentional policy.

Of the two responses just outlined I prefer the second. Both responses are compatible with taking it that the theory of rule-governed practices can explain and accommodate both the transition from (1) to (2) and the transition (3) to (4). It is just that defenders of the first response, which invokes an ambiguity in 'meaning something by a word' would need to make it clear that the reading of (1)

[9] As well as being plausible in itself, this view avoids familiar regresses deriving from thinking that all conformity to a rule is a matter of following an instruction in the way that one follows a recipe.

to which the theory applies is that on which meaning is not a matter of having an intention.

I think we are close to the right way to think about the normativity of meaning—I mean the right way of formulating the claim that meaning is normative. There is, however, a serious problem in the story so far which it is easy to overlook. At the heart of the account is the idea that if you are a participant in a practice, then you ought to act in accordance with the rules. It is natural to take the 'ought' in this conditional claim to modify the consequent of the conditional, so that the entire ought-claim is detachable given that you are a participant in the practice. The problem is that it is not in general true that if you participate in a practice then you ought to accord with the rules of the practice.

Imagine a group of young people who engage in a role-playing game involving stealing cars, ramming them into shop-windows, and stealing the goods. One role is car-stealer, another is car-driver, another is goods-stealer, and so on. Each role, let us suppose, is associated with stylized ways of performing the activity which is definitive of the role. The activity is a practice in which playing a role is governed by a rule requiring that the stylized actions associated with the role be performed. Yet it is not true that just in virtue of participating in the practice one ought to carry out the performances associated with one's role. Something else is true, and this, I think, is what people really mean, or ought to mean, when they say that if one participates in the activity then one ought to carry out the performances associated with one's role. What is true is that *participating in the practice incurs a commitment to carrying out the performances. To say that you have incurred the commitment is to say that you ought either to carry out the performances or abandon the practice.* Understood in this manner the commitment can be discharged in two ways—by carrying it out or by changing the condition which incurs it. Another way to express the commitment would be to say that you ought to bring it about that if you participate in the practice then you carry out the performances of your role. Here the 'ought' modifies a complete conditional and not just its consequent. (As with 'must', an 'ought' attached to the consequent of a conditional does admit a reading on which it modifies the whole conditional.) What matters is that from the assumption that you participate in the practice, and that you ought to bring it about that if you participate in the practice you carry out the performances, it does not follow that you ought to carry out the performances.

The fact that participation in a practice is compatible with its being false that you ought to act as the practice requires should make us suspicious of the explanation of the transition from (1) to (2) which is currently on the table. The suspicion is further justified by reflection on specifically linguistic practices. Indeed, it is sometimes false that you ought to use words in accordance with the rules governing the practice of using those words. Arguably, certain words descriptive of insulting and offensive racial or gender stereotypes ought not to be used expressively at all[10] and therefore ought not to be so used in keeping with their meanings. Yet there are practices of so using those words and the practices are governed by rules requiring that one use the words in keeping with the relevant conditions for correct application. What is true is that participating in a practice of using a word incurs a commitment to using the word in accordance with the relevant rule. As before the commitment can be discharged in two ways—by carrying it out or by changing the condition which incurs it, which in this case would mean withdrawing from the practice.

The kind of commitment I have been talking about is important in connection with belief and intention where it is equally important not to conflate claims as to what one is committed to and claims as to what one ought to do. We can easily find ourselves saying such things as the following: if you believe that p, and the proposition that q is implied by the proposition that p, then you ought to believe that q (at least if a question arises as to whether q). Yet if the 'ought' here really does modify the consequent, the claim is certainly not true. Apart from anything else, it entails the evidently false claim that if you believe that p, and the question arises whether p, you ought to believe that p, since the proposition that p is trivially implied by the proposition that p. What does seem right is that believing something commits you to believing any consequence of that belief, at least if the question arises as to whether it is true. As before that commitment can be discharged in one of two ways—by believing the consequence or by abandoning the belief which incurs the commitment. But having the commitment is compatible with its being false that you ought to believe the consequence. Similarly, we can easily find ourselves saying such things as this: if you intend to φ and ψing is necessary if you are to φ then you ought to ψ. Again, that would imply that if you intend to φ then you ought to φ, since, trivially, φing is necessary if you are to φ, and that just looks wrong. Maybe you ought not to φ. If so, this would not tell against your having the intention to φ. What is true is that if you intend to φ and ψing is necessary if you are to φ then you incur a commitment to

[10] Recall the distinction between expressive and interpretative uses made in section 2.

ψing. You can discharge the commitment either by ψing or by abandoning your intention to φ, but having the commitment does not imply that you ought to ψ.[11]

I propose, then, that we amend the favoured account of the normativity of meaning to reflect the difference between oughts and commitments. The idea now is that

(3) At least on some occasions of use, you mean oak tree by 'oak'

implies

(4') You are committed to using 'oak' on those occasions in accordance with the rule: respect the conditions for true application fixed by its meaning oak tree.

A parallel adjustment is required to (2). Instead of the implication of (2) by (1) we now have it that

(1) 'Oak' has a sense on which it means oak tree

implies

(2') When that sense is in play those who use 'oak' are committed to doing so in conformity with the following rule: use it in ways which respect the conditions for true application fixed by its meaning oak tree.

This is illustrates the version of the normativity thesis with which, in my view, the friend of normativity should work. In the concluding section I consider a couple of lines of thought designed to deflate the pretensions of normativity.

4. Deflationist tendencies

The position I have described captures the idea that *just in virtue of* there being a sense of 'oak' on which it means oak tree, those who use 'oak' in that sense incur a certain commitment. This is the force of the claim that (1) implies (2'), for that amounts to the claim that (2') may be inferred from (1) *without further ado*. A deflationist about normativity, in the sense I have been explaining, would be

[11] I look further into issues surrounding intention and instrumental reasoning in 'Normative Reasons and Instrumental Rationality' in José Luis Bermúdez and Alan Millar (eds) *Reason and Nature* (Oxford: Oxford University Press, forthcoming). John Broome's work on practical reasoning drew my attention to the importance of distinguishing between what one ought to do and what one is committed to doing. See his contribution to the volume just cited.

Alan Millar

someone who denied that (1) implies (2′) in this sense. They may concede that when (1) is true (2′) is true. They think, however, that if (2′) is true that is not just in virtue of (1)'s being true but because something else is true as well. The strategy might be applied to the claimed implication between (3) and (4′) or to the earlier version of the normativity thesis formulated in terms of (1), (2), (3) and (4).)

Paul Horwich is a deflationist in the sense just explained. At any rate, I infer that he is given what he says about the transition from

(5) 'dog' means dog

to

(6) 'dog' ought to be applied only to dogs.[12]

Horwich accepts that (6) is a normative statement and that if (5) is true then (6) is. He denies that (5) implies (6) and seeks to explain why it is that when (5) is true (6) is true.[13] His explanation is in three stages.[14] First, he invokes the idea that truth in belief is something at which we ought to aim—we ought to believe only what is true. Second, he gives a pragmatic account of why we ought to aim at truth: true beliefs are more apt than false ones to facilitate successful behaviour. Third, he argues that since we ought, for the reason spelled out by the pragmatic account, to apply the concept of a dog only to dogs, and since applying the word 'dog' is applying the concept, we ought to apply the word 'dog' only to dogs. The point of the strategy is to show that since the normative claim (6) is grounded, not just on (5), but on (5) in conjunction with the pragmatic considerations about aiming at truth in belief, there is nothing *intrinsically* normative about meaning.

My main objection to Horwich's story is directed at the very idea that the issue is how to account for (6). The problem harks back to the ground-clearing operation conducted in section 2 above, which drew attention to an equivocation in the notion of correctness. As we saw, sometimes when people talk of correct uses they have in mind primarily, if not exclusively, correct applications. Sometimes, though, correct use is conceived as use in keeping with meaning. It seems to me clear that when we are exploring the normativity of

---

[12] *Meaning*, 92f. Horwich appears to conceive of normativity as Boghossian does but with the proviso that the central explanatory consideration is about correct, in the sense of true, application.

[13] Confusingly, at least in relation to my preferred terminology, he says that (5) implies (6), but appears to mean by that only that if (5) is true then (6) is as well.

[14] *Meaning*, ch. 8.

meaning it is the latter notion on which we need to focus. If, contrary to what I have argued, but in line with Kripke and Gibbard, the normative claims we need to focus on are claims about how one ought to use words, then the particular ought-claims which need explaining are claims to the effect that one ought to use words in those ways which are in keeping with the relevant meaning and in *that* sense correct. If that is the issue then the considerations which Horwich adduces are irrelevant and could only seem relevant because of an equivocation over the notion of correctness.[15]

Lying to conceal a mistake I say to you, 'The tree I cut down was an oak' though in fact I cut down a beech. Here I apply the term 'oak' incorrectly (falsely) but I do not misuse it. My use respects the conditions for correct application of the term—it is a use which is entirely consistent with what knowledge of the conditions commits one to. What makes it 'correct' to use the term as I do? Nothing which has to do with what is required for me to achieve the aim of believing only what is true. What makes my use correct, in the sense which matters, is simply that it respects the conditions for true application of the term. Given that I wanted you to take me to be telling you that I had cut down the oak, I needed to use a term for an oak tree, and I did so in keeping with the relevant meaning of the term in question. To vary the example, suppose that in the circumstance in which I cut down a beech I meant to tell you that I'd cut down the oak, but by way of a slip of the tongue I actually said, 'I have cut down the beech'. Here I say something true but I misuse the term 'beech' because knowledge of what 'beech' means commits me, when I am aiming to convey accurate information, to using it to speak of beeches and thus to avoiding using it to speak of oaks. Note that in this case I do know what the term means. My misuse, unlike Fred's, does not derive from a misunderstanding, but simply from

[15] It should be stressed that I sympathize with those who are sceptical about establishing that meaning (or the having of propositional attitudes) is intrinsically normative on the basis of considerations about correct, in the sense of true, application (or belief). In addition to Horwich, see Jane Heal, 'The Disinterested Search for Truth', *Proceedings of the Aristotelian Society* **88**, 1988/89, 97–108, David Papineau, 'Normativity and Judgement' *Proceedings of the Aristotelian Society*, Supplementary Volume **73**, 1999, 17–43, and Fred Dretske, 'Norms, History, and the Constitution of the Mental', in his collection, *Perception, Knowledge and Belief: Selected Essays* (Cambridge: Cambridge University Press, 2000), 242–57. My point here has been that normativity theorists, and their critics, should look elsewhere. So far as linguistic meaning is concerned, the crucial considerations are about use which is correct in the sense of being in keeping with meaning.

the fact it is out of line with what knowledge of the conditions for true application of the term commits me to. With respect to the first of the cases just described, correct use—use in keeping with meaning—is not correct application. With respect to the second, incorrect use—misuse—is not false application. That there can be such cases is no surprise in view of the discussion of section 2. The point which needs emphasis now is that aiming at truth in belief is irrelevant to the explanation of why a speaker *ought* to use a term in those ways which are in keeping with its meaning, and irrelevant therefore to the explanation of failures to use terms in keeping with meaning. With respect to both the cases described, doing what is required to aim at truth in belief is irrelevant because nothing which the user is doing bears on his acquisition of beliefs. What matters is what the user was saying or trying to say and what he means by the words he uses.[16]

A different deflationary strategy would be to concede that the oughts or, as on my approach, the commitments, in which we should be interested are those linked to correct use in the sense of use in keeping with meaning but to argue that these oughts/commitments can still be explained away without invoking the idea that meaning is intrinsically normative. Suppose it is conceded that if 'oak' means oak tree then those who use 'oak' incur a commitment to using 'oak' in those ways which are in keeping with its meaning oak tree, that is, in those ways which are specified by the rule of the relevant practice. Still, it might be said that the reason why these people are so committed is that they are aiming to communicate using 'oak' and so had better use 'oak' in keeping with its meaning oak tree. Again, the point is to invoke a goal which is extrinsic to the term's meaning what it does. This strategy strikes me as being significantly more plausible than the one just considered. Nonetheless, it mislocates the issue. It is true that if you intend to communicate with the folks around here, and propose to use the word 'oak' then, unless you make explicit that you are going to use it in some peculiar way, you are committed to using it in keeping with its meaning oak tree or oak (the wood) as the case may be. It is also true that this commitment is incurred just in virtue of having the intention in question. If you carry out the commitment you will fall in with the prevailing practices of using 'oak'. But the issue is not about what you are committed to in virtue of intending to communicate. There are other

[16] Closely parallel considerations apply with equal force if an aiming-at-truth account of normativity is developed in terms of aiming at truth in assertion and if the strategy is detached from the deflationist aims of Horwich.

commitments on the scene, in particular, those you incur once you are a participant in the prevailing practices. An analogy with rule-governed games helps here. You may be committed to playing a game of soccer. The commitment might be incurred by your saying that you would play, or by your having a standing commitment to play, or some such thing. What explains these commitments is not what explains your commitment to obey the offside rule once playing in the match. The latter commitment is explained by the fact that, as a participant in the game, you incur a commitment to conforming to the rules of the game. The moral is: don't conflate a commitment to participating in a practice with commitments incurred as a participant in a practice. The deflationary strategy under consideration does just that.[17]

The University of Stirling

[17] Work relating to this paper began in 1997 during a research leave part of which was spent as a Visiting Fellow at Clare Hall, Cambridge, and as a Visiting Scholar in the Faculty of Philosophy at Cambridge University. I am grateful to the College and the Faculty for facilities provided, and to Ross Harrison, Jane Heal, Isaac Levi, and Hugh Mellor for stimulating discussion during that stay. The leave was supported by a Research Fellowship from the Mind Association and by a grant from the Carnegie Trust for the Universities of Scotland. I am grateful to both of these organizations. I have benefited enormously from discussion with colleagues at Stirling and with the audience at the lecture based on ideas and arguments in this paper. Thanks are due to José Bermúdez, Bob Hale, Peter Sullivan, Neil Tennant, and Tim Williamson for helpful and encouraging comments.

Two Theories of Names

GABRIEL M. A. SEGAL

0. Introduction

The aim of this paper is to assess the relative merits of two accounts
of the semantics of proper names. The enterprise is of particular
interest because the theories are very similar in fundamental
respects. In particular, they can agree on three major features of
names: names are rigid designators; different co-extensive names
can have different cognitive significance; empty proper names can
be meaningful. Neither theory by itself offers complete explanations of all three features. But each theory is consistent with them
and goes some way towards explaining them.

Both theories are reasonably elegant and economical and make no
undue demands on semantic theory. There doesn't seem to be much
wrong with either of them. For the purposes of this paper, I will
assume that at least one of the theories is on the right track. I will
not offer a detailed defence of this assumption, for my aim is not to
defend either theory against all competitors. Rather it is to assess
the relative empirical plausibility of two particular theories that
agree on the main properties of names, but disagree about their
semantics.

There are theorists with an ecumenical approach to semantics
who would in principle be happy to allow that both theories are
right. Donald Davidson would be a case in point (e.g. Davidson
1977, 1979).

I prefer a more sectarian approach, one that proceeds on the
assumption that at most one of the theories could be right. The sectarian approach generates fruitful enquiry, whether it is demonstrably correct or not.

I will begin by articulating a theoretical background against
which the sectarian approach makes sense. Then I will present a
range of empirical data with a view to assessing its impact on the
two theories. I conclude that one of the theories has a definite lead.
I hope that this exercise provides some vindication both of the sectarian approach itself and of the more specific theoretical assumptions on which the discussion is based.

[1] This use of 'ecumenical' and 'sectarian' is from Quine (1990).

Gabriel M. A. Segal

1. A Realist Cognitivist Framework For Semantics

It is very important that semantic theorizing not proceed in a vacuum. It proceeds best within a framework of assumptions about the nature of semantic facts that allows for some reasonably explicit methodology. One needs to know what sorts of things count as evidence for or against specific semantic theories, and why they do so. So I am about to offer some fairly heavy-duty empirical assumptions to provide the required framework. If you are sceptical about these assumptions, please don't refrain from reading the rest of the paper. The discussion of names should be of interest to semantic theorists of any persuasion. It is just that if you reject the theoretical commitments on which I ground the discussion, then you will need some other way of making sense of the empirical comparison and contrast between the theories of names.

I will assume a basically Chomskian approach to linguistics. On this approach, linguistics is part of cognitive psychology. It studies human linguistic competence. It assumes that this competence consists in largely unconscious cognizance of linguistic rules and principles, where cognizance is conceived of as a representational state, rather like belief, although with a more limited role in cognition. Moreover, and perhaps unlike Chomsky himself, I assume that all this extends to semantic competence, and that semantic competence is owed to largely unconscious cognizance of a compositional semantic theory. I will also assume that semantic facts are determined by the contents of semantic cognizance. To a first approximation what a word or sentence means for a person is just what their internalized semantic theory says it means.[2]

One also needs assumptions about the form of a semantic theory. Here I follow Davidson: it is a truth theory of roughly Tarskian form. The theory consists in (I) axioms attributing semantic properties to atomic expressions, (II) axioms for deriving the semantic properties of complex expressions from their syntax and the semantic properties of their parts, with the aid of (III) a set of rules for constructing the derivations. The apparatus

---

[2] Those who favour a more communitarian approach (e.g. Burge 1989) can regard this last as merely a simplifying assumption for present purposes. We need not disagree about anything important that follows: just assume that I am talking about fully competent speakers, except where I explicitly say otherwise.

allows for the derivation of a T-theorem for each sentence of the object language.[3]

I assume a realist attitude to the above: internalized T-theories (or rather, the internalizations of T-theories) are real phenomena in nature. There are objective facts about each individual's T-theory and about universal, species-wide features of semantic cognizance. These facts are not determined by the explicit cogitations of the academic theorists who study them.

As mentioned above, it is by no means necessary to endorse this heavy-duty framework in order to participate in the discussion of names that follows. However, some sort of theoretical background is required to generate a methodology for semantic theory, and this is the one I am offering. I hope that the ensuing discussion provides a small illustration of the cogency of the general framework I have offered. In general, a good way to assess the validity of a theoretical framework is to see it at work: if it appears to generate legitimate enquiry, the framework is, to that extent, vindicated. If, by contrast, the enquiry bogs down and leads only to subjectivity and irreconcilable dispute, then the framework itself is perhaps at fault.

2. The Theories

The two theories of names to be assessed below are those of Tyler Burge (1973) and Larson and Segal (1995).

2.1 Names As Complex Demonstratives

Burge's account begins with the observation that we can and do use proper names predicatively, as common count nouns. Thus: 'There are two P. Churchlands, which P. Churchland did you mean?' 'I meant the P. Churchland at UCSD.' 'Both P. Churchlands are at UCSD.'

Names in their predicative use would have axioms along the lines illustrated by (1):

(1) $(x)(x$ satisfies 'P. Churchland') iff x is a P. Churchland.

---

[3] The framework of the last two paragraphs is expounded and defended in detail in Larson and Segal (1995). The idea of adopting Davidson's technical insights about the use of truth theoretical semantics for natural languages within a Chomskian cognitivist framework was put forward by Gilbert Harman (1972) and developed in some detail by James Higginbotham, e.g. Higginbotham (1985, 1986).

Gabriel M. A. Segal

Being a P. Churchland is simply bearing the name 'P. Churchland'. There is certainly something circular about (1). However the circle does not appear to be vicious. It is part of our semantic competence to know, in general, what it is for something to bear a name. And we know (partly consciously, partly unconsciously) how names can get attached to individuals by baptisms, cultural conventions and so on. We also know how they stick to individuals over time. (See Evans 1973 and 1982 for discussion). Thus we can establish that something is a P. Churchland without first knowing that it satisfies 'P. Churchland'.

In singular use, Burge suggests, the predicate is concatenated with an implicit determiner, a demonstrative, such as 'that'. So (2) has a logical form along the lines partially depicted in (3):

(2) Aristotle is a shipping magnate.

(3) [[that Aristotle] is a shipping magnate].

Let us call Burge's theory 'DP' (for 'determiner/predicate').

A slight modification can make DP more attractive. In some languages, the presence of an explicit determiner is mandatory when names appear in singular use (Basque, modern Greek) and in some it is fairly prevalent (e.g. Italian, in which it is mandatory in some cases but not all). In these languages, the determiner has the surface form of the term that normally translates as 'the' rather than 'that'.

There is also some intuitive evidence that the implicit determiner would be more like 'the' than 'that'. Suppose that I own a cat, Mina. We hear a commotion at the door. We think it's Mina, but it's another cat, Mog. I say (4):

(4) The cat wants to come in.

The natural intuition is that my utterance would be about Mina, the cat we know and love, rather than about Mog, of whose proximity we are ignorant. Compare (5):

(5) That cat wants to come in.

(5) could be about either to Mina or Mog, depending on the details of the context. If Mog's presence were particularly salient, say if he were manically hurling himself at the door, then the demonstrative in (5) would naturally be taken to refer to him.

We see someone who looks like Fred Bloggs staggering out of a pub. In fact it's Fred Schmidt, I say (6):

(6) Fred has had a little drink.

(6) seems to be a possibly false claim about Bloggs. It is definitely not a true one about Schmidt. This is what DP would predict if it's [the Fred], rather than [that Fred].[4]

If the implicit determiner is 'the', then it is probably a referential 'the'. That would be the simplest and most natural explanation of the genuinely referential nature of proper names, as is suggested by the fact that they are rigid designators. DP thus fits best with an ambiguity theory of the definite article, holding that while 'the' sometimes functions as a quantifier, it can also work as a kind of demonstrative, much like 'this' and 'that'.

Whether DP lends itself to an account of the other two features of names mentioned above obviously depends on the correct account of complex demonstratives. But there certainly are plausible accounts with the right properties. The different cognitive significance of co-extensive names would hinge on their including different predicates: [the Hesperus] and [the Phosphorus], for example, contain different predicates with different extensions. The semantic significance of empty demonstratives would best be accounted for not in terms of truth conditions, but in terms of character, or some T-theoretical reconstruction thereof. (See e.g. Burge 1974 and Larson and Segal 1995 for suggested accounts).[5]

2.2 Names As Constants

Larson and Segal develop (although they do not explicitly endorse) what might be thought of as a sort of quasi-descriptive theory of names. We can call it 'FLIC' (for Free Logic/Individual Concept). The axioms for proper names have the form shown in (7):

(7) (a) (x)(x satisfies 'Boris Karloff' iff x=Boris Karloff).
   (b) (x)(x satisfies 'William Pratt' iff x=William Pratt).
   (c) (x)(x satisfies 'Rumplestiltzkin' iff x=Rumplestiltzkin).
   (d) (x)(x satisfies 'Aristotle$_1$' iff x= Aristotle$_1$ (the philosopher)).
   (e) (x)(x satisfies 'Aristotle$_2$' iff x= Aristotle$_2$ (the magnate)).

In order to keep the meta-theory coherent, it is necessary to adopt a free logic. For we need to avoid, for example, the inference from (7c) to (8):

[4] The argument is due to Higginbotham (1988).
[5] If you think that both empty names and empty demonstratives lack significance, then you can adapt DP to suit yourself. Larson and Segal's theory could also be adapted to disallow empty names, so agreement could be retained on the big issues.

Gabriel M. A. Segal

(8) $(\exists y)(x)(x$ satisfies 'Rumplestiltzkin' iff $x=y)$.

Free logics allow for the coherent use of empty names by modifying the classical rules, for example, by rejecting existential generalization, or restricting it to atomic sentences.[6]

The idea behind (7) is as follows. Recall, first, that semantics is supposed to specify the contents of speakers' internalized theories. Thus the claim is that the axioms in (7) might be part of a typical speaker's internalized T-theory. Hence we are talking about a kind of cognizance-that: for example, the speaker cognizes that $(x)(x$ satisfies 'Boris Karloff' iff $x=$Boris Karloff). A speaker might well cognize that, and yet not cognize that (x) (x satisfies 'Boris Karloff' iff $x=$William Pratt), even though Boris Karloff in fact is William Pratt.[7]

It is natural to think of the cognitive states involved in propositional attitudes, including the sort of cognition involved in linguistic competence, as being structured into component concepts. So somebody who knew the axioms in (7) would have the concepts expressed by the universal quantifier, by 'satisfies', '=' and so on.[8] And they would have the concepts expressed by the meta-linguistic names appearing on the right hand sides. So, for example, someone might have two distinct concepts of the unique individual, Boris Karloff, that are suitably expressed by the names 'Boris Karloff' and 'William Pratt'. Think of someone who knew William as a child, then saw Karloff in a movie. Initially, this person does not realize that the actor was once that little boy, William. She would then have two separate concepts of the individual. And she might, indeed, form a speculation involving these concepts: *maybe Boris Karloff is William Pratt.*

[6] There are a variety of free logics to choose from. See e.g. Burge (1980) and the references therein. Notice that to adopt free logic in this context is not to endorse it as the most suitable for metaphysics or the regimentation of mathematical or scientific discourse. I am attributing (possibly unconscious) cognizance of some principles of free logic to ordinary speakers of natural language. Since we ordinary speakers do reason happily with singular concepts that we know to be empty, the attribution is justified.

[7] This sort of approach to Frege's puzzle within the Davidsonian programme was developed by McDowell 1977 and Evans 1982.

[8] Some people like to draw a distinction between conceptual and non-conceptual or sub-conceptual representations. And they might want to place internalized T-theories on the subconceptual side. I don't mean my use of 'concept' here to conflict with those views. Just take a concept to be a constituent of a structured mental representation. In any event, the claim that people have singular concepts of individuals, like Boris Karloff, is hardly radical.

FLIC thus offers a straightforward account of the cognitive significance of names. The individual concept that a speaker associates with a name will feature in the thoughts she has when interpreting sentences. Roughly speaking, for example, she will take 'Boris Karloff was a fine actor' to mean that Boris Karloff was a fine actor, her *Boris Karloff* concept featuring in the thought she uses to frame an interpretation of the sentence. By contrast, her *William Pratt* concept will feature in the analogous position in the thought she has when interpreting 'William Pratt was a fine actor'. These are different, logically inequivalent thoughts. Hence the speaker might quite reasonably adopt different doxastic attitudes to the two sentences.

Larson and Segal suggest that individual concepts might be accounted for in terms of mental files or dossiers (following John Perry e.g. Perry 1980, and many others). Thus, on encountering a new individual (or what one takes to be such) one opens up a file and there collects information about the individual. The information in the file then determines the cognitive role of the concept, it determines the way one thinks about the individual in question and the way one deploys the concept in thought. One could have two concepts of a single individual if one had two separate files containing information about him.

Under this proposal, there is no special problem about empty names and empty concepts. Empty concepts arise from files that contain information that does not concern—is not information about—any real individual. Empty files can arise either when someone falsely believes in the existence of a corresponding individual, or in cases of abstention, or even in cases where the subject believes that there is no individual answering to the name. You have a concept of Sherlock Holmes, don't you?

The reference of a proper name is not fixed by the information in the dossier. Rather, it is fixed by a separate general theory of naming: the theory of baptisms, reference preservation over time, etc. mentioned above. In this way, FLIC retains the advantages of classical description theories of proper names (significance of empty names etc.) while avoiding the standard objections to them (Kripke 1972).[9]

In the context of FLIC, the axioms in (7) potentially determine two distinct referential paths. The individual concept on the right hand side refers to whatever it refers to. The name mentioned on

---

[9] Notice that if you have more sympathy with the description theory of the reference of a name than Kripke does, you can write this into FLIC: just have the general theory of naming assign a substantial reference-fixing role to the information in the dossier.

the left has its reference fixed by the general theory of naming. The axioms themselves, of course, imply that these objects, the referent of the name and the referent of the concept, are the same.[10]

This doubling of referential paths leads to various possibilities. In some cases, the reference of the concept will be fixed via the name. This sort of case is probably fairly typical where speakers are epistemically distant from the referents. It is plausible, for example, that my individual concept of Cleopatra refers to the Egyptian queen because of its connection with the name 'Cleopatra', and the name's socio-historical link to the referent. In other cases, the reverse is true. In dubbing ceremonies, presumably the reference of the name, in the idiolects of those present, is fixed via their concepts of the person being dubbed.[11]

In other cases, there may be tension. Suppose, for example, that I am well acquainted with a local shopkeeper. Most days, I buy a newspaper from him, and we are in the habit of chatting, exchanging local gossip and so on. This goes on for over three years without my learning his name. Then one day I overhear some people using the name 'Jack' and I mistakenly believe that they are using it to talk about the shopkeeper. My brain encodes this information In the way depicted in (9), where 'α' stands in for my individual concept of the shopkeeper:

(9) $(x)(x$ satisfies 'Jack' iff $x = \alpha)$.

In fact, the shopkeeper's name is 'Bill' and Jack is someone else altogether. Suppose I then say (10), intending to refer to the shopkeeper:

(10) Jack is thinking about retiring.

The shopkeeper is, indeed, thinking about retiring, but Jack is not. Have I spoken truly or falsely, neither or both?

Most people's intuitions tend towards the last option. One way to accommodate the intuition is to distinguish between my I-language (Chomsky 1986) and my sociolect. The former is individuated

---

[10] I am indebted to Takashi Yagisawa and John McDowell for bringing this point to my attention.

[11] Adopting the terminology of Evans (1982), I would suggest as a vague generalization, that in the idiolects of producers, the concept does most of the work in fixing the reference of the name, and in the case of consumers, the name does most of the work in fixing the reference of the individual concept. Notice that cases of the former kind do not conflict with the claim that it is the general theory of naming that fixes the reference of the name. That theory itself determines the reference-fixing role of the concept.

individualistically, the latter is an idiolect individuated partly by social facts. Then when I say (10) I express a claim that is true in my I-language but false in my sociolect.

How well does FLIC fair with respect to rigidity? The axioms in (7) make no mention of possible worlds or counterfactual situations. So they are, in fact, consistent with the possibility of a name's referring to different objects in different possible worlds. Moreover, until the account of names is combined with an account of counter-factuals and other modals, it may not be possible conclusively to demonstrate that FLIC treats names as rigid designators.

However, FLIC is clearly consistent with the rigidity of names. And it does appear to be the right kind of theory to combine with accounts of counterfactuals etc. to generate the desired results. The idea is that axioms like (7) are internalized by speakers, and the contents of these axioms contribute to determining speakers' judgments about the truth conditions of sentences containing names. When a speaker evaluates a counterfactual or other modal sentence, or considers the truth value that the proposition expressed by a non-modal sentence would have had, in this or that counter-factual circumstance, her judgment depends on the axioms she has internalized. One would expect that judgments about the extension of a name in an envisaged counterfactual circumstance would be fixed by the satisfaction conditions given on the right hand sides of the axioms for names. Given the form of the axioms, speakers would then judge that the same object is the extension of a given name in every possible circumstance of evaluation. Nothing other than William Pratt could satisfy the condition of being identical to William Pratt. And, from the cognitivist perspective adopted in this paper, judgments of this sort suffice to render names rigid. If our judgments were not consistent with names being rigid designators, then names would not be rigid designators. Or, if you prefer: then our languages would not contain names.

3. Compare and Contrast

As promised, DP and FLIC agree, or can be brought to agree, on the big issues about proper names: empty names, co-extensive names and rigidity. And there is presumably an isomorphism between the logical forms assigned to utterances by the two theories (i.e. a procedure that, given a sentence, a context of utterance and the logical form assigned by one theory, will derive the logical form assigned to the sentence in the context by the other).

83

Gabriel M. A. Segal

The chief differences are as follows: FLIC has one more semantic species. Under FLIC, proper names feature in a unique form of
axiom. Under DP, proper names are a subspecies of common
nouns, requiring no special type of axiom. FLIC also assigns more
individual lexical items to each idiolect than does DP, seeing, e.g.
many different 'Aristotle's where DP sees just one.

On the other hand, FLIC assigns simpler logical forms to
sentences featuring names as singular terms, logical forms with no
hidden determiners. And it proposes a simpler relation between
underlying and surface forms.

Are there, then reasons, for preferring one theory to the other?

4. Evidence

4.1 Deficit Data

There are intriguing deficit data that certainly indicate that proper
names are somehow special. You will be amazed to learn that
proper names are harder to recall than other kinds of words.[12]
Furthermore, the capacity to recall proper names is more
vulnerable to brain damage than the capacity to recall other types of
expression. For example, a number of cases have been recorded of
aphasic subjects whose production capacities for proper names (e.g.
the capacity to provide the name when shown the face) are significantly more impaired than the analogous capacities to perform with
common nouns.

Interestingly, there are specific aphasias that affect only certain
categories of common nouns, e.g. terms for fruit and vegetables,
body parts or animals. However, it appears that in all these cases
there are further deficits that result in impaired performance in
non-linguistic tasks involving the relevant category. Finally,
although name retrieval is as a rule more vulnerable to damage than
common-noun retrieval, there is some evidence of cases where
proper names are spared relative to other categories. The data are,
however, very limited and not easy to interpret (Valentine *et. al.*
(1996) p. 102).

At first sight, the deficit data might appear to support FLIC over
DP, since proper names differ in important respects from ordinary
common nouns. However, a second look is in order. The data show
that there is something special about proper names. But the special

[12] For an excellent overview of the deficit data and extended discussion
of the processing of proper names, see Valentine *et. al.* (1996). This and
the subsequent five paragraphs owe a great deal to that work.

properties may be ones that would be predicted by or at least consistent with both theories. And, indeed, there is good reason to think that this is case. For the properties of names that seem to be relevant to their processing have to do with features of the name-bearer relationship, a relationship that is, of course, recognized by both theories. The deficits all concern remembering facts of the form: 'individual x bears the name N'. And differences between FLIC and DP don't appear to bear on the nature of such facts.

Consider, for example, the fact that in many cultures, typical individuals have two or more names, and each of these names will be shared with other individuals. Thus 'Jack Nicholson', 'Nicholas Jackson', 'Emma Nicholson' and 'Nicole Jackson' might all be names known to a speaker. Contrast e.g. colour terms. It is not true that a bunch of different colours, with no defining property in common, are all called 'red', while another bunch are all called 'blue' and you have to remember which particular colour is more or less arbitrarily called 'red blue'. It would not be surprising if the distinctive facts about the distribution of names among their bearers made them particularly hard to recall.

Consider also the fact that you can infer rather little about a person's properties from their name. Sometimes one can have a decent shot at sex, religion, age or class. But the reliability of such inferences can be low, and varies considerably across cultures. This may be reflected in the organization of our memories: storage and retrieval mechanisms may be organized so that the name-bearer relation is stored in isolation from other information about the relata, since such information is not likely to be helpful. This may contrast with the storage of semantic information about common nouns, such as 'dog'. If something is a dog, it is also an animal, a quadruped, a possible pet and so on. Our memories may be organized so that connection between 'dog' and doghood is stored in a way that exploits these associated pieces of information.

Merely for the sake of illustration, we might imagine the information stored in a localist connectionist network. The Fido and 'Fido' nodes would be connected by a single bidirectional excitatory link. However the dog and 'dog' nodes would be connected not only by such a link but also by excitatory links to the animal node, the pet node and so on. (See Valentine et. al. (1996) for a fairly detailed proposal of that sort).

There is a lot more work to be done on the explanation of aphasias and their relation to semantics. However, somewhat surprisingly, the signs are that, at least in the case of names, there may be little in the way of evidential connections between them. Let us move on to developmental data.

4.2 Developmental Data

There are some data that are often taken to suggest that infants at the earliest stages of language acquisition anticipate the existence of a class of terms with a special syntax, each of which refers to just one object. This might promise to lend some support to FLIC.

Katz *et. al.* (1974) conducted experiments with the following format. In each instance, a child was introduced to two similar but distinguishable items of the same type, e.g. two similar dolls with differently coloured hair, or two similar but differently coloured blocks. A new term was then introduced in connection with one of the two items. In one condition, the term was always accompanied by a determiner, and in a second, it was always used without one. So, in the first condition they were told things like 'This is a zav, look at the zav now', and in the second: 'This is zav, look at zav now'. It was then tested whether children would apply the new term to the second of the two items, the one to which the term had not previously been explicitly applied. The majority of children refrained from applying the term to the second object when and only when (a) the term had been introduced with no determiner and (b) the object in question was a doll. In all other cases, children tended to apply the term to the second object. This may appear to suggest that children expect there to be terms of two sorts: ones that apply across individuals, presumably on the basis of the some property the individuals possess, and ones that apply each to a specific individual. Syntax can provide a clue to the class, as can the animacy (or surrogate animacy in the case of dolls) of the object named.

However, the evidence does not show that children expect names to have just one bearer each. Once children have inferred from the clues that the new term is a name, their failure to apply it to the second object might be explained very simply by the fact that they have no reason to think that it, too, bears the name.

A further study by Geoffrey Hall (1996) was designed to support the view that children's default assumption is that each name can have but a single bearer. Hall divided four-year-old subjects into two groups. In each group, subjects encountered a new word in syntactic contexts that were consistent with its being either a proper name or an adjective (e.g. 'this dog is zavy'). In one condition, the word was applied to a drawing of a single object with a salient new property (e.g. a dog with a particular striped pattern). In a second condition, the word was applied to drawings of two objects both of which boasted a salient new property (e.g. two dogs with a particular striped pattern). The children were then shown more drawings, including (I) the original object or objects (II) an object of the same kind as the original or originals, but lacking the special property (e.g. stripeless dogs) and (III) an object of a different kind with the special property (e.g. a striped umbrella). The children were then asked which of these would be labelled by the new word (e.g. 'Is this dog zavy?', 'Is this umbrella zavy?'). Children from the first group, who had heard the word applied to only one object, showed a strong tendency not to apply it to the others, and so appeared to treat it as a proper name. Children from the second group, who had heard it applied to two objects, showed a strong tendency to apply it to new objects with the special property, hence appeared to treat it as an adjective describing that property.

Hall's thought was that if children assumed that a name can have only one bearer, then, in the first condition, they might infer that the new word was a name from the facts that (a) it was applied to only one object (b) the object was animate and (c) the word's syntax was compatible with the proper-name interpretation.

It does not seem however, that if children did make the assumption of unique reference, this assumption would be doing any work in their inference that the new term was a name. From the children's point of view, the evidence available to them in the first condition is also consistent with the new term being an adjective describing the new property. Hence they must assign the proper name interpretation as a default. Perhaps they think that a new object is more interesting and important than a new property, hence they are likely to be introduced to the name of the former before the name of the latter. And if they thought that, then they might well assign the proper-name interpretation without any assumption of unique reference.

Notice that datum (a) is not that the new term applies to at most one object. Rather, it is that it applies to at least one. The issue of whether it applies to any other is left entirely open by the evidence available to the child. So the proposition that the term applies to at most one object is not featuring as a premise in the children's inference to the proper-name interpretation. At best, it is the other way around. If they believe the proposition, then they must arrive at it only after having figured out that the term was a proper name.

The experiment does indicate that if children encounter a new term that applies to two individuals who share a salient new property, then the term is an adjective describing that property. (It seems reasonable for us to reject the hypothesis that they think it's a proper name that happens to apply precisely to objects sharing the new property!) But again, the evidence is entirely consistent with the idea that children think that a name can have a plurality of bearers. They need merely assume that it is unlikely that two newly encountered individuals should happen to have the same name. They may well feel that a better explanation of the fact that a new term applies to both individuals with a salient new property is that it is an adjective describing the property.

Suggestive as the experimental developmental evidence is, it does not yet offer any substantial support to FLIC.[13] However, there is anecdotal evidence that is more directly relevant. It seems that at least some small children genuinely do believe that it is impossible for two individuals to have the same name. If they already know someone called 'Jack' and are introduced to someone else as 'Jack', they become distraught and negative: they may object, they may refuse to call the person by the name etc. (Hall 1999). This would make little sense under DP. However, it would be explicable under FLIC.

According to FLIC, it is indeed impossible for two individuals to have the same proper name. 'Aristotle$_1$' and 'Aristotle$_2$' are different names—different syntactic items—that share their surface forms.[14] If the uniqueness of reference is built into UG, then it comes as no surprise that small children are reluctant to accept that a term that they took to be one individual's name could apply also to someone else. In effect, what they have to realize is that names can be ambiguous, that, e.g., the word-form 'Jack' can be the surface realization of two different words. It wouldn't be surprising if it took children some time to come to grips with this rather subtle fact. Hence FLIC could explain the behaviour of both children and adults and the transition between them, where DP would have trouble with the first of these tasks.

A possible reply on behalf of DP would be that FLIC is true of small children's idiolects. But when children do finally realize that homonymous names can apply to more than one individual, they revise their grammar and come to treat them as common nouns. That possibility is consistent with the evidence. And if there were strong evidence in favour of DP, then it might be worth considering more seriously. However, the suggestion is certainly uneconomical and ad hoc as it stands.

[13] See Hall (1999) for further discussion and descriptions of a number of related studies.

[14] I suppose family names by themselves aren't genuine proper names in the relevant sense. 'John Smith' is a genuine proper name, but the family name, 'Smith' alone, is not.

4.3 Syntax

Let us turn now to matters of syntax, beginning with cross-linguistic evidence. As noted above, there are languages in which names are always or often used with an explicit definite article, such as modern Greek and Italian. These languages would appear to offer considerable support to DP. According to DP, they would merely make logical forms more explicit.

But it is not so simple. Native speakers of these languages do not intuitively think of the constructions as being composed of a count noun along with the normal definite article. Indeed, they tend to be surprised at the proposal. This undermines the claim that these languages provide evidence for DP. We have evidence that in these languages, noun phrases containing names bear a superficial resemblance to [determiner [common noun]] constructions, a resemblance at the level of phonology and orthography. But we do not have evidence that the resemblance goes any deeper.

Indeed, these speakers' intuitions appear to provide a tiny piece of evidence against DP. For DP does not by itself offer any immediate explanation of them. If, for example, the 'Il' and the 'Gianni' in 'Il Gianni' were the normal definite article and name-predicate, then why are native speakers not aware of this? FLIC has a natural explanation: speakers aren't aware of it, because it is not so.

English speakers can share the intuitions. Consider 'The Nile', 'The Titanic', 'The Atlantic'. It is not intuitively obvious what the constituents of these expressions are. But English speakers certainly do not have the intuition that e.g. the 'Nile' in 'The Nile' is a common noun.[15]

There are, indeed, clear reasons to doubt that if, in English, names have the logical form [determiner [name]], then this is simply a suppressed version of the surface structure [determiner [common noun]]. Consider (11), for example:

(11) a. The/that Churchland argued for materialism.
     b. Churchland argued for materialism.
     c. The/that philosopher argued for materialism.
     d. *Philosopher argued for materialism.

[15] These are puzzling, quasi-idiomatic constructions. They are not fully idiomatic: witness 'The beautiful Nile', 'Oh, Nile'. But if, as I am suggesting, the name is not functioning as a common noun, then it is not obvious what the 'the' is doing. The origins might have been 'The river, Nile', 'The ship, Titanic', 'The Ocean, Atlantic'. Perhaps now there is a general form along the lines of [DP [D The] [NP [NP F] [DP name]]]) with a suppressed dummy F.

(11c) and d show that in English one cannot drop the determiner 'the' or 'that' from a typical [determiner [common noun]] construction. The result is ungrammatical. So whatever DP's implicit determiner is, it is one that cannot be dropped from the surface when it combines with an ordinary common noun. We must conclude at least that DP's name-predicates form a special category, a category that licenses exceptions to the normal generalizations.[16]

Notice further that, in spite of the parallels noted above, explicit [determiner [name]] constructions do not function exactly like names with no explicit determiner attached. Witness (12):

(12) a. I live in London.
b.?? I live in the/that London.

(12a) provides a perfectly idiomatic response to the question 'where do you live?' posed in an ordinary context, such as when the addressee is visiting Leeds or New York, and when her audience would naturally interpret 'London' as London, England. In the same context, (12b) would sound bizarre.

Contrast (13), uttered in a context in which London, Ontario is not out of the picture.

(13) a. I live in the London that's in S. E. England.
b. I live in that London (pointing from the window of a suitably positioned aeroplane).

And consider finally (14):[17]

(14) a. This is the/that John I mentioned yesterday.
b. *This is John I mentioned yesterday.

If there is a hidden determiner in 12a and 14b, it is evident that there are some special rules governing when it can appear on the surface and when it cannot. DP stands in serious need of a well-motivated account of these rules.

---

[16] See Longobardi (1994) for similar arguments, as well as a subtle and complex syntactic treatment of cross-linguistic data. Longobardi argues that names in singular use occupy the determiner position, leaving no room for an additional determiner expression to feature. If I understand him correctly, he also holds that it is the same syntactic item that functions both as a singular term and as a general one: the semantic interpretation of the item depends on its syntactic position in logical form. This departure from mainstream approaches to semantics appears somewhat undermotivated.

[17] I am indebted to Guy Longworth for examples like (14).

Given the prima facie syntactic evidence against DP and the absence of any good evidence for its hidden determiner, it seems reasonable to conclude that the theory is in trouble.

5. Concluding Remarks

DP and FLIC disagree on two main points. DP holds that proper names in singular use have both the deep syntax and the semantics of complex demonstratives. FLIC holds that they have neither. One could develop compromise positions that adopt elements of both theories. One option would be to combine DP's syntax with FLIC's semantics. Entertaining as the exercise might be, the idea evidently has little to recommend it. The other option would be to adopt FLIC's syntax, but treat names as quasi-meta-linguistic terms of variable reference, as proposed by DP. Thus one might develop axioms along the lines very crudely depicted by (15):

(15) (x)(c)(u)(If u is an utterance of 'Aristotle' in context c, then x satisfies u iff x is the Aristotle determined by c).

'Determined by c' is meant to point towards pragmatic factors that determine which Aristotle is being talked about in a given context. Let's call the theory gestured at by (15) 'VR' (for 'variable reference').

VR accepts that there are at least two different syntactic categories of proper names; singular terms and common nouns. (The meta-linguistic 'Aristotle' on the right hand side of (15) is, of course, a common noun). This move is certainly for the best, since syntax is DP's weakest point. But the price of this empirical plausibility, of course, is DP's elegant economy. Proper names in singular use are no longer subsumed under syntactic and semantic types of axiom that are anyway required for other types of expression.

The crucial difference between VR and FLIC concerns the individuation of words. According to VR, the very same word 'Aristotle' names the great philosopher, the shipping magnate and all the other Aristotles. According to FLIC, each Aristotle has his own name: names as singular terms have at most one bearer each. The intuitions of many philosophers, linguists and psychologists accord with FLIC on this point. And, if the anecdotal evidence is

Gabriel M. A. Segal

to be taken seriously, then so, too, do very young children. This is
all bodes well for FLIC. But the game is not over. [18]

King's College, London

References

Burge, T. 1973. 'Reference and proper names', *The Journal of Philosophy*,
70, 425–39.
Burge, T. 1974. 'Demonstrative constructions, reference and truth', *The
Journal of Philosophy* **71**, 205–23.
Burge, T. 1980. 'Truth and singular terms', in M. Platts, (ed.).
Burge, T. 1989. 'Wherein is language social' in A. George, (ed.) 175–92.
Chomsky, N. 1986. *Knowledge of Language: Its Nature, Origin and Use*,
New York, Praeger.
Davidson, D. 1977. 'Reality without reference' *Dialectica* **31**, 247–53.
Davidson, D. 1979. 'The inscrutability of reference' *The Southwestern
Journal of Philosophy* **10**, 7–19.
George, A. (ed.) 1989. *Reflections on Chomsky*, Oxford: Blackwell.
Higginbotham, J. 1989. 'Wherein is language social', in A. George (ed).
153–79.
Evans, G., 1973. 'The causal theory of names', *Proceedings of the
Aristotelian Society*, Supp. Vol., 47, 187–208.
Evans, G. 1982. *The Varieties of Reference*, Oxford: Clarendon.
Hall, D. G. 1996. 'Preschoolers default assumptions about word meaning:
proper names designate unique individuals', *Developmental Psychology*,
32, 177-86.
Hall, D. G., 1999. 'Semantics and the acquisition of proper names'. In R.
Jackendoff, P. Bloom, & K. Wynn (eds) *Language, Logic, and Concepts:
Essays in honor of John Macnamara*. Cambridge, MA: MIT Press.
Harman, G. 1972. 'Logical form.' *Foundations of Language*, **9**, 38-65.
Higginbotham, J. 1985. 'On semantics', *Linguistic Inquiry*, **16**, 547-93.
Higginbotham, J. 1996. 'Linguistic theory and davidson's programme in
semantics' in E. LePore (ed.), *Truth and Interpretation: Perspectives on
the Philosophy of Donald Davidson*, Oxford: Blackwell 29–48.

[18] An early version of this paper was presented at a conference on the
work of Donald Davidson in Karlovy Vary, 1998. I am grateful to the par-
ticipants there for discussion. A more recent version was presented at a
semantics workshop at Rutgers University, and commented upon by
David Braun. I am grateful to Braun for helpful comments and to partici-
pants for discussion. Thanks are due also to Mark Baker, Paul Bloom,
Donald Davidson, Geoff Hall, Keith Hossack, Kent Johnson, Richard
Larson, Guy Longworth, Friederike Moltmann, Stephen Neale, Mark
Richard, Mark Sainsbury, Barry C. Smith, Jason Stanley, Iannis
Stephanou and Tim Valentine for very helpful comments.

Higginbotham, J. 1988. 'Contexts, models and meaning: a note on the data of semantics' in R. Kempson (ed.) *Mental Representations: The Interface between Language and Reality,* Cambridge, Cambridge University Press 29–48.

Katz, N., Baker, E. and Macnamara, J. 1974. 'What's in a name? A study of how children learn common and proper names'. *Child Development,* 469–73.

Larson, R. and Segal, G. 1995. *Knowledge of Meaning: An Introduction to Semantic Theory.* Cambridge, MA: MIT Press.

Longobardi, G. 1994. 'Reference and proper names: a theory of N-movement in syntax and logical form' *Linguistic Inquiry,* **25:4,** 609–65.

McDowell, J. 1977. 'The sense and reference of a proper name', *Mind,* **86,** 159–85.

Perry, J. 1980. 'A problem about continued belief', *Pacific Philosophical Quarterly,* **5,** 533–42.

Platts, M. (ed.), 1980. *Reference, Truth and Reality,* London: Routledge, Kegan Paul.

Quine, W. v. O. 1990. *The Pursuit of Truth,* Cambridge MA., Harvard University Press.

Valentine, T., Brennan, T and Bredart, S. 1996. *The Cognitive Psychology of Proper Names: On the importance of being Ernest,* London: Routledge.

Relativism and Classical Logic

CRISPIN WRIGHT

I

Let me begin with a reminder of the crude but intuitive distinction from which the relativistic impulse springs. Any of the following claims would be likely to find both supporters and dissenters:

That snails are delicious
That cockroaches are disgusting
That marital infidelity is alright provided nobody gets hurt
That a Pacific sunset trumps any Impressionist canvas

and perhaps

That Philosophy is pointless if it is not widely intelligible
That the belief that there is life elsewhere in the universe is justified
That death is nothing to fear

Disputes about such claims may or may not involve quite strongly held convictions and attitudes. Sometimes they may be tractable disputes: there may be some other matter about which one of the disputing parties is mistaken or ignorant, where such a mistake or ignorance can perhaps be easily remedied, with the result of a change of heart about the original claim; or there may be a type of experience of which one of the disputing parties is innocent, and such that the effect of initiation into that experience is, once again, a change of view. But there seems no reason why that should have to be the way of it. The dispute might persist even though there seemed to be nothing else relevant to it about which either party was ignorant or mistaken, nor any range of relevant experience which either was missing. The details of how that might happen vary with the examples. But in a wide class of cases, it would likely be a matter of one disputant placing a value on something with which the other could not be brought to sympathize; or with her being prone to an emotional or other affect which the other did not share; or with basic differences of propensity to belief, perhaps associated with the kinds of personal probability thresholds which show up in such phenomena as variations in agents' degrees of risk aversion.

Crispin Wright

Intuitively, claims of the above kinds—potentially giving rise to what we may call *disputes of inclination*—contrast with claims like these:

That the snails eaten in France are not found in Scotland
That cockroaches feed only on decomposing organic matter
That extra-marital affairs sometimes support a marriage
That sunset tonight will be at 7:31 pm
That there are fewer professional analytical philosophers than there were
That there are living organisms elsewhere in the solar system
That infant mortality was significantly higher in Victorian times than in Roman.

Any of these might in easily imaginable circumstances come into dispute, and in some cases at least we can imagine such disputes being too awkward to resolve. Relevant data might be hard to come by, and there are also material vaguenesses involved in most of the examples, on which a difference of opinion might turn. Then there is the possibility of prejudice, ignorance, mistake, delusion, and so on, which in certain circumstances—perhaps far-fetched—it might be difficult to correct. But what doesn't seem readily foreseeable is that we might reach a point when we would feel the disputants should just 'agree to differ', as it were, without imputation of fault on either side. Opinions about such matters are not to be excused just by factors of personal inclination, but have to answer to—it is almost irresistible to say—*the facts*.

This crude but intuitive distinction—disputes of inclination versus disputes of fact—immediately gives rise to a problem. Both types of dispute are focused on straightforward-seeming contents expressed in the indicative mood. But all such contents are naturally treated as evaluable as true or false and truth, one naturally thinks, is a matter of how things stand with the relevant facts. So the very expression of disputes of inclination seems tailor-made to encourage the idea that they are disputes of fact after all: disputes in which, *ceteris paribus*, someone is out of touch with how matters really stand. The problem is therefore: how to characterize disputes of inclination in such a way as to conserve the species, to disclose some point to the ordinary notion that there are indeed such things at all, genuinely contrasting with—what the needed characterization had better simultaneously explain—disputes about matters of fact.

II

There would seem to be exactly four broadly distinguishable types of possible response:

i) *Rampant Realism* denies that the illustrated distinction has anything to do with non-factuality. For rampant realism, the surface form of disputes of inclination has precisely the significance just outlined: such disputes *do* centre on truth-evaluable contents, and truth *is* indeed a matter of fit with the facts. So, even in a radically intransigent dispute of inclination, there will, *ceteris paribus*, be a fact of the matter which one of the parties will be getting wrong. It may be that we have not the slightest idea how a particular such dispute might in principle be settled, and that if charged to explain it, we would hesitate to assign any role to ignorance, or prejudice, or mistake, or vagueness. These considerations, however, so far from encouraging relativism, are best attributed to the imperfection of our grasp of the type of subject matter which the dispute really concerns.

I mean this option to be parallel in important respects to the Epistemic Conception of vagueness.[1] The Epistemicist[2] holds that vague expressions like 'red', 'bald' and 'thin' actually denote properties of perfectly definite extension. But we do not (or, in some versions, cannot) know which properties these are—our concepts of them, fixed by our manifest understanding of the relevant expressions, fail fully to disclose their nature. There is thus a quite straightforward sense in which when I say that something is, for instance, red, I (necessarily) imperfectly understand what I have said.[3]

[1] See especially Williamson (1992) and (1994) and Sorensen (1988).

[2] I shall capitalize—'Epistemicist', 'Epistemicism', etc.—whenever referring to views which, like those of Sorensen and Williamson, combine a conception of vagueness as, broadly, a matter of ignorance with the retention of classical logic and its associated Bivalent metaphysics.

[3] Experience shows that Epistemicists incline to protest at this. Suppose 'tall', say, as a predicate of human beings, applies to an individual just if they are precisely 5′11″ tall or more—that *5′11″ tall or more* is the property denoted by the vague, "tall", as actually used. Then why, in saying that an individual is tall, should I be regarded as understanding what I have said to any lesser an extent than when, in circumstances where I do not know the identity of the culprit, I say that whoever broke the clock had better own up? Why should ignorance of what, in fact, I am talking *about* be described as an imperfection of *understanding*?

Clearly there is space for a similar view about the subject matter of a dispute of inclination. It can happen that we express a concept by 'delicious' which presents a property whose nature it fails (fully) to disclose. This property may or may not apply to culinary snails. There is no way of knowing who is right in the dispute, but somebody will be. At any rate, the issue is no less factual than that of whether culinary snails are indigenous to Scotland.

I do not propose to discuss the rampant realist proposal in any detail here. No doubt a fuller discussion of it would recapitulate many of the moves and counter-moves made in recent debates about the Epistemic

---

Although it is not my purpose here to develop criticisms of the Epistemic conception, I'll take a moment to try to justify the charge. The foregoing protest assumes that the epistemicist is entitled to regard us as knowing what *type* of sharply bounded property an understood vague expression denotes, and as ignorant only of *which* property of that type its use ascribes. I know of no justification for that assumption. What type of sharply bounded property does 'red' denote? Something physical? Or a manifest but sharply bounded segment of the 'colour wheel'? Or something else again? On what basis might one decide? And if the understanding of some common-or-garden vague expressions gives rise to no favoured intuitive *type* of candidate for their putative bounded denotations, why should we favour the obvious candidates in cases—like 'tall'— where there are such?

Intuitively, to understand e.g. a simple, subject-predicate sentence is to know what object is being talked about and what property is being ascribed to it. To be sure, the purport of that platitude should not be taken to require that one invariably has an *identifying* knowledge of the former: I can fully understand an utterance of 'Smith's murderer is insane' without knowing who the murderer is. But it is different with predication. Here what is demanded of one who understands is, at least in the overwhelming majority of cases, that they know—*in a sense parallel to the possession of identifying knowledge of the referent of a singular term*—what property the use of a particular predicate ascribes. Since the overwhelming majority of natural language predicates are vague, that is what the Epistemicist denies us. It would be no good for her to reply: 'But you *do* know what property 'red' denotes—it is the property of being red!'. On the Epistemic account, I know neither which property that is, nor what type of property it is, nor even—in contrast to, say, my understanding of '... has Alex's favourite property' where while ignorant in both ways, I at least know what a property has to do in order to fit the bill—what would make it true that a particular property was indeed ascribed by the normal predicative use of 'red'. It is the last point that clinches the observation in the text; if you were comparably ignorant in all three respects about the content of a definite description—thus ignorant, in particular, of what condition its bearer, if any, would have to meet—it would be absolutely proper to describe you as failing fully to understand it.

Conception of vagueness, though there are some interesting additional issues. I shall assume that it is a position of last resort.

(ii) The second possible response to the problem of characterising disputes of inclination is that of *Indexical Relativism*. On this view, truth conditional contents are indeed involved in 'disputes' of inclination, but actually there are no *real disputes* involved. Rather, the seemingly conflicting views involve implicit reference to differing standards of assessment, or other contextual parameters, in a way that allows both disputants to be speaking the literal truth. Snails are delicious *for you*—for someone with your gastronomic susceptibilities and propensities—but they are not delicious *for me*—for one whose culinary taste is as mine is. Hurt-free infidelities can be acceptable to you—perhaps, to anyone inclined to judge the moral worth of an action by its pleasurable or painful effects alone—but they are not acceptable to me—to one inclined to value openness and integrity in close personal relationships for its sake, irrespective of any independently beneficial or harmful consequences.

This, very familiar kind of relativistic move is still supported in recent philosophy—for instance by Gilbert Harman, on morals.[4] Its obvious drawback is that it seems destined to misrepresent the manner in which, at least as ordinarily understood, the contents in question embed under operations like the conditional and negation. If it were right, there would be an analogy between disputes of inclination and the 'dispute' between one who says 'I am tired' and her companion who replies, 'Well, I am not' (when what is at issue is one more museum visit). There are the materials here, perhaps, for a (further) disagreement but no disagreement has yet been expressed. But ordinary understanding already hears a disagreement between one who asserts that hurt-free infidelity is acceptable and one who asserts that it is not. And it hears a distinction between the denial that hurt-free infidelity is acceptable and the denial that it is a generally acceptable by the standards employed by someone who has just asserted that it is acceptable. Yet for the indexical relativist, the latter should be the proper explicit form of the former. In the same way, the ordinary

---

[4] Harman has been, of course, a long-standing champion of the idea. The most recent extended defence of his views is in Gilbert Harman and Judith Jarvis Thomson *Moral Relativism and Moral Objectivity* (Oxford: Basil Blackwell, 1996), Part One. For a many-handed discussion, see Harman, Thomson and others 'Book Symposium on Harman and Thomson,' *Philosophy and Phenomenological Research* LVIII, 1998, pp. 161–213.

understanding hears a distinction between the usual meaning of the conditional, that if hurt-free infidelity is acceptable, so are hurt-free broken promises, and the same sentence taken on the understanding that both antecedent and consequent are to be assessed relative to some one particular framework of standards (that of an actual assertor of the sentence, a framework which might or might not treat infidelity and promise-breaking in different ways.)

Of course there is room for skirmishing here, some of it no doubt quite intricate. But in general it is not clear how indexical relativism might manage to save enough of the normal practice of the discourses within which disputes of inclination may arise to avoid the charge that it has simply missed their subject matter.

(iii) The third possible response to the problem of characterising disputes of inclination is that of *Expressivism*: the denial that the discourses in question deal in truth-conditional contents at all. Of course, on this view there are, again, no real *disputes* of inclination—merely differences of attitude, feeling and reaction. There has been a significant amount of recent discussion of this kind of approach, stimulated by the sophisticated versions of it proposed by writers such as Simon Blackburn and Alan Gibbard.[5] But it confronts a very general dilemma. What is to be the expressivist account of the propositional—seemingly truth-conditional—surface of the relevant discourses? The clean response is to argue that it is misleading—that what is conveyed by discourse about the delicious, the morally acceptable, or whatever this kind of view is being proposed about, can and may be better expressed by a regimented discourse in which the impression that truth-conditional contents are being considered, and denied, or hypothesized, or believed, etc. is analysed away. However it seems fair to say that no-one has shown how to accomplish this relatively technical project, with grave difficulties in particular attending any attempt to reconstruct the normal apparatus of moral argument in such a way as to dispel all appearance that it moves among truth-evaluable moral

[5] Simon Blackburn, *Spreading the Word* (Oxford: Clarendon Press, 1984), Ch. 6: 'Evaluations, Projections and Quasi-realism', still remains the best introduction to his view, but the most recent official incarnation is Simon Blackburn, *Ruling Passions* (Oxford: Clarendon Press, 1998); Alan Gibbard's ideas are developed systematically in his magisterial *Wise Choices, Apt Feelings* (Cambridge, Mass: Harvard University Press, 1990).

contents.[6] The alternative is to allow that the propositional surface or moral discourse, to stay with that case, can actually comfortably consist with there being no genuinely truth-conditional contents at issue, no genuine moral beliefs, no genuine moral arguments construed as movements from possible beliefs to possible beliefs, and so on. But now the danger is that the position merely becomes a terminological variant for the fourth response, about to be described, with terms like 'true' and 'belief' subjected to a (pointless) high redefinition by expressivism, but with no substantial difference otherwise.

(iv) Of the options so far reviewed, the first allows that a dispute of inclination is a real dispute, but at the cost of conceding that one of the disputants will be undetectably wrong about a subject matter of which both have an essentially imperfect conception, while the other two options deny, in their respective ways, that there is any genuine dispute at all. The only remaining option—I'll call it *True Relativism*—must, it would seem, be the attempt to maintain that, while such disputes may indeed concern a common truth-evaluable claim, and thus may be genuine—may involve incompatible views about it—there need be nothing about which either disputant is mistaken, nor any imperfection in their grasp of what it is that is in dispute. Opinions held in disputes of inclination may, in particular cases, be flawed in various ways. But in the best case, the True Relativist thought will be, such a dispute may oppose two opinions with which there is no fault to be found, even in principle save by invocation of the idea that there is an ulterior, undecidable fact of the matter about which someone is mistaken. That hypothesis, distinctive of Rampant Realism, is exactly what True Relativism rejects: for True Relativism, genuinely conflicting opinions about a truth-evaluable claim may each be unimprovable and may involve no misrepresentation of any further fact.

---

[6] For exposition and development of some of the basic difficulties, see Bob Hale, 'The Compleat Projectivist,' *The Philosophical Quarterly* 36, 1986. pp. 65–84; 'Can there be a logic of attitudes?' in John Haldane and Crispin Wright (eds), *Reality, Representation and Projection* (Oxford: Oxford University Press, 1992), pp. 337–63; and 'Can arboreal knotwork help Blackburn out of Frege's abyss?' Forthcoming in a *Philosophy and Phenomenological Research* book symposium on Blackburn's (1988).

Crispin Wright

III

In the light of the shortcomings, briefly noted, of the three noted alternatives—and because it has, I think, some claim to be closest to the common-sense view of the status of disputes of inclination—it is of central importance to determine whether the materials can be made out for a stable and coherent True Relativism. In *Truth and Objectivity*,[7] I proposed—without, I think, ever using the word 'relativism'—a framework one intended effect of which was to be just that. The key was the contrast between areas of discourse which, as it is there expressed, would be merely *minimally truth-apt*, and areas of discourse where, in addition, differences of opinion would be subject to the constraint of *cognitive command*.

To elaborate just a little. The idea that there are merely minimally truth-apt discourses comprises two contentions, about truth and aptitude for truth respectively. The relevant—minimalist—view about truth, in briefest summary, is that all it takes in order for a predicate to qualify as a truth predicate is its satisfaction of each of a basic set of platitudes about truth: for instance, that to assert is to present as true, that statements which are apt for truth have negations which are likewise, that truth is one thing, justification another, and so on.[8] The minimalist view about *truth aptitude*, likewise in briefest summary, itself comprises two contentions:

[7] Wright (1992).

[8] A fuller list might include

: the transparency of truth—that to assert is to present as true and, more generally, that any attitude to a proposition is an attitude to its truth— that to believe, doubt or fear, for example, that P is to believe, doubt or fear that P is true. (*Transparency*)

: the opacity of truth—incorporating a variety of weaker and stronger principles: that a thinker may be so situated that a particular truth is beyond her ken, that some truths may never be known, that some truths may be unknowable in principle, etc. (*Opacity*)

: the conservation of truth-aptitude under embedding: aptitude for truth is preserved under a variety of operations—in particular, truth-apt propositions have negations, conjunctions, disjunctions, etc. which are likewise truth-apt. (*Embedding*)

: the Correspondence Platitude—for a proposition to be true is for it to correspond to reality, accurately reflect how matters stand, 'tell it like it is', etc. (*Correspondence*)

: the contrast of truth with justification—a proposition may be true without being justified, and vice-versa. (*Contrast*) that any discourse dealing in assertoric contents will permit the definition upon its sentences of a predicate which qualifies as a truth predicate in the light of the minimalist proposal about truth;

and

that a discourse should be reckoned to deal with suitable such contents just in case its ingredient sentences are subject to certain minimal constraints of *syntax*—embeddability within negation, the conditional, contexts of propositional attitude, etc.—and *discipline*: their use must be governed by commonly-acknowledged standards of warrant.

A properly detailed working out of these ideas[9] would foreseeably have the effect that almost all the areas of discourse which someone intuitively sympathetic to the 'crude but intuitive' distinction might want to view as hostage to potential disputes of inclination will turn out to deal in contents which, when the disciplinary standards proper to the discourse are satisfied, a supporter is going to be entitled to claim to be true. That however—the proposal is—ought to be consistent with the discourse in question failing to meet certain further conditions necessary to justify the idea that, in the case of such a dispute, there will be a further fact in virtue of which one of the disputants is in error.

What kind of further condition might that be? The leading idea of someone—let's call her the *factualist*—who believes that a given discourse deals in matters of fact—unless she thinks that its truths lie beyond our ken—is that soberly and responsibly to practise that discourse is to enter into a kind of *representational* mode of cogni-

[9] A partial development of them is offered in Wright (1992) Chs. 1–2.

: the timelessness of truth—if a proposition is ever true, then it always is, so that whatever may, at any particular time, be truly asserted may—perhaps by appropriate transformations of mood, or tense—be truly asserted at any time. (*Timelessness*)

: that truth is absolute—there is, strictly, no such thing as a proposition's being more or less true; propositions are completely true if true at all. (*Absoluteness*)

The list might be enlarged, and some of these principles may anyway seem controversial. Moreover it can be argued that the Equivalence Schema underlies not merely the first of the platitudes listed—Transparency—but the Correspondence and Contrast Platitudes as well. For elaboration of this claim, see Wright (1992) pp. 24–7. For further discussion of the minimalist conception, and adjacent issues, see Wright (1998).

tive function, comparable in relevant respects to taking a photograph or making a wax impression of a key. The factualist conceives that certain matters stand thus and so independently of us and our practice—matters comparable to the photographed scene and the contours of the key. We then engage in the appropriate investigative activity—putting ourselves at the mercy of the standards of belief-formation and appraisal appropriate to the discourse in question (compare taking the photograph or impressing the key on the wax)—and the result is to leave an imprint in our minds which, in the best case, appropriately matches the independently standing fact.

This kind of thinking, while doubtless pretty vague and metaphorical, does have certain quite definite obligations. If we take photographs of one and the same scene which somehow turn out to represent it in incompatible ways, there has to have been some kind of shortcoming in the function of one (or both) of the cameras, or in the way it was used. If the wax impressions we take of a single key turn out to be of such a shape that no one key can fit them both, then again there has to have been some fault in the way one of us went about it, or in the materials used. The tariff for taking the idea of representation in the serious way the factualist wants to is that when subjects' 'representations' prove to conflict, then there has to have been something amiss with the way they were arrived at or with their vehicle—the wax, the camera, or the thinker.

That's the core thought behind the idea of cognitive command. The final formulation offered in *Truth and Objectivity* was that a discourse exerts cognitive command just in case it meets this condition:

> It is *a priori* that differences of opinion formulated in [that] discourse, unless excusable as a result of vagueness in a disputed statement, or in the standards of acceptability, or variation in personal evidence thresholds, so to speak, will involve something which may properly be regarded as cognitive shortcoming.[10]

To stress: the constraint is motivated, in the fashion just sketched, by the thought that it, or something like it, is a commitment of anyone who thinks that the responsible formation of opinions expressible within the discourse is an exercise in the *representation* of self-standing facts. Conversely: any suggestion that conflicts in such opinions can be *cognitively blameless*, yet no vagueness be involved of any of the three kinds provided for in the formulation, is a sug-

[10] Wright (1992), p. 144.

gestion that the factualist—seriously representational—view of the discourse in question is in error. Broadly, then, the implicit suggestion of *Truth and Objectivity* was that True Relativism about a particular discourse may be formulated as the view that, while qualifying as minimally truth-apt, it fails to exhibit cognitive command.

IV

However there is an awkwardness to be confronted by any proposal of this general kind. The key to True Relativism, as we have it so far, is somehow to make out that a discourse deals in contents which are simultaneously truth-apt yet such that, when they fall into dispute, there need in principle be nothing wrong with—nothing to choose between—the disputed opinions. But in granting that the contents in question are minimally truth-apt, the relativist allows, presumably, that they are subject to ordinary propositional-logical reasoning. So, where P is any matter of inclination which comes into dispute between a thinker A, who accepts it, and a thinker B, who does not, what is wrong with the following *Simple Deduction?*

1	(1) A accepts P	–	Assumption
2	(2) B accepts Not-P	–	Assumption
3	(3) A's and B's disagreement involves no cognitive shortcoming		Assumption
4	(4) P	–	Assumption
2,4	(5) B is guilty of a mistake, hence of cognitive shortcoming	–	2,4
2,3	(6) Not-P	–	4,5, 3 RAA
1,2,3	(7) A is guilty of a mistake, hence of cognitive shortcoming	–	4
1,2	(8) Not -[3]	–	3,3, 7 RAA

The Simple Deduction seems to show that whenever there is difference of opinion on *any*—even a merely minimally—truth-apt claim, there *is*—quite trivially—a cognitive shortcoming, something to choose between the views. And since this has been proved *a priori*, cognitive command holds for all truth-apt discourses. So the alleged gap between minimal truth-aptitude and cognitive command, fundamental to the proposal of *Truth and Objectivity*, disappears.

Obviously there has to be *something* off-colour about this argument. So much is immediately clear from the reflection that the disagreement it concerns could have been about some borderline case of a *vague* predicate: nothing that happens in the Simple Deduction is sensitive to the attempt made in the formulation of cognitive command to exempt disagreements which are owing to vagueness (one way or another). Yet the deduction would have it that even these too must involve cognitive shortcoming. And the notion of shortcoming involved is merely that of bare *error*—mismatch between belief and truth-value. So if the argument shows anything, it would appear to show *a priori* that any difference of opinion about a borderline case of a vague predicate will also involve a mismatch between belief (or unbelief) and actual truth-value. It would therefore seem that there has to *be* a truth-value in all such cases, even if we have not the slightest idea how it might be determined. We appear to have been saddled with the Epistemic Conception of vagueness! I believe that means, with all due deference to the proponents of that view, that the Simple Deduction proves too much.[11]

So where does it go wrong? A natural suggestion is that the trouble lies with an overly limited conception of 'cognitive shortcoming'. The considerations used to motivate the cognitive command

---

[11] It may be rejoined (and was, by Mark Sainsbury, in correspondence) that we could accept the Simple Deduction without commitment to the stark bivalence espoused by the Epistemic Conception if we are prepared to allow that A's and B's respective opinions may indeed both reflect cognitive shortcoming where P's truth-status is borderline—on the ground that, in such circumstances, both ought to be *agnostic* about P. The point is fair, as far as it goes, against the preceding paragraph in the text. However I believe—and this will be a central plank of the discussion to follow—that it is a profound mistake to regard positive or negative verdicts about borderline cases as *eo ipso* defective. If that were right, a borderline case of P should simply rank as a special kind of case in which—because things are *other than P says*—it's negation ought to hold. In any case the Simple Deduction will run no less effectively if what B accepts is not 'Not-P' when understood narrowly, as holding only in *some* types of case where P fails to hold, but rather as holding in *all* kinds of case where things are not as described by P—*all* kinds of ways in which P can fail of truth, including being borderline (if, *contra* my remark above, that is how being borderline is conceived). So even if Bivalence is rejected, the Simple Deduction still seems to commit us to the more general principle Dummett once called *Determinacy*: that P always has a determinate *truth-status*—of which Truth and Falsity may be only two among more than two possibilities—and that at least one of any pair of conflicting opinions about P must involve a mistake about this status, whatever it is. That is still absolutely in keeping with the realist spirit of the Epistemic Conception, to which it still appears—at least in spirit—the Simple Deduction commits us if unchallenged.

constraint—the comparison with the idea of representation at work in the examples of the photograph or the wax-impression—license something richer: a notion of cognitive shortcoming that corresponds to failure or limitation of process, mechanism or materials, and not merely a mismatch between the product and its object. The two cameras that produce divergent—conflicting—representations of the same scene must, one or both, have functioned less than perfectly, not merely in the sense that one (or both) gives out an inaccurate snapshot but in the sense that there must be some independent defect, or limitation, in the process whereby the snapshot was produced. So too, it may be suggested, with cognitive command: the motivated requirement is that differences of opinion in regions of genuinely representational discourse should involve imperfections of *pedigree*: shortcomings in the manner in which one or more of the opinions involved were arrived at, of a kind that might be appreciated as such independently of any imperfection in the result. Once shortcoming in that richer sense is required, it can no longer be sufficient for its occurrence merely that a pair of parties disagree—it needs to be ensured in addition that their disagreement betrays something amiss in the way their respective views were arrived at, some independently appreciable failure in the representational mechanisms. That, it may be felt, is what the cognitive command constraint should be understood as really driving at.

Such an emended understanding of cognitive shortcoming is indeed in keeping with the general motivation of the constraint. But it does not get to the root of our present difficulties. For one thing, the Simple Deduction would still run if we dropped all reference to cognitive shortcoming—thereby finessing the issue of how that notion should be understood—and replaced line 3 with:

(3*) A's and B's disagreement involves no *mistake*.

The resulting reasoning shows—if anything—that any pair of conflicting claims involve a mistake. If it is sound, it seems there just isn't logical space for any fourth, i.e., true-relativistic response to the original problem. To suppose that P is merely minimally truth-apt in the sense of allowing of hypothesis, significant negation, and embedding within propositional attitudes is already, apparently, a commitment to rampant realism. Surely that cannot be right. But the modified deduction, with (3*) replacing (3), shows that refining the idea of cognitive shortcoming in the manner just indicated has nothing to contribute to the task of explaining why not.

Perhaps more important, however, is the fact that we can run an argument to much the same effect as the (unamended) Simple

Crispin Wright

Deduction even when 'cognitive shortcoming' *is* explicitly understood in the more demanding sense just proposed.[12] One reason why rampant realism is unattractive is because by insisting on a fact of the matter to determine the rights and wrongs of any dispute of inclination, no matter how intransigent, it is forced to introduce the idea of a truth-making state of affairs of which we have a necessarily imperfect concept,[13] and whose obtaining, or not, thus necessarily transcends our powers of competent assessment. This is unattractive in direct proportion to the attraction of the idea that, in discourses of the relevant kind, we are dealing with matters which essentially *cannot* outrun our appreciation: that there is no way in which something can be delicious, or disgusting, or funny, or obscene, etc. without being appreciable as such by an appropriately situated human subject because these matters are, in some very general way, constitutively dependent upon *us*. What we—most of us—find it natural to think is that disputes of inclination typically arise in cases where *were* there a 'fact of the matter', it would have to be possible—because of this constitutive dependence—for the protagonists to know of it. Indeed, the ordinary idea that such disputes need concern no fact of the matter is just a modus tollens on that conditional: were there a fact of the matter, the disputants should be able to achieve consensus about it; but it seems manifest in the character of their disagreement that they cannot; so there isn't any fact of the matter. So for all—or at least for a wide class of cases—of claims, P, apt to figure in a dispute of inclination, it will seem acceptable—and the recoil from rampant realism will provide additional pressure—to hold to the following principle of *evidential constraint* (EC):

P → it is feasible to know that P[14]

and to hold, moreover, that the acceptability of this principle is *a priori*, dictated by our concept of the subject matter involved.[15,16]

---

[12] This point was first observed in Stewart Shapiro and William Taschek, 'Intuitionism, Pluralism and Cognitive Command,' *Journal of Philosophy* 93, 1996, pp. 74–88.

[13] See footnote 3 above,

[14] One substitution instance, of course, is:

Not-P → it is feasible to know that not-P,

[15] To forestall confusion, let me quickly address the quite natural thought that, where EC applies, cognitive command should be assured—since any difference, of opinion will concern a knowable matter—and hence that any reason to doubt cognitive command for a given discourse should raise a doubt about EC too. This, if correct, would certainly augur

Consider, then, the following *EC-Deduction*:

1	(1)	A believes P, B believes not-P, and neither has any cognitive shortcoming	–	Assumption
2	(2)	P	–	Assumption
2	(3)	It is feasible to know that P	–	2, EC
1,2	(4)	B believes the negation of something feasibly knowable	–	1,3
1,2	(5)	B has a cognitive shortcoming	–	4
1	(6)	Not-P	–	2,1,5 RAA
1	(7)	It is feasible to know that not-P	–	6, EC
1	(8)	A believes the negation of something feasibly knowable	–	1,7
1	(9)	A has a cognitive shortcoming	–	8
	(10)	Not-[1]	–	1,1,9 RAA

This time 'cognitive shortcoming', it is perhaps superfluous to remark, must involve less than ideal procedure, and not just error in the end product, since it involves mistakes about feasibly knowable matters.

So: it seems that 1 and EC are inconsistent, i.e. evidential constraint is incompatible with the possibility of cognitively blameless

---

badly for any attempt to locate disputes of inclination within discourses where cognitive command failed but EC held! But it is not correct. What the holding of EC for a discourse ensures is, just as stated, that each of the conditionals

P → it is feasible to know that P

Not-P → it is feasible to know that not-P,

is good for each proposition P expressible in that discourse. That would ensure that any difference of opinion about P would concern a knowable matter, and hence involve cognitive shortcoming, only if in any such dispute it would have to be determinate that one of P or not-P would hold. But of course it is of the essence of (true) relativism to reject precisely that—(and to do so for reasons unconnected with any vagueness in the proposition that P.)

[16] The modality involved in *feasible knowledge* is to be understood, of course, as constrained by the distribution of truth values in the actual world. The proposition that, as I write this, I am in Australia is one which it is merely (logically or conceptually) possible to know—the possible world in question is one in which the proposition in question is true, and someone is appropriately placed to recognise its being so. By contrast, the range of what it is feasible for us to know goes no further than what is actually the case: we are talking about those propositions whose actual truth could be recognised by the implementation of some humanly feasible process. (Of course there are further parameters: recognisable when? where? under what if any sort of idealisation of our actual powers? etc. But these are not relevant to present concerns.)

disagreement. If the EC-Deduction is sound, then it seems that wherever EC is *a priori*, cognitive command is met. And it is plausible that EC *will* be *a priori* at least for large classes of the types of claim—par excellence simple predications of concepts like *delicious*—where relativism is intuitively at its most attractive, and where a gap between minimal truth-aptitude and cognitive command is accordingly called for if we are to sustain the *Truth and Objectivity* proposal about how relativism should best be understood.[17]

V

What other objection might be made to either deduction? Notice that there is no assumption of Bivalence in either argument; both can be run in an intuitionistic logic. But one might wonder about the role of *reductio* in the two proofs. For instance, at line 6 in the Simple Deduction, the assumption of P having run into trouble, RAA allows us to infer that its negation holds. Yet surely, in any context where we are trying seriously to make sense of the idea that there may be 'no fact of the matter', we must look askance at any rule of inference which lets us advance to the negation of a proposition just on the ground that its assumption has run into trouble. More specifically: in any circumstances where it is a possibility that a proposition's failing to hold may be a reflection merely of there being no 'fact of the matter', its so failing has surely to be distinguished from its negation's holding.

Natural though the suggestion is, it is not clear that there is much mileage in it for our present purposes. Let's make it a bit more specific.[18] The idea is best treated as involving restriction of the right-to-left direction of the *Negation Equivalence*.

$$T \neg P \to \neg TP,$$

expressing the commutativity of the operators, 'it is true that' and 'it is not the case that'. In circumstances where there is no fact of the matter whether or not P, it will be the case both that $\neg TP$ and $\neg$

[17] To stress: it is not merely *Truth and Objectivity's* implicit proposal about *relativism* that is put in jeopardy by the EC-Deduction. According to the project of that book, cognitive command is a significant watershed but is assured for all discourses where epistemic constraint fails and realism, in Dummett's sense, is the appropriate view. Thus it appears that if the EC-Deduction were to succeed, cognitive command would hold universally and thus fail to mark a realism-relevant crux at all.

[18] I draw here on a suggestion of Patrick Greenough.

T ¬ P. The proper conclusion, on the assumptions in question, of the reductio at line 6 of the Simple Deduction is thus not that the negation of P holds, but merely that it is not the case that P is true. And from this, since it is consistent with there being 'no fact of the matter' whether or not P, we may not infer (at line 7) that A is guilty of any mistake in accepting P. Or so, anyway, the idea has to be.

Rejecting the Negation Equivalence has repercussions, of course, for the Equivalence Schema itself:

$$T P \to P$$

since one would have to reject the ingredient conditional:

$$P \to TP \ ^{19}$$

That flies in the face of what would seem to be an absolutely basic and constitutive property of the notion of truth, that P and TP are, as it were, *attitudinally equivalent*: that any attitude to the proposition that P—belief, hope, doubt, desire, fear, etc.—is equivalent to the same attitude to its truth. For if that's accepted, and if it is granted that any reservation about a conditional has to involve the taking of some kind of differential attitudes to its antecedent and consequent, then there simply can be no coherent reservation about P → TP.

A more direct way of making essentially the same point is this. At line 6 of each deduction, even with RAA modified as proposed, we are entitled to infer that it is not the case that P is true. By hypothesis, however, A accepts P. Therefore unless that somehow does fall short of an acceptance that P is true, A is guilty of a mistake in any case. But how could someone accept P without commitment to its truth?

Indeed, there is actually a residual difficulty with this whole tendency, independent of issues to do with the attitudinal transparency of truth. Simply conceived, the mooted response to the two deductions is trying to make out/exploit the idea that A and B may each be neither right nor wrong because there is 'no fact of the matter', where this is conceived as a *third possibility*, contrasting with either A or B being right. That idea may well demand some restriction on the form of reductio utilized in the two deductions. But the problem they are bringing to light will persist even after the restriction. For the simple fact seems to be that A is taking matters to be one way, and B is taking them to be another, when in truth they are *neither*—when, precisely, a third possibility obtains. In that case there is indeed nothing to choose between A's and B's respective views, but

---

[19] There will be no cause to question the converse conditional, which is needed for the derivation of the uncontroversial T ¬ P → ¬ TP.

only because they are both equally *off-beam*. We achieve the parity between their views essential to any satisfactory working out of a True Relativism only by placing them in *parity of disesteem*. This general point—broadly, the intuitive inadequacy of 'third possibility' approached to the construal of indeterminacy—is very important.

Anyway, that's our problem. It is the problem of showing how there can indeed be a coherent True Relativism: how there can be a coherent response of the fourth kind—one giving central place to the idea of cognitively blameless disagreement—to the challenge of providing a proper account of the character of disputes of inclination.

VI

Let's take stock of the situation. We may not want to follow Protagoras' example and espouse relativism about everything. Some may not want any truck with relativism anywhere. But it is bad if the position is ruled out right across the board merely for want of any extant coherent formulation. It ought to be possible for there to be a coherent relativism—the kind I'm calling True Relativism—whose thesis, in an appropriate area, is *something like* that there can be genuine differences of opinion which are blameless, differences where the protagonists are entitled to differ, and where ignorance of no further fact is involved. The *Truth and Objectivity* proposal was that a region of discourse may spawn such differences of opinion just if it is minimally truth-apt but fails to exert cognitive command. Yet the two deductions seem to show that the suggestion is incoherent. The Simple Deduction seems to show that any dispute about a truth-apt content involves a mistake, and the EC-Deduction seems to show that any dispute about an evidentially constrained truth-apt content involves some form of procedural cognitive shortcoming—so that, at least for subject matters so constrained, the intended gap between minimal truth-aptitude and cognitive command collapses. Each deduction involves only absolutely elementary and seemingly incontestable modes of inference. Yet their effect is apparently to confound not just my specific proposal about relativism, but the possibility of any coherent True Relativism at all. How can we respond?

I think there is essentially only one way, and I'll close by indicating what it is. As my title suggests, it involves raising a doubt about classical logic, and its associated bivalent semantics.

Sometimes when we don't know the answer to some question, we know how to find out. Sometimes, although we don't know that, we at least know that a way of finding out exists—that experts, for instance, know of one. Sometimes, even if we do not know either of these things, we do at least know that it is possible that an undecided question may come to be decidable—that advances in technology, for instance, may bring the matter within reach. Let us call a *Quandary* any proposition which presents an issue meeting none of these three conditions. More specifically a proposition P presents a Quandary for a thinker T just when the following conditions are met:

   (i) T does not know whether or not P
  (ii) T does not know of any way of knowing whether or not P
 (iii) T does not know that there is any way of knowing whether or not P
 (iv) T does not know that it is (metaphysically) possible to know whether or not P

Note that the satisfaction of each of those four conditions would be entailed if a fifth condition were satisfied:

 (v) T knows that it is (metaphysically) impossible to know whether or not P.

but that is not to be a feature of a Quandary as I intend the notion to be understood; rather, in a Quandary we have uncertainty through and through; so we do not even have the certainty of undecidability. Note also that it is important that the notion of possibility appealed to is of the very weakest—metaphysical—genre.

So characterized, Quandaries are relative to thinkers—one person's Quandary may be part of another's (presumed) information—and to states of information—a proposition may present a Quandary at one time and not at another. There are important classes of example which are acknowledged to present Quandaries for all thinkers who take an interest in the matter. Mathematics throws up plenty of such cases. Fermat's Last Theorem presented a Quandary before Andrew Wiles' recent results. At the time of writing, Goldbach's Conjecture, that every even number is a sum of two primes, is still a Quandary for all of us: we don't know whether or not the conjecture is true, don't know any way of finding out whether or not it's true, don't know that there is any way of knowing whether or not it's true, and do not even know whether it is metaphysically possible to get satisfaction on the matter—whether proof accessible to a finite mind is not here an impossibility. On the other hand, we do not know that it *is* an impossibility—so condition (v) is not met.

Pure mathematics, then, is a source of one type of example of Quandaries. Classically conceived, of course, it is an area where such propositions nevertheless concern quite determinate states of affairs. Classically, there is a fact of the matter whether or not Goldbach's conjecture is true, but it is a fact which is potentially absolutely undecidable for human minds. From the *intuitionistic* point of view originating with Brouwer, however, and subjected to Michael Dummett's powerful and sophisticated general development, the conception of mathematical truth underpinning the classical account is rejected as metaphysical myth. For the intuitionist, truth in mathematics must be constrained by proof—there is no sense in the idea of a mathematical statement's being true beyond all possibility of a finite construction that verifies its truth. The grounds for this claim need not concern us now. The important point is that, intuitionistically, mathematical statements are subject to a general principle of evidential constraint:

P → it is possible to know (prove) that P

It's crucial to realize, however, that this endorsement of evidential constraint does not involve revoking the idea that mathematical statements are apt to present Quandaries. That they are so apt is a solid datum, even for intuitionism, and in its presence an endorsement of evidential constraint cannot be an expression of the conviction that all mathematical statements are decidable. It is the combination of these two considerations—evidential constraint and aptitude for Quandary—that enforces the intuitionistically distinctive revisions of classical logic.

The point is simply appreciated. Suppose, with the classicist, we endorse the Law of Excluded Middle:

P V Not-P

If evidential constraint is in force, that endorsement involves, by routine moves, a commitment to

P is knowable V Not-P is knowable

but the latter is exactly what, if 'P' ranges over statements some of which are Quandaries, we are not entitled to claim. If P is a Quandary we do not know that it or its negation is knowable, even in principle. Accordingly, we have no right to lay claim to the Law of Excluded Middle. It remains, however, that the negation of the Law of Excluded Middle.

Not-(P V Not-P)

is inconsistent by the most elementary logical moves (the only prin-

ciples involved in showing its inconsistency are disjunction introduction and reductio ad absurdum.) So our lack of entitlement to
the Law of Excluded Middle does not equate to an entitlement to
deny it. On the contrary, we are entitled to deny its denial—an entitlement which, under present assumptions, precisely doesn't
amount to an entitlement to lay claim to the Law. So both the Law
of Excluded Middle and the associated principle of double negation
elimination are things we are not entitled to in the presence of evidential constraint and the potentiality for Quandary. Quandary plus
evidential constraint enforces an intuitionistic rejection of classical
propositional logic.

The next thing to note is that there is a good prima facie case for
thinking that the kinds of discourse which give rise to disputes of
inclination are subject to both those conditions. As far as evidential
constraint is concerned, we have already noted that there is, in
effect, a commitment to it in the ordinary idea that, in a difference
of opinion about humour, for instance, or good taste, there need be
'no fact of the matter'—that the antagonists can just as well 'agree
to differ'. This ordinary rhetoric precisely gestures at the thought
that in such a dispute, there is no question of a further, potentially
undecidable fact to make one of the disputants wrong: that here, the
'facts' are essentially open to reception if there are any such facts at
all. That disputes of inclination can present Quandaries is, I
believe, only a little less obviously a commitment of our ordinary
thinking about them. Suppose a dispute about marital infidelity: X
thinks that marital infidelity is alright, provided nobody gets hurt
and Y thinks it is bad, even when no-one gets hurt, because of the
compromise of personal integrity involved. Then such a dispute
can quite properly present a Quandary for a third part, Z, so far
inclined to neither view. Z may be aware of all the considerations
that move X and Y respectively, yet quite permissibly feel unsure
what view to take. She may feel unsure, indeed, that there is or even
could be any justification that would mandate one view at the
expense of the other. So she will meet each of the first four conditions on Quandary. On the other hand, and crucially, she may also
fail to meet the fifth—rejected—condition: she may consider that
she is in no position to exclude the adduction of further considerations which she would want to acknowledge as deciding the dispute;
and even if she cannot envisage what such considerations might be
like, she may also consider that she does not know that the considerations which have respectively moved X and Y are not *already*
good enough to decide the question, so that one of those two verdicts is already knowledgeable.

The point needs further elaboration, but I conjecture that a proper development of the commitments of the intuitions on which the distinction between disputes of inclination and disputes of fact is grounded in the first place will wind up disclosing that they include both evidential constraint and potentiality for Quandary in the discourses in question.

If that's right, then we learn that (something like) intuitionistic logic must be the logic of choice for regions of discourse apt for the expression of disputes of inclination. The final question, then, is how that helps with the problem posed by the two deductions. At this point, someone playing close attention may have noted—perhaps with rising irritation—that there is actually no appeal to a distinctively classical step in either! Line 8 of the Simple Deduction, and line 10 in the EC-Deduction are both derived in an entirely intuitionistically kosher way. Correct. But the twist is that the problem for True Relativism posed by the two deductions has to do not with their conclusions as stated but rather the way in which we unthinkingly allowed those conclusions to be *interpreted*. Take the EC-Deduction. (The point about the Simple Deduction is exactly parallel.) The EC-Deduction effects a reductio ad absurdum of the supposition that a certain dispute involves no cognitive shortcoming. That's a negative existential claim, so the reductio is in the first instance a proof of *its* negation, that is, a proof of the *doubly negated* claim that it is not true that As and Bs conflicting opinions involve no cognitive shortcoming. This much is indeed established *a priori* (provided EC is locally *a priori*.) But it is not yet a demonstration of cognitive command, nor therefore a demonstration that the distinction between minimal truth-aptitude and cognitive command collapses. To show that cognitive command holds, we have to show that it is *a priori* that cognitive shortcoming is involved in any such dispute. And the move to that from the conclusion actually demonstrated at line 10 is precisely a double negation elimination step. If our logic is intuitionistic, we won't be able to make it.

To be sure, in order to find fault with that extra step, we need to have done more than to have motivated dropping double negation elimination from our logic. In addition, we need to show that the transition is suspect in the targeted case. But indeed it is. For if it is to be *a priori* that any disagreement expressed in the discourse in question is to involve some form of cognitive shortcoming, and if that discourse is also *a priori* subject to evidential constraint, then it follows that there must somehow be an *identifiable* shortcoming in A's and B's conflicting opinions—for the shortcoming would have to consist in one or the other of them holding the wrong view about a knowable matter. To insist on the double negation elimination step is thus a commitment to the view that in all cases of conflict of opinion in the discourse in question, a shortcoming may be identified as such—*even if the case is intuitively one of Quandary: even if we do not know the right opinion, do not know how we might know, and have no general reason to suppose that there is, or could be, a way of knowing nonetheless.* The elementary resources involved in the reasoning in the EC-Deduction seem manifestly insufficient to impose any such conclusion.

I am inviting you to make a very fine distinction—fine enough to run the risk that it may seem sophistical. So let me try to be very clear about it. I am proposing that we now concede that the two deductions show that, once a discourse is allowed to be even merely minimally truth-apt—and so apt for the expression of disagreement at all—it cannot coherently be supposed that a disagreement expressed within it is *cognitively blameless*. True Relativism, as originally formulated, is indeed incoherent. But my point is that realising that need not drive us to reconsider the other three distinguished options. Instead we should resist the inference to the conclusion that there has to *be* cognitive shortcoming involved in any difference of opinion within such a discourse. We are not entitled to that conclusion. The reason is because to accept it would be, in the presence of EC, a commitment to a *locatability* claim for which we have no sufficient ground.

Once again: if this is the best that can be done, then we have indeed still failed to map out a space for a coherent True Relativism, so long as the thesis of the possibility of cognitively blameless disagreement is to be of the very essence of that view. We should respond by questioning whether that should be of the essence of the view—whether that interpretation does not exceed anything that is actually supported by the uncontroversial features of the intuitively demarcated range of cases that provide our basic examples of possible disputes of inclination. The two deductions do inescapably teach us that the idea that such a dispute can involve only cognitively irreproachable opinions, both in their contents and their pedigree, is simply incoherent. But the inclination to describe them that way is best seen as an overstated response to the sense that the matter of such a dispute may quite properly be taken—either by a third party, or by the antagonists themselves in a reflective hour—as presenting a Quandary. We do *not* know that any particular such disagreement is cognitively blameless: what we know is, rather, at most that the first four conditions of quandary are met. In the presence of epistemic constraint, that is then—or so I've argued—sufficient to open a distinction between the wholly unwelcome and unjustified seeming thought that such a dispute *has* to involve some specific form of cognitive shortcoming—which is exactly what we want to resist—and the thought, now allowably regarded as weaker in the context of intuitionistic distinctions, that it cannot be that every opinion involved is cognitively blameless.

In sum: in the context of intuitionistic logic, the distinction between cognitive command and minimal truth-aptitude can be saved from the two deductions—or what then emerge as misreadings of the two deductions—which threaten to subvert it. I suggest that, so saved, it offers the best we can do by way of a coherent formulation of (the spirit of) True Relativism, and does provide—what we anyway need—an outlet for relativistic intuition in those areas of discourse and thought where it seems strongest. The relativistic thesis becomes that, in a targeted area of minimally truth-apt discourse, there is—or anyway we have—no *a priori* reason to suppose that any disagreement (prescinding from ones attributable to vagueness) will involve cognitive shortcoming. That approximates[20] to the thesis, not that such disagreements answer to no 'fact of the matter' but rather that there is—or anyway we have—no *a priori* reason to suppose that there is a fact of the matter to which they answer. I do not know whether that would be enough to satisfy Protagoras.[21]

St Andrews and Columbia Universities

[20] Only 'approximates'. Intuitionistically, we have no *a priori* reason to suppose that there is a fact of the matter to which Goldbach's conjecture answers. But pure arithmetic is plausibly a region of discourse exhibiting cognitive command nonetheless, so not one fit for relativism according to the present proposal. (A dispute about Goldbach's conjecture will involve one form of cognitive shortcoming—prejudice—if it occurs in the absence of any purported proof; and if there is a purported proof, the dispute will involve ignorance if the proof is good, or error if it is not.)

[21] This paper presents a self-contained and somewhat elaborated treatment of one strand from my larger 'On being in a Quandary: Relativism, Vagueness, Logical Revisionism,' *Mind* CX, 2001, pp. 45–98. I am grateful to John Broome, Patrick Greenough, Richard Heck, Fraser MacBride, Sven Rosenkranz, Mark Sainsbury, Joe Salerno, Stephen Schiffer, and Tim Williamson for valuable comments and discussion. The research for the paper has been conducted during my tenure of a Leverhulme Research Professorship; I gratefully acknowledge the support of the Leverhulme Trust.

Principles for Possibilia

CHRISTOPHER PEACOCKE

1. The Problem

It seems to be an obvious truth that

(1) There could be something that doesn't actually exist.

That is, it seems to be obviously true that

(1a) ◊∃x(Actually ~ (x exists)).

It is sufficient for the truth of (1) that there could be more people, or trees, or cars, than there actually are. It is also sufficient for the truth of (1) that there could be some people, or trees, or cars that are distinct from all those that actually exist. Do (1) and suchlike statements involve a commitment to possibilia, to things that possibly exist, but do not actually exist? If not, why not? And if so, what is the nature of the possibilia to which (1) and its ilk commit us? These simple little questions are at the tip of an iceberg.

We have to appreciate the size of the iceberg. Some years ago— more than a quarter of a century ago—I thought that there is no commitment to possibilia in this and suchlike statements. We can call this 'the no-commitment view'. My reason for accepting the no-commitment view was that if one starts with an object language containing modal operators and an 'Actually' operator, one can give a truth-theory for this object language in a metalanguage that takes the modal operators as primitive. The theory entails all relevant instances of the schema

'A' is true if and only if A,

including those in which A contains modal operators and occurrences of 'Actually'. That is, the theory is homophonic in Davidson's sense. For the modal operators, the theory has disquotational axioms such as the following:

(Ax □) For any sentence A, and sequence s of objects, s satisfies '□ A' iff □ (s satisfies A).

In this approach, the object-language operator '□' is not treated as a quantifier over worlds. Nor is there outright quantification over the elements of domains of nonactual worlds in the semantic theory.

Christopher Peacocke

The elements of the sequences *s* are all actual objects. Both in the object language and in the metalanguage, the quantifiers not in the scope of any modal operators range only over actual things. Under treatments meeting these specifications, the quantifiers occurring within the modal operators are not assigned a range of nonactual objects. Such treatments are to be found in the writings of Martin Davies, Anil Gupta and myself.[1]

Treatments of this kind seemed to be a natural simultaneous implementation of two tempting philosophical views. The first view is that the contribution of modal operators to the truth-conditions of sentences can be stated without reliance on an ontology of possible worlds. This I thought to be attractive because the notion of possibility seems philosophically explanatorily prior to the notion of a possible world. The second view implemented by the approach is that only actual objects exist. In short, the treatment seemed to embody attractive forms of modalism and actualism.

I thought that one major source of the temptation to reject the no-commitment view was tacit or explicit acceptance of the idea that the Kripke-style model theory for modal operators should also be used to give the absolute truth-conditions for modal statements.[2] In Kripke's treatment, a model structure (**G**, **K**, **R**) contains an element **G** that is intuitively the 'real world' amongst the set of possible worlds **K** on which the accessibility relation relation **R** is defined.[3] The idea behind rejection of the no-commitment view is that the actual world corresponds to some element $G_@$ in the domain of worlds in some model on a model structure containing $G_@$ as its 'real world', and that the philosophical explication of what it is for a modal sentence to be true (simply true, not relative to anything else) is just for it to be true with respect to $G_@$ in that model. The phrase about philosophical explication is present in this formulation in order to prevent the idea from collapsing into a triviality. Virtually any theorist of modality will accept that there is some model such that a modal sentence is true if and only if it is

[1] Martin Davies, 'Weak Necessity and Truth Theories', *Journal of Philosophical Logic* **7** (1978), 415–39; Anil Gupta 'Modal Logic and Truth' *Journal of Philosophical Logic* **7** (1978), 441–72; Christopher Peacocke 'Necessity and Truth Theories' *Journal of Philosophical Logic* **7** (1978) 473–500.

[2] The model theory is that in Saul Kripke, 'Semantical Considerations on Modal Logic' repr. in *Reference and Modality*, ed. L. Linsky (Oxford: Oxford University Press, 1971).

[3] 'Semantical Considerations', p. 64.

120

true in a certain element in that model. What is important is the order of explanation, not the mere truth of this agreed, generalized biconditional. For anyone who accepts that idea, and who accepts that statements like (1) are true, an ontology of merely possible objects will be entailed. The Kripkean model-theoretic semantics quantifies in the metalanguage over possible things that need not exist at the actual world. If the outright truth-conditions for modal sentences are simply given by the truth-conditions for their holding in some designated world G@—the one that corresponds to the actual world—then the truth condition for (1) and (1a) is:

> there is an object distinct from all objects in the domain of the actual world, and which is in the domain of some possible world accessible from the actual world.

I was then, and still am, in agreement with those who say that it is an unstable, indeed incoherent, position to think that you can at the same time use the Kripke-style semantics in the metalanguage to give absolute truth-conditions for modal sentences, count (1) and (1a) as true, yet avoid commitment to the existence of nonactual objects.[4] All these problems were avoided, I thought, if the outright truth-conditions for modal sentences were given in a homophonic absolute truth-theory for a modal language.

No doubt I was a wide-eyed innocent optimist. I still think my earlier attitude is based on a good view of the relative explanatory priority of truth theory and model theory. I also still believe in a form of modalism, the form which states that there are constraints on what is genuinely possible that are explanatorily prior to any legitimate notion of a possible world.[5] What my naïve optimism totally neglected was the need for a theory of understanding. When we look at plausible theories of understanding for modal vocabulary, exactly the same problems as dogged the unstable, incoherent position I just mentioned arise equally for other views of the modal operators. In particular, the same problems arise for a plausible theory of understanding that would need to accompany the homophonic truth-theoretic treatment of the modal operators.

In the special case of metaphysical necessity, the theory of understanding I now favour is one involving tacit knowledge of the

---

[4] In this respect, I am in agreement with Timothy Williamson 'Bare Possibilia', *Erkenntnis* **48** (1998) 257–73, at, p. 263.

[5] For remarks on the varieties of modalism, see my *Being Known* (Oxford: Oxford University Press, 1999) Chapter 4, section 4, and the references therein.

principle-based account of truth-conditions given in *Being Known*. On that treatment, there are certain constraints a world-description must meet if it is to represent a genuine possibility. These constraints, which I called the 'Principles of Possibility', taken together, fix the boundaries of possibility in the following sense: a world-description is a genuine possibility if and only if it satisfies all the constraints. To understand the metaphysical modalities is to have tacit knowledge of these constraints, and to employ them appropriately in evaluating modal claims.

The problem is that if this principle-based conception is developed in accordance with the restriction of all quantifiers to what actually exists, it is easy to see on checking through the truth-conditions offered in the theory that it will count sentences like (1) and formulae like (1a) as false. The principle-based conception introduces the notion of the admissibility of an assignment of semantic values to expressions (or to concepts).[6] Constraints on the notion of possibility are formulated: these are the 'Principles of Possibility'. The theory states that a set of sentences or propositions is possible iff there is some admissible assignment that counts all its elements as true. So, according to the principle-based account, $\Diamond p$ is true iff there is some admissible assignment with respect to which it is true. Under the natural development of this approach, an admissible assignment s will make the sentence

$$\Diamond \exists x (\text{Actually} \sim (x \text{ exists}))$$

true iff there exists an admissible assignment s' differing from s at most in what it assigns to the variable 'x', which assigns to 'x' something within the extension it assigns to 'exists', and with respect to which 'Actually $\sim$ (x exists)' is true. But if admissible assignments can assign only actual objects to variables and singular terms, there will be no such sequence s'. For s' would have to assign an actual object to the variable 'x', and no such assignment will be one with respect to which 'Actually $\sim$(x exists)' is true. In short, when we turn at least to this theory of understanding, there is after all a tension between acknowledging the truth of sentences like (1) and rejecting an ontology of possibilia.

Two roads out of this impasse are blocked. First, it would be quite out of the spirit of the principle-based conception of modality simply to help itself to a domain of non-actual possible

---

[6] The next few sentences briefly summarize the approach of Chapter 4 of *Being Known*.

objects. The claim of the principle-based conception is that our understanding of possibility can be elucidated in terms of our grasp of a set of principles constraining genuine possibility. But if those principles take for granted the notion of a possible, non-actual object, then the idea of a possible object would involve a use of the notion of possibility which has not been explained in terms of the principles of possibility. Perhaps, as Kit Fine remarked to me, a theorist might react by taking the notion of possibilia as basic, but not that of possibility. But the metaphysical and epistemological questions that arise about possibilia seem much too close to those that arise about possibility for the former to be presupposed in any solution to understanding the latter.

A second way out that might be tempting would be not to require for the truth of (1) and (1a) that there exist an admissible assignment s' of the sort described, but to require only that it is possible that there exist such an assignment. This would be within the spirit of the homophonic treatment in my 'Necessity and Truth Theories'. But the price of taking this road would be to fail to answer the questions in the theory of understanding after all—for this is a use of 'possibly' that has not been explained in terms of the principle-based approach. To explain it in turn in terms of the existence of an admissible assignment that assigns only actual objects would take us right back to Square One. (1) and (1a) would again be counted as false.

Can any of the extant analyses of statements about possibilia be used to help out the principle-based conception at this juncture? There are at least two problems with trying to take this way out, one general and one local.

The general problem applies to a wide range of attempted analyses of possibilia, and thereby deserves special emphasis. The problem is simply that whatever the analysis of quantification over, and of apparent reference to, possibilia, as long as there remain modal operators interacting with quantifiers, and we want to count statements like (1) as true, we still have no theory of understanding which does this without incurring a commitment to possibilia. An otherwise attractive style of treatment of possibilia involves explaining away apparent reference to them by using only the 'actualist' quantifiers inside the scope of modal operators. Consider, for instance, the series of papers by Kit Fine offering illuminating proposals about quantification over possibilia. Fine observes that the so-called 'outer' quantifier Ex whose range may include possibilia can be given the following analysis, using Vlach's operators † and ↓:
ExA(x) is equivalent to †◊∃x↓A(x), where '∃x' is the 'inner',

Christopher Peacocke

'actualist' quantifier and †, ↓ are the operators of Vlach.[7] Here we still have modal operators interacting with actualist quantifiers. If this is going to be a solution, we had better have some account of the truth-conditions of sentences of the form ◇∃x....x.... that does not simply say that there is a possible object meeting the condition ...x.... in a world of such-and-such a kind. As we saw, the homophonic truth theory does not by itself provide this, since when we turn to an account of understanding that would mesh with the homophonic theory, that theory of understanding seems to require an ontology of possibilia when we regard (1) as true. So positions of the sort currently in question will not after all have given any reply to the complaint that on further inspection, no truth-condition for ◇∃x....x.... has been given that does not involve a commitment to possibilia. I call this 'the problem of providing acceptable truth-conditions for inner quantifications'. A good solution to this problem of providing acceptable truth-conditions for inner quantifications must be accompanied by a theory of understanding which dovetails with the proposed truth-conditions.

The local problem with many extant analyses of the existence of possibilia is that they take for granted the existence of world-propositions corresponding to possible worlds.[8] A world-proposition consists of or corresponds to a set of propositions, intuitively those that that are true at the corresponding world. The world-proposition will not have been properly specified if it omits propositions about nonactuals that exist at the world to which the proposition corresponds. It would be quite wrong to identify all those possible worlds that disagree only on which nonactual things exist at them, or on what is true of them with respect to those worlds. So the world-propositions themselves seem to re-import a commitment to possibilia.

The chapter in *Being Known* on metaphysical necessity, where it touches on these issues, breezily expresses the hope that some construction of possibilia from actual things can be carried out (p. 153).

---

[7] Kit Fine, 'Postscript' in Arthur Prior, *Worlds, Times and Selves* (London: Duckworth, 1977), pp. 122, 144. As Fine summarizes the semantics of Vlach's operators: '† allows one to keep or "store" a reference to the world of evaluation, while ↓ enables one to pick up this reference' (p. 144).

[8] For discussion of world-propositions and their significance, see *Worlds, Times and Selves*, Chapter 2, Fine's 'Postscript' thereto, and Kripke's Review, in the *Journal of Symbolic Logic*, **48** (1983), pp. 486–88, of Fine's paper 'Failures of the Interpolation Lemma in Quantified Modal Logic' *Journal of Symbolic Logic,* **44** (1979), 201–206.

But it gives no clue as to how this is to be done. Maybe that character trait of unsubstantiated optimism is still present.

There is also a more general lesson here about the limits of the ontological significance of theories of truth for a language. A good truth-theory for a language may attribute truth-conditions for sentences of the language whose fulfillment does not, on the face of it, involve commitment to entities of a certain kind. This fact is of limited significance if a good theory of understanding for the language nevertheless implies that the holding of the truth-conditions does require the existence of entities of that kind.

If we cannot develop an acceptable theory of possibilia which is usable in a credible theory of the understanding of modality, then we would have to accept that talk of metaphysical necessity is after all much more problematic than its more sober defenders have supposed. The pressure on us to move to a fictionalist treatment of metaphysical necessity, of the sort championed by Gideon Rosen, would then be greatly increased.[9] The fictionalist could fairly say that the lack of reasonable, non-fictionalist treatments of apparent quantification over nonactuals is entirely consonant with his position.

In this paper, I propose a solution to this problem within the framework of the principle-based treatment of modality. For reasons I will discuss when we have the proposal before us, the solution appears to be available both to possibilists and to actualists. I will, however, argue that even in its possibilist variant, the solution is free of the features that have made people reject other possibilist treatments.

A theory of possibilia must do more than merely establish that we need to acknowledge such entities. It must also show how the need is to be met. A theory of possibilia must state the existence-conditions and the identity-conditions of possibilia. This must all be done within an acceptable theory of the metaphysics, epistemology and theory of understanding for modal notions.

2. Possibility as Prior to Possibilia

On the treatment I advocate, the truth of propositions involving the notion of possibility is more fundamental than the existence of possibilia. Truths about possibility are used in the explanation of the existence and identity of possibilia. Under some treatments of the

---

[9] Gideon Rosen 'Modal Fictionalism' *Mind* **99** (1990), 327–54.

Christopher Peacocke

notion of a possible world, a possible world is taken to involve possibilia. The present approach will then offer further support for the idea that there are constraints on the notion of possibility that are explanatorily prior to such notions of possible worlds. That is, will be congenial to modalism. If the position I am developing here is along the right lines, it is not only the views I held a quarter-century ago that are entitled to bear the label 'modalist'.

Although the principle-based conception of possibility as it was expounded in *Being Known* quantifies only over actual objects, we understate its resources if we think that its natural development has implications only for actual objects. Take some particular actual object, a man John, say. The principle-based conception, together with plausible possession conditions, entails that no admissible assignment will count as true the proposition *John is a married bachelor*. Hence it explains the metaphysical necessity of the proposition *John is not a married bachelor*. But the implications of the principle-based conception go further. For the Principles of Possibility, together with plausible possession conditions, entail that the open sentence (or concept)

> *x is a married bachelor*

will not be satisfied by any admissible assignment.

This entailment holds regardless of which particular objects exist in the actual world. No information about which objects actually exist is drawn upon in establishing the unsatisfiability of *x is a married bachelor* by an admissible assignment.

This is not merely a technical or formal point. It is symptomatic of the explanation of why there is no admissible assignment that satisfies *x is a married bachelor*. There is no such admissible assignment because of the nature of the rules which determine the actual extensions of *bachelor* and *is married*. The Principles of Possibility (in particular the Modal Extension Principle) carry over these same rules, as constraints on genuine possibility, to nonactual worlds whose domains consist of actual objects. In the same spirit we can equally carry over the same rules again as constraints on genuine possibilities involving merely possible objects. I suggest that in the existence of such constraints we have the philosophical ground of the nonexistence of even a possible object that is both married and a bachelor.

There is a partial structural parallel between the formulation of the Principles of Possibility when they do not explicitly talk about mere possibilia, and physical theories as normally formulated in physics papers and books. Physical laws and principles are

126

normally formulated in purely indicative terms, without any use of modal operators. But it is clearly intended that the laws and principles so stated have consequences for counterfactual circumstances, and can be used in counterfactual reasoning about physically specified circumstances. A structurally similar point applies to the Principles of Possibility. The same constraints on possibility formulated there for actual objects apply equally to merely possible objects.[10]

To generalize the idea, and to capture the point in the formal theory of the Principles of Possibility, we can say the following. There is not even a possible object which is φ if the Principles of Possibility themselves, together with the possession conditions for the concepts in φ, and without any further information about what actually exists, entail that the open sentence

x is φ

is not true under any admissible assignment.

That is a sufficient condition for the nonexistence of a possibile of a given kind. What about sufficient conditions for the existence of a possibile of a given kind? In developing the principle-based conception of modality, I followed the spirit of David Lewis's Principle of Plenitude in accepting a Principle of Constrained Recombination.[11] The Principle of Constrained Recombination amounts to the principle that something is possible if it is not ruled out by the other Principles of Possibility and non-modal truths. This Principle captures the maximalist character of the general notion of metaphysical possibility. We are respecting this maximalist character if we extend a Principle of Plenitude from the possibility of propositions to the existence of possibilia. We can say: for there to exist a possible object that is φ is for it to be consistent with the Principles of Possibility and non-modal truths that there is an admissible assignment under which the open sentence or concept

x is φ

is true. This extends the ontology beyond the realm of actual objects. Suppose N is an element in the periodic table, identified on theoretical grounds from the possibility of its atomic structure, but

---

[10] This point parallels one made by Donald Davidson concerning the indicative character of theories of truth, and their possible role as meaning-theories in his 'Reply to Foster' in *Truth and Meaning* ed. Gareth Evans and John McDowell (Oxford: Oxford University Press, 1976).

[11] David Lewis, *On the Plurality of Worlds* (Oxford: Blackwell, 1986), esp. pp. 87–92.

Christopher Peacocke

of which there are actually no instances anywhere. It is possible that there exist a quantity of N. But it is plausible that no actual quantity of matter could be a quantity of N. It is consistent with the Principles of Possibility and non-modal truths that there is an admissible assignment under which the open sentence or concept

x is a quantity of N

is true. Hence the account correctly implies that there is a possible quantity of N, and any possibile verifying this will not be an actual quantity of matter.

Such is the solution that the principle-based conception of modality offers to the problem of truth-conditions for inner quantifications. The dovetailing position in the theory of understanding is that in understanding these inner quantifications, a person has tacit knowledge of this sufficient condition for the existence of a possible object which is φ. This knowledge is manifested in multiple ways in our actual assessments of whether there is a possible object that is φ, for various particular φ's. Since the condition for there to be a possible object that is φ involves a negative existential —that there is no derivation of a certain sort from the Principles of Possibility—there is an open-endedness in our commitments in accepting that there is a possible object that is φ. We should be, and in fact we are, always rationally ready to consider putative facts that entail that there is such a derivation in assessing whether we should accept that there is a possible object that is φ.

To give necessary and sufficient conditions for the existence of a possibile that is φ is not yet to supply existence and identity conditions for individual, particular possibilia. The preceding account of the truth-conditions of a sentence containing an existential quantification inside a modal operator do not by themselves settle the question of what it is for a *de re* sentence about a possibile to be true. We need to know how a particular possible is individuated, in such a way that we can use that information in evaluating such sentences as, for instance, (1) and (1a).

Ruth Marcus formulates one approach.[12] It is an approach that she explicitly rejects; but we can take it as a starting point in the process of building up an account. She writes:

> Putative possibilia are familiar artifices; we concatenate some set of properties attached to a uniqueness condition and endow it with reference to some kind of shadowy object (p. 197).

[12] Ruth Marcus 'Possibilia and Possible Worlds', in her *Modalities: Philosophical Essays* (Oxford: Oxford University Press, 1993).

128

The context of the discussion makes it clear that these are meant to be properties that are compossible.[13] So this starting idea is that for each possibile, there is some combination of properties (which might be relational properties) $F_1,..., F_n$ such that the possibile is individuated by a true condition of the form

$$\Diamond\exists x(F_1 x \ \& \ .... \ \& \ F_n x \ \& \ \forall y((F_1 y \ \& \ .... \ \& \ F_n y) \supset y = x)).$$

This leaves a lot open (when, for instance, do two such true conditions determine the same possibile?). But there are two fundamental problems with this approach. The first is that the uniqueness condition evidently involves quantification over possibilia. If it does not, the approach does not work, for quantification over actuals will be too weak to capture all the possibilia we need. But the uniqueness condition presupposes understanding of identity between possibilia. In the above version, the identity sign occurs between variables ranging over possibilia. But it was identity and individuation of possibilia that was to be explained by this account, not presupposed. We could, however, hardly omit some form of uniqueness condition, explicit or implicit, if we are really giving an account of the identity of a particular possibile. We can call this 'the problem of circularity in the uniqueness condition'.

The second problem, or rather cluster of problems, with the idea is that it does not distinguish sharply between these two things:

a uniqueness condition that is possibly fulfilled

and

the individuation of a possible object.

Giving a uniqueness condition that is possibly fulfilled falls short of individuating a possible object. The first reason it falls short is that the relation between a possibly-fulfilled uniqueness condition and possible objects is, in general, one-many. There certainly could be a unique final President of the United States. The United States might politically dissolve; or there might be a nuclear winter that extinguished human life; and so forth. But in the various different ways in which it could come about that someone is the last US President, it will be different possible people who are the final occupants of that office. The possibility of a uniquely holding condition does not give us a unique possible object.

The other reason the proposal falls short is that even in the

---

[13] See the last but one paragraph before that containing the displayed quote.

special case in which the possible uniqueness condition does give us a unique object—if, for example, we circumscribed the predicates F_i sufficiently so that only one particular possibile could satisfy them—then there is a possible object meeting this condition only because there is a possible *person* meeting them. But on the question of the individuation of this particular person—the conditions under which he or she exists in various possible circumstances, this proposal is quite silent.

This initial attempt is failing to separate out the level at which the possibilia themselves are individuated. Once we have that individuation, we can discuss what uniqueness conditions the possibilia so individuated may fulfil. But an entirely generic formulation like the one displayed is too unspecific to supply an individuation of the objects that may verify such uniqueness conditions.

To fix on a particular kind of case, we can consider possible human beings. In the sense of individuation relevant to existence and identity in any given possible world, each actual human being x is individuated by the sperm y and egg cell z from whose fertilization by y he or she originated. (Here I assume origins in a process without meiotic division.) That same actual human being x exists in some merely possible state of affairs just in case in that state of affairs a human being develops from y and z (again without meiosis).[14] It is wholly natural to apply the same principle to merely possible human beings. For each possible human being x, it is possible there is some sperm y and some egg cell z such that x develops from y's fertilization of z. We can abbreviate this $\Diamond\exists y\exists z Rxyz$. A merely possible human being is individuated by this relation R and the possible (or actual) objects y and z that verify the existential quantifications in $\Diamond\exists y\exists z Rxyz$. This is simply to extend to possible human beings the way in which actual human beings are individuated. This extension of principles from actual to possible cases is wholly within the spirit of the principle-based conception of modality given in *Being Known*. Just as the extension of a concept in a possible world is determined by applying the same rules as fix its extension in the actual world, so the individuation of nonactual things of a given kind is determined by applying the same principle as determines the individuation of actual things of that kind.

[14] Henceforth I ignore the case of meiotic division. Although taking it into account complicates the correct formulations, it does not bring new issues of principle. An individual who results from meiotic division originates essentially in the first cluster of cells that is not subject to later meiotic division. No individual who results from non-meiotic division could result from meiotic division.

We can distinguish three cases that can arise in respect of the objects y and z which individuate a possible human x.

(a) Both the sperm y and egg cell z may be actual objects.

(b) One or both of y and z may be individuated by its relations to things which are in turn individuated by their relations to actual things; and so on. We can take the relation *x is chain-related to y* to be the ancestral of the relation *x is individuated in part at least by its relations to y*. Then we can say that this second case (b) is the one in which x is chain-related to actual things.

It is sometimes said that possible objects are merely general, that no particular objects enter their individuation. Taken literally and without any qualification, this doctrine seems to me too strong. Actual objects enter directly or indirectly the individuation of any possible person who is chain-related to actual things. It is, however, fair to say that once we fix the identity of possible sperm y and egg cell z from which a possible human may develop, the remainder of what is involved in individuating a merely possible person is general. By analogy to Charles Parsons' (1971) use of the notion of relatively substitutional quantification, we might call the possible individuals individuated in these first two cases (a) and (b) 'relatively general'.[15]

(c) There is a third kind of case, for not every example falls under headings (a) and (b). The universe could have had a totally different history. There could have been a world with a history that shares no initial segment with ours. Human life, or something biologically equivalent to human life—if you think the origins of a species are essential to being a human—could have evolved in such a world. There are possible human beings in such a world, or possible human-like beings (I will henceforth ignore this qualification). In this third kind of case, we have possible human beings who are not chain-related to actual sperm and egg cells. For such a possible human x, some condition of the form

$$\Diamond \exists y \exists z (Rxyz \ \& \ \varphi!y \ \& \ \psi!z)$$

holds, where φ and ψ are purely general, in the sense that they make no reference to actual objects or anything chain-related to them. For this to be possible, under the principle-based conception of modality, is for it to be consistent with the Principles of Possibility and non-modal truths that there is an admissible assignment under which the open sentence '$\exists y \exists z Rxyz \ \& \ \varphi!x \ \& \ \psi!z$' is true.

---

[15] Charles Parsons, 'A Plea for Substitutional Quantification' *Journal of Philosophy* **68** (1971), 231–37.

Christopher Peacocke

This formulation makes it clear that the identity of a possible individual who is not chain-related to actual things has a determinacy only up to the level of determinacy with which we individuate a possible state of affairs. If we employ a richer family of concepts in canonically characterizing possible states of affairs, richer concepts than φ and ψ may be available for fixing the possible sperm and egg cells from which a possible human being develops. Two richer specifications of worlds may be incompatible, yet not disagree in respect of what is true of them when characterized in a less rich family of concepts. In such a case, a possible human being individuated at the less rich level may not be identifiable with either of the possible individuals characterizable in the richer family of concepts. There is no more determinacy in these possible individuals than there is in the apparatus used to individuate them. For any given purpose we may have in discussing possible individuals, we may need to proceed only to a given level of richness of characterization, one which serves the purpose in question.

The treatment of possible individuals that I propose simply generalizes what I have just said about possible human beings to other possible concrete objects, and to other possible objects individuated by their relations to possible concrete objects (such as sets of objects). I call this treatment 'the principle-based account of possibilia', and to a first approximation it runs as follows:

For each possibile $\mathbf{x}$, there is some condition $R(\mathbf{x}, y_1, ..., y_n)$ that individuates $\mathbf{x}$, where

(I) $y_1, ..., y_n$ are actual or possible objects;
(II) $\Diamond \exists z\, R(z, y_1, ..., y_n)$, where for this possibility-proposition to be true is for it to be consistent with the Principles of Possibility and non-modal truths that there exist an admissible assignment under which

$$R(v, y_1, ..., y_n)$$

is true (here 'v' is a free variable); and
(III) there is some fundamental kind K such that each object of kind K is individuated by a condition of the form $R(v, u_1, ..., u_n)$.

In the case in which K is a kind with instances in the actual world, the principle-based account of possibilia, in adopting clause (III), extends to the merely possible Ks the same conditions for individuation as apply in the actual world.

It is clause (II) that makes this approach one which treats possibility as prior in the order of philosophical explanation to the existence of possibilia. That clause represents the solution offered by the principle-based account of possibilia to the problem of provid-

132

ing acceptable truth-conditions for inner quantifications. The principle-based approach does not deny that 'Possibly there is an F distinct from all actual F's' is true if and only if there is a merely possible F, a possibile. But the existence of such a possibile comes to no more than the consistency of a certain proposition with the Principles of Possibility and non-modal truths. The principle-based account thus attempts to answer the question that remains unaddressed by those approaches that simply take the truth-conditions of sentences containing quantifiers inside the scope of modal operators for granted.

The principle-based account of possibilia is really a conjunction of two theories. One is a metaphysical theory about possibilia; the other is a principle-based theory of what is involved in the holding of the modal propositions used in the metaphysical theory of possibilia. It would be possible in principle to accept the metaphysical theory without accepting the principle-based theory; and vice versa. For our purposes, however, both elements are essential. The second component is essential in addressing the question of what it is to understand statements apparently about possibilia. The second component also gets a grip in addressing this question only because of the role of modality in clause (II), that is, in the metaphysical theory about possibilia.

The principle-based account of possibilia can operate recursively. The variables $y_1,\ldots, y_n$ may range over mere possibilia, as well as actual objects. This does not imply, however, that any possibile acknowledged by the principle-based account is chain-related to some actual object. It is entirely consistent with the Principles of Possibility, and hence genuinely possible under the principle-based conception, that there exist a universe which shares no initial common temporal segment with the actual universe. There can in such a universe be possible objects that are not chain-related to any actual object.

I said that the displayed criterion is a only a first approximation because there are possible objects which are not of kinds that are instantiated in the actual world, and which may even be of kinds that do not exist themselves in the actual world. Such possible objects are individuated by the condition that in turn individuates the possible kind under which they fall in worlds in which they exist. This possible kind is then individuated in the same way as other possibilia, by the possibility of an existential quantification. The condition that is existentially quantified depends on the correct theory of individuation for kinds.

The condition that individuates a given possible object is, like the condition that individuates an actual object, something at the level of objects, properties, and relations. It is a Russellian proposition, rather than a Fregean Thought. When we individuate either an actual or a possible human by his or her relations to the objects from which it develops biologically, we are individuating the object, however it is picked out, by that relation, however it is picked out, to certain objects, however they are picked out.

It may be that certain possible entities can be individuated only by their relations to one another. These are entities that would be indiscernible if we ignored their relations to one another. If we want to allow for this, we can broaden the formulation of the principle-based conception to allow for the simultaneous individuation of an n-tuple of possiblia $x_1,..., x_n$. Instead of speaking of a condition $R(x, y_1,..., y_n)$ that individuates the single possibile x, we would speak of the condition $R(x_1,..., x_n, y_1,..., y_n)$ that individuates the n objects $x_1,..., x_n$; and we would make corresponding changes in the other conditions (II) and (III).

The principle-based conception of possibilia is meant to be answerable to those of our pre-theoretical intuitions about what possibilia there are that survive theoretical reflection. The principle-based conception is acceptable only if just those possibilia that we are prepared, on reflection, to acknowledge as possibilia are ratified as such by the principle-based account of possibilia. According to the principle-based treatment, only those possibilia exist for which there exists a relation R meeting the conditions given in the criterion. The principle-based criterion is not something trivial or stipulative.

It is a by-product of the principle-based criterion that certain distinctions that someone might attempt to draw for possibilia do not correspond to genuine differences. Suppose someone suggests that if a given sperm fertilizes a given egg cell, and there is non-meiotic development from the fertilized cell, we can nevertheless distinguish two possible people who might have so developed, say one who would have developed if the fertilization had taken place at one time, and a second who would have developed if it had taken place at a second time. Under the principle-based conception, this is a distinction without a difference. These are in fact two possibilities for the same possible person. The thinker who postulates two possible persons here will have no answer to the question of why there are two. All the considerations that, for an actual individual, make it plausible to say that we have two possibilities for that one single actual individual seem to apply equally to a possible individual. All these points are consequences of the principle-based account of possibilia.

We could make similar points in a range of other hypothetical

134

examples. Under the now rejected steady-state theory in cosmology, matter is spontaneously created. If that theory were correct, it is always possible that a hydrogen atom spontaneously comes into existence at a given place and time. Do we really understand the idea that one and the same particular possible atom comes into existence at a certain place and time is the same as the atom which, in a different possible circumstances, came into existence a thousand years earlier at a different place? I suggest that we do not. The obvious explanation of why we do not is that for such spontaneously created particles, their spatio-temporal origin contributes to their individuation. Carrying this principle over to possibilia, in the manner of the principle-based account of individuation, we obtain a principle which entails that if a possible particle of a given kind is created at a given place and time, it could not have been created at a totally different time and place.

Some theorists may object that we should have one account of what it is for a possibile to exist, and another account of what distinctions between possibilia involving identity represent genuine differences. If the principle-based approach is correct, however, the two accounts cannot ultimately be completely separate. Under that approach, the conditions for individuation—the conditions crucial to settling identity questions—fix the very existence-conditions of possibilia. That said, we can still make sense of a dispute between two theorists who have the same general background conception of what it is for a possibile to exist, but differ over identity conditions. Such theorists may be agreeing on the principle-based criterion for the existence of a possibile of a given kind, while disagreeing on the relation that individuates members of a given kind.

Under the principle-based conception, mere possibilia may be regarded as having *derivative* existence. As derived objects, the existence of each one of them is derivative from the consistency of a corresponding proposition with the Principles of Possibility and non-modal truths. There is a partial parallel in this respect between mere possibilia and the existence of natural numbers under 'Fregean Platonist' conceptions. It is natural to say that under the latter approaches, the existence of the natural number 6 is derivative from a certain fact, that there is a condition for the number of F's, for any arbitrary sortal F, to be 6.[16]

The derivative character of possibilia under the principle-based approach seems to me to undermine any deep parallelism between

---

[16] See Crispin Wright, *Frege's Conception of Numbers as Objects* (Aberdeen: Aberdeen University Press, 1983), and my paper 'The Metaphysics of Concepts' *Mind* **100** (1991), 525–46.

Christopher Peacocke

merely possible objects in the modal case, and past objects that no longer exist in the temporal case. Nathan Salmon writes, 'It might be thought that past individuals and past states of affairs are in some way more real than possible individuals that never come into existence and possible states of affairs that never obtain'; and he eventually concludes that 'As far as the present is concerned, past individuals and states of affairs, future individuals and states of affairs, and forever merely possible individuals and states of affairs are all on a par: they are now equally unreal'.[17] The propositions that Salmon cites in support of his conclusion are not propositions that I would at all dispute. But there is a respect in which merely possible individuals and no-longer existent past objects are not on a par, even when we consider them from the standpoint of the present. A merely possible object has derivative existence. Its existence is, constitutively, a matter of what is consistent with a certain set of principles. It is not at all plausible that a no-longer existent past object, a material object such as the ancient library at Alexandria, for instance, or a past event of pain, has merely derivative existence. I doubt that there is any set of nontrivial principle with the property that the existence of the library at Alexandria, or the past occurrence of the pain-event, consists in the relation of either of these objects to some set of nontrivial principles involving them. That such an object or such an event existed is a brute fact that does not consist in the existence of facts about what is or is not deducible from a set of principles.

The past object will have its individuating condition, of course—that is not the issue. The difference between possibilia and objects that existed only in the past lies rather in the nature of their respective individuating conditions. What it is for a past object to exist is not a matter of what is consistent with a certain set of principles.

Before I close this section, I should note that, though I have disagreed with the letter of the original formulation of Ruth Marcus by which I introduced these issues about individuation, from the standpoint of the principle-based conception of possibilia, there remains something right about the position she identified. The idea that the possibility of a proposition is explanatorily prior to the existence of a possibile is central to her proposal; and that is something endorsed by the principle-based conception. In fact, her proposal can be transformed into something wholly within the spirit of the principle-based conception if we make one restriction and one

---

[17] Nathan Salmon 'Existence', *Philosophical Perspectives* **1** (1987), 49–108, at pp. 91 and 92 respectively.

modification. The restriction is that in her proposal, the condition F_1x & .... & F_nx be something that individuates an entity which is of the kind of the possible object being introduced. The modification is the deletion of the uniqueness condition, which the restriction makes redundant. The 'artifice' so introduced need not be regarded as a fiction.

3. Commitments, Actualism and Some Varieties of Possibilism

What precisely then are the commitments of our original sentences (1) and (1a) on the present view? Before we can answer this question properly, we first must distinguish two ways in which the principle-based conception of possibilia may be developed. The first way is non-reductionist and not actualist. The second way is reductionist and actualist.

On the non-reductionist option, the condition that, under the principle-based account, individuates a possibile is a condition which legitimizes talk about a genuine entity, viz. the possibile so individuated. So this option is a mild variety of possibilism: it is in the spirit of 'modal possibilism' in the sense of Fine's 'Postscript'.[18] If actualism is the thesis that the most general quantifiers we can legitimately use range only over what actually exists, then this non-reductionist option is not an actualist position. Under the non-reductionist option, we can have general quantifiers that range both over actual objects and over these possibilia. If the quantifier 'everything' has that wide range, the Barcan formula 'If everything is necessarily F, then necessarily everything is F' is valid. Anything within the range of the second occurrence of the quantifier in the formula is already in the range of the first occurrence, when the quantifiers are understood so generally. The converse of the Barcan formula will also be valid. On these points, the non-reductionist option will be at one with Williamson's position in 'Bare Possibilia'.

The fact that the principle-based conception of possibilia can be developed in such a possibilist variant shows that I was wrong when in *Being Known* I wrote that the principle-based conception 'has to be' an actualist conception (p. 153). The non-reductionist option

[18] Though it is not within the letter of that doctrine, which requires that modal operators be primitive. The spirit is retained by the weaker position that there are constraints which something must satisfy to be a possible world, and which are explanatorily prior to the notion of a possible world.

Christopher Peacocke

seems to me to be fully within the spirit of the principle-based conception.

The other way of developing the principle-based conception of possibilia is reductionist, and is a form of actualism. The materials for giving a translation scheme for statements apparently about possibilia into statements that do not mention possibilia are already present in the exposition of the principle-based conception of possibilia. To say, for instance, that there is a merely possible man who is eight feet tall is to say that it is consistent with the principles of possibility and non-modal truths that the open sentence or concept

x is a man distinct from all actual men and x is eight feet tall

is satisfied by some admissible assignment. One could proceed similarly through the other constructions in which reference to possibilia features. If the principle-based conception is correct, the reductionist will insist, as a point of metaphysics, that these translations do show that one can assert sentences that seemingly quantify over mere possibilia without thereby being committed to their existence. Under this option, actualism is preserved, and there is a rationale for rejecting the Barcan formula and its converse, even when the quantifiers are given their most general range. This reductionist, actualist option is one that would provide philosophical underpinning for the species of homophonic truth theory I gave in 'Necessity and Truth Theories'.

Why would anyone adopt the non-reductionist, mildly possibilist option if the reduction really is available? Without trying to resolve this issue (if there is a real choice), I mention two considerations to give some sense of the apparent disagreement. First, the reduction is cumbersome. Natural language employs the apparatus of quantification, identity, and numerical quantifiers for possibilia. All these natural-language predicational and quantificational sentences about possibilia can properly be regarded as having the logico-semantical structure that they seem to have if we take the first, non-reductionist option. This argument for the non-reductionist position is analogous to one of those found in the philosophy of arithmetic for construing numerals as making reference to natural numbers, and taking quantification over numbers at face value, even when those numbers are individuated by their role in numerical quantifications.[19] Second, it is an old issue in ontological disputes why a successful reduction cannot be seen as one means, amongst others, of legitimizing an ontology. If this stance is accepted, it then makes available the ontology of possibilia required in the smooth

---

[19] Wright, *Frege's Conception of Numbers as Objects*.

semantics for natural-language quantification over possibilia mentioned in the first motivation.

Now we can return to the question of the commitments of (1) and (1a) once we adopt the principle-based account of possibilia. Since, as we just saw, the principle-based conception can be developed in an actualist form, it cannot be an entailment of the principle-based account itself that (1) and (1a) are committed to the existence of mere possibilia. Equally, since the principle-based conception of possibilia can be developed in a possibilist form, it cannot be an entailment of that conception that (1) and (1a) have only actualist commitments. It follows that we need some better articulation, consistent with, but not entailing, each of the further ways of developing the principle-based conception, of what that conception implies about the commitments of (1) and (1a).

I suggest that the implication of the principle-based conception of possibilia is that the existence of a certain kind of truth is indispensable in the explication of what it is for a sentence of the form $\Diamond \exists x Fx$ to be true, in the case in which the sentence is not verified by an actual thing that is possibly F. The kind of truth which is indispensable to the explication is fixed by the two conditions that (i) truths of this kind are apparently about possibilia (whether or not these are given an actualist reduction), and (ii) truths of this kind are not in turn explained in terms of the truth of some proposition of the form $\Diamond \exists x Gx$, taken as not further explicable. The principle-based account does of course take propositions of that last form as indeed further explicable, in terms of the properties of the principles of possibilia.

The indispensability in question here is not that of an ontology, but of truths of a certain kind (i) and (ii), truths apparently about possibilia. The claim is then an instance of the form: truths of such-and-such kind with specified features are indispensable in the explication of the truth of statements of so-and-so kind. To the best of my knowledge, there is in the extant literature no name for this indispensability claim, and I suggest that it be called *propositional possibilism*. The indispensability in question concerns propositions of a certain kind, propositions apparently about possibilia. Although the non-reductionist and the reductionist developments of the principle-based treatment of possibilia disagree about whether these propositions have an actualist reduction, they have the following in common: they both rely on such propositions in their explication of what is involved in the truth of a proposition of the form $\Diamond \exists x Fx$, in the case in which it is not verified by the modal properties of an actual thing.

Christopher Peacocke

Does this mean that the principle-based account of possibilia as developed here is simply a variety of pure possibilism, an admission of bare possibilia? I would dispute that. We are in the realm of terms of art at this point, but one thing that might be meant by 'pure possibilism' is the two-part thesis that (a) possibilist quantifications are true or false in virtue of truths about possibilia, and that (b) there is no further elucidation of what it is for these truths about possibilia to hold. The first component, (a), will be present in any possibilist view. The second component, (b), will be denied by the principle-based account of possibilia. The existence or nonexistence of a possibile meeting certain conditions unfolds into facts about what is and what is not consistent with the Principles of Possibility and non-modal truths. The objects which make true or false possibilist quantifications are, in the sense of the previous section, derivative objects. This distinguishes the principle-based conception from pure possibilism so understood.

4. What is it for a Possibile to be Actual?

There is another issue, besides that of the correct theory of understanding, on which the principle-based account has a significant advantage. The issue can be introduced by the question: what does it mean when we say that a merely possible object might have been actual? An answer is needed, on any view. In the case of the principle-based approach, someone might ask: since on that view a possible person (for example) is individuated by a condition which may hold, but does not in fact hold, a possible person is not a concrete object. But how is it even possible that something that is not concrete be concrete? Isn't any entity that is not concrete essentially not concrete?

The answer to this question is that under the principle-based account, and some cognate theories, for a possible object to be actual is simply for the existential quantification of its individuating condition to hold in the actual world. For the possible person who would have resulted from the non-meiotic development following the fertilization of actual egg cell b by sperm c to be an actual person is just for there actually to be someone who non-meiotically develops from such a union of b and c. According to the principle-based account, for each possibile x there is an individuating condition $R(x, y_1,..., y_n)$ that individuates x. So we can say quite generally that for x to be actual is for it to hold in the actual world that there is something z such that $R(z, y_1,..., y_n)$. We can call this 'the individuating-condition analysis'. With the individuating-condition analysis, we can explain what it is for a possible person to be actual without any commitment to the intelligibility of the idea that an entity that is not a concrete entity might have been concrete. Modal thinkers manifest tacit knowledge of the individuating condition analysis in their acceptance of certain conditions under which a possible human would have been actual.

The individuating-condition analysis of what it is for a possible entity to be actual seems to me to capture what is right in the widely-felt sense that is articulated by Ruth Marcus when she writes of a merely possible object that 'It isn't a thing waiting in the wings to take its place among the actuals when called' (pp. 206–7). It really is literally the same thing that was in the wings and is later on stage, when a concrete object moves from the wings to the stage. By contrast, under the individuating-condition analysis, the possibile, the merely possible person for instance, is not the same thing as is the concrete person in the world with respect to which the possibile is actual. All that it means for a world to be one with respect to which that possibile is actual is for the relevant existential quantification of possibile's individuating condition to hold in that world.

In fact even the idea of a merely possible *person* has to appeal to the same resources. A merely possible person is not something that is both possible and a person, since such an entity is not a person at all (all persons are actual).[20] An entity is a possible person only because in any world in which the existential quantification $\exists z R(z, y_1,..., y_n)$ of its individuating condition $R(\mathbf{x}, y_1,..., y_n)$ holds, the thing which stands in relation R to $y_1,..., y_n$ is a person.

The plausibility of the individuating-condition analysis needs to be taken into account when one is considering philosophical analyses of possibilia. Some approaches identify possibilia with their essences, or at least individuate them by their essences. Kit Fine has articulated and illuminated theoretical options of this sort.[21] Since an essence can always be extracted from a possibile's individuating condition under the principle-based approach, treatments of this style dovetail with the principle-based approach I have offered. Now consider the particular variant of this essence-based treatment of possibilia under which a possibile is said to be identical with its essence. Is it an objection to such a treatment that since an essence

---

[20] That is, in the terminology of Williamson, we are concerned not with the 'predicative' but with the 'attributive' sense of 'possible person'. See his paper 'The Necessary Framework of Objects', *Topoi* **19** (2000) 201–8.

[21] 'Postscript', pp. 122–3.

could not be a real concrete person, it follows that no possible person is an essence? If the individuating-condition analysis is correct, that is not a good objection. What it is for a merely possible object to be actual is in need of philosophical explanation in any case, as we saw. If we identify possibilia with their essences, the correct analysis is simply that for a possibile to be actual is for its essence to be instantiated in the actual world. This is equivalent to the individuating-condition analysis, under the natural assumption that the essence with which the possibile is identified is determined by the relational property $\lambda z R(z, y_1,..., y_n)$ fixed from the individuating condition for the possibile.

Which objects are actual, and hence which objects have non-derivative existence, varies with which world is actual. There is therefore one clear respect in which the extension of the predicate 'has non-derivative existence' varies with which world is actual. But it does not follow from this that there is one and the same thing that in one world has non-derivative existence, and in another has merely derivative existence. If we consider a world w with respect to which you do not exist, we do not need to postulate a merely possible object that exists there as a mere possibile, and with which you are identical. There is no need to say that you might have been a derivative object. With respect to that world w, it is true that it is possible you exist (whether or not any denizens of that world are capable of having relational thoughts about you). Any thinking inhabitants of that world may in thought make reference to a possibile **a** that has an individuating condition which, in the actual world, latches on to you. It does not follow that **a** could have been you, nor that you could have been **a**. As before, the possibility at w of **a**'s being actual consists simply in the possibility, with respect to w, of there being something meeting **a**'s individuating condition. You are in fact that thing.

The individuating-condition analysis of what it is for a mere possibile to be actual is also germane to what I call 'the Actualization Puzzle'. The puzzle is illustrated in propositions (A) through (D):

(A) A merely possible human being is not a physical object.
(B) Anything which is not a physical object is necessarily not a physical object.
(C) A merely possible human being could exist and be a human being.
(D) Necessarily, any human being is a physical object.

I take the predicate 'human being' in this example just for illustrative purposes. The puzzle can be reproduced for a vast range of other predicates. The Actualization Puzzle is also one that must be solved by all theories, of whatever stripe. It is not a product of the Principle-Based treatment. (There is no commitment to the Principle-Based treatment of modality in (A) through (C).) Now suppose (A)–(D) are regarded either as being, or as entailing, propositions of the following form, where **a** is a possible human being:

(A1) ~**Pa**
(B1) ∀x(~Px ⊃ □ ~Px)
(C1) ◊(E**a** & H**a**)
(D1) □∀x(Hx ⊃ Px).

(A1) through (D1) form an inconsistent set. (C1) and (D1) imply that ◊P**a**. But (A1) and (B1) imply that □ ~P**a**. This is a contradiction.[22]

I suggest that the culprit is the formalization of (C) as (C1). To say that the merely possible human being **a** could exist cannot be merely to say that it is possible **a** exists. It is true even of a mere possibile that if it is an object, it already exists. In accordance with the individuating-condition analysis, what is required for the truth of the claim that the merely possible human could exist is rather that the existential quantification of its individuating condition could be true. That is, the correct formalization of (C) is instead something of the form

(C2) ◊∃z(Rzuv & Hz)

where R is the relevant relation involved in the individuation of human beings. The set of propositions consisting of (C2) together with propositions (A1), (B1), and (D1) is a consistent set. I myself would say the members of this set are true under their intended interpretations.

Are there other solutions to the Actualization Puzzle? Denying (C) is no way out: (C) merely states what is involved in being a possible human. Denying (D) is unattractive: a biological entity such as a human being could hardly be non-physical. Denying (A) leads to a bizarre conception. If a merely possible human is physical, does this mere possibile have location? Could it interact physically with actual physical entities? If it could not interact with actual physical entities, in what sense is it physical?

---

[22] 'E(ξ)' is a first-level existence predicate. For anyone uneasy about its use, it would suffice for present purposes to replace it by '∃y(y=ξ)', where the existential quantifier has the inner, actualist reading within modal operators. The points of the text still go through under this replacement.

Christopher Peacocke

Denying (B) is not at all so bizarre. But either the denial is limited, to deal only with the problems of possibilia, or it is unrestricted. Nothing in the present considerations seems to me to lead to unrestricted rejection of (B). Nothing in these considerations suggests that we can make sense of an alleged possibility that a natural number is a tree, or a country. So suppose the rejection of (B) is confined to possibilia. The restrictions on the conditions under which (B) is false need to mention those merely possible entities which are individuated in terms of the conditions required for them to exist not as mere possibilia. So this approach would be using the same resources and distinctions to solve the Puzzle as those I have been advocating. The theorist who rejects (B) would also have to introduce some further complexities to block the unattractive consequence that you could have been a derivative object (or at least a mere possibile). The approach that endorses all of (A) through (D), but says that their correct formalization involves (A1), (B1), (C2) and (D), is not ad hoc and seems, prima facie, to be simpler.[23]

5. Concluding Remarks on Modal Validity

In modal thought, we often use the standard Kripke-style semantics for assessing the validity of modal arguments. In doing so, we are rightly keen to allow domains for nonactual worlds that may not be subsets of the domain of the actual world. One of the consequences of drawing the distinction between the principle-based account of possibilia and bare possibilism is that we should not think that, in using the Kripke semantics thus, we are thereby committed to any variety of bare possibilism. It is indeed true that, if we are to use the Kripkean model-theoretic semantics in assessing the validity of a modal argument without engaging in doublethink, the actual world must correspond to some world in the range of worlds recognized in the model theory, and something must correspond to the elements of the domains of nonactual possible objects recognized in the model theory. Under the present approach, those elements are possibilia, derivative objects with individuating conditions of the sort acknowledged by the principle-based account. The principle-

[23] This prima facie impression could be overturned if the opposing view could cite some other cases, outside issues of possibilia, that give us reason to reject (B). Considerations of uniform theory might then point in a different direction.

based account of possibilia can then be seen as a contribution to the task of making the standard semantics metaphysically acceptable. This approach allows us to use the Kripkean model theory in assessing matters of modal validity with a clear conscience.[24]

New York University

[24] I thank Gideon Rosen and Timothy Williamson for stimulating discussions on modal matters, and to Justin Broackes and Kit Fine for valuable comments on an earlier draft of this paper.

What are these Familiar Words Doing Here?

A. W. MOORE

My title is a quotation from Davidson's essay 'On Saying That'.[1] And although my concerns are at some remove from his, they do connect at one significant point. We (non-philosophers as well as philosophers) find ourselves under the continual pressure of theory to deny that ordinary familiar semantic features of ordinary familiar words equip them to serve certain ordinary familiar functions. One of Davidson's aims is to resist that pressure as far as the function of reporting indirect speech is concerned.[2] In similar vein I want to look at some common things that we do with words and show how we can hold fast to a simple common-sense view of what we are doing despite the doubts to which reflection is apt to give rise. In fact I want to look at six things we do with words, six linguistic moves we make.[3] These six moves are related in a number of important ways. Even so, they are really the subjects of six separate essays (six separate sketchy essays at that), and I am well aware that treating them together in the way that I shall be doing—worse still, trying thereby to make some headway with solving one or two extremely difficult philosophical problems, as I shall also be doing—will mean that in each case I can at best produce something highly programmatic.

The theoretical pressure that particularly concerns me comes from a certain compelling picture of linguistic behaviour, which I will call the Governing Picture.

The Governing Picture: Linguistic behaviour is *messy*. It is a vast baroque labyrinthine structure, constituted by millions upon millions of diverse but connected episodes, sometimes differing crucially but imperceptibly from one another, each dependent for its significance in all sorts of subtle and indeterminate ways on context, between them putting language to an inexhaustible

[1] Donald Davidson, 'On Saying That', reprinted in his *Inquiries into Truth and Interpretation* (Oxford: Oxford University Press, 1984), 94.
[2] See esp. 108.
[3] This way of putting it is an allusion to Ludwig Wittgenstein, *Philosophical Investigations*, trans. G. E. M. Anscombe (Oxford: Basil Blackwell, 1974), Pt. I, §§7 and 22.

variety of uses, and between them subject to constant processes of essentially unpredictable evolution which combine to give them a corporate life of their own, beyond the reckoning of any individual speaker.[4]

This picture is pretty much undeniable, certainly undenied, even by those who entertain a rigidly formalistic conception of the mechanisms that underlie all these messy surface phenomena. (Remember Wittgenstein's claim in the *Tractatus* that 'everyday language is part of the human organism and is no less complicated than it.'[5]) But there are those who use the Governing Picture to argue as follows.

The meaning of a word is never, or hardly ever, something precisely defined that regulates applications of the word. Rather it is something that develops along with applications of the word, as they in turn both exploit and extend the possibilities that it affords. It has an open-ended dynamic. But this means that talk of 'linguistic moves', with all its connotations of bounded rule-governed games, is quite inappropriate. There is not one piece of linguistic behaviour, except in highly stylized contexts such as the actual playing of a game, that has its own delineated significance in isolation from the sprawling spawning socio-linguistic history to which it belongs; not one that should be thought of on the model of bidding Three No Trumps, or castling.[6]

To many who argue in this way I think Murdoch's admonitory reply is apt. She writes:

Here truism, half-truth, and shameless metaphysics join to deceive us. Yes, of course language is a huge transcendent structure, stretching infinitely far away out of our sight, and yes, when

[4] For endorsement of the Governing Picture, along with many interesting references, see Paul Standish, *Beyond the Self: Wittgenstein, Heidegger and the Limits of Language* (Aldershot: Avebury, 1992), Ch. 2: see esp. the quotation from Charles Taylor, *Human Agency and Language* (Cambridge: Cambridge University Press, 1985), 231, which Standish gives on 74.

[5] Ludwig Wittgenstein, *Tractatus Logico-Philosophicus*, trans. D. F. Pears and B. F. McGuiness (London: Routledge & Kegan Paul, 1961), 4.002. Cf. Donald Davidson, 'Criticism, Comment, and Defence,' reprinted in his *Essays on Actions and Events* (Oxford: Oxford University Press, 1980), esp. 123 and §H; and Donald Davidson, 'What Metaphors Mean', reprinted in his op. cit., note 1.

[6] There is something of this line of thought in Derrida: see e.g. Jacques Derrida, 'Signature, Event, Context', in his *Margins of Philosophy*, trans. Alan Bass (Brighton: Harvester Press, 1982).

we reflect, we realize that often we cannot say quite what we mean or do not quite know what we mean. Common-sense does not usually take the trouble to reflect as far as this, or if it has done so realizes that nothing is really being changed and meaning and truth are what they have always seemed.[7]

We do ordinarily think of ourselves as making various linguistic moves: as describing, requesting, commanding, greeting, thanking, and the like. True, the Governing Picture should serve to remind us that making these moves is subject to all sorts of indeterminacy; that it is not always rigidly bound by rules; that language is versatile enough for sentences with the same surface grammar to be used to make quite different moves, indeed, very often, for the self-same sentence to be used to make quite different moves; and that the stock of moves we can make is not something clearly circumscribed, but is indefinitely large and changing all the time. But we need not feel any pressure from the Governing Picture to renounce talk of linguistic moves altogether.

In saying these things I take myself to be following a more or less Wittgensteinian line.[8] Yet some of those who argue in the way I indicated above take themselves to be doing the same. They see Wittgenstein as likewise recoiling from (what they see as) the hopeless artificiality of dividing our use of sentences into different linguistic moves, and, at least as far as our use of *declarative* sentences is concerned, as acquiescing rather in its 'homogeneity': always simply to say how things are.[9]

[7] Iris Murdoch, *Metaphysics as a Guide to Morals* (Harmondsworth: Penguin, 1993), 188–189.

[8] See e.g. Wittgenstein, op. cit. note 3, Pt. I, §§23– 24, and 224, third and fourth paragraphs from the bottom. Concerning the point about sentences with the same surface grammar being used to make quite different moves, cf. the volte-face between the first and second editions of Hacker's *Insight and Illusion*, respectively P. M. S. Hacker, *Insight and Illusion: Wittgenstein on Philosophy and the Metaphysics of Experience* (Oxford: Oxford University Press, 1972) and P. M. S. Hacker, *Insight and Illusion: Themes in the Philosophy of Wittgenstein* (Oxford: Oxford University Press, 1986); see in particular ix of the latter.

[9] See e.g. Sabina Lovibond, *Realism and Imagination in Ethics* (Oxford: Basil Blackwell, 1983), §§6 ff. For a backlash, somewhat more in keeping with my reading, see Simon Blackburn, 'Wittgenstein's Irrealism', in *Wittgenstein: Eine Neuerberwehrung*, Johannes L. Brandl and Rudolf Haller (eds.) (Vienna: Holder-Richler-Temsky, 1990). A third possible position, of course, is to see in this divergence of interpretation fuel for cynicism, either about Wittgensteinian exegesis or indeed about Wittgenstein.

A. W. Moore

In fact the matter is complex. Wittgenstein says things that fit with both readings.[10] The mistake is to try to extract some single pithy thesis from what he says. Wittgenstein is not offering us a thesis. He is trying to clear away confusions that he has discerned. There are certainly elements in what he says that should make us wary of comparing saying hello with bidding Three No Trumps. He has warnings against *various* models of our linguistic practices that we adopt. But the point is not to spurn the models, still less to spurn them in favour of equally flawed alternatives. The point is simply to heed the warnings. There is nothing in Wittgenstein, it seems to me, to suggest that we cannot realistically think of ourselves as making all sorts of linguistic moves.

Nor is there anything in the Governing Picture to suggest this. I am certain of that. In fact, however, that is not what I want to argue in this essay. My concern is not with the idea that we cannot realistically think of ourselves as making all sorts of linguistic moves. My concern is rather with the idea that there are some particular linguistic moves, the six to which I have alluded, such that we cannot realistically think of ourselves as making *them*. What I want to argue is that there is nothing in the Governing Picture to suggest that *this* is the case.

I

The appearance of ambivalence in Wittgenstein that I have just been talking about brings us nicely to the first of these six moves, which is this. We sometimes state rules of representation. For instance, we say, 'Aunts are female,' meaning thereby that we are not to count somebody as an aunt unless we also count that person as female. Aunts *have to be* female.

Why do I associate this particular move with the appearance of ambivalence in Wittgenstein? Well, there are many places in which Wittgenstein himself alludes to this move, emphasizing the ways in which it differs from making an empirical claim about how things are, for instance when he distinguishes between giving the criteria for a disease and giving its symptoms.[11] On the other hand the distinction between making this move and making a true empirical

[10] In support of the opposed reading see e.g. Wittgenstein, op. cit., note 3, Pt I, §402—cited by Lovibond in her op. cit. note 9, 26—and Ludwig Wittgenstein, *The Blue and Brown Books: Preliminary Studies for the 'Philosophical Investigations'* (Oxford: Basil Blackwell), 25.

[11] E.g. Wittgenstein, op. cit., note 10, 24–25.

claim about how things are is very reminiscent of the distinction between uttering an analytic truth and uttering a synthetic truth, and there is much in Quine's famous assault on the latter[12] that is in turn very reminiscent of Wittgenstein. Thus Wittgenstein is every bit as suspicious as Quine is of the idea of Platonically conceived meanings, attaching to our words by dint of our linguistic behaviour and determining, by themselves, that certain assertions are true— 'true in virtue of meaning'—while others need the corroboration of experience for their truth.[13] Furthermore he shares Quine's sense of the constant erosion of our use of words over time, an erosion brought about by a variety of pragmatic forces working away against forces of conservatism, whereby the very sentences we use at one time to say how things must be we may later find ourselves using to say how they are not.[14] For now, I simply register this apparent tension in Wittgenstein's thinking. In due course I hope it will be clear that it is only apparent.

Quine, meanwhile, thinks that we do best to treat all declarative sentences, or more strictly all utterances of declarative sentences, as homogeneous assertions about how things are: in so far as there is anything like an analytic/synthetic distinction to be drawn, then it is simply a matter of how likely we are to retract our assertions when we subsequently discover that things are not how, in making those assertions, or better in making that whole body of assertions, we took them to be. Quine seems precisely to be using the Governing Picture, or at least one part of it—that language-use evolves in fluid and unpredictable ways—to challenge the idea that we ever state rules of representation. We say, 'Aunts are female,' simply because that currently looks like a correct thing to say. We are not thereby legislating for what to say in the future, irrespective of how our view of things may change. There is no question that aunts *have to be* female.

Thus Quine. But now consider. Is Quine saying simply that there *is* no analytic/synthetic distinction, or is he denying its very coher-

---

[12] The *locus classicus* is W. V. Quine, 'Two Dogmas of Empiricism', reprinted in his *From a Logical Point of View: Logico-Philosophical Essays* (New York: Harper & Row, 1961).

[13] See e.g. Ludwig Wittgenstein, *Philosophical Grammar*, ed. Rush Rhees and trans. Anthony Kenny (Oxford: Basil Blackwell, 1974), 54.

[14] See e.g. Ludwig Wittgenstein, *On Certainty*, ed. G. E. M. Anscombe and G. H. von Wright and trans. Denis Paul and G. E. M. Anscombe (Oxford: Basil Blackwell, 1969), §§96–99. Indeed such thoughts are present in the very place where he draws the distinction between giving criteria and giving symptoms: see again his op. cit., note 10, 25.

A. W. Moore

ence? Dummett, commenting on Quine's essay 'Two Dogmas of Empiricism',[15] insists on the former. He writes:

> In the last third of the article, Quine employs notions in terms of which it is quite straightforward to define 'analytic' and 'synthetic': in these terms, an analytic sentence is one such that no recalcitrant experience would lead us to withdraw our assignment to it of the value true, while a synthetic one is one such that any adequate revision prompted by certain recalcitrant experiences would involve our withdrawing an assignment to it of the value true. The position arrived at at the conclusion of the article is not in the least that there would be anything incorrect about such a characterization of the notions of an analytic and a synthetic sentence, but simply, that these notions have no application: as thus defined, there are no analytic sentences, and there are no synthetic ones.[16]

Yes and no.[17] Obviously Dummett, in this passage, is not construing sentences purely phonemically. If he were, there would need to be some explicit caveat to discount change of meaning. Otherwise it would be entirely trivial that 'analytic' and 'synthetic', thus defined, had no application. Dummett must therefore be construing sentences as having a semantic component, as being identified, in part, by their meaning. Now on any construal that would be acceptable to Quine, Dummett is quite right: Quine's position is that there are no analytic sentences and no synthetic ones, as defined. But this is not the end of the matter. For, on any such construal, the proposed definitions are not faithful to the distinction as traditionally conceived. As traditionally conceived, the distinction presupposes a much more robust conception of meaning than would be acceptable to

---

[15] Op. cit., note 12.

[16] Michael Dummett, 'The Significance of Quine's Indeterminacy Thesis', reprinted in his *Truth and Other Enigmas* (London: Duckworth, 1978), 375. Note that, because Dummett couches his discussion in terms of sentences rather than in terms of their utterances, we must presume that attention is being restricted to sentences that can be classified as true or false without reference to individual utterances of them—sentences of the kind that Quine elsewhere calls 'eternal' (W. V. Quine, *Word and Object* (Cambridge: The MIT Press, 1960), §40).

[17] Some of what I am about to say is anticipated by Dummett later in his discussion: see 411 ff. Cf. also Rudolf Carnap, 'Quine on Analyticity', in *Dear Carnap, Dear Van: The Quine-Carnap Correspondence and Related Work*, R. Creath (ed.) (Berkeley: The University of California Press, 1990).

Quine. On the traditional conception, given any analytic sentence, recalcitrant experience can certainly lead to its rejection in the way that Quine envisages; it is just that the sentence will thereby have undergone a change of meaning.[18] Very well; suppose that the proposed definitions are suitably reconstrued, so as to bring them into line with the traditional conception. *Now* Quine's position is that they are incoherent.[19]

What Quine is really attacking, then, is the more robust conception of meaning. This is a conception whereby meanings are clearly discriminable monadic entities that stand to words in something like the relation of exhibits to labels,[20] the Platonic conception to which I alluded earlier and to which Wittgenstein is equally hostile.

It seems to me that Quine is absolutely right to attack this conception. Certainly there is much in the Governing Picture to challenge it. But what does it have to do with the idea that we sometimes state rules of representation? There is simply no obvious connection.[21] Can we not adopt a rule whereby it is incorrect to apply one

[18] So too, on the traditional conception, given any synthetic sentence which is held true, and given any recalcitrant experience, the sentence can continue to be held true *vis-à-vis* that experience, in the way that Quine envisages; but again, sometimes, only by undergoing a change of meaning. If meaning is kept fixed, then there will never be any choice about whether or not a sentence which is held true should be rejected *vis-à-vis* any possible recalcitrant experience: if the sentence is analytic, it never should be; if the sentence is synthetic, it sometimes should be. This is why, on the traditional conception, the distinction is both exclusive and exhaustive, a fact that Dummett's discussion somewhat obscures.

[19] I have borrowed material in this paragraph from A. W. Moore, 'The Underdetermination/Indeterminacy Distinction and the Analytic/Synthetic Distinction', in *Erkenntnis* **46** (1997), 8–9. Note that in his op. cit., note 12, Quine does describe the word 'analytic' as 'un-understood' (34) and later relates the idea of analyticity to another idea which he describes as 'nonsense, and the root of much nonsense,' (42): I am grateful to Alexander George for drawing my attention to these two passages.

[20] Cf. W. V. Quine, 'Ontological Relativity', reprinted in his *Ontological Relativity and Other Essays* (New York: Columbia University Press, 1969), 27.

[21] Cf. Quine's concession in his op. cit., note 12, 25–26, that we sometimes stipulatively define novel terms, and that, whenever we do, 'we have a really transparent case of synonymy': I am grateful to Timothy Williamson for drawing my attention to this passage. (Not that I want to claim that Quine would be happy with everything I say in this section. Stating rules of representation covers far more than stipulatively defining novel terms. When I talk about 'what Quine is really attacking', I do not mean this exegetically. I am making a point about the force of his arguments.)

153

word, 'aunt', and at the same time to deny application of another, 'female', without this in any sense requiring the existence of meanings as clearly discriminable monadic entities, without its rendering anything we say 'true in virtue of meaning', indeed without its even precluding a natural evolution in our language-use whereby we later allow talk of 'non-female aunts'? (If we do later allow talk of 'non-female aunts', this will simply mean that we are no longer abiding by the same rules.[22])[23]

II

The second move we sometimes make is to represent things 'categorically', by which I mean in a way that involves neither systematic context-dependence nor implicit relativization of any kind.[24] (These, where they occur, indicate that the representation is from a particular point of view.) It is an aspiration of physicists, I believe, to make this move as extensively as they can.[25] For it is a working presupposition of physicists that the most fundamental physical laws look the same from every point of view. Thus consider Newton's first law of mechanics: a body continues in a state of rest or of uniform motion in a straight line unless it is compelled to change that state by forces acting upon it.[26] This statement of the

[22] Will it also mean that we no longer have our current concept of an aunt? Or will it mean that our current concept of an aunt has undergone a change?—When, some time in the fifteenth century, the Pawn was first allowed to move forward two squares in chess, did this create a new game, what we now call chess? Or did that very game undergo a change?—It is relatively clear what is going on in these cases. Say what you will as long as you do nothing to threaten such clarity.

[23] Cf. again Wittgenstein, op. cit., note 14, §§96–99—esp. §98, where he denies that his famous river-bed analogy makes logic 'an empirical science'. And cf. Wittgenstein, op. cit., note 3, Pt. I, §354. For some extremely helpful material on the ideas in this section see various essays in Robert L. Arrington and Hans-Johann Glock (eds.), *Wittgenstein and Quine* (London: Routledge, 1996), esp. P. M. S. Hacker, 'Wittgenstein and Quine: Proximity at Great Distance' and Christopher Hookway, 'Perspicuous Representations' the former of which is an abbreviated version of the even more helpful P. M. S. Hacker, *Wittgenstein's Place in Twentieth-Century Analytic Philosophy* (Oxford: Basil Blackwell, 1996), Ch. 7.

[24] Cf. above, note 16: precisely what an 'eternal' sentence is is a sentence that equips us to make this move.

[25] Cf. Wittgenstein, op. cit., note 3, Pt. I, §410.

[26] Isaac Newton, *Mathematical Principles of Natural Philosophy*, trans. Andrew Motte and Florian Cajori (Berkeley: The University of California Press, 1947), Bk. I, Law I.

law holds only relative to an inertial frame. The earth, for example, is not an inertial frame. With the earth as frame, the sun describes something approximating to a colossal circle once every twenty-four hours even though there are no relevant forces acting upon it. It was in large part because of his dissatisfaction with the suppressed relativization in this statement of the law, and the partiality which this in turn implied, that Einstein was impelled to look for something more universal, and eventually to formulate his general theory of relativity.[27]

However, the Governing Picture seems to preclude our representing things categorically—in pretty much the same way as it seemed to preclude our stating rules of representation. (This is quite apart from the fact that it expressly includes the idea that episodes of linguistic behaviour depend for their significance in all sorts of subtle ways on context, which some people would say should already give pause.) The point is this. Granted the Governing Picture, it seems impossible for the meaning of a word to be anything apart from its continued usage, so that any word has, at any stage in its history, different possibilities of further meaning-preserving use woven into it. The use of a word can always be continued in different ways, for different purposes, to different effects. It has what was called earlier 'an open-ended dynamic'. Thus there is no legislating in advance for the success of metaphors, which may be contrived to describe situations completely unlike anything that anyone has ever encountered before and which may then give way to new, previously unimagined, literal uses: consider, for instance, the smooth adaptation of the word 'hear' to cover what we do to somebody's voice over the telephone. But it seems to follow that there is no representing things except in a way that depends at the very least on temporal context. For no application of a word can be understood except as occurring at a particular stage in its development. Consider the following sentence:

(1) Earshot of somebody is the distance within which it is possible to hear his or her voice.

---

[27] See Albert Einstein, *Relativity: The Special and the General Theory*, trans. Robert W. Lawson (London: Methuen, 1960), 11, 61, 71–72 and 99. For more on the aim to transcend perspective (of this and any other kind), and for an argument that this aim is achievable, see A.W. Moore, *Points of View* (Oxford: Oxford University Press, 1997), esp. Chs. One–Four.

This was once more or less definitional. In the terms of the last section, it would once have been used to state a rule of representation. If someone were to utter the sentence now, on the other hand, then they would be saying something at best false. Yet it seems unsatisfactory, in accounting for this, just to say that (1), or more particularly the word 'hear', has undergone a change of meaning. That would be far too simplistic. As intimated above, it seems better to say that the meaning of the word 'hear' has evolved to accommodate its current usage.

Well, yes; it is certainly unsatisfactory *just* to say that the word 'hear' has undergone a change of meaning.[28] But *some* change has occurred. To pick up the theme of the last section: we are no longer abiding by the same rules. And this means, in particular, that we cannot draw conclusions about the categoricity of any of our representations by comparing current uses of the word 'hear' with erstwhile uses of it. To say that someone has represented things categorically is not to deny that the sentence they have used to do so might also be used, in another context, metaphorically perhaps, to say something quite different. Nor is it to deny that various processes of attrition and accretion might eventually ensure that the sentence can no longer effectively be used *except* to say something quite different. The point is only that their sentence is free of the sort of systematic context-dependence that attends the use of, say, the word 'now'; the sort of context-dependence that would need to appear in an account of the semantics of the word. They have represented things in a way which is, at least in these narrowly semantic terms, from no point of view.

III

The third move we sometimes make is to employ expressions in such a way as to make *them* our subject matter. In the standard terminology, we sometimes *mention* expressions. This is in contrast to the more usual way of employing expressions, which, again in the standard terminology, is to *use* them: when we use expressions, in this quasi-technical sense, our subject matter (if we have one) is not them, but something determined by their semantics. There are a number of conventional devices for mentioning expressions. The commonest of these is the use of inverted commas. Thus, whereas

[28] Cf. above, note 22: even if allowing the Pawn to move forward two squares did create a new game, it would be unsatisfactory *just* to say that chess was invented in the fifteenth century.

cats have four legs, 'cats'—note the singular verb coming up—has four letters.

What I have just proffered is basically a grammatical characterization of the distinction between using expressions and mentioning them. A more pragmatic characterization, it seems, would be this. Using expressions involves employing them in a way that exploits whatever meaning they have, so as to draw attention to something determined, in part, by that meaning; mentioning expressions involves employing them in a way that waives whatever meaning they have, so as to draw attention to the expressions themselves.

But now the Governing Picture casts doubt on whether any such distinction can be drawn. For given the Governing Picture, the grammatical characterization and the pragmatic characterization signally fail to accord with each other. According to the former, the distinction is a clear-cut one with clearly recognizable grammatical criteria of application. According to the latter—at least if the Governing Picture is correct—the question whether one is using an expression or mentioning it on any given occasion (as with any other question about what one is drawing attention to by means of an expression on any given occasion) is a complex, vague and unruly matter that depends in all manner of ways on the particular circumstances: it certainly does not depend in any straightforward way on one's use of devices such as inverted commas.

Thus consider the following two sentences, and the underlined expressions that occur in them:

(2) Christopher can never remember his nine-times table; he always says that <u>eight nines are seventy-four</u>

(3) The only word for this is '<u>preposterous</u>'.

On the grammatical characterization, the underlined expression in a (typical) use of (2) would be used, and that in a (typical) use of (3) mentioned. But on the pragmatic characterization, the reverse would be true. Again, consider this sentence:

(4) Albert, who remembers virtually nothing of the physics he once knew, does remember that electrons have negative charge.

On the grammatical characterization, 'negative' would be used in a (typical) use of (4). The pragmatic characterization, on the other hand, yields no clear verdict at all. On the pragmatic characterization, (4) illustrates how using an expression and mentioning it can merge imperceptibly into each other—the distinction is one of

A. W. Moore

degree—whereas on the grammatical characterization, the distinction is one of kind.[29]

Does the Governing Picture entail the disintegration of the distinction then, and with it the illegitimacy of the idea that we ever mention expressions? Not at all. What it entails is that the two characterizations should be kept apart; and that, if we are going to talk about mentioning expressions, then we should be clear about which of the two characterizations we are operating with.[30] My own preference, for various reasons, is to operate with the grammatical characterization, which I proffered at the beginning of this section and which I think is more in line with received practice. It is also more appropriate, in many ways, to the idea that mentioning an expression counts as making a linguistic move. But that is by the by. Both characterizations give clear content to the idea that we sometimes mention expressions. (And both characterizations, come to that, give important content to this idea. The grammatical characterization, for example, allows us to say that one of the greatest intellectual achievements of the last century, namely Gödel's proof that arithmetic cannot be consistently and completely axiomatized, would not have been possible without due appreciation of the distinction between using expressions and mentioning them.[31])[32]

[29] Another notable example would be a use of the sentence 'Aunts are female' to state a rule of representation. On the grammatical characterization, this would involve using both 'aunts' and 'female'. On the pragmatic characterization, it would involve mentioning them both (roughly—though it is a very nice question how roughly (cf. G. P Baker and P. M. S. Hacker, *Wittgenstein: Rules, Grammar and Necessity*, Volume 2 of *An Analytical Commentary on the Philosophical Investigations* (Oxford: Basil Blackwell, 1985), Ch. VI, §3(ii))).

[30] This is a main theme of A. W. Moore, 'How Significant is the Use/Mention Distinction?', in *Analysis* **46** (1986), which contains a fuller discussion of these issues.

[31] Kurt Gödel, 'On Formally Undecidable Propositions of *Principia Mathematica* and Related Systems I', trans. Jean van Heijenoort, in *From Frege to Gödel: A Source Book in Mathematical Logic, 1879–1931*, Jean van Heijenoort (ed.) (Cambridge: Harvard University Press, 1967), e.g. 601. See also W. V. Quine, 'Gödel's Theorem', in his *Quiddities: An Intermittently Philosophical Dictionary* (Harmondsworth: Penguin, 1990), 84. Indeed I think the grammatical characterization allows us to go further and say that one of the great achievements, in turn, of analytic philosophy is to have made due appreciation of the distinction possible. Even the most rigorous writings in mathematics often flout it: cf. W. V. Quine, 'Use Versus Mention', in his ibid., 232. (For an indication of the significance of the distinction on the pragmatic characterization, see Moore, op. cit., note 30.)

IV

The fourth move we sometimes make is quite simply to say, truly or falsely, how things are (where the truth or falsity of what we say is taken to be one of the defining characteristics of our making this move). It may seem fantastic to include this move on my list. Could anybody really think that the Governing Picture poses any threat to the idea of our doing anything as basic as this? Well, if truth and falsity are understood in even a moderately ambitious way, then our philosophical heritage, extending back to Plato and beyond, is in fact replete with challenges to this idea, based on features of linguistic behaviour highlighted in the Governing Picture.[33] However, these challenges raise metaphysical issues that are not really my current concern. I have in mind much less heady worries about the idea of our making this move, worries based on the countless ways, again highlighted by the Governing Picture, in which, when we use a declarative sentence that equips us to make the move, the conditions might nevertheless not be right for us to do so: we end up not saying anything true or false at all. Examples include cases of reference failure, as when someone says, 'That dagger is covered in blood,' and is hallucinating. They also include cases of what Travis calls natural

[33] For a tiny sample, see: Plato, *Theaetetus*, trans. M. J. Levett and Myles Burnyeat and ed. Myles Burnyeat (Indianapolis: Hackett, 1990), 183a4–b8; Friedrich Nietzsche, *The Will to Power*, trans. Walter Kaufmann and R. J. Hollingdale and ed. Walter Kaufmann (New York: Random House, 1967), §616; and Jacques Derrida, *Dissemination*, trans. B. Johnson (London: Athlone Press, 1981), 168.

[32] It is interesting at this point to consider Derrida again. His attitude to the distinction between using expressions and mentioning them is a curiously ambivalent one. He often seems to make play with words, and indeed to make philosophical points, precisely by flouting the distinction: see e.g. Derrida, op. cit., note 6, 320–321. (This is a complaint that Searle levels against him in his commentary on this essay, J. R. Searle, 'Reiterating the Differences: A Reply to Derrida', in *Glyph* 1 (1977), 203.) Furthermore there are places where Derrida seems to be overtly hostile to the distinction. Cf. his comment, 'I try to place myself at a certain point at which... the thing signified is no longer easily separable from the signifier,' quoted in David Wood and Robert Bernasconi (eds.), *Derrida and 'Différance'* (Evanston: Northwestern University Press, 1988), 88. Cf. also Jacques Derrida, *The Post Card: From Socrates to Freud and Beyond*, trans. Alan Bass (Chicago: The University of Chicago Press, 1987), 97 ff. However, in his reply to Searle—Jacques Derrida, 'Limited Inc a b c...', trans. S. Weber and reprinted in his *Limited Inc*, ed. G. Graff (Evanston: Northwestern University Press, 1988)—he writes (81), 'I agree that [the confusion of "use" and "mention"] might very well be [a radical evil].'

A. W. Moore

isostheneia,[34] as when—this is Austin's delicious example[35]—someone says, 'He is not at home,' and the person referred to is lying upstairs dead. Anyone who has anti-realist qualms about the law of the excluded middle[36] might also want to include all those cases in which we have no procedure for telling, even in principle and even with some margin of error, whether what has been said is true or false. (Anti-realism challenges the idea that something can be true or false though we have no procedure for telling which.[37]) One such case might be someone's saying, 'Descartes would have loved Marmite.'

But of course, the mere fact that there are countless ways in which we can use a declarative sentence and fail to say something true or false does not, on its own, show that there are not also ways in which we can use a declarative sentence to *succeed* in saying something true or false. So long as there is no reason to think that known impediments to our making this move are somehow symptomatic of unknown impediments to our doing so, there does not yet seem to be any threat to the idea that we sometimes—indeed, often—say truly or falsely how things are.[38]

[34] Charles Travis, 'Sublunary Intuitionism', in *Grazer Philosophische Studien* **55**, a special issue entitled 'New Essays on the Philosophy of Michael Dummett', Johannes L. Brandl and Peter M. Sullivan (eds.), (1998), which includes an extensive (and superb) discussion of such cases.

[35] J. L. Austin, 'Truth', reprinted in his *Philosophical Papers*, eds. J. O. Urmson and G. J. Warnock (Oxford: Oxford University Press, 1970), 128.

[36] See e.g. Michael Dummett, 'Truth', reprinted in his op. cit., note 16; and Michael Dummett, 'Realism and Anti-Realism', reprinted in his *The Seas of Language* (Oxford: Oxford University Press).

[37] I do not say that anti-realism challenges the idea that something can be true though we have no procedure for telling that it is. That way of putting it (though often found in the writings of anti-realists themselves) saddles anti-realism with the paradoxical consequence that there can be no unknown truths (see F. B. Fitch, 'A Logical Analysis of Some Value Concepts', in *Journal of Symbolic Logic* **28** (1963)). The version in the main text does not (see Joseph Melia, 'Anti-Realism Untouched', in *Mind* **100** (1991)). (Our having a procedure for telling whether x is true or false is to be understood as allowing for the following possibility: that, although x is in fact true, the actual carrying out of the procedure would render it false (and would accordingly put us in a position to tell that it was false).)

[38] For different but related reservations about the idea of our making this move (in fact of our making *any* move), based on suspicion of the very contrast between situations in which there are impediments to our doing so and situations in which there are not, see Derrida, op. cit., note 6. It may be that Derrida is insufficiently open to the possibility that one and the same sentence can be used in one situation to make one move and in another situation, inimical to the making of *that* move, to make another.

What then are we to say about someone who utters a declarative sentence in an *attempt* to make this move, though the circumstances are in fact unsuitable? Just that. This is someone who has uttered a declarative sentence in an attempt to make the move; but, because the circumstances are unsuitable, the attempt is a failed attempt. It is not that they have made the move in a way that is somehow deficient. Rather they have not made the move at all.[39]

Herein, I think, is a clue as to how to respect anti-realist qualms about the law of the excluded middle without surrendering to them. What we can do is to hold fast to the law, as part of what constitutes the very making of this particular linguistic move;[40] then, when someone utters a declarative sentence where we have no procedure for telling whether they have said something true or false, to say simply that they have failed to make the move. For if they have failed to make the move, then questions about the law of the excluded middle, in respect of what they have done, do not so much as arise— any more than such questions arise in respect of orders given or oaths expressed. In particular, what this person has done need not incline us either to abandon the law of the excluded middle or even to have reservations about re-affirming it. I realize, of course, that there is far more to be said about this. Some of it I have tried to say elsewhere.[41] For now, I am content merely to advert to this way of

[39] Is this idea perhaps negotiable? Could we eliminate the category of failed attempts to make this move, by simply extending our notion of falsity and assimilating all such cases to cases in which something false has been said (cf. Dummett, 'Truth', op. cit., note 36)? For reasons why we may not be able to do this see again Travis, op. cit., note 34.—Note: there is also the question, on which Strawson is sometimes alleged to have equivocated in P. F. Strawson, 'On Referring', reprinted in *Meaning and Reference*, A. W. Moore (ed.) (Oxford: Oxford University Press, 1993), whether someone who utters a declarative sentence in an unsuccessful attempt to make this move thereby makes a statement that is neither true nor false or fails to make a statement at all: see e.g. G. Nerlich 'Presupposition and Entailment', in *American Philosophical Quarterly* **2**. That seems to me to be an unimportant point of terminology.

[40] Cf. Wittgenstein, op. cit., note 3, Pt. I, §136.

[41] Moore, op. cit., note 27, Ch. Ten, §4: see in particular the discussion of what I call 'partial realism', 245–249. For a fascinating discussion which in effect raises problems for this position, see Timothy Williamson, 'Never Say Never', in *Topoi* **13** (1994). Williamson ends his essay by asking whether these problems constitute a *reductio ad absurdum* of the position with which he has been concerned in the essay, namely intuitionism (143). We can also ask whether they constitute a *reductio ad absurdum* of partial realism: I think not.

holding fast to the law of the excluded middle even while insisting that nothing can be true or false without our having some procedure for telling which. I think it has the potential to defuse a number of reactionary worries about anti-realism.[42]

But does it not also entail that we cannot always *tell* whether someone has made this move? For surely there are times when, even though we do not know of any procedure for telling whether someone has said something true or false, we cannot rule out the possibility that there *is* one.

This question betrays a misunderstanding. By our having a procedure for telling whether someone has said something true or false, I *mean* our knowing of such a procedure.

Very well; suppose someone says, 'Descartes would have loved Marmite.' And suppose that archaeological-cum-technological advances eventually put us in a position, currently beyond our ken, to have a decent stab at ascertaining whether or not Descartes *would* have loved Marmite. Suppose, finally, that someone then utters the sentence anew. (This is, of course, the sort of possibility that the Governing Picture puts us in mind of.) Are we really to say that the first of these utterances is a failed attempt to say something true or false, but the second a successful attempt? Surely the advances in question give the first utterance (retrospectively) as much title to the claim of being a successful attempt as the second. Or if we *are* to distinguish between the two utterances in this way, are we also to accept that *what* is said on the second occasion depends on the nature of the advances and may yet differ from what is said on some third occasion when further advances allow us to address the question even more efficiently? That seems very counterintuitive.[43]

These concerns are reminiscent of concerns expressed above in §§I and II. And my response is effectively as it was before. Certainly it is unsatisfactory *just* to say that the different utterances of this sentence differ in these ways, especially granted the evident constancy in the sentence that makes the differences possible. But this is not to say that there are not these differences. It is to say only that the full semantic story does not begin and end with them.

---

[42] For a superb discussion of related issues in connection with Wittgenstein, see Hacker, the second edition of *Insight and Illusion*, op. cit. in note 8, Ch. XI, §4.

[43] For discussion of such questions see Cora Diamond, 'How Old Are These Bones? Putnam, Wittgenstein and Verification', in *Proceedings of the Aristotelian Society* Sup. Vol. **73**.

V

The fifth move is a special case of the fourth (where I mean 'special' only in the sense of species and genus: instances of the fifth move all but exhaust instances of the fourth). We sometimes say, truly or falsely *and imprecisely*, how things are. That is, we sometimes make the fourth move by using a sentence which, in some contexts, cannot be used to say anything clearly true or clearly false—or clearly neither. Call such a sentence a *vague sentence*. And call an utterance of a vague sentence, in such a context, a *vague utterance*. Examples are: the sentence, 'You are a child'; and an utterance of it addressed to a fourteen-year-old, in the absence of anything serving to hone its sense (such as a context-specific stipulation).

Now the phenomenon of vagueness has recently spawned a massive literature.[44] It is here more than anywhere else in this essay that I am conscious of being able to make only a tiny contribution to the issues that arise. But I include this move because I see important connections with the rest of what I have been saying.

How is the Governing Picture relevant here? Principally in serving to remind us that there *are* vague sentences, and that there are vague utterances of them. For unless we can give a coherent account of these, then we risk having to admit that there is no coherent account of non-vague utterances of vague sentences (say, an utterance of 'You are a child,' addressed to a five-year-old). This is partly because of the infamous sorites paradoxes,[45] which I shall discuss in the next section, and partly because of the fact that what counts as a vague utterance of a vague sentence is itself, of course, vague. The very idea of our saying how things are by using vague sentences is under threat.

Now it seems to me that there are all sorts of things that might reasonably be said about vague utterances, each more or less appropriate in any given case. One of these is that the truth of the

[44] Pre-eminent is Timothy Williamson, *Vagueness* (London: Routledge, 1994). An excellent collection is Rosanna Keefe and Peter Smith (eds.), *Vagueness: A Reader* (Cambridge: The MIT Press, 1997). Each of these contains extensive bibliographies.

[45] The sorites paradoxes are a family of paradoxes modelled on the following, from which their name derives (the Greek adjective '*sorites*' corresponds to the noun '*soros*', meaning 'heap'). One grain of sand does not make a heap; for any number n, if n grains of sand do not make a heap, then $n + 1$ grains of sand do not make a heap; therefore, there is no number of grains of sand that make a heap.

A. W. Moore

utterance is secured by the very fact of its being made. This allows for the possibility that a subsequent utterance of the negation of the same sentence, in the same context, or in a relevantly similar context, should also count as true. This is not incoherent. The idea is that there is a degree of freedom in the use of vague sentences whereby vague utterances of them can function somewhat like performatives, or somewhat like jurors' verdicts: they can be true, in a way, by virtue of being made.[46] ('You could say she's a child; you could say she's not a child. It's up to you.'[47]) The Governing Picture, in reminding us of the huge variety of ways in which sentences can work, makes us open, or should make us open, to the possibility of this sort of latitude.

Another thing which might be said about a vague utterance, and which might indeed be said when the 'performative' tag just suggested seems appropriate but the utterer's endorsement cannot be said to carry its usual authority, is that the utterance is neither true nor false; that it is a failed attempt to say something true or false, of the sort considered in the previous section. ('Look, you haven't said a single true thing about her! I agree, you *could* say she's a child. But you said that only because you thought she was seven. In fact she's fourteen. So that doesn't count.') The same thing might also be said when the 'performative' tag seems inappropriate and what matters is simply to register that the utterance is vague. ('You predicted that the next person to come into the room would be a child. But actually this is a borderline case. Your prediction wasn't really correct, and it wasn't really incorrect either.') Would *this* be coherent?

A familiar argument due to Williamson purports to establish that it would not be.[48] Williamson's argument, if successful, shows that calling a vague utterance neither true nor false would commit one to

[46] Austin, in J. L. Austin, *How To Do Things With Words*, eds. J.O. Urmson and Marina Sbisà (Oxford: Oxford University Press, 1975), introduces the notion of a 'performative' by means of examples: these include an utterance of 'I do' in the course of a marriage ceremony, and an utterance of 'I bet you sixpence it will rain tomorrow' (5–6). He expressly denies that performatives are either true or false (6). Others have subsequently adopted his notion, but have amended it so as to grant performatives truth: on the amended account, performatives make themselves true (see e.g. W.V. Quine, 'On Austin's Method', reprinted in his *Theories and Things* (Cambridge: Harvard University Press, 1981), esp. 90). In invoking performatives here, I am obviously presupposing this amended account.

[47] Cf. R.M. Sainsbury, 'Concepts Without Boundaries', reprinted in Keefe and Smith (eds.), op. cit., note 44, §6.

[48] Williamson, op. cit., note 44, §7.2

a contradiction. (In the example given, the contradiction would be that the person in question was neither a child nor not a child—or perhaps, if it were a case where the 'performative' tag seemed appropriate, that the person in question was neither what the utterer would then and there call a child nor not what the utterer would then and there call a child.)

I shall not rehearse Williamson's argument in full here. All that matters for my purposes is that it rests on the assumption that the utterance concerned 'says something'. Can this assumption be resisted?

Consider a case of reference failure. Think again about the case in which an hallucination victim says, 'That dagger is covered in blood.' There is a sense in which their utterance says something. There is a *sense* in which it says that some dagger is covered in blood. But there is also a sense in which it does not. In particular, of course, granted that the utterance is neither true nor false, it does not say anything in any sense that requires us to regard *in propria persona* mimicry of it as true or false: that is a platitude. Thus when I say that the utterance is neither true nor false, and in particular that it is not true, I do not thereby commit myself to the claim that the dagger is *not* covered in blood. There *is* no dagger. There is no such claim. Can the same sort of assessment be given of a vague utterance?

To be sure, given that what counts as a vague utterance is itself vague, the same sort of assessment cannot be given of a vague utterance unless what counts as saying something is also vague, that is unless the sentence 'This utterance says something' is a vague sentence. But it surely is. That is one consequence of the Governing Picture that we surely have to accept.

Williamson himself has three arguments against the view that a vague utterance says nothing (in the relevant sense).[49] One is that, had circumstances been different in such a way that the utterance had been non-vague, it would have said something; and more to the point, it would have said the same thing. Another is that there is no obstacle to understanding the utterance parallel to the obstacle to understanding an utterance involving reference failure. Both of these strike me as question-begging. By far the most powerful of the three arguments turns on the apparent contribution that the content of the vague utterance can make to more complex utterances. Thus consider again an utterance of 'You are a child,' addressed to a fourteen-year-old without any suitable sharpening. Whatever we are to

[49] Ibid., 195–197.

say about this, it seems that we must accept the truth of an utterance of 'If you are a child, then any younger sibling of yours is also a child,' addressed to the same fourteen-year-old.[50] But, Williamson would insist, 'the conditional says something only because its antecedent and consequent also do.'[51]

However, I think there is a corrective to this thought, which is to look beneath the forms of the sentences involved to the moves made with them.[52] It is no accident that the truth of the conditional is itself no accident. The person making this utterance is stating a rule of representation: a prohibition against counting the addressee as a child without also counting any younger sibling of theirs as a child.[53] But accepting this rule is quite compatible with giving each of various individual verdicts on the matter. In particular, I cannot see how it precludes refusing to count the addressee as a child *and* refusing to count the addressee as not a child. The truth of the conditional (that is, the holding of the rule) allows for, among other things, the lack of truth or falsity of an isolated appearance of its antecedent.[54]

In sum then: that a vague utterance is neither true nor false is another of the many things that might reasonably be said about it. And this carries no threat to the idea that we are forever using vague sentences to say, truly or falsely, how things are.

[50] Let us take for granted that childhood is age-determined, at least to this extent. In fact, this is something of an idealization. (See further below, note 56.)

[51] Ibid., 196.

[52] Cf. again Hacker's volte-face, referred to above in note 8.

[53] If the person making the utterance knows that the addressee has a younger sibling, Stephen say, then he or she could also state what might be called an *applied* rule of representation, by saying, 'If you are a child, then Stephen is a child.' While the truth of the original utterance is necessary, the truth of this utterance would enjoy a sort of conditional necessity—conditional on Stephen's being the addressee's younger sibling. What I am about to say in the main text about the original rule would hold of this applied rule too.

[54] It might be said, in defence of Williamson, that he expressly forestalls this counter-argument by talking about 'material' conditionals (ibid., 196), where a material conditional, unlike a conditional used to state a rule of representation, is precisely one whose truth or falsity is determined by the truth or falsity of its antecedent and consequent. But in that case it is question-begging to suppose that there *are* any relevant conditionals that are both material and true (or material and false).

VI

This reference to rules of representation brings my essay full circle. It is a variation on the idea of a rule of representation that I want to consider in this final section, but still in connection with vagueness. I want to suggest an approach to the sorites paradoxes. (Nothing I said in the previous section really touches on them.)

We sometimes—this is the sixth move—rule out cut-off points in connection with vague concepts. (By vague concepts I mean the concepts, like that of a child, that make vague sentences vague.) Thus consider Ellen, who is ten years old. We are prepared to endorse the following:

(5) No particular day will mark the end of Ellen's childhood.

(Being prepared to endorse (5) is part of what it is to have a full grasp of the concept of a child.) The Governing Picture itself suggests that we do well to have such rules, to safeguard the flexibility and the connection with casual observation that help to give these concepts their point.[55]

But of course, Ellen *will* stop being a child. And this creates a paradox. For her passage from childhood into adulthood seems, on reflection, to be impossible *without* a cut-off point. It seems that she cannot stop being a child unless there is a *last day* on which she is a child.[56] This is a classic sorites paradox.

Let us look a little more closely at how the paradox arises. (5) seems to be equivalent to the following:

(6) For any day on which Ellen counts as a child, she will still count as a child the following day.

But (6), combined with the premise that Ellen is a child today, yields the conclusion that she will remain a child ever after: her childhood will pass unchecked from one day to the next. So if Ellen is to stop being a child, then it seems that we must reject (6)—and thus (5).

---

[55] Cf. Michael Dummett, 'Wang's Paradox', reprinted in Keefe and Smith (eds.), op. cit., note 44, 109.

[56] Not that the age at which Ellen stops being a child need be the same as the age at which any other person stops being a child. Cf. above, note 50: it is something of an idealization to think of childhood as age-determined at all, even to an extent that precludes children having younger siblings who are not children, or adolescents reverting to childhood for that matter; but it would be a far greater idealization, with which we need have no truck, to think that, for any two people of the same age, one is a child if and only if the other is a child. Childhood is more contextual than *that*.

A. W. Moore

In fact, however, this does not follow. Certainly we must reject (6). What does not follow is that we must reject (5) as well.

In order to see how (5) and (6) come apart, consider this: in rejecting (6), do we commit ourselves to endorsing (7)?

(7) There will come a day on which Ellen counts as a child, even though she will no longer count as a child the following day.

No. Think about what it is to endorse or to reject a sentence like (6) or (7). On their most natural interpretation, if such sentences are true, then they are necessarily true.[57] To endorse such a sentence is to accept a rule of representation. To reject it is to decline to accept that rule. There is no reason whatsoever why we should not reject *both* (6) *and* (7). To insist otherwise would be a little bit like insisting that either 'The opening move shall be a Pawn move' or 'The opening move shall not be a Pawn move' must be a rule of chess. We can decline to have a rule of representation whereby we are not to count Ellen a child on any given day unless we also count her a child on the following day—on pain of having to admit that she will never stop being a child. But we can also, quite consistently with that, decline to have a rule of representation that forces us to acknowledge that there will come a last day on which she is a child—on pain of violating the very vagueness of our concept of a child.[58] Ellen will *gradually* stop being a child.[59]

[57] Cf. what I said about 'If you are a child, then any younger sibling of yours is a child' in the previous section. But cf. also note 53: it is more accurate to speak here of conditional necessity than of necessity *simpliciter*. Ellen might never have been born. She might (God forbid) not survive her childhood. (The latter possibility is one from which I am prescinding throughout this section.)

[58] Cf. Bernard Williams, 'Which Slopes are Slippery?', reprinted in his *Making Sense of Humanity and Other Philosophical Papers: 1982–1993* (Cambridge: Cambridge University Press, 1995), 217. Cf. also Ludwig Wittgenstein, *Remarks on the Foundations of Mathematics*, eds. G. H. von Wright and G. E. M. Anscombe and trans. G. E. M. Anscombe (Oxford: Basil Blackwell, 1978), Pt V, §13.

[59] In the previous section I tried to give some indication of the free play which our concept of a child allows for, alluding in particular to the way in which vague utterances that use this concept can function like performatives. Part of what it means to say that Ellen will gradually stop being a child, in semantic terms, is that this free play, applied over the course of her life, will first gradually increase, then gradually decrease. (Part of what this in turn means is that the sentence 'Ellen is old enough for an utterance of "Ellen is a child" to function like a performative' is every bit as vague as the sentence 'Ellen is a child.' This seems to me to rebut an argument

But to reject (7)—to decline to have that rule—is itself to have a rule. It is to have a second-order rule that we are not to adopt that first-order rule, or any other that commits us to it (for instance, the first-order rule that a person stops counting as a child on his or her fourteenth birthday). This second-order rule might be called a rule of *rule of* representation. It does not preclude our imposing precision on the concept of a child for certain specific and restricted purposes, say in legal contexts. We would not be violating the rule if we said that, for such and such purposes, we were going to count anyone under the age of fourteen as a child and anyone else as not a child.[60] But we would be violating the rule if we saw this as binding on all subsequent uses of the concept of a child. The second-order rule precisely safeguards our entitlement to impose such precision, but with a different cut-off point, on some later occasion.[61]

We can accept and state this rule of rule of representation then. And *that*, I submit, is what we are doing when we endorse (5). (This

[60] My 1993 edition of *The Chambers Dictionary* defines 'child' as 'a very young person (up to the age of sixteen for the purpose of some acts of parliament, under fourteen in criminal law)'.

[61] This is another example of the free play that our concept of a child allows for (see above, n. 59). Cf. once again Sainsbury, op. cit., note 47, §6.

in Williamson, op. cit., note 44, §7.3, in favour of the view that the concept of a child has *some* sort of cut-off point. (Williamson actually couches the argument in terms of the concept of a heap.) This argument can be broached by considering the two following situations. In the first, there are two co-operative omniscient speakers who are asked to say whether Ellen is a child at various future dates. They diverge in when they stop calling her a child. In the second, there are again two co-operative omniscient speakers who are asked to say whether Ellen is a child at various future dates, *but they are also instructed to use any discretion they are allowed as conservatively as possible* (that is, roughly, they are told to stop calling her a child as soon as they can). They too diverge in when they stop calling her a child. The argument turns on the thought that, whatever sense we can make of the first of these situations, the second is unintelligible. For if it is, then there must after all be some sort of cut-off point for the concept of a child. But in fact, granted what I said about the vagueness of the sentence 'Ellen is old enough for an utterance of "Ellen is a child" to function like a performative', the second situation is no more unintelligible than the first. Or if it is, then this is because the instruction given to the two speakers—to use any discretion they are allowed as conservatively as possible—is meant to apply even to itself, in which case I think we have reason to locate the unintelligibility of the situation, not in the fact that there is some sort of cut-off point for the concept of a child, but in the unintelligibility of the instruction.)

is why I said at the beginning of this section that I wanted to consider a *variation* on the idea of a rule of representation. The sixth move is like the first. Nevertheless, it is importantly distinct.) To think that (5) is equivalent to (6), or rather that endorsing (5) is equivalent to endorsing (6), is to confuse levels. There is no obstacle to our endorsing (5) and rejecting (6). Nor does our endorsing (5) lead to paradox: this is precisely because it does not involve our endorsing (6).

An objector might say, 'This is all very well, but suppose we consider uses of (5), (6) and (7), not to make the moves that you have been talking about, but to make simple empirical claims about how things are. What then?'

Well *what* then? It is not obvious from the sentences themselves what empirical claims are being envisaged. If what I have been urging about the flexibility of our concept of a child is right—if some applications of the word 'child' to Ellen can count as correct just by virtue of being made, while others count as neither correct nor incorrect—then it is of no avail here just to appeal to our understanding of the words in the sentences and then to try somehow to invoke compositional semantics. That simply does not deliver any suitable interpretations. The fact is that these sentences cannot be used to make empirical claims about how things are without a considerable amount of supplementary gloss.

Some utterances of them, on some suitable glosses, will be unproblematically true; others will be unproblematically false; and others again, granted what I said in the previous section, will be neither true nor false. For instance, an utterance of (6) will be unproblematically true if it means that, for any day on which Ellen counts as a child, the ensuing twenty-four hours will make no appreciable difference to any of the characteristics in virtue of which she does so. It will be unproblematically false if it means that, for any day on which Ellen counts as a child, the ensuing twenty-four hours will make no difference at all to any of these characteristics. An utterance of (5) will be unproblematically true if it means that we shall not, as a matter of fact, have a special day to mark the end of Ellen's childhood. A corresponding utterance of (7) will then be unproblematically false. Conversely, an utterance of (7) may be unproblematically true if it means that there will come a last day on which everyone in a certain group (or a majority of people in that group, or at least one person in that group, or the utterer himself) is prepared to say, without hesitation, that Ellen is a child. And a corresponding utterance of (5) will then be unproblematically false. Or it may be that neither of these utterances will be true *or* false, given

170

that whether someone is prepared to say, without hesitation, that Ellen is a child is itself a vague matter. None of this, so far as I can see, threatens paradox.

A principal lesson of this section, then, as of all the others, is that there is elucidation to be gained from diverting attention away from the forms of sentences to the moves made with them. And despite the discouraging messiness of linguistic behaviour, the moves are there to be discerned. In particular, we sometimes state rules of rules of representation—just as we sometimes make each of the other five moves that I have focused on in this essay. The Governing Picture does not gainsay this. On the contrary, due appreciation of the Governing Picture can enhance our understanding of all six moves, and can help us to see our way round some familiar philosophical conundrums.[62]

St. Hugh's College Oxford

[62] I am very grateful to Uri Henig for a number of helpful discussions, and to Peter Hacker, Oswald Hanfling and Timothy Williamson for comments on an earlier draft. I have also profited from Uri Henig, *Meaning and Negation*, unpublished M. Litt. thesis, Oxford University (1994).

Particular Thoughts & Singular Thought

M. G. F. MARTIN

A long-standing theme in discussion of perception and thought has been that our primary cognitive contact with individual objects and events in the world derives from our perceptual contact with them.[1] When I look at a duck in front of me, I am not merely presented with the fact that there is at least one duck in the area, rather I seem to be presented with *this* thing (as one might put it from my perspective) in front of me, which looks to me to be a duck. Furthermore, such a perception would seem to put me in a position not merely to make the existential judgment that there is some duck or other present, but rather to make a singular, demonstrative judgment, that that is a duck. My grounds for an existential judgment in this case derives from my apprehension of the demonstrative thought and not vice versa.

The cognitive role of experience is also mirrored in its phenomenology: that I am presented with a particular rubber duck, or a particular event of, say, the duck coming off the production line, is reflected in how things now visually appear to me. It looks to me as if there is a particular object before me, or that some given unrepeatable event is occurring. Hence we should expect a theory of sensory experience which aims to give an adequate account of phenomenology to accommodate and explain how such experience can indeed be particular in character.

An *Intentional Theory of Perception* (as I shall use this phrase) seeks to explain aspects of the phenomenal character of our perceptual experience in terms of the experience's possession of representational properties or, in other words, through its possession of an intentional content. On such a view, an experience's having the phenomenal properties it does (at least, with respect to those aspects of it directed at the external world) is not constitutively dependent on any object, event, or property-instance which the experience presents to the subject. One's experience would be just the way it is, presenting to one just the kind of state of affairs it does, whether or not such a

[1] This is a notable theme of (Strawson 1959), Chapter One. But one can trace it back even to Moore's early discussions of perception and judgment, for example (Moore 1922).

state of affairs genuinely obtained and was perceived. The phenomenal character of the experience is constituted or determined by the representational properties themselves, which we pick out by reference to what they represent, and is not constituted by the objects represented. An intentional theory of perception exploits this supposed independence of experience from its subject matter in accounting for the possibility of hallucination. That is to say, an intentional theory of perception is committed to three claims: (a) that our sensory experiences possess intentional properties; (b) that at least some phenomenal aspects of experience, namely those which relate to the objects of perception, are to be explained by those intentional properties; and (c) the same account is to be given of veridical perception and perfectly matching hallucination by appeal to their common possession of the same intentional properties.[2]

However, the phenomenon with which we started, the particularity of sensory experience, poses a fundamental challenge to intentional theories of perception. According to one popular conception of thought and representation, associated in particular with Gareth Evans and John McDowell, where an intentional content is directed on a particular object or event and is 'singular', such a content is 'object-dependent': one can think thoughts of this kind only where an appropriate object to be thought about actually exists.[3] Since hallucinations are taken to be paradigm examples of the absence of any such candidate object of reference, object-dependent accounts of intentional content will ascribe no intentional content to hallucinations. Given this assumption, an intentional theory of sensory experience faces a dilemma: either to reject the particularity of experience and thereby to give up the pretension of explaining the phenomenal character of experience in terms of intentional content; or to embrace the singularity of such content and thereby to forsake the motivation of giving a common account of both perception and hallucination. Hence, one might think that proper attention to the

---

[2] For advocates of such theories see, for example, (Harman 1990), (Tye 1995), (Burge 1986). Endorsing an intentional theory of this form is consistent with claiming that there are also sensational aspects to experience (see Peacocke 1983). We can call a theory a 'pure intentional' theory which seeks to explain all aspects of phenomenal character by reference to intentional content; Harman and Tye argue for such pure intentional theories.

[3] This simplifies matters with respect to Evans who insists on the *variety* of reference—he also wants to allow for the existence of non-object-dependent, non-Russellian modes of reference using descriptive names. This would not apply to the case of perceptual demonstrative reference, however.

particularity of experience offers us a motivation for embracing what has come to be called a disjunctive conception of sensory experience: the denial that we can give a common account of perception and hallucination.[4]

The route to solving this problem takes us through another question about the particularity of experience concerning identical twins. The ambition of intentional approaches, as I have glossed them above, is to explain sameness and difference in phenomenal character of experience in terms of the intentional contents that experiences possess. So two experiences with the same intentional content should be taken to be phenomenologically the same, at least with respect to those aspects explicable in intentional terms, and two experiences which are phenomenologically the same in intentional aspect should possess the same contents. But now when one perceives identical twins, the experience of each alone can be phenomenologically indistinguishable from the experience of the other. This is not merely a matter of not being able to note the difference between the two: rather what makes one twin the individual it is and not the other need not be perceptually detectable, so the properties experientially present in both cases are the same. But if the two experiences are phenomenologically the same, then presumably they must possess the same intentional content. Yet each of the experiences presents a distinct individual and so any content in common between the experiences must be object-independent. The arguments against reconciling intentional theories with the particularity of experience seem multiple. But in fact the solution to this problem shows the way to answering our initial challenge.

In the first section of the paper, I outline the doctrine of object dependence for singular thought and isolate the key element which presents the problem for intentional theories of perception. In the second, we review the question of indiscriminable twins. In the third section I explain how the theory can embrace the conclusion that experiences of identical twins have the same phenomenal character without having to deny that individual experiences have particular objects as part of their phenomenal nature. This leads us to distinguish between those aspects of a psychological episode which it essentially has in common with any other episode of fundamentally the same kind, and those aspects of it which are proprietary to it as an individual, unrepeatable event. Discussion of the issues

---

[4] Just such a challenge can be found in (McDowell 1986), though not explicitly directed at intentional theories of perception. It seems to be offered as one of the main motivations for disjunctivism about perception in (Snowdon 1990), and is suggested by (Soteriou 2000).

raised by identical twins shows how to answer our initial problem of reconciling the particularity of experience with the intentional theorist's need to appeal to object-independent content. In the closing section of the paper, I then draw out some of the consequences of this approach to the metaphysics of contentful psychological episodes through contrasting the model elaborated here with Evans's own view of experience which is in sharp contrast to his view of singular thought.

1. In *The Varieties of Reference,* Gareth Evans introduces what he there calls 'Russellian' thoughts, but what have come to be known by others as 'object-dependent' thoughts. Evans defines Russellian thought so:

> A thought is Russellian if it is of such a kind that it simply could not exist in the absence of the object or objects which it is about.[5]

McDowell discusses the same idea in his paper 'Truth-Value Gaps' and, in introducing it, draws an immediate consequence:

> ... a singular thought is a thought that would not be available to be thought or expressed if the relevant object, or objects, did not exist. It follows that if one utters a sentence of the relevant sort, containing a singular term that, in that utterance, lacks a denotation, then one expresses no thought at all; consequently neither a truth nor a falsehood.[6]

That Evans himself also endorses this consequence is reflected in the following passage later in the book:

> Consequently, demonstrative thoughts about objects, like 'here'-thoughts, are Russellian. If there is no one object with which the subject is in fact in informational 'contact'—if he is hallucinating, or if several different objects succeed each other without his noticing—then he has no Idea-of-a-particular object, and hence no thought. His demonstrative thought about a particular object relies upon the fact of an informational connection of a certain kind, not upon the thought or idea of that connection; and hence it is unconstruable, if there is no object with which he is thus connected.[7]

So we have here two aspects to the idea of Russellian or object-dependent thought: First, that the existence of a thought-content,

[5] (Evans 1982), p. 71.
[6] (McDowell 1982), p. 204 in reprint.
[7] (Evans 1982), p. 173.

and hence the existence of an episode of thinking that content, is constitutively dependent on the existence of the object or objects that the thought-content is about,[8] second, that where we have a case putatively of this kind but in which no appropriate object of thought is present, then the subject thinks no thought at all.

The second claim places an emphasis on what one has to say about the 'empty' case, where no appropriate object is present, rather than on any feature of the central case where there is an object. And that has caused a certain amount of discussion about psychological states present in the case of hallucination.[9] In some passages, Evans appears to commit himself to the view that there is no episode of thinking in the empty case, in others what he has to say is ambivalent; the same is true of McDowell in his commentaries on Evans.[10] For our purposes here, however, it is more important to focus on the commitments which concern only the case in which an appropriate object is present and hence to bracket assess-

[8] It seems to me as plausible to put the thesis just in terms of the conditions for the existence of episodes of thought rather than the existence conditions for the contents of those thoughts (we could allow that Russellian thought-contents existed in all worlds but were inaccessible to thought in worlds where the object thought about does not exist). However Evans defines it first in terms of condition for existence of the thought-content.

[9] Here see (Noonan 1993), (Segal 1989) and (Carruthers 1987) for an extensive discussion.

[10] Cf. (Evans 1982), on pp. 45–6 he states, 'It is not part of this proposal that his mind is wholly vacant; images and words may clearly pass through it, and various ancillary thoughts may even occur to him'; and on p. 71 the stress is simply on the claim that no thought of the Russellian kind could be had in the absence of an object, in contrast to the passage on p. 173. In an appendix to Ch. 6, the authorship of which may be more due to McDowell as editor than the text proper, it is claimed 'It is a consequence of the realism with which we have just mentioned that when a person hallucinates, so that it appears to him that he is confronting, say, a bus, then, whether or not he is taken in by the appearances, there is literally nothing before his mind.', pp. 199–200. However, in McDowell's own commentary on this in (McDowell 1986), he writes, '[a subject] may think that there is a singular thought at, so to speak, a certain position in his internal organization although there is really nothing precisely there.' Continued in footnote 17: 'Nothing precisely there; of course there may be all sorts of things in the vicinity' (p. 145). The discussion in the footnote seeks to rebut a suggestion of Blackburn's in (Blackburn 1984), Ch. 9, that Evans would be committed to the view that the mind is 'empty' or has a 'void' in the hallucinatory case.

ment of what one says about the empty case, and whether the claim made about cases in which the thought depends on an object really does have the consequence McDowell claims it does for the empty case.

We should then define the notion of object dependence so. A proposition or thought content is *object-dependent* where the thought content concerns a given object and a mental state or episode which has the thought content in question as its content could only occur given the existence of the object being referred to or thought about. Certainly no such thought content could then be entertained in a case of hallucination as normally conceived, where no appropriate candidate for the object of thought exists. Whether that should mean that no thought content at all could then be entertained, and in turn whether that means that no mental state or episode could then be occurring is a further matter.

Correlative to the idea of object dependence, we might also define a notion of *object-involvingness* for the mental states or episodes which have such contents. Let us say that a mental state or episode is object-involving where a state or episode of that very kind could only occur given the existence of a suitable object for the state or episode to be related to. In the absence of such an object, then there will be no instance of that mental kind. We can interpret Evans's and McDowell's position here to be that acceptance of object dependence for content leads also directly to acceptance of object-involvingness for mental episodes and states. Against this, I shall argue in this paper that while the connection between object dependence and object involvingness holds for a wide range of thought contents, the defender of an intentional theory of perception will insist that there are some states of mind which have an object-dependent truth condition associated with them but which are not object-involving.

To see how this possibility can arise, we need to notice a distinction among the kinds of capacities we have for thinking about objects. Evans's talk of 'Ideas' is intended to direct our attention to the fact that we have capacities for thinking about objects which underlie our capacities for entertaining whole thought contents. For our purposes we need to focus on the case of perceptual demonstrative thoughts and those ways of thinking about objects which are essentially tied to our perceptual encounters with objects. Such capacities might be contrasted with those we have for thinking about objects in their absence, as when reading a newspaper account of someone's endeavours, or simply wondering what an absent friend may now be doing. Here the idea of a capacity of thought for an individual is taken to be (in part) individuated by the object thought about: capacities to think about distinct individuals must be distinct capacities. Yet they are also conceived of as more fine-grained than capacities which would be counted as the same or different solely by reference to the objects they are capacities to think of: we are to contrast perceptually demonstrative capacities to think about individuals tied to current perceptual contact with them, with capacities grounded simply in one's knowledge of those individuals which can persist beyond any momentary encounter.

One can think of the latter sort of capacities as what one might call *standing* capacities: a thinker possesses such a capacity over time and is capable of exercising the very same capacity on different occasions. The possession of such a capacity reflects the fact that a thinker can entertain the very same thought content on different occasions of thinking even where thought content is individuated more finely than by appeal to the objects, events and properties that it concerns.

In the case of demonstrative thoughts, however, we need to recognize the presence of more than any such standing capacities for thinking about objects. We need to note the possibility of someone on a given occasion being capable of thinking about a particular object or event just given the circumstances present in that particular situation. Such an ability or capacity to think about a given object in a particular circumstance should be thought of as a one-off, unrepeatable capacity: an episodic capacity. If such a capacity arises on a given occasion, no other thinking, even by that very same thinker would involve the very same episodic capacity, even if it concerned the very same individual.

Such episodic capacities are plausibly attributed only where there is a corresponding standing capacity. We would be reluctant to attribute to a subject the capacity to make demonstrative judgments, unless he or she was able to make more than one such judgment. Unlike the standing capacities for thought about individuals introduced above, these standing capacities for demonstrative thought are not be thought of as abilities to think (repeatedly) about some given individual item, but might rather be thought of as capacities to think about whatever is suitably placed when the appropriate occasioning event for the capacity occurs. That is, as an object-independent capacity to acquire the episodic capacity to think about an object when suitably placed on a given occasion.

This is to put the basic contrast in very abstract terms. We can make it more concrete with examples. Suppose then that I have a way of thinking about Ken Livingstone, as reflected in the way that I can recognize his face, and respond to uses of his name in news reports, gossip columns and the like to associate with the history of one given individual. If I have such a capacity, we will appeal to it to explain how different occasions of thinking what I would express by, 'Ken Livingstone never travels on the No. 19 bus' can all be expressions of the very same thought content. Contrast this with a case of demonstrative thought, where one's accidental encounter with one object rather than another explains which object it is one is thinking about. For example, think of a production line at a rubber-duck factory. In judging what I express with the words, 'Now that's yellow!' pointing in the direction of the first duck in line, call it 'Huey', the thought I entertain is one available to me because Huey is peculiarly visually salient to me at that time. The situation allows me to exploit a general capacity I have for forming a particular capacity for thinking about related to whatever is perceptually salient at a time in making the judgment. But had the circumstances been slightly different, and another, indistinguishable duck come off the line at that moment, then I would have thought about the other duck and not Huey. The background standing capacity for thinking about a perceptually salient object would have been operative in the same way, but a different episodic capacity would have been engaged.

Now, Evans's and McDowell's conception of object-dependent thought and correspondingly object-involving psychological states goes neatly with the former example and the idea of standing capacities for thinking about particular individuals. Parallel to the modal intuitions which may convince us that the truth conditions of the judgments are object-dependent, intuitions about whether someone is thinking the same thing on different occasions or at different times should convince us that what singles out different occasions of thinking as relevantly of the same kind will just be that they are all exercises of the same standing capacity to think about Ken Livingstone in a given manner. In that case, no thinking which concerned some other entity alone and did not concern Ken Livingstone could really be of the same kind. There would be no room, then, to suppose that the thoughts I would have been entertaining had Ken Livingstone not been known to me but only some double with the same name would have been cases of thinking in just the same way, exploiting the very same capacities for thought.

But the same conclusion is really not forced on us for perceptual demonstrative thoughts, given the role of episodic capacities for thought. The very object I happen to be perceiving at this one time, Huey, is all that is relevant to the question whether my thoughts are true and under what conditions they would be true. But if this is a one-off capacity to think about Huey, then there is no reason to think that any other distinct episode of thinking must involve the very same capacity for thinking about Huey, as opposed to the general capacity for thinking about whatever is salient to one. So there is no license to judge that episodes of thought are of exactly the same kind just because they concern Huey presented in a certain manner. Rather, if we are to group different episodes of thinking together as of the same kind when focusing on perceptually grounded judgments, then it is plausible to suppose that episodes of thinking which concern different objects, but similarly presented, should be counted together. If this is right, then we see the need to make room for truth conditions of thought episodes which are tied to the objects the thoughts are about, yet for which we do not get object-involving mental states or episodes as we have defined above.

This gives the general framework which we will use below to expand on and then address the problems facing the intentional theory of perception. If perceptual experiences are to be treated analogously to episodes of thinking, then the model appropriate would arguably be that of perceptual demonstrative thought. If we can make sense of the latter as relating to objects without being object-dependent, then we can show how the intentional theorist can allow for the particularity of experience without giving up on the pretension of explaining hallucinatory experience in the same terms as perceptual experience. The point can be made more forcibly once we look at the case of perceiving indiscriminable twins and the grounds that some have found in this for supposing the content of experience to be existentially general in form.

2. The relevance of perceptually indiscriminable twins to the question whether experience can have a particular or object-involving content has been raised before. Colin McGinn and Martin Davies have both argued that the content of perceptual experience must be general on just this ground

> ... when we are describing the content of an experience we should not make singular reference to the object of the experience ... In fact it seems right to uphold a stronger thesis about experiential content: that an accurate description of the phenomenological content of experience will employ only general terms to specify how the experience represents the world.[11]

Davies, who endorses this view, offers the following brief argument in its favour:

[11] (McGinn 1982a), p. 39.

... in the case of perceptual content, it is plausible that if two objects are genuinely indistinguishable for a subject, then a perceptual experience of the one has the same content as a perceptual experience of the other. The source of this plausibility is the thought that the perceptual content of experience is a phenomenal notion: perceptual content is a matter of how the world seems to the experiencer... If perceptual content is, in this sense, 'phenomenological content' ... then, where there is no phenomenological difference for the subject, there is no difference in perceptual content.

If perceptual content is phenomenological content then, it seems, it is not object-involving. But from this it does not follow that perceptual content is not truth conditional—not fully representational; for we can take perceptual content to be existentially quantified content. A visual experience may present the world as containing *an* object of a certain size and shape, in a certain direction, at a certain distance from the subject.[12]

As suggested above, these claims would seem to be at odds with the simple thought that our experiences ground demonstrative judgments about particular objects. As Moore was keen to stress, a glance at one's desk may lead to the judgment, *'That* (directing one's attention at one thing on one's desktop) is an inkstand'. One is not stuck with merely the possibility of judging that there is some inkstand in the vicinity, one can pick out the very inkstand in question and make a demonstrative judgment about it. If experience makes reasonable such demonstrative judgments, surely how things are presented as being must reflect the fact that it is one particular thing rather than another that one perceives. So surely the content of the experience cannot itself be entirely general in character.

Neither McGinn nor Davies wish to deny that our experiences prompt, and justify, singular judgments about particular objects. Their claim is rather that the experiences themselves lack such particularity in their content. So they would dispute the further contention that the rationalizing role of experience requires that it have a content matching the singular demonstrative judgment that issues from it.

Leave that issue to one side. For we can instead press the question in terms of how the phenomenal character of our experience relates to our intuitions about whether the scene before us is presented correctly or illusorily. It is arguable that assessing experience in this way requires us to take into account which object

[12] (Davies 1992), pp. 25–6.

is being presented to the subject, and this fact cannot properly be accommodated on a view on which the content of experience is purely general.

Now in defence of the idea that the content of experience is purely general, some have appealed to the possibility of 'veridical hallucinations'. If I have the visual hallucination of an orange on the table in front of me, my experience may match how things are before me without thereby being a perception. Someone may simply place an appropriately sized orange on the table without thereby restoring my sight. In the relevant sense of veridicality here we appeal solely to a general content: that there should be some orange or other on the table before the subject if his experience is veridical.[13]

But this does not exhaust all of the judgments we are prepared to make about the veridicality of experience. We also make judgments about one's misperceiving an object to be a certain way, and that the object is presented to one as being a way that it is not. Consider, for example, a slight modification of a Gricean example. One views a scene through a rose-tinted prism, under slightly unusual lighting. Directly ahead of one is a pink candle. A white candle is placed to the right of the pink candle. Intuitively, in this case one sees the white candle, although it looks to one as if there is a pink candle before one. So far, in parallel with the case of veridical hallucination, we can judge this to be a misperception of one object while also being a veridical experience with respect to how one's environment is represented. But now suppose that we change the situation somewhat and bleach out the coloured light. It now looks to one as if there is a white candle before one. Where the experience was veridical before, it is now illusory: for it is as if there is a white candle before one when in fact there is a pink one. On the other hand, we can also recognize a sense in which the experience is also now more accurate. In the first example it misrepresents the location and colour of a candle, now it merely misrepresents its location. These assessments of veridicality require reference to the particular object of perception, and not just the kind of state of affairs in the subject's environment.

A similar moral can be drawn from cases involving perception over time. Suppose one is staring at a thin piece of paper with a blue cross on it. Unbeknownst to one, there is in fact a densely packed ream of paper crosses before one, and each in turn is imperceptibly dissolving. Over a period of time it will look to one as if there

[13] Such thoughts are prompted by Grice's famous discussion of the causal theory of perception, (Grice 1961).

continues to be a blue cross before one. This is in fact correct, for throughout the period there is a blue cross there, albeit there is no one blue cross which one continues to see. There is some inclination here to think of the experience as involving an illusion of persistence. But unless we bring in reference to some particular thing we have no way of distinguishing this illusory course of experience from a veridical case in which one sees just one cross over time.[14]

Neither example is conclusive. For instance, it would be open to McGinn and Davies to grant that we can make these judgments about the accuracy of experience but then insist that in doing so we import considerations which are external to the phenomenological character of the experience. To make such an assessment of one's experience, it might be claimed, goes beyond the phenomenal character and appeals to causal considerations about which is the object of perception, a question which depends on matters external to phenomenology.

I'm not too concerned to settle the merits of this debate here.[15] Whether we can conclusively show that experience has the relevant phenomenological particularity, one would be mistaken to think that it is simply obvious that its character is existentially general in form. So there is as much interest in focusing on the arguments that McGinn and Davies can offer in favour of their interpretation of experience. Must the intentionalist commit to the view that experience is general in its content, given that there is at least some *prima facie* evidence to the contrary? This leads us back to Davies's argument for his conclusion.

It is clear that we can perceive distinct but qualitatively identical objects. Distinct objects can possess the very same visible properties; two objects can look exactly the same as each other. Such objects are visually indistinguishable. Their distinct identities may be detectable by other means but not by simply looking. For example, if one was presented consecutively with two rubber ducks off the same production line, one might be unable to tell from inspecting each in turn which of the two it was: whether one had

[14] Cf. here also (Soteriou 2000) for arguments for the particularity of the character of experience, and why an intentional theory of perception should be committed to this.

[15] I also ignore the attempt to explain these phenomena in terms of a descriptive condition picking out the object of perception as the cause of the experience—see (Searle 1983) for the proposal, and (Burge 1993) and (Soteriou 2000) for scepticism about its merits.

been given the same duck twice, or viewed a different duck on each occasion. In this case not only would the two objects be visually indistinguishable, but the two experiences of the objects would be indistinguishable for their subject through introspection of them. Moreover, and this does not simply follow from the former claim, we would be inclined to say that the experiences are the same in phenomenal, or qualitative, character. Both of the experiences are experiences of an object looking duck-shaped and yellow-tinged in the region of space before the subject. So there is no difference in how the objects perceived are presented as being.

None of this, I take it, is open to dispute. But Davies's reasoning contains two further moves in order to arrive at his conclusion that the content of both experiences is general in form. And each of these moves is open to question. The first involves Davies's claim that, given that the two experiences are phenomenally the same, their contents must be the same, since the content of experience is 'phenomenological content'. The second move is the claim that if the contents of the two experiences are the same, then that content must be general in form. We need to consider each in more detail.

In support of the first move, one might claim that the phenomenology or qualitative character of an experience is nothing more than its similarities or differences from some other experience. Hence if two experiences are exactly alike in their qualitative character, as the reasoning above appears to concede, then any difference between them must be a difference in some non-phenomenological aspect. So, any notion of content which is intended to capture the sameness or difference of the two experiences should be attributable to both, since they are qualitatively alike.

On at least one conception of experience, this conclusion is unavoidable. According to an 'adverbialist' conception of experience, the qualitative character of experience is conceived simply as a matter of the presence of certain qualia or qualities. To experience a red square, say, is to experience in a certain determinate manner: redly-coincidingly-with-squarely. An understanding of what it is for one's experience to be so requires us to make no appeal beyond the ways or manners in which one experiences, where we are to think of that as the subject or the experience instantiating some simple mental quality. Our ascriptions of experience, of course, make reference to the objects or putative objects of experience, and so appear relational, but for an adverbialist this reflects the fact that in order to find terms rich enough to express the variation in character we may make reference to the typical causes of such experience.[16] On such a conception of experience, it is possible, in principle at least, for distinct sensory episodes to possess the same qualia. And what it is for experiences to be qualitatively the same or different is simply for them to share or differ in the qualia they have. So there can be no room, on this conception, for experiences to differ in their phenomenology apart from sharing or failing to share such qualia. Such a conception of experience would endorse the move from qualitative identity of the two sensory episodes to the claim that any difference between them would have to be non-phenomenological, since all phenomenology could be would be something qualitative and hence general in form.

Elsewhere I have laboured the inadequacies of any such conception of the phenomenal character of experience.[17] What is distinctive of experience, and central to our understanding of the problems of perception, is that in having an experience, a subject is presented with a particular subject matter; how things are in some part of the subject's body or environment is given to him or her in having the experience. We cannot understand what an experience is like independent of its subject matter. The phenomenal nature of a given experience is a matter of what is presented to the subject and the manner in which it is presented, and the similarities or differences among experiences are a matter of similarity or difference among these complex phenomenal natures. So similarity and difference of experiences can be just a matter of similarity or difference of their subject matter.[18] Once we appeal to the distinction between the subject matter of an experience (the objects and qualities as presented to the subject in so experiencing) and the qualitative characteristics of the experience itself, then the conclusion drawn above by the adverbialist no longer follows from our assumptions.

Moreover, intentional approaches to perception want to acknowledge precisely the aspect of experience highlighted above: that the phenomenal nature of experience is, at least in part, the presentation of a subject matter. After all, the need for appeal to intentional content is precisely to bring out the connection between what an experience is like and the mind-independent entities putatively present to a subject even in a case of hallucination. So an intentional theorist of perception ought to reject the adverbialist conception of

[16] For an example of such adverbialism see (Tye 1984).

[17] See (Martin 1998).

[18] Note the qualification 'can be': it is quite consistent with the points made here that there is more to the phenomenal character of an experience than its subject matter, so that two experiences which share a subject matter may nonetheless be phenomenologically different from each other.

experience and so Davies cannot appeal to that conception of qualitative similarity of experience in support of his reasoning against an intentionalist.

We can not only question the reasons for making the move. In addition, we can offer positive reason to reject it. For one may claim that what it takes for an entity to be an aspect of the phenomenology of an experience is just that it be among the presented elements of that particular episode. Such an experience could be entirely qualitatively identical with another experience involving a distinct object and yet still differ in its phenomenal nature solely in this respect. In this way, the one experience of one rubber duck, of Huey, say, may be the presentation of that very toy, while the experience of the other rubber duck, Dewey, is the presentation of the other toy. There is a difference between the two experiences—that is a difference between the two particular unrepeatable events— namely that the one is the presentation of one object and the other the presentation of another object. And this difference between them is quite consistent with there being no qualitative difference between the two experiences. For, of course, to look at them as *qualitatively* the same or different is precisely to abstract away from any particulars involved in either situation. One is merely asking what qualities the two have in common. Both experiences are presentings of yellow, duck-shaped objects.

Davies's opponent can insist that the difference in content between the two experiences shows up only in the differences between the particular experiential episodes and not in the phenomenal properties the episodes share. So there can be a difference in content between two phenomenally identical experiences without that difference having to be non-phenomenological.

This is, I suggest, sufficient to block Davies's argument as given. We have blocked the first move. But the argument is worth exploring further, nonetheless. Can we find further justification behind Davies's explicit words in order to press the argument on? Elsewhere, I've explored and rejected arguments based on the idea that the ascription of content here is constrained by the subject's powers of discrimination.[19] But there is a deeper and more interesting set of considerations, or so I shall argue, which would bolster Davies's position here and which seem to operate implicitly in much of the discussion of the content of utterances and thoughts.

Our aim is to reconcile the claim that two experiences of distinct objects could be phenomenologically the same with the claim that particulars should figure in the phenomenal character of an

[19] (Martin 1997).

187

experience. To do this we suggested that particular objects are relevant to the phenomenal nature of a particular episode of experiencing on its own, rather than to the phenomenal character of the experience which it would share with distinct experiences of the same kind. When we ask whether two experiences are phenomenally the same or different, we abstract away from any concern with which particular object or event is being apprehended. We are solely interested in whether objects or events of a certain kind were presented to the subject. Reconciling the two claims in this way requires us to rely on a contrast between the phenomenal nature of individual experiential events and the phenomenal character they share with other experiences of the same kind. But can we appeal to this contrast if we also assume that the phenomenology of experience is determined by its intentional content?

For, one might claim, the commonest conception of psychological content is as that which individuates psychological states and divides experiences into fundamental categories or kinds. Part of the import of Frege's contrast between thought as objective and ideas as subjective seems to be to draw out the role of thought in classifying distinct episodes or states of thinking into common kinds. Hence we may conceive of content as objective in being potentially the object of distinct psychological episodes. If this is how we are to conceive of content, as essentially shareable across episodes of thinking or experiencing, then if two psychological states differ in their contents, they must be fundamentally of different kinds; while if they are the same, then they must have the same content. In general, sameness and difference among intentional states will be a function of the content of those states and the attitude the subject takes towards that content in being in that state.[20]

Just such principles are at work in the debate between, for example, Evans and Perry on Fregean thought. Perry, following Kaplan's work on demonstratives and indexicals, insists that there are two notions of content: one, *psychological role,* which goes with cognitive states; and the other, *propositional content,* which has truth conditions. For Perry, it is clear that two agents, Barry and Harry, who both think, 'I am hungry' have relevantly the same psychological episodes with respect to psychological explanation, although the truth conditions of their thoughts differ. At the same time, if it is Barry who says, 'I am hungry', then the thought he expresses has the same truth conditions as my utterance then of 'Barry is hungry',

[20] For one discussion of this role of content see (Peacocke 1992), Ch. 5. for a general critique of these assumptions about content see (Travis, 1994) and (Travis 1998).

even though the thinking of that needn't have the same psychological role as the first-personal thought. Barry and Harry are in states with the same content with respect to psychological role, but the truth conditions of the two states differ. According to Perry, truth-conditional content alone would treat as alike cases which ought to be seen as different, and distinguish cases which are relevantly the same. It is psychological role which individuates psychological states, and hence Frege was just confused to think that any notion of content could both play the individuating role and be a bearer of truth values.[21]

In contrast, Evans wishes to work with a single notion of content which is truth-conditional but more fine-grained than Perry's conception of truth conditions. On Evans's view there is an important similarity between the two agents: they are thinking similar thoughts. But nonetheless there is an important difference between the two situations and hence the thoughts are nonetheless distinct because they concern different individuals and that is fundamental to psychological explanation. So, according to Evans, it is this fine-grained notion of content which is needed to delimit the fundamental similarities and differences among psychological states. There is both a difference between the two propositions about Barry, since entertaining them involves different modes of thinking about Barry, and differences between Barry's and Harry's thoughts, since they are thinking of different things.

At one level, one might think that Perry's position is simply a variant of Evans's position, and vice versa. We can model the notions of content that each uses by logical construction from the notion of content that the other uses. Evans's Fregean contents could be treated as ordered pairs of Perry's truth-conditional content and his psychological roles; while Perry's psychological roles can be treated as one set of equivalence classes of Fregean contents, and its truth conditions as a different set of equivalence classes of those contents. To pinpoint what is at issue here we need to think in terms of which notion of content is most fundamental to giving an account of the kind of thing these psychological states are: what is essential to how they differ or are the same? That is just to assume that there is a notion of content which matches these questions, and so Perry and Evans differ about which kind of content should play that individuative role. This deep issue between them consists of a disagreement about what is fundamental to psychological explanation and psychological kinds.

In the case of interest to us, given an assumption that there is

[21] (Perry 1993).

such a notion of content for the case of sensory experiences, the question becomes, 'Which experiences should we treat as of the same fundamental kind?'. Those which are of the same kind should be attributed the same content. Episodes of distinct fundamental kinds, with different contents, may nonetheless be similar to each other: they may fall under some more general kind. But the main question to be pursued is, 'How fine-grained, at base, does our ascription of content need to be for a given kind of experience?' To attribute distinct contents to two experiences is to treat them as being of fundamentally different kinds. Conversely, where one has independent compelling reason to treat two experiences as of exactly the same kind, then one should attribute to them the very same content.

We can reconstruct Davies's first move so. Consider three possible sensory experiences. Two of these experiences are presentations of Huey on the table in front of the perceiver, the third is a presentation of Dewey. If the presence of a different object makes for a different content, then the first two experiences may be attributed the same content, but the third experience must have a different content. So the first two experiences are similar in a way that the third is not. Now, of course, everyone should grant that there is a similarity which the first two have but which the third lacks, for example being caused by Huey as opposed to being caused by Dewey. The point at issue is whether that can be a difference in the phenomenal kind, the phenomenal character, of the experience. Does the fact that a different object is perceived make a difference to the kind of experiential event one is having? After all, not all properties that an event has need thereby be aspects of the phenomenology of that event. And here Davies can simply point out that our intuition is that, given the perceptual indistinguishability of Huey and Dewey, the way things are presented in all three cases must just be the same. There does not seem to be anything about what the first experience is like which allies it more closely with the second than with the third experience.

So, we might put the point so. The intuitions that we already have about sameness and difference of sensory episodes leads us to treat all three experiences as of the same kind, and not to discriminate the first two from the third. If these judgments about sameness and difference of kinds of experience are to be reflected in the contents that we ascribe to the experiences, then all three experiences should be ascribed the very same content.

Hence we seem to have restored cogency to Davies's first move, as long as we accept the general principle about the individuative role of content and the intuitions about fundamental similarity and difference among experiences. What now of Davies's second move? The claim that if the experiences have the same content when one is presented with distinct objects, then the content in question must be general.

Davies himself closes the gap by talking of the experience being 'truth conditional' and 'fully representational', but the import of these qualifications is not entirely clear. However, we might expand on them through a simple line of reasoning to this conclusion. First, assume that the correctness conditions of the experience are essential to it and the same in both cases. In the first situation, when presented with Huey, the correctness, or veridicality, of one's experience will be determined by how things are with Huey. Given that it looks to one as if there is a yellow duck-shaped object present, one's experience will be veridical just in case Huey is both duck-shaped and yellow. On the other hand, in the second situation, when presented with Dewey, whether one's experience is veridical is sensitive to how things are with Dewey, whether Dewey is duck-shaped and yellow. So neither Huey nor Dewey is essential to determining the correctness of the content but each in turn, in one of the situations but not the other, is relevant to the truth of the content. Now this pattern of relevance to truth and truth conditions is exactly what we would predict on the basis of a view which supposes that the content of an experience merely lays down a general condition which an object must meet in order to fix the correctness of that content. Huey is relevant in the first situation because in that situation Huey meets the relevant condition; while in the second situation Dewey meets the condition and hence is relevant to the correctness conditions in that situation. So, we might supplement Davies's argument simply with the thought that ascribing a general content to the experiences best explains this pattern of relevance.

However, there is an alternative to this. We could instead suggest that the correctness conditions for the experiences are not the same across both situations but are rather to be assessed in each of the contexts in which an experience occurs.[22] The content of the sensory experiences, given the above argument, is context-insensitive: distinct sensory episodes which could have occurred at different times or with the presentation of distinct objects, possess the same

[22] Does this make the experiences not 'fully representational' or not 'truth conditional'? Perhaps that is what Davies has in mind, but there is really no reason to think that a contextually assigned truth condition renders a state not fully representational other than by stipulation.

content. But content can be context-insensitive without its correctness conditions being so: for the content may determine a correctness condition relative to a context.

Tyler Burge recommends just such a conception of perceptual content. Burge suggests that we can specify the content of a perceptual state so:

> (a') that F is G [where one indicates the relevant F, and where 'that F' is not only used, but stands for the mode of indication used in the statement (or visual experience) whose truth conditions are being given].
>
> ... The Intentional content involves a demonstrative occurrence (or type individuated in terms of a demonstrative occurrence) that governs F-predication and that in fact is applied to the relevant physical object.[23]

Given Burge's general approach to the semantics of demonstratives this conception assigns a truth condition involving a particular object only to given applications of the content in particular contexts. As Burge goes on to comment:

> On my view, demonstrative elements—which I contrasted with conceptual elements—should be taken as primitive in mental states, or their Intentional contents. In order to have reference, demonstrative elements must be part of a particular thinker's thought or experience in a particular context ... demonstrative elements contrast with conceptual elements, which have a constant reference or extension regardless of who thinks them or when they are thought.[24]

In the one situation, when presented with Huey, the contextual factors determine that the reference of the demonstrative element of the content expressed by 'That is duck-shaped' is Huey. So in this case the truth conditions of the judgment on this application concern how things are with Huey. However, in that situation Dewey rather than Huey could have been present. Had that been so, then the reference of the demonstrative element would have been Dewey and not Huey, so the truth conditions of the judgment would have concerned Dewey and not Huey. In this way we can see the visual experience being so characterized as having a content in common to the two occasions.

This conception matches the same pattern of dependence on the objects of the experience that we had with treating the content of

[23] (Burge 1993), p. 200.
[24] (Burge 1993), p. 208.

the experience as purely general. In contrast to that, though, it continues to treat the content as irreducibly demonstrative. So it can hold on to the pretensions that our experiences are indeed of particular objects, and provide for our singular, demonstrative judgments about them. Again we have a means of resisting Davies's and McGinn's position. This time we can refuse to make the second move.

But does this really save the spirit of the position that Davies is arguing against? Can't Davies hit back by reminding us that the whole point of intentionalism concerning experience is to explain the phenomenology of experience, its phenomenal nature or character, in terms of its intentional content. But now, he may insist, if the content of the experiences is the same in both cases, then their phenomenology must be the same. Although, in each context, the truth of the content depends on something different, that difference is not reflected in the phenomenal nature of the experience. After all, he may insist, it is the representational aspects of experience which are to explain its phenomenal nature. So this alternative account of content to Davies offers no alternative account of the phenomenology of experience—it no more respects the intuition that the character of a particular episode involves particular objects than does Davies's account in terms of existentially general truth conditions.

This response takes us back to the point made against Davies's first move. If we are interested in specifying the phenomenal nature of a given sensory episode as it occurs, then we should specify its content as applied in that context. That means in that situation picking out the object perceived in the relevant demonstrative way. In this way, correctly to specify what the perceiver's experience is like one needs to demonstrate the object which is in fact perceived. This aspect of the experience is not common across different occurrences of experiences with that intentional content, for in so doing we would shift the context in which the content is applied. But as things stand, with the objects so arrayed in the environment, the proper characterization of the experience if it is a veridical perception should mention them. This is so consistent with the intentionalist's claim that the intentional content alone and not the objects perceived constitute the phenomenal character of the experience, conceived as that which can be common across different occurrences.

The underlying point here requires us to reflect on how our metaphysical commitments in the notion of content interact with our conception of sensory experiences having a subject matter. There is something inherently general in the conception of a particular episode of thought or experience having a content. Given a conception of content as something shareable across distinct episodes of thought, the having of a content will be a general attribute of each episode of thought. Once we reflect on the way in which an experience has a subject matter, the presentation of a particular scene, then we need a way of making room for the essentially or inherently particular aspects of this as well as the general attributes of experience. We need to contrast the unrepeatable aspect of its phenomenology, what we might call its *phenomenal nature,* with that it has in common with qualitatively the same experiential events, what we might call *its phenomenal character.*

A given individual event may involve one set of particular entities rather than another. But when we come to type events as falling into kinds, we abstract away from the particulars involved in the individual events and just consider the general attributes that the particulars exhibit. For example, consider someone investigating the flaws in the rubber duck manufacturing process. Perhaps a certain shape of stain is present on both Huey and Dewey as they come off the production line. We may hypothesize that there is a specific design fault, at a given stage of the process, which leads to this kind of flaw. In that case, we are concerned to treat the event of producing Huey as of the same kind as the event of producing Dewey. That the two events involve distinct particulars is irrelevant to what kind the events are. It is just the same intuition at work, I suggest, when we are moved to think of the three experiences, two of Huey and one of Dewey. That is what explains the consistency of our intuitions: that each experience has a particularity about it relating to the very objects or events apprehended; and that at the same time, the three experiences are all entirely of the same type.

An intentional theory of perceptual experience will reject the thought that the objects of perception are literally constituents of an experiential episode, because hallucinatory experiences which are taken to be of the same kind will lack any such constituents (hence it cannot be essential to this kind of experience that it has its subject matter as a constituent). Nonetheless, an intentionalist will still be moved by a concern with one's first-person perspective on experience. From that point of view, it is as if the scene before one is a constituent of the experiential event. So no articulation of what the experience is like would be adequate if it did not make mention of the particular objects and events experienced in the case of genuine perception. Hence, an intentionalist should best think that the particular phenomenal nature that a particular experiential episode has is determined just in the context in which the experience occurs.

To sum up our discussion of perceptually indiscriminable twins. We can respect the idea that distinct objects and events can be presented in phenomenally exactly the same way, and that consequently such experiences are phenomenally the same in nature. Furthermore, one can accept as a consequence of this that such experiences will share exactly the same content. This is quite consistent with supposing that there is an aspect of the phenomenology of experience which is inherently particular, that the subject matter of a given experience involves particular objects and events. The two are reconciled where we see the subject matter of a particular experience as being context-determined, given by the context-invariant content and the particular circumstance in which the experiential event occurs.

3. In applying Burge's model to the case of indiscriminable twins, it is easy to see also how it can apply to the problem case of hallucinations. For the account does not make contentful states *per se* object-involving. Indeed, Burge has long developed accounts of thought *de re* designed explicitly to accommodate the possibility of thought about the non-existent. For a long time he has advocated the use of a negative free logic in giving the truth conditions of statements, on which atomic predications containing an empty term are not considered meaningless, as Evans would insist for Russellian terms, but simply false.[25] In relation to the present kind of case, involving demonstrative thought about perceived objects, he draws the following moral:

> It is possible for an applied demonstrative element to fail to have a referent. Since thoughts are individuated in terms of their contents (including the token applications of demonstrative elements in thought), some demonstrative thoughts are not *de re*. Moreover, since some demonstrative token applications that in fact have a referent might have failed to have had one (if the contextual circumstances had been different), some thought tokens that are in fact *de re* are not essentially *de re*. The very same thought content might have lacked a referent if the world beyond the thought had been different.[26]

[25] For one exposition of the account see (Burge 1983). For applications to the case of empty demonstratives see (Burge 1983). For more on belief *de re* see his (Burge 1977). For our purposes the adoption of a *negative* free logic is not required, though the idea that there can be contents where no appropriate object is present is.

[26] (Burge, 1993), p. 208.

M. G. F. Martin

Applying this in the terms we have used of the phenomenal nature of particular experiential episodes and their intentional content, we might extrapolate so. When one has a veridical perception, the particular experiential episode one has then has a phenomenal nature which is only adequately articulated by making reference to the very objects and events which are appropriately related to the occurrence of the experience in that very context. In so describing how things are presented as being we specify the conditions under which the experience is veridical relative to that very context. Nonetheless, there can be an exact qualitative duplicate of this experience in another context where no appropriate object of perception is present. Such an experience can share the very same intentional content with the perceptual experience, since that content, in being given in a manner analogous to an open sentence is object-independent. In that context, one cannot specify what the object of perception is, since there is none, other than in a conniving way which makes apparent reference to something which necessarily does not exist (the hallucinated object of perception).

For the hallucination and perception to warrant the same explanation we only require that they be of the same qualitative kind: this is captured by the common, object-independent content. In order to do justice to the intuition that the very object one is perceiving is an aspect of the phenomenology of one's experience, we must recognize that such objects figure within any adequate specification of the particular phenomenal nature of the experience one has at a time, and this is reflected in giving the truth conditions of how things are presented relative to that context.

In fact, Burge's own development of an account of perceptual demonstrative reference goes beyond this set of claims. He claims that it is inessential to a token demonstrative thought that it is *de re*. The very same demonstrative thought or utterance could have occurred on an occasion on which there was no appropriate object to be thought about. If we are thinking of utterances, then it is plausible to suppose that the production of speech or an inscription is independent of the distal environment in which the utterance is made, and hence it might seem arbitrary to individuate the use of words in a particular way relative to the presence or absence of objects in the environment. So perhaps Burge is warranted in the modal commitments he avows for the example he is looking at. However an intentionalist concerned with experiential events should be wary of affirming this additional claimed independence. The identity of individual events in the stream of consciousness may well not be independent of their causal history.

So, once we have addressed the intuitions relating to indiscriminable twins, we can see that the relevant notions of context-independent content and context-dependent correctness or truth conditions provides us with the materials for both marking what is distinctively particular about the phenomenology of experience while attributing an object-independent content to these experiences.

4. The intuitions that we appealed to in the case of indiscriminable twins has directed us towards an account of the intentional content of sensory experience which would seem to answer our initial queries about how intentionalism allows for the particularity in the phenomenology in our perceptual experience. Yet one might still be worried whether Burge's account really secures objects the correct role in experience. Just such a worry is expressed by McDowell. He associates Burge's conception of *de re* belief with 'two-factor' views of content, and against these complains:

> Once the subject's cognitive world has been segregated from his involvement with real objects this merely terminological move cannot restore genuine sense to the idea that we can get our minds around what we believe—even when the belief is *de re*.[27]

It is not clear whether the objection here to two-component views is supposed to tell equally against Burge's account, however McDowell does present matters as if one has no option but to adopt McDowell's position in response, so if we are to find an argument against a Burge-like view, it will be located here. McDowell elaborates on the ideas a bit more in a later paper, where he complains of such accounts of intentionality that:

> ... if we try to see intentionality as at most partly determining what it is that a subject thinks, we leave ourselves without anything genuinely recognizable as a notion of intentionality at all. The two-component picture of mind ... aims to codify the idea the thesis that in these cases intentionality is only a partial determinant of what the subject thinks; and the complaint can be focused by noting that the internal component is the only place in a two-component picture for the ideas associated with that aspect of intentionality which concerns the directedness of thought to specific objects... Directedness towards external objects enters the picture only when we widen our field of view to take in more

[27] (McDowell 1984), p. 293.

than the internal component. So on this conception there is no object-directed intentionality in cognitive space.[28]

Given our current concerns, one might restate this worry so. If we assume that the generalist thesis of McGinn and Davies is false, our perceptual experience in cases of veridical perception is experience of the very objects which we can then perceive. In describing the experience from the subject's point of view, one should demonstrate those very objects in one's specification of what this experience is like. Yet, according to Burge, one could have such an experience with the same content and yet be hallucinating. In such a case no such objects would be presented to the mind, since one would be perceiving nothing. But if there is nothing before the mind in the case of hallucination, and if what determines the phenomenological nature of the experience in this case is the same as in the perceptual case, then surely it does not determine the presence of objects to the mind even when veridically perceiving. Perceptual experience, then, when conceived from the subject's point of view would lack appropriate direction on an object.

This worry assimilates a metaphysical claim about the status of experience with a phenomenological claim about it. The phenomenological claim is that particular objects figure within the phenomenal nature of our experiences. There is a *this-such* presented to one when one's eye are open and one's attention is directed out at the world. The metaphysical claim is just a specific version of what I label elsewhere, 'Actualism': that the objects of perception, in figuring as the presented elements of one's experience (i.e. the phenomenological claim), must actually be constituents of the experience. But an intentionalist who adopts the line suggested here will simply deny that these two claims have to go together.

For such a theorist, the proper description of the phenomenal nature of experience when one does perceive some object is to be given partly by reference to the very object before one then. In that context, the correct expression of the demonstrative content of the experience is to make reference to the actual object which can be referred to in that situation. This is quite consistent with recognizing that in some other circumstance a state of mind with the very same content would not be expressible in the same way, i.e. by demonstrating that very object. Qualitatively the two experiences would be the same. As we saw in discussion of Davies, the fact that

---

[28] (McDowell 1986), p. 165. The main target of his criticism here is identified as McGinn in (McGinn 1982b). In the earlier paper McDowell associates Burge's approach to *de re* belief with McGinn's conception.

two experiences are qualitatively the same does not force us to deny that in the one case a particular object must be picked out in relation to the phenomenal nature which is not picked out in the other.

McDowell will only get his conclusion if he insists that the phenomenal nature of a given experience can be specified in a context-invariant way, and hence from the recognition of object-free instances such as those of hallucination, we must conclude that even in the case of perception, an intentionalist will have to claim that the nature of experience is object-free as well. But this is to ignore the possibility of the kind of account we have sketched above: one on which an aspect of the phenomenal nature of an experience is not something guaranteed to be replicated in any other experience of the same kind.

The room for this response would not be available had we focused on aspects of phenomenology which are repeatable across times or possible situations. When we have a repeatable element of the phenomenology, an element which will thereby turn up in the shared phenomenal character of two experiences of the same kind, we can ask of that element whether it can occur in the absence of the corresponding feature in the world. If it can, then presumably there is some adequate description to be given of it which makes no reference to the actual object of the experience. So the phenomenal nature of such an experience is describable independent of this subject matter, as McDowell complains. Indeed, many of the two-factor theories of content assume that some form of generalization from the case of indexical thought to all aspects of thought is possible. These theories precisely ignore the importance of those aspects of experience or thinking which are repeatable from those which are tied to a particular occasion. Nothing I have said here undermines the questions that McDowell can press against such views.

Could one press McDowell's objection further? What would be the consequences of embracing Burge's actual position and allowing that the very same experiential event could on one occasion possess an object and on another lack one? McDowell might press that, after all, some adequate description can be given of the phenomenal nature of the experience which makes no mention of the object perceived—namely a description available in the merely possible situation in which that very event occurred as an hallucination. Even if that description would not be available in our actual context of veridical perception, it would nonetheless report the very same facts in the context it which it was truthfully available.

I suggested above that this aspect of Burge's position is optional.

If instead we insist that the cause of the individual mental event was essential to it, we can deny that there are any such circumstances. At the same time, conceding this would not force one to deny that events of just the same type could occur but with different antecedent causes. One will agree with Burge that it is not of the essence of the perceptual event that it is *de re*: events of just the same psychological kind occur without an object. But with respect to the individual event which did occur we insist that the object perceived is necessarily an element of the experience's causal history. If this is so, then there would be no possibility of having the very same individual experience, and hence phenomenal nature, without the very same object as part of its subject matter. Although the intentional theorist will deny that the object is a constituent of the experience, that is not revealed by finding a situation in which the very same experience presents a different object, or none at all.

Note also that here I am rejecting McDowell's arguments, and not his resting place. Like McDowell, I think it plausible to claim that we conceive of our veridical perceptions as having among their constituents the objects and events we then perceive. It follows from this that we can have no experience of this kind when we hallucinate and no appropriate objects are present for us to perceive. Hence, if we can show that we have grounds for accepting this constitutive role of the objects of perception, intentionalism must be misguided.

What I have resisted here, though, is the claim that there is any simple move from the recognition that particular objects and events figure in the phenomenal nature of particular experiential episodes to the conclusion that they must thereby be constituents of the experience. The latter claim concerns the metaphysical status of experience and our modal and constitutive intuitions about experience. It is here that a Naïve Realist about experience and an intentionalist will disagree. I doubt that simple introspection of one's experience, unaided by further theorizing could reveal which view has a better grip on this issue.

To that extent, recognizing the particularity of perceptual experience should not thereby lead one simply to reject intentionalism. It should, however, make one reflect more about the general metaphysics of ascription of content to psychological states and the ways in which one can be lead to have genuinely singular thoughts or experiences.

5. The picture that we have drawn and re-modelled from Burge's account of demonstrative content is not the only form of object-independent account on offer. But is the appeal to the idea of experiences as particular episodes contrasting with experiences as kinds of event legitimate here? To pursue this question further it is useful to contrast the account elaborated above with Gareth Evans's sketch of the informational content of experiential states. Although Evans is associated with the idea of object-dependent content, in fact he only argues for the thesis with respect to conceptual states of mind, Russellian singular thoughts. He contrasts perceptual states and other states of what he calls 'the informational system' with conceptual judgments and beliefs. The way in which experiences come to be about or of individuals contrasts with the way in which our thoughts can be directed at an individual.

Evans first contrasts belief and experience so:

> In general, it seems to me preferable to take the notion of *being in an information state with such-and-such content* as a primitive notion for philosophy, rather than to attempt to characterize it in terms of belief... a fundamental (almost defining) property of the states of the informational system ... [is] their 'belief-independence'.[29]

For Evans, the informational system is in play in perception, memory and testimony. The information one acquires through perception or testimony and is preserved through memory or testimony underpins our ability to keep track of individuals and succeed in having conceptual thoughts about them.

One of the key elements of the picture, which Evans elaborates and later exploits in his accounts of demonstrative reference and of conniving uses of empty terms, is the manner in which an informational state can be of, or about, a given individual:

> We can speak of a certain bit of information being of, or perhaps from, an object, in a sense resembling the way in which we speak of a photograph being of an object...
> The sense in which a photograph is of an object is as follows. A certain mechanism produces things which have a certain informational *content*. I shall suppose for the moment that this content can be specified neutrally, by an open sentence in one or more variables...
>
> Red (x) & Ball (x) & Yellow (y) & Square (y) & On Top Of (x, y).
>
> ... Notice that I have explained the sense in which a photograph is of an object, or objects, without presupposing that a specification of its *content* must make reference to that object, or those objects. (op. cit., pp. 124–5.)

[29] (Evans 1982), p. 123.

Now this presentation has an obvious parallel with Burge's discussion of demonstrative reference in the appeal to the use of open sentences in specifying the content of the state in question. However, there are also a number of key differences. Perhaps the most obviously salient one is Evans's claim that this account holds for non-conceptual states of information and not for beliefs and judgments, whereas there is no such restriction on Burge's view. There are also other, metaphysical, differences which are germane to the discussion we have had above of the import of choosing a context-dependent construal of the correctness conditions for perceptual states. Briefly I will review one aspect of Evans's argument for non-conceptual content which has been neglected before focusing on the metaphysical issues about the relation between information and psychological states.

One of the ways in which Evans's views were novel was the introduction of the idea of a non-conceptual content to experience in particular, and informational states in general. Both the coherence of the idea of non-conceptual content and Evans's arguments for his own conception have been much discussed, yet there is a key motivation for it, presented in the passages we have been discussing which seems almost entirely to have been ignored or misunderstood.

Evans offers three main reasons for accepting the idea that there are non-conceptual states of mind. One concerns the similarities between us and creatures who lack the conceptual sophistication we have but yet seem capable of experiencing the world as we do—the idea of non-conceptual content is then intended to capture this similarity. The second concerns the way in which experience can present the world as being one way or another in a more fine-grained manner than we typically have concepts for. This we can think of as relating to the predicative aspect of the content of informational states, what Evans initially models in terms of open sentences. It is this ground which has caused the greatest amount of comment in discussions of non-conceptual content, since it has been attacked and defended in recent work by McDowell and Peacocke.[30]

The third, however, has been neglected and this relates to the non-predicative aspect of an informational state and how it relates to a particular object or event as its source. At the outset of sketching Evans's position I noted the appeal to belief-independence as a fundamental and significant mark of the difference between the

---

[30] See (McDowell 1994), (Peacocke 1998), (Peacocke 2001).

informational system and conceptual states such as belief and judgment. Some discussions of non-conceptual content have sought to use the idea of belief-independence as a ground for attributing non-conceptual content to experiential states.[31] However no appeal to the brute idea that one can disbelieve one's experiences and hence experience things to be a certain way without so believing them to be is at all plausible. This is for two reasons. First, there are plenty of belief-independent psychological states which we have no reason to think of as essentially non-conceptual. Take the case of preference: one may very well prefer that Manchester City should end up being top of the league in 2002 while remaining entirely agnostic about their chances of doing so. Such a preference would be belief-independent if any psychological state is, yet it is surely not a non-conceptual state, if there is to be any interesting contrast between conceptual and non-conceptual contentful psychological states. Indeed, at first blush, the mere fact that one can disbelieve one's senses reflects something about the attitude involved in experiencing, that it is not one of believing or simply accepting, rather than anything about the contents to which one takes that attitude.

Second, it would be a misreading of Evans to attribute to him the view that all informational states are exhaustively non-conceptual. He does, it is true, explicitly hold this view for perceptual informational states, but he clearly identifies episodes of testifying and hearing testimony as examples of the operation of the informational system. Such linguistic episodes plausibly have a conceptual content, when one indicates to someone that such and such is the case; and nothing in Evans's own discussions of testimony indicates that he thinks that the same grounds for the nonconceptual character of the predicative component of experiential states should carry over to the case of testimony. Furthermore, where we have genuine testimony exploiting a language, we certainly lack Evans's other general motivation for supposing states to be non-conceptual, namely that we can share them with non-language using non-human animals and human infants.

Taking these together suggests we need to find a more fine-grained appeal to belief-independence in Evans's thought, since it is clear from the passages quoted earlier that Evans does believe that there are grounds tracing to belief-independence for the non-conceptual nature of informational states. Where we need to look, I suggest, is in Evans's conception of how conceptual states can be properly singular and relate one to or be about a particular object.

[31] See (Crane 1992).

For example, in his discussion of communication and information, Evans puts forward the following claim:

> ... in order to understand [a Russellian] term, one must oneself believe that there is something to which the term refers. (This thesis is in fact implicit in my claim that such singular terms require information-based thoughts for their understanding, since, according to my explanation of the notion of information-based thoughts, such thoughts commit the subject to the existence of something as their object ...)[32]

The discussion which then ensues concerns the problems brought about for this claim by precisely considering cases of putative hallucination in which a subject disbelieves their experience and yet is able to exploit the information that it contains about its source—this being a potential counter-example to the claim that one does need to have the belief in question.

So I suggest that Evans means the following by belief-dependence. In relation to any conceptual psychological state, such a state can genuinely contain an object-dependent singular concept, or in Evans's terminology Idea, where the thinker believes that there is something which the concept picks out. When one prefers that Manchester City top the league in 2002, one may be agnostic about whether this really will be the case, but one cannot be agnostic about the existence of the football club if that is what one really prefers. This stands in stark contrast to what Evans called informational states. For these psychological phenomena (both experiences and cases of testimony) can be related to particular objects of events, that is, they can give one information relating to some particular object or event, and yet their occurrence is belief-independent in the sense just introduced: one *can* he in such a state (i.e. have an experience, or understand what someone has said) while lacking the requisite existential belief concerning the object the information is about. So, if informational states which are belief-independent in this sense are about, in some sense or other, particular objects or events, then they are directed on them, or about them in a non-conceptual manner. So the non-predicative aspect of informational states, according to Evans, is non-conceptual precisely for this reason.

If Evans's argument is sound, then this marks a significant difference between him and Burge: for Burge hopes to extend his account to all demonstrative thought, but Evans seems to give reason to restrict the account to those special cases where the

[32] (Evans 1982), pp. 326–7.

204

occurrence of the state is independent of the relevant existential belief. Whether this is a fundamental difference between the two approaches once we have modified Burge's position in the way indicated above is a moot point, though. For one might hold that demonstrative thought proper, in contrast to the corresponding experiential state, should allow of repeatability, the entertaining of the very same thought content on a different occasion. In the end, for both, perception may be a special case, even if for different reasons.

Moreover, it is questionable whether Evans's argument for non-conceptual content is sound; and for a reason that Dummett notes in his discussion of Evans on existence. Evans concedes in his discussion of make-believe that two thinkers who mistakenly take themselves to be hallucinating a little green man may actually succeed in referring to him within the scope of pretence when commenting on their joint hallucination:

> ... let us switch to the other version of the story, in which the subject and his companion are *mistaken* in believing that their senses deceive them—there *is* a little green man on the wall. It seems clear that a subject in this situation, thinking within the scope of the pretence in the way I have outlined, would actually be thinking of that little green man—entertaining various thoughts concerning him. In allowing his thoughts to be controlled by the information, he is in fact responding to the properties of the little green man.[33]

Dummett objects to this concession on Evans's part:

> Evans thus appears to be mistaken in claiming that the speakers engaging in make-believe discourse on the basis of what they take to be an illusion are referring to something actual if they are not in fact victims of any illusion; this claim is incompatible with his own principle making intention a necessary condition for reference.[34]

An alternative response here is to see Evans's reaction to his own example as a natural and plausible one, however it conflicts with the details of his overall theory. For, one might elaborate the point so. What matters in one's coming to refer to a given object is that one have a capacity for picking it out in thought or talk and that one can rationally exercise it. We cannot exploit such capacities in inten-

[33] (Evans 1982), p. 362.
[34] (Dummett 1992), p. 302.

tionally thinking about such objects without thereby taking the objects to exist, for one can only try to do what one thinks is possible, but if one believes there to be no object there one could not be referring to it if one was hallucinating. However, make-believe is a special case: one can employ actual abilities to refer in pursuit of purely make-believe ends. So one may exercise a genuine capacity to refer to an object even if one only make-believedly takes the object referred to to exist without really believing it to exist.

Yet in recognizing the plausibility of this position, Evans undermines one of the main claims for such states to be non-conceptual with respect to their referential component. For if one can say that a singular concept is present through one's possessing the capacity to refer to the object, then the particularity of experience could nevertheless be conceptual despite the belief-independence that Evans notes. Rather than marking the non-conceptual nature of the referential component of informational states, Evans's observations may rather reflect the passivity of such states. One does not come to have an experience with a particular content intentionally, so that one could not intentionally engage a referential capacity without intending to would not stand in the way of an experience exploiting that capacity coming about.

To force this move on Evans would be to press his account of reference at a fundamental point, for in highlighting the idea of our possessing referential capacities independent of our belief in the existence of what is picked out, one challenges Evans reliance on what he calls 'Russell's Principle', that to refer to an object one must know which thing it is. If we assume that such knowledge requires corresponding belief, one can know which object a given thing is only given that one believes that it exists. One can hardly think that the observations made above about make-believe can really settle the matter here. To make proper progress one needs to review the foundation of Evans's broader views about reference. For our purposes it suffices to point out that Evans's arguments are not decisive.

But let us turn to the other issue, that of the metaphysical status of information and informational states. Evans fleshes out his account of informational states and bits or pieces of information throughout chapter five, and sums up the view of information so:

> ... [this] introduces a use of the notion of the same (bit or piece of) information which deserves explanation, even though it is common. We want to be able to say that two informational states (states of different persons) embody the same information,

provided that they result from the same initial informational event..., even if they do not have the same *content:* the one may represent the same information as the other, but *garbled* in various ways. Conversely, and obviously, it is not sufficient, for two informational states to embody the same information, that they have the same content. When two states embody *the same information*, they are necessarily such that if the one is of an object *x*, then so is the other.[35]

This introduces a rather different conception of how psychological states relate to their contents from that we discussed above. Recall that in discussing object-dependent conceptual content of thoughts and experiences we noted a general methodological principle that there should be some notion of content, 'psychologically real' content, which plays an individuative role for thinkings. Once we have factored in the attitude taken by a subject towards a content, sameness and difference of kind of thinking are mirrored in sameness and difference of the thought content that the subject has an attitude towards. Parallel with this, the essential properties of such propositional attitudes is simply the attitude a subject has and the content towards which the subject has that attitude. For states of the informational system, Evans employs a three-fold distinction: there are states or episodes of individual thinkers which are the concreta of the system's operation—the having of an experience, the recalling of a past event, the telling of a story; there is the bit or piece of information which the state embodies; and there is the content of that bit of information. The first thing to emphasize is that for Evans informational states are not individuated by contents but rather by the bits of information that they carry; while bits or pieces of information are in turn not individuated by content.

What is the force of claiming that the content of a piece of information does not individuate it? What is Evans making us focus on when we think of content as neither necessary nor sufficient for the bit of information to be the same? One way of construing this is simply in terms of the metaphysics of content and psychological states we introduced with the methodological principles. Where a psychological state is individuated by its content, its having that content is a general attribute of it. We can make no sense of two psychological states being entirely alike in their general characteristics and yet differing in their content. In contrast, Evans wants to stress the intuitive force of the idea that one might have two pieces of information about distinct individuals, each of which

[35] (Evans 1982) (pp. 128–9).

characterizes the individuals in the same way while the pieces of information are different simply because each traces back to a distinct individual. Bits of information, then, are not to be construed as, so to speak, universals, but individuals. What marks one piece of information from another is a particular historical fact, where it originates, which cannot be read off from how things are qualitatively presented as being.

At the same time, even if pieces of information are individuals, they are not particulars. For the same piece of information can be present in the minds of different subjects at the very same time, for example when we both witness a scene from the same point of view, or you pass on your titbit of gossip to me. Moreover the same piece of information can be present in different psychological states of an individual at different times. The same piece of information can be embodied in my current perceptual experience of a rubber duck before me, and in my experiential recall of the scene some days hence. So pieces of information are neither uniquely located at one time as concrete individuals are, nor are they unrepeatable at different times, as particular events are.

If we stick at the level of content then there is an obvious similarity between Evans's approach and Burge's (*modulo* the issue of content being non-conceptual). For in both cases the content is specified by using an open sentence, and hence is contrasted with a purely existential content.[36] But for Burge the content is individuative of the episode of thinking, and he claims as noted above, that it is inessential to a token demonstrative thought that it should be *de re*. Evans takes the content neither to be individuative of the state nor of the piece of information it conveys. Rather pieces of information are individuated by their source, so it is essential to a piece of information that it come from the source that it does.

Though pieces of information are essentially tied to their sources, this does not lead Evans to deny that a piece of (mis)information can be present in a case of hallucination. Necessarily such information will not be sourced in any object, even any merely possible object, but since the content of a piece of information can be akin to a mere open sentence, the lack of an appropriate object does not show that the piece of information could not exist. So to this extent as well, Evans, like Burge, allows for object-independent informational states.

[36] Though in fact, Evans does allow for informational states to have a purely existential content and yet to be sourced in an object, at least in the case of testimony, see pp. 127–8.

As I indicated above, Burge's attitude to the modal independence of a token experience from its object is not essential to his view; and we have already seen reason to reject it. An intentionalist can quite consistently accept both claim that the object of an experience has no constitutive role within it and the claim that the experience itself could only have occurred in the given context in which it happens. In that case, one will happily allow that an experience of just the same kind could occur in a case of hallucination, but yet deny of the very token experience one enjoys when perceiving that it could have occurred in another context. There would still be a difference between this position and Evans's, but the difference is more subtle and suggestive than a simple one about trading modal intuitions about object dependence or independence of information.

Evans's idea of a piece of information is something that can recur in different psychological states and which has a definite history: two psychological states can both embody the same piece of information only if they are causally connected in the right way. For this reason alone, we cannot conceive of Evans's pieces of information on the model I suggested earlier for the particular phenomenal nature of a perceptual episode. In that discussion I exploited the idea of there being an unrepeatable aspect of an experiential episode which could be determined by a context-limited aspect of the intentional content. But for Evans, the piece of information must be repeatable across psychological states of different individuals and those of the same individual at different times. So the aspect in which we explain its particularity must be consistent with this repeatability. Here we have the key difference between the picture of experiential content elaborated above and Evans's account in terms of information and information states.

Having isolated the difference, the question to raise now is which picture the intentionalist should really prefer. There is not enough space here to assess properly how successful Evans's alternative picture is. Perhaps two comments might suffice. The first is that Evans is clearly tapping in to intuitions that we have about how information, in some broad construal, can come to be disseminated across a population of thinkers, and preserved within the mind of one thinker. It is another thing to claim, though, that the intuitions can together be used to develop a useful theory of information. That theory would not only require us to have some conception of what the right causal connections ought to be across thinkers and within a thinker for the information to be preserved, but also to make work for the idea of the very same piece of information being transmitted, rather than simply appealing to the causal connections between each of the states in the system and the initial event which is the source.

Secondly, in the view articulated here much weight has been placed on the idea that perceptual experiences are particular, unrepeatable events. This opens room for the idea that there is an aspect of the phenomenology of such events, their particular phenomenal nature as we might say, which we ignore when we discuss their qualitative character as something they could share with other experiential events, events of the same phenomenological kind. The contrast between the particular phenomenal nature of an experience and its kind, I then suggested, can be modelled by an intentional theorist in terms of the context-dependent correctness conditions on the one hand and the context-invariant content that all experiences of that phenomenal kind will share on the other. However, following Evans, we may question whether there really can be a useful notion of the phenomenal nature of a particular experience which is unrepeatable in this way. For, in his discussion of the informational system, Evans stresses the idea that a perceptual experience and a later memory experience can present the very same piece of information to a subject to be exploited in thought. Whatever it is about the perceptual experience which makes it the presentation of the very objects or events it is the perception of, that same feature is to be found in a later memory of those objects and events. As I have stressed above, it is the need for this common element between the experience and the memory which leads to Evans's modification of the connection between psychological state and what individuates it. Instead of using content to individuate informational states, we have the appeal to pieces of information which are not themselves purely contents. But is Evans right to suppose that the way in which both perception and memory relate to the same particular event requires that we have a notion of content or information which is repeated between the distinct episodes?

It certainly is plausible that our memory experiences can in some way preserve our abilities to refer to particular objects which we have perceived earlier.[37] So it would be objectionable if a theory cannot accommodate in the right way our intuitions about how these connect. In sketching how the picture of the informational system captures the intuition, Evans uses the model of a photograph, where we have the intuition that two indistinguishable photographs may

[37] Evans himself suggests that there are restrictions on how the information in memory can be exploited for past reference, see the discussion of Russell's Principle and the Photograph Model in Chapter Four of *The Varieties of Reference*.

yet be of different scenes, having been caused by exposure to different events. At the same time, we think that copies of either photograph can be made by appropriate causal processes from one print to another. This is what is to give us the picture of how a memory may derive its content from a previous perception. As Evans wishes to stress, 'memory and testimony are ... *recursive* elements of [the informational system] structure' (p. 127). While it is highly intuitive that the way in which an experiential memory relates one to a past event is in some way dependent on a past experience of that event—what has been called the Previous Awareness Condition for personal memory—it is equally intuitive that such a derivativeness is, in some sense or other, internal to the phenomenological content of the memory. Remembering is not phenomenologically the same as first perceiving some object or event, rather the object or event is presented as being in one's own past, in one's own experienced past. This aspect of derivativeness, or recursiveness, is not really captured by Evans's notion of a piece of information embodied by an informational state. For in this sense, both the perception and the memory will embody the very same piece of information, just as a copy of a photograph can look entirely like the original if reproduced accurately enough.

If this is right then what the memory of an event needs to do is to represent something which is unrepeatable and particular about the original perceiving from which the memory derives. So we should want an account of how the particularity of experiential memory is secured which exploits a different account of how the particularity of the initial perceptual experience is secured. Since Evans account of information seems to offer us a uniform account of this for both experience and memory, that account is flawed, and in itself gives us no reason to reject the Burgean-type model offered here.

That suggests that the parallel between episodic memory content and perceptual content does not in the end give sufficient reason to prefer Evans's approach over the one elaborated here. We should after all hold on to the idea that the way in which a perceptual experience connects us to some particular individual or unrepeatable event involving that individual is peculiar to the perception itself and not replicated as such in the memory of that experience.

But the problem for Evans's view of the parallel between remembering and perceiving does not just raise a problem for his approach. Even if the intentionalist does not seek to explain the particularity of episodic memory in terms of the repeated content from the prior perceptual experience, he or she still needs to give some account of the relation between these two states. Elsewhere I suggest that there is indeed a more general problem here for intentionalism.[38]

Despite Evans being the focus of discussion of object-dependent thoughts, his conception of the informational system offers us an example of how perceptual experiences can be object-independent states (though the basis of object-dependent perceptual demonstrative judgments). The picture that he offers is an alternative to the Burgean account we have been presenting. However, I have offered a couple of reasons for resisting the Evans approach, although nothing that is decisive in itself. Both approaches seek to do justice to the particularity of the phenomenology of perception without thereby making the psychological episodes object involving. So the initial worry can be resisted by an intentional theorist. Nonetheless, the deeper worry with Evans's account I have finished with may turn out to present a more serious problem for an intentional theory. That is a topic for further discussion elsewhere. The more general morals to draw relate to questions about the conditions for having the same kind of psychological state or event again, and the question of how that relates to our ascription of the same or different intentional contents to a psychological state. We need to a get a proper overview of the way in which mental states do and do not replicate aspects of others and how that leads us to attribute the same or different contents to them.[39]

University College London

Bibliography

Blackburn, Simon. 1984. *Spreading the Word*. Oxford: Clarendon Press.
Burge, Tyler. 1973. 'Truth and Singular Terms', *Journal of Philosophy*.
Burge, Tyler. 1977. 'Belief *De Re*', *Journal of Philosophy*, 338–62.
Burge, Tyler. 1983. 'Russell's Problem & Intentional Identity', In *Agent,*

[38] For a more detailed discussion of this see my (Martin 2001) and (Martin 2002).

[39] Earlier versions of this material were presented at seminars at the University of Glasgow, the University of Sussex, the Autonomous University of Barcelona, Inter University Centre Dubrovnik, University College London, Princeton University and the Royal Institute of Philosophy. I am grateful to those audiences for discussion and in particular to Kent Bach, John Campbell, Naomi Eilan, Josep Macia, Susanna Siegel, Matt Soteriou, Scott Sturgeon, for discussion and Charles Travis for extended discussion of these themes and very detailed comments on an earlier draft.

Language & the Structure of the World, edited by J. Tomberlin. Indianapolis: Hackett Publishing Co.

Burge, T. 1986. 'Cartesian Error and the Objectivity of Perception', In *Subject, Thought & Context,* edited by P. Pettit and J. McDowell. Oxford: Clarendon Press.

Burge, T. 1993. 'Vision and Intentional Content'. In *Colin Searle and his Critics,* edited by R. v. Guhck and E. LePore. Oxford: Basil Blackwell.

Campbell, John. 1997. 'Sense, Reference and Selective Attention', *Proceedings of the Aristotelian Society, Supplementary Volume 97.*

Carruthers, Peter. 1987. 'Russellian Thoughts', *Mind,* Vol. 96, No. 381, 18–35.

Crane, Tim. 1992. 'The Nonconceptual Content of Experience', In *The Contents of Experience,* edited by T. Crane. Cambridge: Cambridge University Press.

Davies, M. 1992. 'Perceptual Content and Local Supervenience', *Proceedings of the Aristotelian Society XCII,* 21–45.

Dummett, Michael. 1992. 'Existence', In *The Seas of Language.* Oxford: Clarendon Press.

Evans, G. 1982. *The Varieties of Reference.* Edited by J. McDowell. Oxford: Clarendon Press.

Frege, Gottlob. 1977. 'Thoughts', In *Logical Investigations.* Oxford: Basil Blackwell.

Grice, H. P. 1961. 'The Causal Theory of Perception', *Aristotelian Society* Supplementary Volume XXXV.

Harman, G. 1990. 'The Intrinsic Quality of Experience', In *Philosophical Perspectives 4,* edited by J. Tomberlin: Ridgeview Publishing Co.

Martin, M. G. F. 1997. 'The Reality of Appearances', In *Thought and Ontology,* edited by M. Sainsbury. Milan: FrancoAngeli.

Martin, M. G. F. 1998. 'Setting Things Before the Mind', In *Current Issues in Philosophy of Mind,* edited by A. O'Hear. Cambridge: Cambridge University Press.

Martin, M. G. F. 2001. 'Out of the Past: Episodic Memory as Retained Acquaintance', In *Time and Memory,* edited by C. Hoerl and T. McCormack. Oxford: Clarendon Press.

Martin, M. G. F. 2002. 'The Transparency of Experience', *Mind & Language,* 17.

McDowell, John. 1982. 'Truth-Value Gaps', In *Logic, Methodology and Philosophy of Science VI: Proceedings of the Sixth International Congress of Logic, Methodology, and Philosophy of Science,* Hannover, 1979, edited by L. J. C. et. al. New York: NorthHolland Publishing Co. Reprinted *Mind, Thought & World*

McDowell, John. 1984. *De Re Senses. Philosophical Quarterly.*

McDowell, John. 1986. 'Singular Thought and the Extent of Inner Space', In *Subject, Thought and Context,* edited by P. Pettit and J. McDowell. Oxford: Clarendon Press.

McDowell, J. 1994. *Mind and World.* Cambridge, MA: Harvard University Press.

M. G. F. Martin

McGinn, C. 1982a. *The Character of Mind*. Oxford: Oxford University Press.

McGinn, Colin. 1982b. 'The Structure of Content', In *Thought and Object*, edited by A. Woodfield. Oxford: Clarendon Press.

Moore, G. E. 1922. Some Judgments of Perception. In *Philosophical Studies*. London: Routledge & Kegan Paul.

Noonan, H. M. 1993. 'Object-Dependent Thoughts: A Case of Superficial Necessity But Deep Contingency', in *Mental Causation*, (eds) John Heil and Alfred Mele. Oxford: Clarendon Press.

Peacocke, C. A. B. 1992. *A Study of Concepts*. Cambridge MA: MIT Press.

Peacocke, C. A. B. 1998. 'Non Conceptual Content Defended', *Philosophy and Phenomenological Research* LVIII, 381–8.

Peacocke, C. A. B. 2001. 'Does Perception Have a Nonceptual Content?', *Journal of Philosophy* 98, 239–64.

Perry, John. 1993. *The Essential Indexical and other Essays*. New York: Oxford University Press.

Searle, John. 1983. *Intentionality*, Cambridge: Cambridge University Press.

Segal, Gabriel. 1989. 'The Return of the Individual', *Mind,* Vol. 98, No. 389, 39–57.

Snowdon, P. F. 1990. 'Perception and its Objects', *Proceedings of the Aristotelian Society, supplementary vol.*

Soteriou, Matthew. 2000. 'The Particularity of Experience', *European Journal of Philosophy.*

Strawson, P. F. 1959. *Individuals*. London: Methuen.

Travis, Charles. 1994. 'On Constraints of Generality', *pas* XCIV, 165–88.

Travis, Charles. 1998. Pragmatics. In *A Companion to Philosophy of Language,* edited by C. Wright and R. Hale. Oxford: Basil Blackwell.

Tye, Michael. 1984. 'The Adverbial Approach to Visual Experience', *Philosophical Review* XCIII (April), 195–225.

Tye, Michael. 1995. *Ten Problems about Consciousness*. Cambridge, MA: MIT Press.

Conditional Belief and the Ramsey Test*

SCOTT STURGEON

1. The Issue

Consider the frame

S believes that —.

Fill it with a conditional, say

If you eat an Apple, you'll drink a Coke.

What makes the result true? More generally, what facts are marked by instances of

S believes (A→C)?

In a sense the answer is obvious: *beliefs* are so marked. Yet that bromide leads directly to competing schools of thought. And the reason is simple.

Common-sense thinks of belief two ways. Sometimes it sees it as a three-part affair. When so viewed either you believe, disbelieve, or suspend judgment. This take on belief is *coarse-grained*. It says belief has three flavours: acceptance, rejection, neither. But it's not the only way common-sense thinks of belief. Sometimes it's more subtle: 'How strong is your faith?' can be apposite between believers. That signals an important fact. Ordinary practice also treats belief as a fine-grained affair. It speaks of levels of confidence. It admits *degrees of belief*. It contains a fine-grained take as well. There are two ways belief is seen in everyday life. One is coarse-grained. The other is fine-grained.

Both are used in formal treatments of reason. When belief is viewed in the coarse-grained way, an overall epistemic state is modelled by a *set of sentences*. It's said to codify what one accepts. Reason is then modelled by constraints on such sets and shifts

* Public Lecture given to the Royal Institute of Philosophy. Thanks to Dorothy Edgington for getting me interested in conditionals and teaching me so much about them. Thanks also to Anna Mahtani, Mike Martin, David Papineau and Maja Spener for helpful discussion. Technical Facts are discussed in the appendix.

between them. When belief is viewed in the fine-grained way, an overall epistemic state is modelled by a *probability function*. It's said to measure how much one accepts. Reason is then modelled by constraints on such functions and shifts between them. This Janus-faced approach spills over to the belief-in-conditional schema. We face two questions: what are its truth-makers when belief is viewed in the coarse-grained way? what are they when belief is viewed in the fine-grained way?

The most influential remark on this comes in a footnote. Frank Ramsey wrote:

> 'If two people are arguing "If p will q?" and are both in doubt as to p, they are adding p hypothetically to their stock of knowledge and are arguing on that basis about q.' (1929: 143)

Both coarse- and fine-grained epistemology take inspiration from this passage. Both find in it a 'Ramsey Test' for conditionals. Such a Test is used to say when one believes a conditional. In making theirs precise, however, each school of thought is hit with a technical Bombshell. Peter Gärdenfors used one Ramsey Test to derive absurdity within coarse-grained epistemology.[1] David Lewis used another to do so within fine-grained epistemology.[2] This makes one wonder: why do such Tests lead to trouble? Why do they generate conflict within precision epistemology? My question is this: what is the underlying assumption about conditionals, if any, which leads to Gärdenfors' result when Ramsey is read in the coarse-grained way and Lewis' result when he's read in the fine-grained way? That is my question. Now for its background.

2. The coarse-grained Bombshell

Suppose we model belief with sentences. We see an overall epistemic state as a set of them. We see it as a *theory* in the technical sense. Within such a framework, the Ramsey Test is said to be this:

$(A \rightarrow C)$ belongs to an agent's theory T iff C belongs to the minimal revision of T induced by the addition of A.

The basic idea is that a rational agent accepts $(A \rightarrow C)$ when C belongs to the minimal disturbance of her view brought on by A.

[1] 'Belief Revision and the Ramsey Test for Conditionals', *The Philosophical Review* (1986).
[2] 'Probabilities of Conditionals and Conditional Probabilities', *The Philosophical Review* (1976).

This is not only a coarse-grained take on Ramsey, it's a *belief-revision* take. It spells out his idea with that of a 'minimal revision'.

Let **min-rev** be a function which so revises belief. The coarse-grained Ramsey Test is then

(RT) (A→C) belongs to an agent's theory T iff C belongs to **min-rev**(T by A).

It's unclear what **min-rev** comes to. But we need just two assumptions about it to set off Gärdenfors' Bombshell. One is a principle of Contradiction Avoidance. It says

(CA) If an agent's theory T is self-consistent, and her input I is too, then so is **min-rev**(T by I).

The other is a principle of Epistemic Conservatism. It says

(EC) If an agent's theory T contains Ø, and her input I doesn't conflict with Ø, then **min-rev**(T by I) contains Ø.

The first principle aims at the idea that rational agents do not endorse contradictions unless forced to do so. The second aims at the idea that such agents do not throw out information unless prompted to do so. Both thoughts look good at first blush.

Yet with these resources Peter Gärdenfors dropped a Bombshell on the coarse-grained belief community. Through a complex derivation he showed their Ramsey Test, Contradiction Avoidance and Epistemic Conservatism lead to absurdity. In particular, he showed they generate contradictory predictions about belief revision. But he did not diagnose why. We'll do so in §4.

3. The fine-grained Bombshell

Suppose we model belief with probability functions. We see an overall epistemic state as measured by one. Within such a framework, the fine-grained Ramsey Test says that when $\mathbf{P}(A)$ is non-zero:

(ℜ𝔖) $\mathbf{P}(A{\to}C) = \mathbf{P}(C/A)$.

The basic idea is that a rational agent accepts (A→C) to the degree she has confidence in C on the supposition that A. In other words, credence in the conditional equals conditional credence. This is a fine-grained take on Ramsey. And it joins with a framework to yield *another* internal link between conditional belief and belief revision. But this takes some explaining.

Scott Sturgeon

The fine-grained epistemology used by Lewis says one should update credence in C after learning A by **Conditionalization** (C). And it runs that process off the right-hand side of (ℜℑ). The resulting picture agrees with the coarse-grained model: one's take on (A→C) aligns with belief revision. Specifically, it aligns with how one should view C after learning A. The main difference is the rule of revision. Whereas Gärdenfors' model uses **min-rev**, Lewis' uses Conditionalization.

There's a pictorial way to understand the latter. It proves useful in diagnosing Lewis' Bombshell. We'll work with it throughout. To begin, suppose you've got a marble for each 'percent of credence' you have to lend; and you distribute them like this:

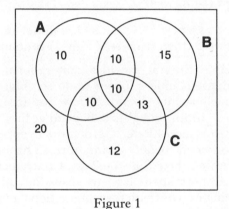

Figure 1

Think of the box as logical space, its points as possible worlds. Circles collect worlds at which propositions are true. They partition the space into mutually exclusive and jointly exhaustive cells (which correspond, of course, to lines in a three letter truth-table). Numerals within each cell show your spread of credence. They indicate, amongst other things, that you see four ways A might be true: with B and C, with neither, and with just one of them. They also show that within A-worlds you see only symmetry:

$$P(A\&B\&C)=P(A\&\neg B\&\neg C)=P(A\&B\&\neg C)=P(A\&\neg B\&C)=10\%$$

You're 40% sure A will happen, 60% sure it won't.

Now suppose you learn A. Conditionalization says in becoming certain that A you must preserve credal structure within it. Intuitively, you must scoop-up credence lent to ¬A, distribute it within A, and preserve credal symmetry on show. The easiest way to picture this is to lop off the non-A bit of Figure 1 and reinterpret the marbles. In other words: zoom in on the A-bit:

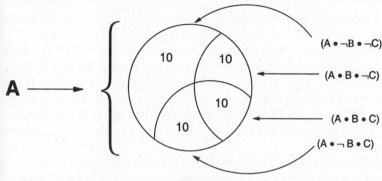

Figure 2

Now we have 40 marbles in our model. Each represents 1/40th of your revised credence. Note it preserves symmetry within A. Your old credence lent equal weight to four ways A might be true. Your new credence does so as well. It says

$$P_A(A\&B\&C)=P_A(A\&\neg B\&\neg C)=P_A(A\&B\&\neg C)=P_A(A\&\neg B\&C)=25\%.$$

Pictorially, then, Conditionalization is a 'zoom in' rule of belief revision. It takes a credence distribution as input and yields another as output. That output is focused on one of the original distribution's cells. It's got by zooming in on a cell corresponding to what is learned. Conditionalizing on A is the minimal way to become certain that A without disrupting prior-to-learning credal structure within it.

Thus it is that this fine-grained epistemology has a belief-revision take on Ramsey. It marks one's view of $(A{\to}C)$ by one's view of C after zooming in on A. With these resources David Lewis dropped a Bombshell on the fine-grained belief community. Through a complex derivation he showed their Ramsey Test and updating rule lead to absurdity. In particular, he showed they're consistent only if credence is utterly trivial (in a way to be glossed). But he did not diagnose why. We'll do so in §5. Before that we locate the coarse-grained difficulty.

4. Diagnosing Gärdenfors' Bombshell

The key to this explosion is a technical property of belief revision. We can unearth it by considering two arguments:

(A)	(B)
1a *All* Texans have an accent	1b *Most* Texans have an accent.
2 Fred's a Texan.	2 Fred's a Texan.
C ∴ Fred has an accent.	C ∴ Fred has an accent.

The arguments share a conclusion. And they both support it. But they do so in different ways. The premises of (A) link to C in an 'unbreakable' way. Those of (B) do not. You can revise the latter with new information, add nothing which makes for conflict, yet break the link to C. That would happen, for instance, were you to learn that Fred was not raised in Texas. Although (B)'s premises support C, they allow for consistent revision to wipe out the support. (A)'s premises don't. They support C no matter how they're embellished.

Think of it this way. Suppose you build a column of claims. First you list a set of claims S. Then you draw a line. Under it you list S's deductive consequences D(S). Next you build a new column just to the right. This time you start with S plus a new claim N. Then you draw a line. Under it you list (S+N)'s deductive consequences. Since (S+N) contains S, you're guaranteed D(S+N) contains D(S). You're guaranteed everything below your first line appears below your second.

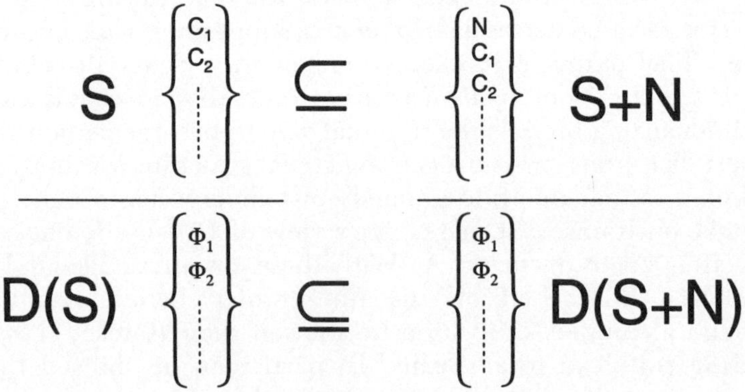

Figure 3

Induction isn't like that. Start a column with S. Draw a line and list what's inductively supported by S. Start a new column with (S+N). There'll be no guarantee I(S+N) contains I(S). There'll be no guarantee what's below your first line appears below your second.

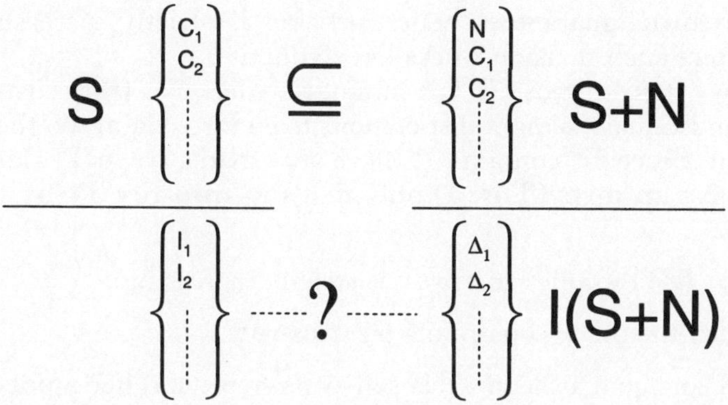

$$S \left\{ \begin{matrix} C_1 \\ C_2 \\ \vdots \end{matrix} \right\} \subseteq \left\{ \begin{matrix} N \\ C_1 \\ C_2 \\ \vdots \end{matrix} \right\} S+N$$

$$\left\{ \begin{matrix} I_1 \\ I_2 \\ \vdots \end{matrix} \right\} \text{----?----} \left\{ \begin{matrix} \Delta_1 \\ \Delta_2 \\ \vdots \end{matrix} \right\} I(S+N)$$

Figure 4

This is a basic difference between induction and deduction. It proves the key to Gärdenfors' Bombshell. Let's say

A revision rule **R** is *strictly increasing* $=_{df.}$ when theory T is contained in theory T*, **R**(T by I) is contained in **R**(T* by I).

In other words, **R** is strictly increasing when its picture looks thus:

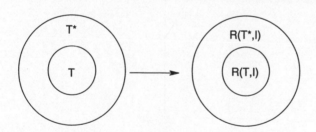

Figure 5

Deduction is strictly increasing. Induction is not.
  Recall the coarse-grained Ramsey Test:

(RT) (A→C) belongs to an agent's theory T iff C belongs to **min-rev**(T by A).

It says, in effect, that a rational agent is disposed to infer C upon learning A exactly when her theory *marks* the disposition. More specifically, it says a rational agent is so disposed when her theory marks the disposition with (A→C). That's tantamount to the idea that such dispositions are *part* of her overall epistemic state. And *that*, in turn, guarantees belief revision is strictly increasing. It guarantees such revision works like deduction.

To see this, suppose T is contained within T*. **(RT)** ensures T uses conditionals to mark dispositions to endorse claims on the basis of input. Since T* contains T, those very marks are in T*. Hence a claim is in **min-rev**(T by I) only if it's in **min-rev**(T* by I). We have

Fact 1: **(RT)** implies **min-rev** is strictly increasing.

But recall the other constraints on **min-rev**:

(CA) If an agent's theory T is self-consistent, and her input I is too, then so is **min-rev**(T by I).

(EC) If an agent's theory T contains Ø, and her input I doesn't conflict with Ø, then **min-rev**(T by I) contains Ø.

They imply **min-rev** is *not* strictly increasing. They imply **min-rev** works like induction. That's why putting them with **(RT)** sets off an explosion.

To see this, suppose three guys are walking down a road. They come to a three-way fork:

Figure 6

Leftie thinks 'Either we're going left or down the middle'. Rightie thinks 'Either we're going right or down the middle'. Middleman thinks 'We're going down the middle'. These guys are boring. That's all they think. Their theories consist in such thoughts and their consequences. Note each has a consistent view. Note also Middleman's *contains* Leftie's and Rightie's. For his logically implies theirs. But consider what happens when Oracle says Middleman is wrong. How should our heroes update?

Well, the new information is internally consistent. And all three began with consistent views. Hence Contradiction Avoidance says their views must remain consistent after taking on board that Middleman is wrong. Yet the new information is compatible with both Leftie's and Rightie's initial view. Hence Epistemic Conservatism ensures they add it to their stock of belief. Logic then leads them in opposite directions (as it were). Leftie thinks 'We're going left'. Rightie rejects that. Since Middleman must be consistent after revision, his revised view *cannot* contain both of his cohorts's. Although he began with a view which did so, after revision he can no longer hold a consistent view which contains Leftie's and Rightie's. Thus we have

Fact 2: (CA)&(EC) imply **min-rev** is *not* strictly increasing.

Gärdenfors' Bombshell has a simple source: Contradiction Avoidance, Epistemic Conservatism and the coarse-grained Ramsey Test place *inconsistent demands* on belief revision. The first two jointly force it to contract as well as expand. The last forbids contraction. The result is contradiction. That's why the model generates conflicting predictions about belief revision.

5. Diagnosing Lewis' Bombshell

The key to this explosion is Conditionalization. Recall it's a zoom in rule of belief revision. Suppose you start with this distribution of credence:

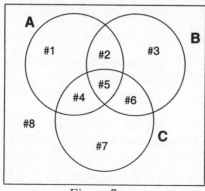

Figure 7

Scott Sturgeon

Conditionalizing on A amounts to zooming in on A without disrupting credal structure within it. Conditionalizing on B amounts to zooming in on B without disrupting credal structure within it. And so forth. This means Conditionalizing on A *and then* Conditionalizing on B yields the same thing as Conditionalizing *once* on (A&B). After all: zooming in on A and then zooming in on B yields the same thing as zooming in once on (A&B). Pictorially put: lopping off the non-A bit of Figure 7 and then lopping off the non-B bit of the result yields the same thing as lopping of the non-(A&B) bit of the original Figure. Either way you get

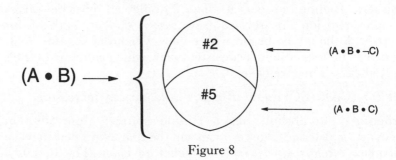

Figure 8

This is a key fact about Conditionalization. Running the process twice over equals doing so once on a conjunction.

But recall the fine-grained Ramsey Test. When **P**(A) is non-zero:

(ℜ𝔍) P(A→C) = **P**(C/A).

It says, in effect, that (A→C) *marks within* **P** the view of C taken after learning A. This is because **(ℜ𝔍)**'s right-hand side *is* that view. It's the view of C had by Conditionalizing **P** on A. Yet we've just seen two Conditionalizations equal one on a conjunction. This means **(ℜ𝔍)**&(C) imply that when **P**(A&B) is non-zero:

Fact 3:   **P**[A→(B→C)] = **P**[(A&B)→C].

This is a probabilistic analogue of a widely discussed rule. It echoes the so-called Import-Export law:

[A→(B→C)] ⇔ [(A&B)→C].

Alan Gibbard has shown this rule implies → has material truth conditions if any.[3] His argument can be mimicked to show Fact 3 implies

[3] 'Two recent theories of conditionals', in *Ifs*, edited by Harper *et al.*, Reidel (1980).

Fact 4: $P(A \rightarrow C) = P(A \supset C)$.

In light of **($\mathfrak{R3}$)** this means

$$P(C/A) = P(A \supset C).$$

But it's a fact about probability that whenever $P(C/A)$ equals $P(A \supset C)$ either

(i) $P(A) = 1$

or

(ii) $P(A \& \neg C) = 0$.

This means **P** fails to spread across regions like

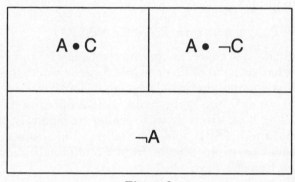

Figure 9

After all, if it did neither (i) nor (ii) would hold. Lending credence to $\neg A$ would violate (i). Lending credence to $(A \& \neg C)$ would violate (ii). In a nutshell, then, **P** fails to spread across more than two disjoint cells built from A and C. Yet A and C were chosen at random. Hence we have

Fact 5:   **($\mathfrak{R3}$)**&(C) imply that **P** carves possibility into less than three disjoint cells.

We can now explain Lewis's initial 'triviality results'. The fine-grained Ramsey Test plus Conditionalization entail probabilistic Import/Export (Fact 3). This ensures conditional probability aligns with probability of material truth-conditions. The only way *that* can happen, however, is if credences spread across less than three disjoint cells. That's why **($\mathfrak{R3}$)** and (C) jointly lead to absurdity. That's why they imply credence is trivial.

Scott Sturgeon

6. The rumpus

Here's what we've seen. Two precision epistemologies latch onto Ramsey's footnote. They use it to forge an internal link between conditional belief and belief revision. They run into trouble by doing so.

This suggests there's no such link. It suggests conditional belief and belief revision are independent. It doesn't *prove* as much, of course. But it burdens those who think otherwise. It obliges them to source Bombshells without fingering the link between conditional belief and belief revision. This holds for Ramsey Test loyalists in coarse- and fine-grained epistemology. To this point there's symmetry.

But it stops here. Recall both Tests:

(RT) (A→C) belongs to an agent's theory T iff C belongs to **min-rev**(T by A).

(ℜℑ) When **P**(A) is non-zero: **P**(A→C) = **P**(C/A).

(RT)'s left-hand side concerns conditional belief. Its right-hand side concerns belief revision. The principle forges a direct link between the two. **(ℜℑ)** does not do that. Although its left-hand side concerns conditional belief, its right-hand side concerns conditional credence. The link from that to belief revision is forged by Conditionalization. **(ℜℑ)** yields an indirect link from conditional belief to belief revision. It's got from Conditionalization plus the fine-grained Ramsey Test.

When hit with Bombshells, therefore, Ramsey Test loyalists enjoy different lines of defence. Coarse-grained loyalists must defend a belief revision take on Ramsey. That is the hallmark of their view. Fine-grained loyalists needn't do so. They can reject an internal link between conditional belief and belief revision. They're not forced to do so, of course; but they can if they choose. Fine-grained loyalists need only defend an internal link between conditional belief and conditional credence. That is the hallmark of their view. When dodging Bombshells they have more wriggle room than their coarse-grained cousins.

Needless to say, escape routes have been investigated in both schools of thought; and a great deal of work has gone into it.[4]

---

[4] Within coarse-grained epistemology see Sven Hansson's *A Textbook of Belief Dynamics,* Kluwer Academic Publishers (1999) and its references. Within fine-grained epistemology see Alan Hájek and Ned Hall's 'The Hypothesis of the Conditional Construal of Conditional Probability' and its references, in *Probability and Conditionals,* edited by Ellery Eells and Brian Skyrms, Cambridge University Press (1994).

226

Assumptions have been exposed. Their denial has been costed. Lots of moves are now known. Some preserve an internal link between conditional belief and belief revision. Others do not. Yet durable reactions have one thing in common. In one way or another they all treat conditionals *as factually-defective discourse*.[5] They all say conditionals do not target the world, do not report how it is. And this, I submit, is the true price of loyalty to Ramsey. It has no direct bearing on conditional belief and belief revision. It turns on whether conditional belief is factual. I close by glossing the view it is not.

7. Non-Factualism.

Factualists about conditionals say those sentences express propositions. In particular they say conditionals express propositions which link other propositions. Let

L = the proposition that *L*ewis didn't kill Leibniz,

and

S = the proposition that *S*omeone else did.

Suppose L and S are associated with the antecedent and consequent of

(*) If Lewis didn't kill Leibniz, someone else did.

Factualists then say (*) expresses a proposition of the form CON(L,S). More generally they say conditionals are factually-effective discourse. On their view, producing a conditional is like producing an unconditional. It puts forward a proposition as true. It results in propositional assertion. It marks acceptance by a believer of a thing accepted.

Non-Factualists reject this picture. They deny conditionals express propositions. They say conditionals are factually-defective discourse. On their view, producing a conditional is not like producing an unconditional. It does not put forward a proposition as true. It does not result in propositional assertion. It does not mark acceptance by a believer and a thing accepted. Rather, conditionals mark *sui generis* types of thought and speech, irreducibly conditional types of thought and speech.

[5] A phrase drawn from Hartry Field's 'Disquotational Truth and Factually Defective Discourse', *The Philosophical Review* (1994).

The difference is marked by a question: *where* is conditionality within practice? Factualists find it in one place. Non-Factualists find it elsewhere. To wit:

- Factualists say believing (A→C) is a relation of acceptance which holds between a believer and a thing accepted. Non-Factualists say it's a relation of conditional acceptance which holds between a believer, A and C. The former deal with belief by invoking one type of belief-like attitude— acceptance—and two types of content-conditional and unconditional. The latter do so by invoking two types of belief-like attitude—acceptance and conditional acceptance— and one type of content— unconditional.

- Factualists say asserting (A→C) is a relation of putting forward which holds between an assertor and a thing asserted. Non-Factualists say it's a relation of conditionally putting forward which holds between an assertor, A and C. The former deal with assertion by invoking one type of assertion-like act—putting forward—and two types of content—conditional and unconditional. The latter do so by invoking two types of assertion-like act—putting forward and conditionally doing so—and one type of content—unconditional.

And so forth. In a nutshell: non-Factualists reject the view that conditionality is found within contents of thought, speech and action. They see it within acts of conditional-thought, -speech and -action. Rather than see conditionality within objects which *are* contents, non-Factualists see it within acts which *have* content. That is the hallmark of their view. And if they're right, of course, conditionals won't behave like factual discourse. They won't have truth-conditions. Nor will they embed like sentences that do. Conditionals will behave like durable reactions to Bombshells say they do. They'll behave like factually-defective discourse.

Recall the frame with which we began:

S believes that —.

Bombshells force Ramsey Test loyalists to say conditionals are factually defective. Yet those very sentences slot into the frame to yield truth. It follows their view must be the frame is ambiguous: when truths are got from it by filling the blank with unconditional sentences, those truths build from a relation of acceptance which holds between S and a proposition; and when truths are got from it by filling the blank with conditional sentences, they build from a relation of conditional acceptance which holds between S and two propositions. Ramsey Test loyalists must say "belief" is ambiguous. Sometimes it stands for acceptance. Sometimes it stands for conditional acceptance. Reflection on belief, then, leads to competing schools of thought twice over. It leads directly to coarse- and fine-grained epistemology. It leads indirectly to Factualism and non-Factualism about conditional belief.

Proofs and Comments

Fact 1: (RT) implies **min-rev** is strictly increasing.

Proof: Suppose T is included in T* and C is in **min-rev**(T by A). The right-to-left direction of **(RT)** ensures (A→C) is in T. Since T is included in T*, (A→C) is in T*. Hence the left-to-right direction of **(RT)** ensures C is in **min-rev**(T* by A). Thus **min-rev**(T by A) is included in **min-rev**(T* by A). **min-rev** is strictly increasing. ▨

Comment: The proof relies on nothing but the idea that one's epistemic state includes two-place updating dispositions. It does not rely on the idea those dispositions are part of one's *theory*, that something one accepts marks them. It just needs the thought one's epistemic state *includes* two-place updating dispositions (however managed).

To see this, suppose we model epistemic states with sentences. This time, though, we embellish those states with two-place updating dispositions. We say an epistemic state E is a combination of sentences and such dispositions. The former codify what one accepts. The latter mark tendencies to accept specific claims on the basis of specific input. E will then look like this:

E = {T + D}.

T will be the worldview of those in E. D will be their two-place updating dispositions. And E will be included in epistemic state E* iff T is included in E*'s worldview T* and D is included in E*'s disposition set D*. Now, suppose we endorse the Ramsey-like view

(RT)* D(A,C) belongs to an agent's epistemic state E iff C belongs to **rev**(the T in E by A).

In the event, **(RT)*** implies **rev** is strictly increasing. And the proof goes just as before:

Scott Sturgeon

Proof: Suppose E is included in E* and C is in **rev**(the T in E by A). The right-to-left direction of **(RT)*** ensures D(A,C) is part of E. Since E is included in E*, D(A,C) is in E*. Hence the left-to-right direction of **(RT)*** ensures C is in **rev**(the T* in E* by A). Thus **rev**(the T in E by A) is included in **rev**(the T* in E* by A). **rev** is strictly increasing. ▨

In a nutshell: **(RT)*** entails **rev** works like deduction. The lesson is stark. Induction requires updating dispositions to be tertiary. It obliges them, basically, to be relative to one's background theory.

The lesson can be used to block Gärdenfors' Bombshell. The idea is to insist conditionals have a tacit indexical element which is a function of what else one accepts. In the event, Gärdenfors' proof will not go through. For the coarse-grained Ramsey Test will look thus:

(RT!) $(A{\rightarrow}C)_T$ belongs to an agent's theory T iff C belongs to **rev**(T by A).

This principle does not support the line used to show **rev** is strictly increasing. Consider the analogue steps:

Bogus Proof: Suppose T is included in T* and C is in **rev**(T by A). The right-to-left direction of **(RT!)** ensures $(A{\rightarrow}C)_T$ is in T. Since T is included in T*, $(A{\rightarrow}C)_T$ is in T*. Hence the left-to-right direction of **(RT!)** ensures C is in **rev**(T* by A). Thus **rev**(T by A) is included in **rev**(T* by A). **min-rev** is strictly increasing.

The break down occurs at the fourth sentence. The mistake is to think

(+) $(A{\rightarrow}C)_T$ is in T*

is an instance of **(RT!)**'s left-hand side. It's not. That side speaks to the case in which a conditional's tacit element and the theory to which it belongs are identical. That's not so at (+). The 'proof' is bogus.

This is a coarse-grained analogue of something proved by van Fraassen within fine-grained epistemology.[6] He showed one can give truth-conditions to conditionals, endorse standard rules for probability, yet accept the fine-grained Ramsey Test. One need only say a conditional's truth-conditions vary from probability function to probability function. In other words, one can side-step Lewis'

---

[6] 'Probabilities of Conditionals', *Foundations of Probability Theory, Statistical Inference, and Statistical Theories of Science* (1976).

Bombshell by emphasizing a tacit semantic element in (A→C). It must vary from psychological context to context. The same holds true for Gärdenfors' Bombshell.

Fact 2: (CA)&(EC) imply **min-rev** is *not* strictly increasing.

Proof: Let A be a contingent proposition. Consider three theories:

  T1 = the consequences of A
  T2 = the consequences of (A v C)
  T3 = the consequences of (A v ¬C).

T2 and T3 are included in T1. Consider the minimal revision of each by ¬A. Since ¬A is consistent with (A v C), Epistemic Conservatism ensures both are in **min-rev**(T2 by ¬A). So C is in **min-rev**(T2 by ¬A) too. But similarly: ¬A is consistent with (Av¬C). So Epistemic Conservatism ensures both of them are in **min-rev**(T3 by ¬A). Hence ¬C is in **min-rev**(T3 by ¬A). Yet Contradiction Avoidance implies the minimal revision of T1, T2 and T3 by ¬A are each consistent. So it *can't* be that **min-rev**(T2 by ¬A) and **min-rev**(T3 by ¬A) are each included in **min-rev**(T1 by ¬A). That would mean C and ¬C are both in **min-rev**(T1 by ¬A), in conflict with Contradiction Avoidance. **min-rev** is *not* strictly increasing. ▨

Fact 3: (ℜℑ)&(C) imply that when $P(A\&B)$ is non-zero:

$P[A{\to}(B{\to}C)] = P[(A\&B){\to}C]$.

Proof: Suppose(ℜℑ), (C) and $P(A\&B)$ is non-zero. Then

$P[A{\to}(B{\to}C)]$	=	$P[(B{\to}C)/A]$	by (ℜℑ)
	=	$PA(B{\to}C)$	by (C)
	=	$PA\ (C/B)$	by (ℜℑ)
	=	$P[(C\&B)/A]{\div}P(B/A)$	by (C)
	=	$P[C\&B\&A]{\div}P(B\&A)$	
	=	$P[C/(A\&B)]$	
	=	$P[(A\&B){\to}C]$	by (ℜℑ). ▨

Fact 4: (ℜℑ)&(C) imply that when $P(A\&C)$ is non-zero:

  $P(A{\to}C) = P(A{\supset}C)$.

Proof: Assume $P(A\&C)$ is non-zero. Since (A&C) is truth-function-ally equivalent to [(A⊃C)&A], it follows $P[(A{\supset}C)\&A]$ is non-zero. An instance of Fact 3 is thus

Scott Sturgeon

$$\mathbf{P}[(A \supset C) \rightarrow (A \rightarrow C)] \quad = \quad \mathbf{P}\{[(A \supset C) \& A] \rightarrow C\}.$$

Now apply **(ℜ3)** to both sides:

$$\mathbf{P}[(A \rightarrow C)/(A \supset C)] \quad = \quad \mathbf{P}\{C/[(A \supset C) \& A]\}.$$

The right-hand side of this equation is unity. Hence

$$\mathbf{P}[(A \rightarrow C) \& (A \supset C)] \quad = \quad \mathbf{P}(A \supset C).$$

This entails

$$\mathbf{P}(A \supset C) \quad \leq \quad \mathbf{P}(A \rightarrow C).$$

By **(ℜ3)**, then,

$$\mathbf{P}(A \supset C) \quad \leq \quad \mathbf{P}(C/A).$$

Yet $\mathbf{P}(C/A)$ cannot exceed $\mathbf{P}(A \supset C)$. Hence

$$\mathbf{P}(A \rightarrow C) \quad = \quad \mathbf{P}(A \supset C). \; \maltese$$

Birkbeck College, London

Necessary Existents

TIMOTHY WILLIAMSON

It seems obvious that I could have failed to exist. My parents could easily never have met, in which case I should never have been conceived and born. The like applies to everyone. More generally, it seems plausible that whatever exists in space and time could have failed to exist. Events could have taken an utterly different course. Our existence, like most other aspects of our lives, appears frighteningly contingent. It is therefore surprising that there is a proof of my necessary existence, a proof that generalizes to everything whatsoever. I will explain the proof and discuss what to make of it. A first reaction is that a 'proof' of such an outrageous conclusion must contain some dreadful fallacy. Yet the proof does not collapse under scrutiny. Further reflection suggests that, suitably interpreted, it may be sound. So interpreted, the conclusion is not outrageous, although it may not be the view you first thought of.

1. The proof rests on three main claims.[1] The first is that my nonexistence strictly implies the truth of the proposition which states my nonexistence:

(1) Necessarily, if I do not exist then the proposition that I do not exist is true.

For that things are so-and-so is just what it takes for the proposition that they are so-and-so to be true. The second main claim is that the truth of the proposition strictly implies its existence:

(2) Necessarily, if the proposition that I do not exist is true then the proposition that I do not exist exists.

For if the proposition did not exist, there would be nothing to be

---

[1] The argument reworks for another purpose material from A. N. Prior, *Past, Present and Future* (Oxford: Clarendon Press, 1967), 149–151. See also Kit Fine's 'Postscript' to A. N. Prior and K. Fine, *Worlds, Times and Selves* (London: Duckworth, 1977), 149-150, and his 'Plantinga on the Reduction of Possibilist Discourse', *Alvin Plantinga*, J. E. Tomberlin and P. van Inwagen (eds) (Dordrecht: D. Reidel, 1985), 160–180, and A. Plantinga, 'On Existentialism', *Philosophical Studies* **44** (1983), 9–10, and 'Reply to Kit Fine', *Alvin Plantinga*, op. cit., 341–349. My interest in the argument was aroused by the work of my pupil, David Efird.

true. The final main claim is that the existence of the proposition strictly implies my existence:

> (3) Necessarily, if the proposition that I do not exist exists then I exist.

For if I did not exist, there would be nothing for the proposition to state the nonexistence of.

Given (1)–(3), the rest of the proof is easy and more or less uncontroversial. For if p strictly implies q, q strictly implies r and r strictly implies s then p strictly implies s by the transitivity of strict implication. Thus (1), (2) and (3) entail (4):

> (4) Necessarily, if I do not exist then I exist.

Consequently, my nonexistence strictly implies a contradiction and is therefore impossible. Hence my existence is necessary; (4) entails (5):

> (5) Necessarily, I exist.

Of course, any thinker could go through (1)–(5) to prove their own necessary existence. Indeed, nothing in the proof depends on the use of the first person 'I'; other names and demonstratives would do in its place. Indeed, we can generalize the proof by substituting a variable for 'I' to derive the result that for every x, necessarily x exists (a result which we might prefix with a further 'necessarily').

One can construct a parallel proof with the phrase 'at all times' in place of 'necessarily' throughout (1)–(5). It would prove eternal rather than necessary existence. That conclusion seems even more obviously wrong. Surely I did not exist as a soul before my conception. Moreover, a variant of the argument with 'this body' in place of 'I' would prove the eternal existence of this body. Surely this body did not exist as a foreshadow of itself before conception, and will not exist as a ghost after death. Arguably, if these are counterexamples to the proof of eternal existence, then they are also counterexamples to the proof of necessary existence, for the latter entails the former. Something exists necessarily only if it exists in all possible situations; but all past, present and future situations are possible, so it exists in all past, present and future situations, so it exists eternally. Therefore, if I did not exist before my conception or will not exist after my death, then my existence is not necessary. In any case, with or without this temporal corollary, (5) looks counterintuitive enough.

2. As already noted, (5) is a fairly uncontroversial consequence of (1)–(3). The obvious strategy is to examine the grounds for those three premises in the hope of finding a weak link. First, however, it will be useful to clarify the notion of a proposition used in all three premises.

We can refer to propositions with 'that' clauses, such as 'that it is snowing' or 'that I do not exist'. Propositions are bearers of truth and falsity. The proposition that it is snowing is true if and only if it is snowing, and false if and only if it is not snowing. Propositions are the objects of propositional attitudes, such as believing, hoping and saying. One can believe that it is snowing, hope that it is snowing, or say that it is snowing. Propositions are expressed by the sentences in the corresponding 'that' clauses, although the same proposition can be expressed by different sentences and the same sentence can express different propositions in different contexts. I can express the proposition that I am tired by saying 'I am tired' in English or 'Ja sam umoran' in Serbian. But if you say 'I am tired' you say that you are tired, not that I am tired; the proposition which you express with that sentence is the proposition that you are tired (or something like it), not the proposition that I am tired. To express the proposition which you express with the sentence 'I am tired', I must use a sentence with a different linguistic meaning, such as 'You are tired'. A proposition can also be a premise or conclusion of an argument. For example, someone who says 'John is taller than James; therefore James is not taller than John' is expressing an argument in which the premise is the proposition that John is taller than James and the conclusion is the proposition that James is not taller than John. This preliminary explanation will be amplified below.

Now consider premise (1). It is one half of one instance of a quite general principle which characterizes truth for propositions:

(1+) Necessarily, the proposition that P is true if and only if P.

Here 'P' may be replaced by any declarative sentence which says that something is the case, in the instance of (1) 'I do not exist'. The principle 'The proposition that P is true if and only if P' is the standard characterization of propositional truth; (1+) adds that it holds of necessity.[2]

To motivate (1+), consider a standard notion of a valid argument as one in which, necessarily, if the premises are true then the conclusion is also true. This is not the purely logical notion of validity,

---

[2] In his defence of the unnecessitated principle, Paul Horwich suggests that the necessitated version might be derivable from the assumption that the unnecessitated version is explanatorily fundamental: *Truth*, 2nd ed., (Oxford: Clarendon Press, 1998), 21.

Timothy Williamson

since it does not require the truth-preservation to be guaranteed by the logical form of the argument; the connection between premises and conclusion might be an informal one. It is nonetheless a useful notion to apply, particularly when we want to use arguments in order to draw out what follows from a counterfactual supposition. For example, although we know that space has at least three dimensions, we may still wonder what would have been the case if space had had only two dimensions; then we need to know what conclusions follow from the supposition that space has only two dimensions, in the sense that necessarily they are true if the supposition is. Now the argument from the premise that P to the conclusion that Q passes the test of necessarily preserving truth on condition that necessarily, if the proposition that P is true then the proposition that Q is true. But the usefulness of this test depends on the equivalence of that condition with the simpler condition that necessarily, if P then Q. For example, when we argue 'John is taller than James, therefore James is not taller than John', our interest is primarily in the comparative heights of John and James, and in the truth of the propositions only to the extent to which it correlates with our primary interest. We want to know whether necessarily, if John is taller than James then James is not taller than John. Our question is answered by the information that necessarily, if the proposition that John is taller than James is true then the proposition that James is not taller than John is true, *provided* that principle (1+) holds, for then, necessarily, the proposition that John is taller than James is true if and only if John is taller than James, and the proposition that James is not taller than John is true if and only if James is not taller than John. Without (1+), we have no obvious reason for using a notion of a valid argument as one in which the truth of the premises necessitates the truth of the conclusion. Thus our ordinary way of thinking about the validity of arguments assumes the correctness of (1+).

Arguably, many other aspects of our use of the notion of propositional truth also depend on (1+). For example, what would it have been like had all Napoleon's (actual) hopes come true? He hoped that Russia would be conquered, so in the relevant circumstances Russia is conquered. But that assumes that, in the counterfactual circumstances in which all his hopes come true, the proposition that Russia is conquered is true if and only if Russia is conquered. Our confidence in that equivalence rests on (1+).

Schema (1+) does not commit us to any particular theory about the nature of propositions. For instance, it is neutral as to whether propositions are in some loose sense linguistic items. However, it does exclude some theories. For example, it is inconsistent with a

236

theory on which, with respect to any possible circumstances, the phrase 'the proposition that dogs bark' simply denotes the string of letters 'Dogs bark', with whatever meaning it has in those circumstances, for the string could have meant what 'Cats philosophize' actually means, and been false even though dogs barked. Thus a theory on which propositions are linguistic items would need somehow to hold the relevant meanings fixed across such circumstances in order to accommodate (1+). That is not intuitively surprising.

None of this makes (1+) as unassailable. Some argue that it must be revised in the light of the semantic paradoxes such as the Liar. For example, suppose that by some self-referential device we can construct a proposition p to be the very proposition that p is not true. By an instance of (1+), the proposition that p is not true is true if and only if p is not true; but the proposition that p is not true just is p, so (since identical items have the same properties) p is true if and only if p is not true, which implies a contradiction. However, it is by no means clear that any proposition p can be the very proposition that p is not true. Perhaps sentences which appear to express such propositions do not really succeed in saying that anything is the case, and therefore cannot be substituted for 'P' in (1+). The resolution of the semantic paradoxes remains a matter of considerable obscurity. It is not obvious what kind of qualification, if any, (1+) requires. At any rate, it should be qualified only where absolutely necessary. In premise (1) of our argument, the sentence 'I do not exist' replaces 'P'; this substitution has no special link with the semantic paradoxes. Appeal to them does not destroy the strong presumption in favour of (1). Let us therefore proceed on the revocable basis that premise (1) holds.

Premise (2) is an instance of the principle that existence is a precondition of truth:

(2+) Necessarily, if the proposition that P is true then the proposition that P exists.

For consider a possible world in which the proposition that P does not exist. If that world had obtained, there would have been no proposition that P. *A fortiori*, there would have been no true proposition that P. Thus a counterexample to (2+) seems ruled out. Given that (2+) holds, so does (2).

It is sometimes said that a proposition can be true *of* a possible world without being true *in* that world.[3] We can express

---

[3] Fine makes a similar distinction between outer and inner truth, 'Plantinga on the Reduction of Possibilist Discourse', op. cit., 163.

propositions in one world about another world. Thus a proposition might be true of a possible world without existing in that world. But this idea does not address the case for (2+), for (2+) does not say that the proposition exists in any possible world of which it is true. We could paraphrase (2+) thus: for any possible world w, if the proposition that P would have been true if w had obtained, then the proposition that P would have existed if w had obtained. We can abbreviate that by saying that for any possible world w, if the proposition is true in w then the proposition exists in w. The antecedent concerns truth in w, not truth of w, so the distinction poses no threat to (2+).

Does the distinction pose a threat to (1+)? Someone might suggest replacing (1+) by the schema: for any possible world w, the proposition that P is true of w if and only if, in w, P. In particular, the proposition that I do not exist is true of w if and only if, in w, I do not exist. That does not yield (1), which requires that if, in w, I do not exist then, *in w,* the proposition that I do not exist is true. Thus the argument for (4) and (5) would fail. Since (1+) was motivated by the use of the condition that necessarily the conclusion is true if the premises are as the standard for a valid argument, the replacement of (1+) would require a corresponding replacement of that standard by the condition that the conclusion is true *of* any possible world *of* which the premises are true.

But now a threat of circularity emerges. For the concept of a possible world is a technical one, itself in need of explanation. What is a possible world? A natural answer is that it is a consistent and complete class of propositions. A class X of propositions is consistent if and only if for every pair of contradictory propositions p and $\sim p$, there is not both a valid argument from X to p and a valid argument from X to $\sim p$. X is complete if and only if for every pair of contradictory propositions p and $\sim p$, there is either a valid argument from X to p or a valid argument from X to $\sim p$. Thus the concept of a possible world is explained in terms of the concept of validity. But, on the envisaged view, the concept of validity is explained in terms of the concept of a possible world!

That objection is not immediately decisive, for there are rival explanations of the concept of a possible world. But the distinction between truth in a world and truth of a world faces another problem. We say that the open sentence 'x is a capital city' is true of London and not of Oxford because London is a capital city and Oxford is not. The true-of relation between an open sentence and an object depends on the assignment of the object to a variable in the open sentence. Different propositions result from different assignments. The proposition that London is a capital city is true, the proposition that Oxford is a capital city false. Can we apply this model to the postulated true-of relation between propositions and worlds? Consider the contingently true proposition that Blair was Prime Minister in 2000. It is supposed to be true of the actual world @ and false of some other possible world w. On the model, the sentence contains a tacit variable; if @ is assigned to the variable, a truth results, if w is assigned, a falsehood. But that does not make the resulting propositions contingent. There is genuine contingency in how things are only if, once values have been assigned to *all* variables, the resulting proposition could still have differed in truth-value. It is not contingent that Blair was Prime Minister in 2000 in @ and that he was not Prime Minister in 2000 in w. What is contingent is simply that Blair was Prime Minister in 2000. Its contingency requires it not to have a variable waiting to be assigned a world. The reply 'But contingency just is variation in truth-value with variation in the value of the world variable' betrays a failure to grasp what contingency is.

According to David Lewis's modal realism, contingency consists in differences between possible worlds, which are conceived as equally real, mutually disconnected spatiotemporal systems.[4] Consider the common sense claim 'It is contingent that there are no talking donkeys' ($\sim\exists x(Tx \& Dx) \& \Diamond\exists x(Tx \& Dx)$). If one interprets the quantifier as unrestricted, modal realism makes the claim false by making its first conjunct false: the modal realist holds that there really are talking donkeys, in spatiotemporal systems other than ours. For modal realism to make the claim true as uttered in the actual world, one must interpret the quantifier as implicitly restricted to the objects in a world. Our spatiotemporal system contains no talking donkeys but, on Lewis's account, other spatiotemporal systems do contain talking donkeys. The restricted quantifier is given an implicit argument place for a world. Intuitively, however, a difference between spatiotemporal systems in itself constitutes no contingency at all. For all that has been said, it is necessary that another spatiotemporal system contains talking donkeys while this system does not, in which case the matters at issue are not contingent. A necessary difference between spatiotemporal systems constitutes no contingency. Even if there are mutually disconnected spatiotemporal systems such as Lewis postulates, they are not the distinctive subject matter of modal discourse. They are simply more of what there is, about which we can ask genuinely modal

[4] D. K. Lewis, *On the Plurality of Worlds* (Oxford: Blackwell, 1986).

239

Timothy Williamson

questions: for instance, whether there could have been more or fewer spatiotemporal systems than there actually are.

To put the point another way, the modal realist claims that one can fully specify how things are in an extensional language without modal operators, restricted quantifiers or other expressions indexed to worlds. Yet, still according to modal realism, nothing stated in that language is contingent. Thus the view implies that it is not genuinely contingent how things are. Of course, the view also implies that one may truly say 'It is contingent that there are no talking donkeys'; that shows that it is also wrong about the truth-conditions of modal statements. Lewis misidentifies contingency as a special kind of indexicality, just as Berkeley misidentified material objects as special groups of sense impressions.

The modal realist's postulation of an implicit argument place for worlds is not faithful to our understanding of modal vocabulary. Since there is no argument place for worlds of the required kind, the postulated true-of relation between propositions and worlds does not behave like the standard true-of relation. Absent some special explanation, the postulate rests on a false analogy.

We can grasp a distinction between truth in a world and truth of a world for utterances. An utterance of the sentence 'There are no utterances' in this world is true of a world in which there are no utterances. For the way the utterance says things to be is the way they are in that world. But that is just a notational variant of the point that the utterance actually expresses a proposition which would be true if that world obtained; in other words, the proposition is true in that world. The utterance need not exist in that world in order to be true of it because the proposition which it expresses in this world exists in that one. We need not carry the utterance across from this world to that one precisely because we can carry the proposition across instead. There is the illusion of a distinction between truth in a world and truth of a world for propositions because we appear to be able to model such a distinction on a corresponding distinction for utterances, forgetting that the presence of the latter depends on the absence of the former. On critical reflection, both (1+) and (2+) withstand the threat from the purported distinction.

Finally, consider premise (3). It too is a special case of a more general principle, roughly, that a proposition about an item exists only if that item itself exists:

(3+)   Necessarily, if the proposition that P(o) exists then o exists.

Here 'o' is to be replaced by a referring singular term such as a simple demonstrative, indexical or ordinary proper name, whose

240

function is to refer in a given context to a particular object (o) and enable us to say something about it; 'o' is not to be replaced by a definite description. 'P(o)' is to be replaced by a sentence which has that singular term as a constituent and says that something is the case. In (3), 'I' replaces 'o' and '... do[es] not exist' replaces 'P(...)'; 'I' is a referring singular term of the requisite kind, a non-descriptive indexical and a constituent of 'I do not exist'.

A simple defence of (3+) is based on the Russellian view that the proposition that P(o) is a structured entity of which one constituent is the object o. For example, the proposition that that dog is barking is a complex consisting of that dog and the property of barking. On this view, the terms that may replace 'o' are *directly referential* in David Kaplan's sense; the contribution of such a term to the proposition expressed by a sentence in which it occurs is simply its referent.[5] If a structured object has a given constituent, then necessarily the former exists only if the latter is a constituent of it and therefore exists too. Since o is a constituent of the structured proposition that P(o), necessarily, the proposition that P(o) exists only if o exists. On Kaplan's view, 'I' is a paradigm of a directly referential term. It is being used as such rather than mentioned in the sentence 'I do not exist', so (3) is a genuine instance of (3+).

However, (3+) is plausible even independently of the direct reference view. For example, on a more Fregean view propositions ('Thoughts') are structured objects, but the constituent corresponding to the term 'o' is a mode of presentation of o rather than the object o itself, a sense of which o is the referent. Thus the sense of the demonstrative 'that dog' in the present context, but not that dog itself, is a constituent of the proposition expressed in the present context by the sentence 'That dog is barking'. Even so, how could something be the proposition that that dog is barking in circumstances in which that dog does not exist? For to be the proposition that that dog is barking is to have a certain relation to that dog, which requires there to be such an item as that dog to which to have the relation. The argument is quite general; it does not even require propositions to be structured objects. Necessarily, if o does not exist then there is no such item as o, so there is no such item as the proposition that P(o), so the proposition that P(o) does not exist. It is crucial to the argument that the function of the singular term 'o' is

[5] D. Kaplan, 'Demonstratives: An Essay on the Semantics, Logic, Metaphysics, and Epistemology of Demonstratives and Other Indexicals', *Themes from Kaplan*, J. Almog, J. Perry and H. Wettstein (eds) (Oxford: Oxford University Press, 1989).

Timothy Williamson

to refer to a particular object, and not merely to introduce a description, for otherwise the existence of the proposition might imply only the existence of the description, whether or not anything satisfied it. But the function of the indexical 'I' evidently is to refer to a particular object (in a given context) and not merely to introduce a description. 'I' does not function like the definite description 'the actual producer of this utterance': one might be under the illusion 'I am not the actual producer of this utterance' without being under the illusion 'I am not me'.[6] Although some remarks in Frege suggest a purely descriptive conception of singular terms, more recent developments from his views acknowledge the kind of object-dependence which the present argument requires. Thus it is not only on a Russellian view that (3) is one of the instances of (3+) to which the argument applies. Necessarily, if the proposition that P(o) exists then o stands in some kind of relation to it (such as being a constituent or being the referent of a constituent), and therefore exists.

Nevertheless, a subtle objection might be made to (3+), and correspondingly to (3). The argument for (3+) assumes that when we use the phrase 'the proposition that P(o)' in speaking of a counterfactual situation (in the scope of 'necessarily'), we thereby refer to something which would have the corresponding property (of being a proposition to the effect that P(o)) *in the counterfactual situation*. But there is another possibility. Perhaps we are using the phrase 'the proposition that P(o)' to pick out the object which has that property *in the actual situation* and then talking about how things could have been with that very object in a counterfactual situation, whether or not it had the property in the counterfactual situation. In other words, the argument treats 'the proposition that P(o)' like the definite description 'the winner' in a typical utterance of the sentence 'The winner could have been someone else': with respect to a counterfactual situation the description denotes whoever won in that situation (the description has narrower scope than the possibility operator in 'could have'). An alternative is to treat 'the proposition that P(o)' like 'the winner' in a typical utterance of 'The winner could have lost': with respect to a counterfactual situation the description denotes whoever won in the actual situation (the description has wider scope than the possibility operator). Let the actual proposition that P(o) be p. Thus p actually has a relation to o. Suppose, however, that in some counterfactual circumstances p

[6] Even the description 'the producer of this utterance' contains the demonstrative 'this utterance', which is not purely descriptive, but 'I' does not refer to the utterance.

242

lacks the property of being a proposition to the effect that P(o). In those circumstances, p might lack the relation to o, so we lose our reason for expecting the existence of p to necessitate the existence of o. But, on the alternative reading, (3+) says that, necessarily, if p exists then o exists; thus we lose our reason for accepting (3+), and with it our reason for accepting (3). Perhaps the object which actually has the property of being a proposition to the effect that I do not exist would have lacked that property if it had been true.

Although the objection may initially sound plausible, it is hard to substantiate. If the actual proposition that I do not exist would not have been a proposition to the effect that I do not exist if I had not existed, why should it have been true in those circumstances? What would its content have been? The point is general. Consider again the truth schema (1+). Let p be the proposition that P. On the reading which the objection requires, (1+) says that, necessarily, p is true if and only if P, even if p could have lacked the property of being a proposition to the effect that P. But in circumstances in which p is not to the effect that P, why should it be true if and only if P? That is, the motivation for (1+) requires that, with respect to counterfactual circumstances, the phrase 'the proposition that P' denotes something which *in those circumstances* would have the property of being a proposition to the effect that P, which is exactly what the objection treated as optional. The most natural view is that the proposition that P is essentially a proposition to that effect, so that the distinction between the two readings makes no difference to the argument. Alternatively, the phrase 'the proposition that P' might pick out a different object with respect to counterfactual circumstances, but one with the property in those circumstances of being a proposition to the effect that P. Either reading fits (3+) and (3) in fitting (1+) and (1).

It is quite unclear what could have been the proposition that I do not exist (if I had not existed) other than the actual proposition that I do not exist. Moreover, on the natural reading of the standard for validity, 'Necessarily, if the premises are true then the conclusion is true', the descriptions 'the premises' and 'the conclusion' are understood rigidly, as denoting the same propositions with respect to all circumstances. Since that test for validity is well-motivated only if we can unpack the truth-conditions of premises and conclusion by means of something like (1+), the natural suggestion is that 'the proposition that P' is to be understood as rigidly designating something which is essentially a proposition to the effect that P.

We can make the same point in other terms. Consider the special case of (1+) in which 'P' is replaced by something of the form

Timothy Williamson

'P(o)': necessarily, the proposition that P(o) is true if and only if P(o). For any possible circumstances, (1+) requires an item which in those circumstances is true if and only if P(o). That equivalence is guaranteed only if the item has a relation to o in those circumstances. If o did not exist in those circumstances, then there would be nothing for the item to have the relation to. Thus the motivation for (1+) underpins (3+) too. Since the objection to (3+) did nothing to show how (1+) could fail, the objection is not sustained.

So far, the argument for necessary existence has withstood scrutiny. Each of the three premises (1)-(3) has highly plausible grounds. Moreover, the grounds for different premises are mutually reinforcing; they do not pull in different directions in the way characteristic of sophistical arguments. That point has just been noted in one respect for (1) and (3), and will be reinforced below in another respect for (2) and (3). We should therefore take seriously the possibility that the argument is sound, its conclusion strange but true. How can its conclusion be true, though? What is supposed to be wrong with the apparently compelling grounds for regarding its conclusion as false?

3. We can make some progress by considering how the concept of existence was applied in the motivation for (2) and (3). In both cases, the argument was that if a given item had not existed, then there would have been no such item as it, and therefore nothing to have a property or a relation to something. Here 'property' and 'relation' are understood in a broad sense in which any predication ascribes a property or relation. If the proposition that P had not existed, there would have been no such item to be true. If the object o had not existed, there would have been no such item to be constitutively related to a proposition. Existing was taken as a necessary precondition of having any properties or relations whatsoever.

The motivation assumes that, necessarily, if x does not exist then there is no such item as x. By contraposition: necessarily, if there is such an item as x then x exists. The converse is scarcely controversial. Thus a necessary and sufficient condition for x to exist is that there be such an item as x. We can therefore symbolize 'x exists' by the familiar formula $\exists y\ x=y$, where the quantifier is not restricted to any particular kind of thing. In particular, it must not be restricted merely by definition to what has spatial or temporal location.[7] Call that the *logical sense* of 'exist'.

The motivation for the argument further assumes that a given

[7] For a defence of unrestricted quantification see my 'Existence and Contingency', *Aristotelian Society* **100** (2000), 117–139.

object o could not have had a property or relation without existing in the logical sense, without there being such an item as o to have the property or relation. That point is sometimes challenged by appeal to past objects. For example, it is said, Trajan's Column in Rome is now a trace of the Emperor Trajan, and the name 'Trajan' refers to him, so various objects now stand in causal and semantic relations to Trajan. By the same token, Trajan now stands in causal and semantic relations to various objects. He still has relations, but does not still exist.

Such examples are not decisive. Doubtless, *in some sense* Trajan no longer exists. Specifically, he is no longer anywhere; he lacks spatial location. Although atoms which once composed him may still be spatially located, he is not identical with those atoms. More generally, we may say that he is no longer *concrete*. But he still counts for one when we ask 'How many Emperors of Rome were there?'. Suppose that in fact there were n Emperors of Rome. The past tense formulation with 'were' of course does not mean that at some past time there were then n Emperors of Rome, for they were not all Emperor simultaneously. Rather, it means that the number of objects with the property of having been Emperor of Rome at some time or other is n. If there are m apples in the bowl, then the number of objects with the property of either being an apple in the bowl or having been Emperor of Rome is $m+n$. Whatever can be counted exists at least in the logical sense: there is such an item. Past objects are no counterexamples to the principle that having properties or relations entails existing in at least the minimal sense. 'Trajan does not exist' is true when 'exist' is used in the nonlogical sense of concreteness, not when it is used in the logical sense. Existence in the sense of concreteness is of crucial significance for metaphysics; for logic it is just one more property, which objects may have or lack.

Fictional objects threaten the argument still less. The question is whether some object could have had a relation without existing in the logical sense. A positive answer could not be supported by a claim such as 'Satan does not exist, but he has the relation of being-worshipped-by to Satanists'. For the name 'Satan' yields a verifying instance of the claim that something could have had a relation without existing in the logical sense only if the name refers to something, in which case 'Satan exists' is true in the logical sense of 'exists' in the very world in which the name putatively refers to something which has the relation of being-worshipped-by to Satanists: the actual world.

Nonexistence in the logical sense is a very radical matter indeed, for it entails having no properties or relations whatsoever. It is not obvious that I could have failed to exist *in the logical sense*. The argument for (5) depends on reading 'exist' in the logical sense, for that is the one needed to make (2+) and (3+) plausible. Its conclusion is therefore to be interpreted as the claim that it is necessary that I am something. What is surely not necessary is that I 'exist' in the sense of being concrete:

(6) Possibly, I am not concrete.

From (5) and (6) we can deduce by standard modal reasoning that existing in the logical sense does not necessitate being concrete:

(7) Possibly, I exist and I am not concrete.

We should not assume that the only alternative to being concrete is being abstract. When Trajan died, he did not become an abstract object, although he ceased to be concrete. He did not become the value of some abstraction operator. He became something neither abstract nor concrete, but something that had once been concrete. Trajan is an ex-concrete object. Similarly, if my parents had never met, I would have been something neither abstract nor concrete, but something that could have been concrete.[8] I would have been a possible concrete object. I would not have been a physical object, but I would have been a possible physical object.

We must be clear what we mean by phrases of the form 'possible F', such as 'possible physical object'. They are sometimes given a *predicative* reading, on which '*x* is a possible F' is equivalent to the conjunction '*x* is possible and *x* is an F', just as '*x* is a spherical stone' is equivalent to the conjunction '*x* is spherical and *x* is a stone'. Then '*x* is possible' is in turn read as something like '*x* could exist'. On the predicative reading, a possible physical object is a physical object, one which could exist. Thus if each physical object could exist, the possible physical objects are simply the physical objects. But the predicative reading is irrelevant to the preceding

---

[8] The underlying assumption is that since I am concrete, it is necessarily possible that I am concrete (so even if I had not been concrete it would still have been the case that I could have been concrete). This is an instance of the so-called Brouwerian principle $p \supset \Box \Diamond p$ in modal logic, which is plausible when $\Box$ and $\Diamond$ stand respectively for metaphysical necessity and metaphysical possibility. The principle corresponds to the symmetry of the accessibility relation in possible worlds semantics. It is a theorem of the attractively simple modal system S5, a good candidate for the logic of those notions, but also of much weaker systems without the S4 principle $\Box p \supset \Box \Box p$, which corresponds to the transitivity of accessibility.

claims, for they imply that I could have been a possible physical object without being a physical object. The relevant reading here is an attributive one, on which 'x is a possible F' is equivalent to 'it is possible that x is an F' ($\Diamond Fx$), just as 'x is a pretended cure' is equivalent to 'it is pretended that x is a cure', not to the scarcely intelligible 'x is pretended and x is a cure'. On the attributive reading, a possible physical object need not be a physical object; it may qualify simply because it could have been a physical object. We may define a *merely* possible F in the attributive sense as a possible F that is not an F. For example, if you are not a government minister but could have been, then you are a merely possible government minister. If my parents had never met, I would have been a merely possible physical object. Since I am actually a physical object and actuality implies possibility, I am a possible physical object; but I am not a merely possible physical object.

Someone might still ask 'What *kind* of thing is a merely possible physical object?'. The answer that 'possible physical object' already demarcates a kind is liable to elicit the complaint 'I asked what it *is*, not what it *could have been*'. Presumably, the complainant wants an answer in non-modal terms. But what justifies the presumption that there should be such an answer? When we think of past physical objects, we are content to classify them in terms of what they were; we do not insist on a classification in terms of what they are now, without reference to the past. Why should possible physical objects be different?

One source of unease may be an inability to imagine what a merely possible physical object would be like. But what exactly is it that we cannot do? We can intellectually grasp the concept of a merely possible physical object; in effect it has just been defined by the open sentence 'x is not a physical object but x could have been a physical object'. Consequently, we can formulate the general existential thought that there are merely possible physical objects. We cannot perceptually imagine a merely possible physical object as such, just as we cannot imagine a number, but that has no more tendency to show that there are no merely possible physical objects than it has to show that there are no numbers. It is impossible to perceive numbers or merely possible physical objects, for they lack spatiotemporal location and causal relations.[9] Perception does not exhaust our contact with reality; we can think too. We have been given no reason to accept the empiricist prejudice that what cannot be perceptually imagined is thereby suspect. Of course, good ques-

[9] If the objects of perception are not all physical then the objection will need to be stated with more care, but that is the objector's problem.

tions arise about our ability to grasp and apply modal concepts; if something is not actually the case, how do we know whether it could have been the case? Since we do have such knowledge, those questions must have answers. It is still far from clear what those answers are. We should not assume that they will make knowledge of (1), (2) and (3) more problematic than knowledge of more familiar claims of necessity, or knowledge of (6) more problematic than knowledge of other claims of possibility. From those premises, and others like them, the relevant conclusions follow.

Even the claim that merely possible physical objects are unperceivable must be formulated with care. What is true is the *de dicto* claim that it is impossible that someone perceives some merely possible physical object. But the corresponding *de re* claim is false, that for some merely possible physical object it is impossible that someone perceives it. For a merely possible physical object could have been a physical object; in normal cases it could have been a perceived physical object. Merely possible physical objects are unperceivable only in the sense in which unperceived physical objects are unperceivable. Of course, for physical objects the difference between being perceived and being unperceived may be purely extrinsic, whereas the difference between being a physical object and being a merely possible physical object is intrinsic in some sense. That suggests a different objection.

On the envisaged view, two very different states are possible for one object. It is capable of being an embodied person, knowing, feeling and acting in space and time. It is also capable of being a merely possible person, disembodied, spatiotemporally unlocated, knowing nothing, feeling nothing and doing nothing. Is so radical a difference in properties consistent with the identity of the object? But the two sets of properties are not wholly disparate. The person actualizes the potential to have properties characteristic of a person. The merely possible person has the unactualized potential to have such properties. What they share is the potential. Why should that not suffice?

Consider identity and distinctness for persons and merely possible persons. If person A is somewhere person B is not, then A is distinct from B. But if A is a merely possible person, then A is nowhere, and therefore does not satisfy that condition for distinctness from B. Nevertheless, A still *could have been* somewhere B was not; in those circumstances, A would have been distinct from B. By the necessity of identity, if A could have been distinct from B then A is distinct from B, for if A and B are identical and A could have been distinct from B then A could have been distinct from itself (by the indiscernibility of identicals), which is impossible. Thus the mere potential for A to be somewhere B is not suffices for the actual distinctness of A and B. Quite generally, suppose that, necessarily, Fs are identical if and only if they stand to each other in a relation R. Then, necessarily, possible Fs are identical if and only if they could both be F and stand to each other in R. For let A and B be possible Fs. If they are identical then, in possible circumstances in which A is an F, B is the same F and they stand to each other in R. Conversely, if A and B could both be F and stand to each other in R, then they could be identical, and therefore are identical, by the necessity of distinctness (if A and B are distinct, they could not have been identical).[10] To the extent to which one can state identity conditions for Fs, one can state identity conditions in correspondingly modalized terms for possible Fs.

A different sort of complaint about the envisaged view is that it has a massively inflationary effect on our ontological commitments. Any human sperm S and egg E could have united to result in a person, who would have existed necessarily; therefore, given the view, there actually is a possible person who could have resulted from S and E.[11] Arguments of this type yield an infinity of merely possible animals, vegetables and minerals. Is this an objectionable cluttering or crowding of our ontology? Of course, the spatial metaphor of clutter is misleading, for it is crucial to the new objects that they lack spatial location. The nonmetaphorical complaint is that the theory commits us to too many objects. At this point appeals may be made to Ockham's Razor: 'Do not multiply entities without necessity'. Of course, it is objectionable to postulate without reason that there are entities of some kind. It is also objectionable to postulate without reason that there are no entities of some kind; it is objectionable to make any postulate without reason. But merely possible animals, vegetables and minerals have not been postulated here without reason; the argument explained above for necessary existence gives a reason for postulating them. Underlying Ockham's Razor we can also discern the insight that simplicity of theory is a virtue. But the simplicity of a theory is not proportional to the size of its ontology. Zermelo-Fraenkel set theory postulates a high infinity of sets but is comparatively simple; with *ad hoc* modifications one could massively reduce the size of its commitments while massively increasing its

---

[10] On the necessity of identity and distinctness see my 'The Necessity and Determinacy of Distinctness', *Essays for David Wiggins: Identity, Truth and Value*, S. Lovibond and S. Williams (eds) (Oxford: Blackwell, 1996).

[11] The reasoning again depends on the Brouwerian principle.

Timothy Williamson

complexity. The proposed conception of necessary existence effects a major simplification of both the proof theory and semantics of quantified modal logic. It simplifies the proof theory because it validates certain formulas (such as the Barcan Formula and its converse) which are derivable in the simplest axiomatizations; other views invalidate those formulas, and must therefore complicate the proof theory in order to block their derivation. The conception simplifies the semantics because it obviates the need to associate each possible world with a domain of quantification containing just those objects which exist at that world. If Ockham's Razor amounts to a preference for simple theories, it tells strongly in favour of the proposed conception. As for any preference for theories that estimate numbers of entities as low rather than high as such, it seems to carry no independent weight. For example, if two cosmological theories of equal simplicity estimate the number of galaxies in the universe, and one estimate is twice the other, that by itself seems to be no reason at all for preferring the theory with the smaller estimate.[12]

There are few knockdown arguments in philosophy, and the foregoing argument for necessary existence is not one of them. Someone determined to reject its conclusion at all costs can surely reject one of its premises, perhaps by abjuring the very idea of a proposition.[13] The argument is directed to those with more open minds, who are willing to rethink the status of its superficially implausible conclusion in the light of the argument itself and of the proposed metaphysics. The cost of rejecting a premise may be higher than the cost of accepting the conclusion.

On the view defended here, an object is essentially a locus of

[12] The view defended in this paper is put forward in my 'Necessary Identity and Necessary Existence', *Wittgenstein—Towards a Re-evaluation: Proceedings of the 14th International Wittgenstein-Symposium*, vol. 1, R. Haller and J. Brandl (eds) (Vienna: Holder-Pichler-Tempsky, 1990), and elaborated and given further support in my 'Bare Possibilia', *Erkenntnis* **48** (1998), 257–273, and 'The Necessary Framework of Objects', *Topoi* **19** (2000), 201–208. For a somewhat similar view see B. Linsky and E. Zalta, 'In Defense of the Simplest Quantified Modal Logic', *Philosophical Perspectives 8: Logic and Language*, J. Tomberlin (ed.) (Atascadero: Ridgeview, 1994) and 'In Defense of the Contingently Nonconcrete', *Philosophical Studies* **84** (1996): 283–294.

[13] If the rejection of propositions nevertheless permitted some way of simulating them, the argument for necessary existence might still be simulated by a sound argument to the same conclusion. For example, quantification over propositions might be simulated by nonsubstitutional quantification into sentence position; for the latter see my 'Truthmakers and the converse Barcan formula', *Dialectica* **53** (1999), 253–270.

potential. How far it actualizes its potential may be a radically contingent matter. But the existence of that object with that potential is wholly noncontingent. Logical properties and relations such as existence and identity are not subject to contingency.[14]

[14] Thanks to audiences in Oxford and at the Royal Institute of Philosophy for comments on earlier versions of this paper.

Ambiguity and Belief[1]

S. G. WILLIAMS

1. This paper is concerned with the notion of ambiguity—or what I shall refer to more generally as homonymy—and its bearing upon various familiar puzzles about intensional contexts.[2] It would hardly of course be a novel claim that the unravelling of such puzzles may well involve recourse to something like ambiguity. After all, Frege, who bequeathed to us one of the most enduring of the puzzles, proposed as part of his solution an analysis of intensional contexts according to which all expressions change their sense when embedded in such contexts. (Indeed they change their sense with each embedding.) And many contemporary philosophers who have discussed the puzzles, while not perhaps endorsing Frege's own somewhat extreme view, nevertheless take ambiguities in the contained sentences to be the key to the puzzles. In this paper, however, I wish to follow those who take the crucial source of homonymy, at least in the most difficult of the puzzles, to lie primarily not in the embedded sentences, but rather in the intensional verbs that embed them. I begin with a brief examination of certain aspects of ambiguity and homonymy.

2. An expression is ambiguous if it has more than one meaning. So the ways of specifying ambiguities will be at least as various as the ways of specifying the meanings themselves.[3] For example, just as certain expressions, such as 'vixen' (female fox) or '∅' (the empty set), admit of analysis or definition, so also expressions such as

[1] I am very grateful to Sabina Lovibond for detailed, constructive comments on an earlier draft; I would also like to thank members of the lecture audience, particularly Gary Jenkins, for helpful remarks during the discussion period.
[2] By an intensional context, I shall here mean any sentential context generated by a sentence of the form 'X F that p', where X is a grammatical subject and F is either a psychological verb such as 'believes', 'hopes', 'fears', etc., or a speech act verb such as 'says', 'denies', 'explains', etc. I shall speak of the psychological verbs here as propositional attitude verbs, and the intensional contexts they generate as propositional attitude contexts.

[3] I here ignore forms of non-linguistic meaning such as Gricean non-natural meaning or speaker meaning.

'port',[4] which admit of more than one analysis or definition, are ambiguous. Or again, given that the meanings of genuine proper names and successful uses of singular indexicals and demonstratives, expressions which will prove to be of special interest to us, are best understood in terms of what Frege called 'modes of presentation', and Gareth Evans called 'ways of thinking', of their referents,[5] so they will be ambiguous when they have more than one mode of presentation or way of thinking associated with them. Typically they will be ambiguous when they have more than referent, though because different ways of thinking may become associated separately with different uses of the same name, this isn't strictly required.[6] Finally, a full specification of the meaning of a complex expression will have to advert to the modes of combination of the words involved; and the corresponding ambiguities will obviously be structural ambiguities in which different modes of combination are adverted to.[7]

[4] Meaning (amongst other things) either a certain type of fortified dessert wine or a town or place by navigable water where ships can load or unload.

[5] See G. Frege 'On Sense and Reference', *Translations from the Philosophical Writings of Gottlob Frege*, P. T. Geach and M. Black (eds. and trans.) (Oxford: Basil Blackwell, 1952); and G. Evans, *The Varieties of Reference* (Oxford: Oxford University Press, 1982), ch. 1. Although Frege applied his model quite generally, I here restrict myself to applying it to singular terms.

[6] In discussions of context-sensitive terms, it is also important to distinguish what David Kaplan calls *character* and *content* (see e.g. his 'Thoughts on Demonstratives', *Demonstratives*, P. Yourgrau (ed) (Oxford: Oxford University Press, 1990). Abstracting from his particular semantical framework, we may view the character of a term as consisting of the general, context-free rules governing its use, while its context-specific content will be what it means in that context, on that occasion of its use. My concern is primarily with the latter—though of course an expression may be ambiguous in character as well as in content. (Thus the pronoun 'she', which is sometimes used in accordance with a convention to refer to a previously mentioned female, and sometimes in accordance with a convention to refer to an unspecified human being, is ambiguous in character.)

[7] This is obviously not meant to be exhaustive. For example, some expressions, notably the logical constants, are arguably best elucidated in terms of their inferential role, which is perhaps most appropriately specified in terms of their introduction and elimination rules, or their incompatibility rules. And expressions may be correspondingly ambiguous by virtue of having different inferential roles; for examples, see S. G. Williams 'Ambiguity and Semantic Role', *Identity, Truth and Value: Essays for David Wiggins*, S. Lovibond and S. G. Williams (eds) (Oxford: Blackwell, 1996).

Now to the extent that different concepts, or different arrangements of concepts, figure in the alternative specifications of the meanings of an ambiguous expression, ambiguity embodies a form of conceptual disunity.[8] It is important to recognize, however, that there is a second kind of conceptual disunity that is easy to confuse with ambiguity but which should be kept separate. This may be seen in unambiguous expressions, or at least relevantly unambiguous expressions, which record what I shall call 'essentially disjunctive concepts'—concepts whose natural, perhaps canonical specification, is disjunctive.

Trivial examples are provided by artificial Goodmanian oddities such as the predicate 'chable', defined as either a chair or a table. This predicate is clearly unambiguous; it does not express one concept on one occasion, a second on another. But because there is no unitary principle that will bring under a single concept what people sit round and what they sit on, other than something tantamount to the disjunction itself, it still expresses something essentially disjunctive. Doubtless it could turn out that tables and chairs are just the pieces of furniture that (say) the Queen Mother likes; but if that is to be used as a unifying principle for tables, then the definition of 'chable' must be different.

Of course, if the only terms for essentially disjunctive concepts are those recorded by Goodmanian oddities, then all we need do is record their existence and move on. Since there are many other examples, however, some of considerable philosophical interest, we cannot safely ignore them. As we shall see, what marks them out is the fact that they have been introduced, or at least have been in circulation or use, in part because of similarities or conceptual connections between the disjuncts or their satisfiers; crucially, however, such similarities or conceptual connections fall short of unity.

A simple example is provided by the figure of speech known as *synecdoche*, defined as using the whole to represent the part or the part to represent the whole.[9] This term nicely expresses certain

[8] It may be that singular senses are not always wholly conceptual, but involve, at least in part, a form of non-conceptual content. I do not subscribe to this view myself. But I do not see any great obstacle to replacing conceptual content by a more general notion of conceptual or non-conceptual content in most of what follows. For a general defence of the conceptualist position, see J. McDowell, *Mind and World* (Cambridge, Mass.: Harvard University Press, 1994) and B. Brewer, *Perception and Reason* (Oxford: Oxford University Press, 2000).

[9] 'England won the Test Match' would be an example of the whole representing the part, and 'All hands on deck' of the part representing the whole.

kinds of part-whole relations through the symmetrical nature of the disjuncts of the *definiendum*. But the disjuncts nevertheless remain conceptually disunited: there is no non-trivial, fundamentally non-disjunctive principle that unites them. Philosophically more familiar examples are traditional family resemblance terms such as 'game'[10] or 'number' (at least in some of its uses). Like 'synecdoche' they will be characterizable (if at all) in terms of an irreducible disjunction, though unlike 'synecdoche' their characterizing disjunctions tend to be much more open-ended. They will often require one of their disjuncts to be something like 'or is relevantly similar'. But perhaps the most surprising group of examples consists of terms defined essentially by means of mathematical induction. Take, for example, '+', the symbol for numerical addition, defined in terms of successor ('):

$$a + n = b =_{df} [[n = 0 \ \& \ b = a] \text{ or } (\exists m < n)[n = m' \ \& \ b = (a + m)']]$$

This definition is clearly disjunctive: it tells us first how to define '+' for zero, and then how to define it for other natural numbers. But assuming adequate non-inductive definitions of '+' are not possible, it is also *essentially* disjunctive.[11] For although there is a conceptual dependence of the second disjunct on the first—one cannot apply the second to obtain a determinate answer to a particular sum without having already applied the first—this only provides a pattern that mitigates the disunity, it does not remove it altogether.

An expression, then, may embody conceptual disunity in two ways, one if it means more than one thing, the other if it has a meaning that is essentially disjunctive. I shall reserve the term 'homonym' for expressions of one or other of these two types. It will also be useful to have a term which applies both to the different elucidations of an ambiguous expression and to the elucidations of the different disjuncts of a non-ambiguous homonym. For this purpose, I shall employ the term 'account'. It follows that although only ambiguous homonyms have more than one meaning, both sorts have more than one account.[12]

It should be noted that it is sometimes quite difficult to decide whether in certain of its uses an expression is an ambiguous or a non-ambiguous homonym. There are, however, a number of

[10] In the sense roughly of what one plays, not in the sense of a kind of animal hunted for food or sport.

[11] If an adequate, non-inductive definition of '+' is possible, then it may or may not express an essentially disjunctive concept.

[12] The Aristotelian echo is deliberate, but I do not commit myself to Aristotle's own account of 'account'.

inferential tests that will sometimes serve. For instance, we may distinguish the ambiguous 'port' from the (relevantly) unambiguous 'game' by virtue of the fact that the sentence 'Smith had a port after dinner and the QEII docked at a port' does not entail that there is something that Smith had after dinner and the QEII docked at (namely, a port), whereas the sentence 'Cribbage is an exciting game and lacrosse is an exciting game' entails that there is something exciting that both cribbage and lacrosse are (namely, a game). Equally, while 'Cribbage is an exciting game and lacrosse is an exciting game' entails the perfectly sensible 'Cribbage is an exciting game and so also is lacrosse', 'Smith had a port after dinner and the QEII docked at a port' does not entail 'Smith had a port after dinner and so also did the QEII dock at one'. Indeed, it scarcely makes sense.

3. Having made these remarks about what I take to be the primary division within the category of homonyms, I now want to add some more detailed, though certainly not exhaustive, taxonomic comments which cut across this division. At root are what Aristotle called *chance homonyms*. These are homonyms which have not been introduced or been in circulation or use because of similarities or conceptual connections between any of the salient accounts of the expressions or the things that satisfy the accounts. These are of the 'port'/ 'port' or 'chable' type, and are perhaps the least interesting kinds of homonymy. Much more important are those homonyms which are or have been in use because of such connections. Allowing myself a little latitude, I shall call all such expressions family resemblance terms.[13] As we noted above, 'synecdoche' and arguably the traditional examples of 'game' and 'number' (in some of its uses) are illustrations of non-ambiguous homonyms that function in this way. But given the implausibility of almost all set theoretic reductions of the natural numbers, 'number', as it is used in ordinary conversation and in text books on set theory, is ambiguous as well.[14]

Now an important species of family resemblance term (as I have interpreted the notion) is provided by what are sometimes known as

[13] The idea of a family resemblance term comes from L. Wittgenstein, *Philosophical Investigations*, G. E. M. Anscombe, (ed. and trans.) (Oxford: Blackwell, 1967), sect. 66. It is often taken to be a condition on something's satisfying such a term that its characterizing disjunction be open-ended; cp. the examples of game and perhaps number above. For reasons of taxonomic simplicity, I do not insist on any such restriction here.

[14] Cp. '3 is an odd number and so is the set consisting of the empty set'.

focal homonyms.[15] In effect, a homonym is focal if some or all of its associated accounts are elucidated in terms of a fixed account of the term itself or of some expression cognate with it. Thus 'healthy' is a focal homonym, since the expressions 'healthy body', 'healthy diet', 'healthy complexion', 'healthy scar', and so on can all be defined in terms of their (different) relationships to the concept recorded by the cognate term 'health': a healthy body possesses health, a healthy diet is conducive to health, a healthy complexion is indicative of health, and a healthy scar is perhaps indicative of flesh that has recovered its health. Here the focus of the term 'healthy' is (the concept recorded by) the term 'health'; and what we might term its *satellites* are (the concepts recorded by) 'healthy body', 'healthy diet', 'healthy complexion' and 'healthy scar'.[16] Notice that in the first three of these examples, 'healthy' is almost certainly a non-ambiguous homonym. At any rate, they seem to pass the inferential tests above. (It is perfectly acceptable, for instance, to deduce 'My diet is healthy and so is my complexion' and 'My diet and my complexion have something in common' from 'My diet is healthy and my complexion is healthy'.) But the last example may well introduce an ambiguity. Certainly it is very odd to say, 'My scar is healthy and so is my diet'.[17]

My primary interest, however, is in a species of focal homonymy which I shall call *ideal use homonymy*. This involves providing different accounts of a homonym by reference to an ideal or absolute use of the term. If the homonym is ambiguous, the different

[15] Or *'pros hen'* homonyms, as Aristotle called them, homonyms directed towards one thing. The term 'focal' we owe to Owen; see G. E. L. Owen, 'Logic and Science in Some Earlier Works of Aristotle', *Logic, Science, and Dialectic*, M. Nussbaum, (ed.) (London: Duckworth, 1986).

[16] Sometimes I speak of the terms being the focus and the satellites, and sometimes of the concepts recorded by those terms; no confusion, I think, arises.

[17] Cp. also 'My body is healthy and so is my curiosity'. It is worth remarking that there is scope for extending focal homonymy to include what might be called *pros polla* homonymy, homonymy directed towards many things. For example, consider the terms 'headsman' and 'headhunter'. The former may be characterized as the head of a whaling vessel or as an executioner whose *modus operandi* consists in chopping people's heads off; while the latter may be characterized as someone who collects heads or as someone who finds heads (i.e. people) for jobs. In these cases, the prefix 'head' is focally related to different, but metaphorically or analogically related uses of 'head': head as part of body, head as top of an organization, and head as representative of the whole body. This would be an example of *pros tria* homonymy, homonymy directed towards three things.

accounts will be framed in terms of whatever account is associated with the ideal use; if it is not ambiguous, the different accounts will be framed in terms of the account associated with the disjunct corresponding to the ideal use.

To illustrate the idea, consider the much derided but perfectly intelligible dispute between Sir Arthur Eddington and Susan Stebbing about the concept of solidity.[18] According to Eddington, tables and chairs are not solid, since nothing that is composed primarily of empty space can be solid, and tables and chairs are composed primarily of empty space. According to Stebbing, on the other hand, tables and chairs are paradigms of what it is to be solid. If *they* are not solid, then the notion of solidity has no practical application or content; but it does. Now it has not escaped students of this debate that Stebbing and Eddington seem to be talking at cross-purposes, working with different conceptions of solidity. Eddington is employing a strict notion of solidity, according to which nothing is solid if it contains any empty space; whereas Stebbing is using a much more informal everyday notion, one which allows for something to be solid even if it contains some empty space, provided that it is reasonably hard and cannot commingle with other reasonably hard objects. But these notions are scarcely unrelated. Something is solid in the everyday sense if it in some way approximates to the strict or ideal notion, the degree of approximation being determined by the discursive context. And it is this relation of the everyday to the ideal that makes the term 'solid' an ideal use homonym.[19]

Ideal use homonymy is intimately related to what David Lewis calls 'score-keeping in a language game'.[20] According to Lewis, we use terms in conversation with varying degrees of precision, or in varying registers, and sometimes these will change in the course of a conversation. Furthermore, as Lewis observes, such changes are in some measure rule-governed. (Indeed, Lewis indicates some of the implicit rules himself.) And we may expect the meanings of ideal

[18] See A. Eddington, *The Nature of the Physical World* (London: Dent, 1928) and L. S. Stebbing, *Philosophy and the Physicists* (Harmondsworth: Penguin, 1944), ch. 3.

[19] Notice that it is not plausible to treat the term 'solid' as univocally expressing a relation between objects and degrees of precision. For whatever conception of solidity is recorded by a true sentence of the form 'X is solid', it remains intuitively the case that 'solid' expresses an intrinsic property of X. So although there may well be such a relation, it will at best be an abstraction based on the ideal use and the particular approximations to the ideal use that are fixed, however vaguely, by the context.

[20] See D. Lewis, 'Scorekeeping in Language Games', *Collected Papers*, I, (Oxford: Oxford University Press, 1983).

use homonyms to vary with the changes in degree of precision or in register broadly in accordance with such implicit rules. Sometimes it will be the general background which effects the changes—perhaps from a conversation in a school corridor to the pronouncements of a teacher in an applied mathematics lesson. At other times, a change may be signalled by means of an explicit register-shifter such as 'strictly', 'ideally', 'roughly', 'partly', 'wholly', and so on. (Compare the teacher who says, 'Strictly, my chair is not solid': this shifts the register from the imprecise and informal to the (more) precise and formal.) And occasionally—as with Stebbing and Eddington—we must fix on a level of precision to avoid an apparent contradiction or a discussion that is at cross-purposes.

4. This completes my brief discussion of homonymy. I now want to turn to the question of its bearing on certain puzzles generated by the presence of intensional contexts. What I shall suggest is that the puzzling nature of some of them derives at least in part from a failure to appreciate the homonymy—and in particular, the ideal use homonymy—of the relevant intensional verbs. I shall begin with Frege and the puzzle he constructed which sparked off much contemporary debate about intensional contexts. Frege took it to be a consequence of his solution to the puzzle that words within such contexts inevitably mean something different from what they mean outside. Such a consequence seems to me thoroughly counterintuitive. But since I wish to endorse in modified form what he says about the original puzzle, I had better say why I think the ambiguity claim does not follow.

Consider then the two sentences 'Hesperus = Phosphorus' and 'Hesperus = Hesperus'. It seems clear that the first sentence may be informative, even to someone who fully grasps it, while the latter will not be. But since Hesperus is in fact Phosphorus, this cannot be due to differences in what 'Hesperus' and 'Phosphorus' refer to. Some other feature of the names is needed to explain the asymmetry. According to Frege, this feature consists in their different senses—that is (using the terminology we noted earlier) in the different (non-linguistic) modes of presentation or ways of thinking of the planet Venus that are associated with the two names.[21]

[21] Cp. Frege op. cit., 56–7. As Frege himself does in the passage cited, I take for granted that the reference of a (non-empty) name is what it is a name of. For a brief discussion of the kinds of ways of thinking that may be wholly or partially constitutive of the sense of a name, see sect. 16. Note also that I sometimes speak of (identifying) information concerning the referent rather than ways of thinking of it.

Now Frege uses such considerations to explain how intensional verbs function. Because the substitution of coreferential singular terms within intensional contexts does not always preserve truth, a sentence such as 'Galileo believes that Hesperus is a planet' cannot express a relation between (*inter alia*) Galileo and the planet Hesperus. If it is to express a relation, therefore, the relation must be between a believer and something else. In the light of his solution to the original puzzle, it is natural to take the alternative relatum to be the sense of the contained sentence (or what Frege called the *thought* that sentence expresses). And since the sense of a sentence is a function of the senses of its components, the whole sentence can then equally well be taken to express a relation between the believer and the senses that make up the thought that the contained sentence expresses.

Frege of course takes this to mean that the words in the contained sentences refer to their customary senses; and so (by a variant on the original puzzle) they must each have a different ('indirect') sense. But given that 'believes that' is indefinitely iterable, these considerations lead to the highly implausible conclusion that every expression is automatically ambiguous in infinitely many ways. And even if we try to resist this argument by insisting that no additional senses are needed beyond the first two—perhaps because substitution of expressions with the same customary sense even within iterated contexts seems always to preserve sense—we are still left with the counterintuitive conclusion that expressions automatically mean one thing within belief contexts and something else outside them. The word 'planet' is surely not ambiguous in the sentence 'Not only does Galileo believe that Hesperus is a planet, it *is* a planet'.

Happily, however, in accepting Frege's solution to the original puzzle, we are not forced to the conclusion that every word is thereby ambiguous in this way. It is possible to accept that the suggestion that certain expressions have a property, sense, distinct from their reference, is at least part of the proper way to explain e.g. the informativeness of certain identity claims, while at the same rejecting the view that such expressions refer to their customary senses in intensional contexts, and so are automatically ambiguous. One way— which still allows intensional verbs to express relations between subjects and senses—would be to take the thoughts expressed by the contained thoughts in sentences apparently of the form e.g. 'X believes that p' to be specified demonstratively, in accordance with some version of Davidson's paratactic theory. According to this suggestion, the sentence 'Galileo believes that Hesperus is a planet' is construed in logical form as two sentences, 'Galileo believes that' and 'Hesperus is a planet', where the word 'that' in the first sentence is taken to be a demonstrative referring not to the second sentence (or an utterance thereof, as Davidson thought), but rather, by means of what Quine once referred to as 'deferred ostension', to the thought expressed by the second, namely the thought that Hesperus is a planet.[22] A second way—one which I myself prefer—takes 'believes that' ('doubts that', 'says that', etc.) to be a combination of a predicate true of subjects and a sentential operator—though being meaning-functional rather than reference-functional, such operators will of course require a different background semantic theory from the kind of truth-theoretic framework envisaged by Frege.[23]

5. Although Frege's own considerations about intensional verbs do not compel us to acknowledge the importance of homonymy for our understanding of such verbs, it is still (I think) crucial. As I indicated above, what I wish to suggest is that intensional verbs are ideal use homonyms, and that this fact may be used to explain some of the puzzles generated by such verbs.

[22] For Davidson's account, see 'On Saying That', *Inquiries into Truth and Interpretation*, (Oxford: Oxford University Press, 1984). The suggestion that the demonstrative may be taken to refer to the Fregean thought expressed by the second sentence is a variant on a suggestion made by S. Boër and W. Lycan, *Knowing Who* (Cambridge, Mass.: MIT Press, 1986).

[23] In such a framework, a clause for 'believes' would have to parallel those for standard sentential operators such as 'not', and would be something like:

$\forall S \forall t \forall a$[t refers to a → 't believes that S' is true iff a believes that S is true];

but this is obviously false. A truth theory of sorts could of course be constructed, using an axiom like:

$\forall S \underline{\forall} p \forall t \forall a$[[S is true iff p & t refers to a] → 't believes that S' is true iff a believes that p],

where the underlined quantifier is substitutional and the associated substitution class sufficiently large to prevent the axiom from being falsified by linguistic impoverishment. But with the resources of substitutional quantification available, we may just as well use as an axiom something like:

$\forall S \underline{\forall} p \forall t \underline{\forall} a$[[S means p & t means a] → 't believes that S' means a believes that p],

in which meaning itself is taken to be the basic semantic notion, and the underlined quantifiers are again substitutional. (For details, see M. K. Davies, *Meaning, Quantification, Necessity* (London: Routledge, 1981), esp. chs. 1 and 5.)

Restricting myself initially to propositional attitude verbs, I begin with two commonplaces, one about the propositional attitudes that such verbs in context express, the other about understanding. The first commonplace is that one's grasp of the meaning of an expression, and in particular the thought a sentence expresses, can stretch from the negligible to the essentially complete. The second is that the extent to which one believes a thought, doubts it, etc. is partly a function of one's grasp of the thought. Plainly if my grasp of a thought is extremely slight, then I cannot be said to believe or doubt it; but equally one obstacle to attributing to me such a belief or doubt is overcome if my grasp of it is complete.

Now in the course of ordinary conversation a person's grasp of a thought, while not perfect, may be sufficiently good for someone to attribute corresponding propositional attitudes. For example, if I say to a friend that all cars have sumps, it would normally be perfectly acceptable for him to attribute to me the belief that all cars have sumps, even if he knows that my conception of a sump is of a metal gizmo in a car that has something to do with the distribution of oil. But should the conversational context change, so may the standards of understanding; and it may then cease to be correct for him to attribute such attitudes. If my friend wants to check how much I know about cars with a view to offering me a job, he may ask me to elaborate. In such circumstances, if all I can muster by way of reply is that they've all got a metal gizmo that has something to do with the distribution of oil, then we may be inclined to say that strictly speaking I don't believe that all cars have sumps, but only something approximating to that thought. In saying this, we are using a stricter notion of belief, one more nearly correlated with full understanding. But this suggests that expressions of both understanding and belief are ideal use homonyms, with expressions of full understanding and of belief that has been fully grasped as foci. And similarly with other propositional attitudes.[24]

Notice that nothing in the above entails that I didn't strictly *say* that all cars have sumps. As many philosophers have pointed out,

[24] The present proposal does of course require a general treatment of the ways in which thoughts, and their constituent senses, approximate to one another. And given the variety of ways of specifying the meanings of different types of expression, we may expect a similar variety of ways of specifying sense approximation. In the examples I give, however, it should be clear roughly in what relevant approximations consist. Notice that I construe 'X believes something approximating to the thought that p' more or less as follows: there is some thought to the effect that q that approximates to the thought that p, and X believes that q.

we often say things without having a clue what we're talking about. Equally, however, this doesn't mean that speech act verbs don't exhibit similar properties to the propositional attitude verbs. For example, if I say to a car mechanic, 'The oil gizmo in the car is leaking', he might report this to his mate by saying, 'SGW said his sump's leaking'. But while this would normally be good enough, it need not always be. A stickler for accurate reportage might insist that since 'sump' is a much more precise term than 'oil gizmo', the mechanic has been too generous in his reporting. In accordance with the more precise register, he should have reported something closer to the content of my actual words. 'Says', therefore, is arguably an ideal use homonym as well, with an interpretation of 'X says that p' at its focus according to which what is substituted for 'p' is exactly synonymous with X's words.

6. It is a consequence of the view I am advocating that in the circumstances entertained the sentence

(1) SGW believes that all cars have a sump

is strictly false. But many philosophers sympathetic to something like Frege's notion of sense would be tempted to try to avoid this conclusion by saying that 'sump' connotes my inadequate conception of a sump, rather than (say) the full technical concept. Such a relativist view, however, leads to certain familiar and telling difficulties.

For example, suppose that I tell the mechanic above, who has a much better grip on what a sump is than I do, that I think that all cars have a sump, and that I do so in just those words. Suppose also that he agrees. Then both (1) *and*

(2) The mechanic believes that all cars have a sump

are true. But for the relativist, this is impossible. For although (1) and (2) clearly entail:

(3) The mechanic and SGW both believe that all cars have a sump,

the relativist can provide no interpretation of 'sump' according to which it is true. It can hardly connote my conception, since my conception includes something the mechanic will not accept, namely that sumps are invariably metal; but equally, it cannot connote his, since his is much more sophisticated than mine. And finally it cannot connote that of a third party who utters (3), since, whoever that is, the mechanic and I would still have to have the same conception.

Of course, according to the view I am advocating, no such problems arise. For suppose first that in the above context small differences of conception are of little or no importance. Then all of (1), (2) and (3) will be true: to all relevant intents and purposes, both the mechanic and I believe that all cars have sumps. But now suppose that the standards of precision are raised sufficiently to make (1) strictly false. All I strictly believe is something that approximates to the thought that all cars have a sump. Then (3) will also be strictly false. What is strictly true is that each of us believes something—though not necessarily the same thing—that approximates to the thought that all cars have sumps. (I assume here that approximation does not exclude identity.)[25] So either way we do not have a situation in which (1) and (2) are true, and (3) is false.

7. By exploiting the idea that propositional attitude verbs are ideal use homonyms, we can sidestep certain difficulties that beset relativized notions of sense. I want now to turn to a problem which anyone sympathetic to Frege's notion of sense must eventually come to terms with. It can be taken as an argument for the view that coreferential singular terms are substitutable *salva veritate* in propositional attitude contexts; but it may equally be taken to show that even if such substitution is not always permitted, the failure cannot be attributed to differences in sense. This is Kripke's puzzle about Pierre.[26]

According to this puzzle, a Frenchman, Pierre, having read a number of well-informed and lavishly illustrated articles in French about a city called 'Londres', comes sincerely to endorse the sentence 'Londres est jolie'. Since this sentence translates into English as 'London is pretty', it seems to follow that Pierre believes that London is pretty. However, Pierre now arrives in England and decides to pay a visit to a city called 'London', but without realizing that it is the very same city that he has been calling 'Londres'. After some considerable sightseeing (and a little bit of language learning[27]), he comes sincerely to endorse the sentence 'London is not pretty', and hence (it seems) to believe that London is not pretty. So Pierre now apparently has the inconsistent beliefs that London is

[25] The assumption is required, since (2) may still be strictly true. Whether it is will depend upon how good the mechanic's conception of a sump really is.

[26] See S. A. Kripke, 'A Puzzle About Belief', *Propositions and Attitudes*, N. Salmon and S. Soames (eds) (Oxford: Oxford University Press, 1988).

[27] Though not enough for him to realize that 'Londres' is the French for 'London'.

pretty and that it is not pretty. But as Kripke points out, it is surely wrong to convict Pierre of having inconsistent beliefs in such circumstances.

Now it is at least formally possible to insist that in these circumstances the standards of belief attribution must be raised, and hence that strictly speaking Pierre doesn't believe that London is pretty or that London is not pretty, since by not having a perfect grasp of the terms 'London' and 'Londres', he doesn't understand the corresponding thoughts (viz. that London is pretty and that it isn't). All he believes is something approximating to these things; and so no inconsistency is attributable to him. What we need, however, is a good reason for saying this.

It is perhaps tempting to argue that, as Kripke sets up the example, the ways of thinking of the city, the pieces of identificatory information, that Pierre associates with 'Londres' are different from those he associates with 'London'. So he doesn't fully understand one or both of the names. (To understand both, he would have to associate the same pieces of information with both.) But we have to recognize that not only does Pierre seem to possess information associated with 'Londres' that would make anyone who had stayed at home in France amongst monoglot French speakers a perfectly competent user of the name 'Londres'; he also seems to possess information associated with 'London' that would make any visitor to the capital a perfectly competent user of the name 'London'. And in any case, according to Kripke, Pierre could perfectly well associate exactly the same information with 'Londres' as with 'London'— it's just that the information is in French in the first instance, and he doesn't make the connection. (As Kripke points out, such facts as that 'Buckingham' is pronounced differently in the French phrase 'Palais de Buckingham' from how it is pronounced in English may be enough to throw Pierre off the scent.)

8. In spite of these remarks, however, I still wish to defend the view that even in the amended circumstances Pierre does not fully understand either 'Londres' or 'London', or the thoughts that they can be used in sentences to express; and that consequently the thoughts he believes are at best only approximations to the thoughts that London is pretty and that London is not pretty. In fact, in the abstract, this follows from the observation that although it would be wrong to convict Pierre of believing inconsistent things, he should, by virtue of his explicit endorsement of the two sentences 'Londres est jolie' and 'London is not pretty', be convicted of *saying* inconsistent things. For this means that what he says and what he thinks are not the same. But the challenge remains to explain what exactly Pierre says but doesn't believe, or what it is about his words that he doesn't fully understand.[28]

9. It will help if we consider an example similar to Kripke's puzzle but one involving singular terms of a different kind, namely vision-based perceptual demonstratives.[29] It is much easier to understand what is going on in this example; and although the details do not carry over straightforwardly to Kripke's puzzle, they do point us in the right direction.

The example involves a pair of individuals, A and B, who are sitting on a hillside gazing at a particular sheep, some 50 yards away, in a flock. After some time, B, who is just behind A, says, 'That sheep is benign ... ', whereupon A turns round and nods his head in agreement. B, however, then continues, '... but is that sheep benign?', after which A turns his gaze back to the flock to find B referring to a sheep that looks, for all A can tell, exactly like the one they've both just been gazing at, and from which the others appear to have run away. Now since there are quite a few sheep in the flock with just such an appearance, A cannot tell whether the sheep they were looking at before is the same as the one they're now looking at. (The original sheep may have been nudged out of the way.) But since further A thinks that B would hardly ask the question if it were the same sheep, A responds to B's question by saying, 'No'. Unfortunately B, who has kept his gaze fixed firmly on the original sheep, is playing games and is consciously referring to the same sheep. And this means that the sense of both occurrences of 'that sheep' is the same. Hence if A genuinely understood B's whole remark, he must have been thinking contradictory thoughts: first that that sheep is benign, and secondly that that sheep is not benign. But whatever else A is guilty of, it is surely not the crime of inconsistent thinking. It wouldn't even be correct to say that he has changed his mind.

[28] Faced with a divergence between belief content and corresponding speech act content, certain philosophers are apt to introduce the distinction between the 'narrowly psychological' content of the belief states, and 'world-involving' content of the speech acts. The problem with this response, however, is that in the version of the example according to which Pierre is put off by different pronunciations of 'Buckingham', etc., even the narrow psychological states should on the face of it be inconsistent. The picture I ultimately want to endorse does not require this distinction: the contents of both the belief states and the speech acts can both perfectly well be 'world-involving'.

[29] Henceforth, I shall omit the qualification 'vision-based'.

Now the right response here must be to deny that A genuinely understood the whole of B's remark. This follows from the fact that in the circumstances envisaged B would have been thinking contradictory thoughts if he had thought that that sheep is benign and that that sheep is not benign. So evidently B grasps something that A does not. But what is it? It is accepted by a good many neo-Fregeans that to understand a thought of the form 'That is G', or 'That F is G', where the demonstrative is perceptual, one must be able to discriminate via the relevant sense modality which object that, or that F, is from all other objects. (This is a consequence of what Gareth Evans calls *Russell's Principle*.[30]) But if this right, we may conclude that in respect of one or other of the two uses of the demonstrative, A does not possess, by the time B completes his utterance, the relevant discriminative capacity. (And in the circumstances described, it must be the capacity associated with the former.) But what is that has undermined this capacity? In virtue of what is he no longer able to discriminate the referent of the first use of 'that sheep'? Clearly it isn't in virtue of a change in visual appearance. (Since the sheep is the same, this is so whether visual appearances are individuated in part by reference to how things are in the world, or purely phenomenologically.) Nor—we may assume—is it that A has forgotten what it is to be a sheep.[31] But then what is left?

One answer is based on Gareth Evans's observation that to have demonstrative thoughts of the kind we are interested in, and hence to understand sentences expressing such thoughts, one must be able to locate the referents of the relevant demonstratives egocentrically—to locate them as over there, to the left, and so on.[32] For in the circumstances described the moment A looks away he loses the ability to locate the referent of the first occurrence of 'that

[30] See Evans, op. cit., 89–92.

[31] Grasp of some demonstratives of the form 'that F' may also require one to know that their referents are F. I doubt this applies to 'that sheep', however, since one could perfectly well grasp an utterance of 'That sheep is frisky', even if the utterer were in fact referring to a goat; but let us assume in any case that A has not forgotten that the referent of the first use of 'that sheep' is a sheep.

[32] Evans, op. cit., ch. 6, esp. sect. 6.4. I here take egocentric location to allow (as in this case) that the specification of the place may be relative to more than one person. Thus each of A and B is interested in the location of the sheep relative to *them*. For a detailed discussion of further complexities relating to egocentric location, see Brewer, op. cit., ch. 6, who differs from Evans on a number of matters of detail not crucial to the present paper.

sheep' relative to himself. Even when he looks back, the presence of the other sheep, together with the fact that any one of them might have nudged it out of the way, undermines his ability to locate it as (say) *over there*. Hence if Evans is right, A loses his understanding of the first occurrence of 'that sheep'. At best, all he can think in relation to the first utterance is what is expressed by e.g. 'The sheep we were referring to a moment ago is benign', something that merely approximates to his original thought.[33] Of course, none of these considerations applies to B, since B has kept his gaze firmly on the salient sheep, and so is still in a position to locate the referent of the first use of the demonstrative as over there.

10. The puzzle about the sheep can be solved therefore by uncovering a feature which is coordinate with the visual appearance of the sheep (i.e. with the appropriate way of thinking of it), and A's inability to identify which explains his failure to retain his understanding of the first occurrence of 'that sheep'. This feature is the egocentric location of the sheep.[34] Can we say anything similar about proper names that would enable us to tackle Kripke's puzzle, even in its modified form? If we can, then by the same token we must be able to discover some feature which is coordinate with the identical ways of thinking that Pierre associates with both 'Londres' and 'London', and his inability to identify which explains his failure to grasp one or both of the names. Of course, if there is such a feature, it clearly cannot be egocentric location. I can have a pretty good grasp of the name 'Judi Dench' (say) without having the remotest idea how to locate her relative to myself. And that even applies to names for cities. No matter how disoriented I might be—perhaps I have been knocked out, kidnapped, and placed in a dark-

---

[33] This means that 'A is unable to locate x egocentrically' is implicitly intensional. (Otherwise, A would still be able to locate the referent of the first demonstrative egocentrically, since the referents of the demonstratives are the same, and he can certainly locate the referent of the second egocentrically.) To bring out the intensionality, we may say, as a first approximation, that for A to be unable to locate the referent of the first demonstrative egocentrically, there must be no place specified egocentrically as s (say), such that A knows that the sheep he was referring to is at s.

[34] Bill Brewer speaks of the perceptual experience of an object as 'display[ing its] spatial location' (op. cit. 187). With this in mind, we may take the sense of a perceptual demonstrative to consist precisely in a way of thinking of its referent that displays (at least potentially) the location of its referent egocentrically.

ened room—I can still understand the name 'London'. So what could the feature be?[35]

11. Help may be at hand here in what Evans calls 'a proper-name-using practice'.[36] For Evans, such a practice arises when a putative name for an object is introduced to a linguistic community by certain individuals who, by virtue of their (perceptual) acquaintance with the object, have stipulated or learnt 'a truth which they could then express as "This is NN", where "This" makes a demonstrative reference to [the object]'[37], and 'NN' is the intended name. As such individuals make further judgments of the form 'This is NN', in part by virtue of exercises of their capacity to recognize the object, eventually this particular use of 'NN' becomes entrenched, and 'NN' becomes a name for the object.[38] The individuals who introduce 'NN' and entrench its use in the manner described, Evans calls 'producers'. And the practice of using 'NN' in this way we may refer to as the practice of *calling the object 'NN'*—though since many different objects may be called 'NN', *which* practice this is of calling the object 'NN' must, in a full specification of the practice, be given by reference to the relevant producers. Of course, the name can also be used in accordance with this practice by people who have not been acquainted with the object, or by those who have forgotten that they have. Such people, who will have got the name from others in some way, Evans calls 'consumers'. Over a period of time, the number of consumers of a given name may well come to exceed the number of producers. Indeed, when the producers die out, and the

[35] A second suggestion would be the location of the referent in one's personal history of encounters with things, a proposal that Evans makes in connection with recognitional demonstratives; see Evans op. cit. 299-301. However, whether or not this is a viable proposal for such demonstratives, I doubt that an ability to identify this feature is necessary for understanding names. I may have forgotten every occasion when I encountered London, but still be able to understand the name 'London'.

[36] See Evans op. cit., ch.11, esp. sect. 11.2. Henceforth, I shall use the expression 'name-using practice' as shorthand for 'proper-name-using practice'.

[37] Op. cit., 376.

[38] Note that although initially the recognitional capacities exercised by the producers will doubtless enable them to place their encounters with the object in question in their own personal histories, the ability to do so need not be retained. As we observed in fn. 35, people can understand a name without being able to remember any of the occasions when they encountered its referent. This negative aspect of understanding a name is also important for the communality of the sense of a name; see sect 16.

referent ceases to be available, the name may eventually be used only by consumers. Evans refers to this as 'the late phase' of the name-using practice.

It is evidently an important feature of name-using practices that they allow certain people who are not acquainted with the referent of a name nevertheless to refer to it. Such people may even be able to use a name to refer to something, despite having inadequate or fundamentally incorrect information about the referent.[39] In fact, it would be no exaggeration to say that name-using practices are in this way indispensable to successful reference in a world of fragmented acquaintance with things. But what I wish to suggest further is that they are also essential to the understanding of names. We asked earlier whether there might be a feature that is coordinate with the partially sense-constituting ways of thinking associated with a name (or use of a name), and which is required for complete understanding of it. What I propose is that this feature is its associated name-using practice.[40] In effect, for a given (use of a) name, both the associated ways of thinking and the name-using practice are components of its sense. So understanding (a use of) a name is tantamount to knowledge of both the appropriate ways of thinking of its referent that are associated with it and which name-using practice it belongs to.[41]

[39] This is what is established by Kripke's examples of Feynman, on the one hand, and Gödel and Schmidt, on the other; see S. A. Kripke, *Naming and Necessity* (Oxford: Blackwell, 1980), Lecture II. See also Evans, op. cit., ch. 11, where he repeatedly stresses the dangers of confusing understanding a name with being able to use it successfully to refer. *Pace* Evans, however, it is not clear that a speaker can refer to something only if 'he manifest[s] which name-using practice he intends to be, and to be taken to be, participating in' (op. cit., 384). For it is surely possible that someone could succeed in referring to something even if he's forgotten which practice he's participating in, provided that his audience realizes which it is. (Imagine someone who has been told to inform a certain audience that NN is in town. By the time he comes to blurt this out to the relevant audience, he may have forgotten not only who NN is, but also who told him to relay the message or even whether it is a message at all. But the audience can still know perfectly well which practice is being manifested by his utterance.)

[40] It is therefore the feature that is at least roughly analogous to the egocentric location of the referent when the referring expression is a perceptual demonstrative.

[41] But why are the ways of thinking and the name-using practice separated? If I call something 'NN', am I not thinking of the referent of 'NN' as being called 'NN'? Yes; but it is still important to separate them since being called 'NN' isn't a recognitional way of thinking of the referent. And

S. G. Williams

12. If this proposal is correct, then sameness of sense for (uses of) names requires sameness of name-using practice. So it might seem that we could very quickly deal with Pierre. For since 'London' and 'Londres' must be associated with different practices—one with the practice of calling London 'London', the other with the practice of calling it 'Londres'—they must have different senses. And if they have different senses, we cannot properly attribute to Pierre the belief that London is pretty, on the basis of his sincere endorsement of the French sentence 'Londres est jolie'.

As we shall see, if circumstances had been different, this might well have been the right conclusion to draw. But the argument itself cannot be right. For at the very least it falsely entails that 'London' and 'Londres' cannot be translations of one another, and so incorrectly requires the example to be a version of the 'Hesperus'/'Phosphorus' puzzle. But where does it go wrong? The flaw, I think, lies in the implicit assumption that different names for the same object automatically belong to different name-using practices—an assumption that is almost certainly wrong in the case of 'London' and 'Londres'. Indeed, it is the fact that they do belong to the same practice that provides the key to Kripke's puzzle.

13. So why might 'London' and 'Londres' be thought of as belonging to the same practice? The first thing to note is that it was always part of Evans's conception of a name-using practice that a practice associated with a given name can sometimes be associated with certain ancestors of the name as well. 'A single practice of referring to something by name [may be] preserved despite the change in the form of the name'.[42] And of course something similar applies synchronically, given that particular names can be pronounced or spelt differently. In the right context, the same practice is associated with the name 'Newcastle' whether it is pronounced "Newcastle' or 'New'castle'; similarly the same practice would have been associated with Locke's name whether it was spelt with an 'e' or without.

Now one reason why these different pronunciations and spellings

[42] Op. cit., 393.

---

with the exception of being called 'NN', it is those ways of thinking, at least in the phases of a name-using practice when the input of producers remains central to the practice, which are the partially sense-constituting ways of thinking of the referent. Or so I shall suggest in sect. 16. In the late phase of a name-using practice, however, there seems no reason not to treat being called 'NN'—or more strictly being actually called 'NN'— as just one more way of thinking of the referent amongst the rest (see sect. 16 again).

might be thought to belong to the same name-using practice is that they are different forms of a single name for the same object. Indeed, we might even offer a similar justification for taking 'London' and 'Londres' to belong to the same practice. After all, they both derive etymologically from the Latin 'Londinium'. However, it would be a mistake to take being forms of the same name for a given object, where names are individuated in terms of their etymological sources, as being either necessary or sufficient for belonging to the same name-using practice. It is not sufficient, since coreferential forms of a name, which have a common etymological source, and perhaps identical orthography and pronunciation, could, by virtue of the contingencies of history and geography, belong to distinct and wholly isolated name-using practices. And it is not necessary, since commonly known different spellings of someone's name might (*per accidens*) have different etymological sources. I should add that a criterion grounded in etymology is unlikely to be acceptable if, as I maintain, belonging to a single name-using practice is the key to Kripke's puzzle. For the puzzle could just as well have been constructed using names that have no etymological connection. Suppose, for example, that the French for 'London' had been 'Le Grand Goitre'.[43]

Despite these considerations, however, the examples involving different pronunciations and spellings do point to another reason for treating 'London' and 'Londres' as part of the same practice. For in addition to their phonetic and orthographic similarities, they also have in common the fact that anyone who is aware that the different pronunciations and spellings are of the same word for the same object will associate exactly the same information with one as with the other, and immediately, i.e. non-inferentially, associate with one of the pronunciations or spellings any new information or misinformation that is associated with the other.[44] And the same seems to apply to 'London' and 'Londres'. For anyone who knows that the French for 'London' is 'Londres' will associate the same information with the one as with the other, and any new information he associates with the one he will non-inferentially associate with the other. It is this fact, I suggest, that gives an acceptable conception of a name-using practice according to which 'Londres' and 'London' do belong to the same practice.

[43] London was once known as the Great Wen.

[44] Clearly, someone who is aware of both pronunciations of 'Newcastle' will not, on hearing that 'Newcastle is F, reason that since 'Newcastle is New'castle, New'castle is F. In the language of certain theorists, there is, for that individual, just one 'dossier of information' associated with both pronunciations.

In order to make this more precise, let us say that names (or uses of names) are *informationally transparent to an individual x* iff information associated by x with one is thereby (i.e. non-inferentially) associated by x with the other. Then I propose that name-using practices be individuated by reference to informational transparency as follows: the practice of calling something 'NN' is the same as the practice of calling something 'NN'', as instigated and/or appropriately reinforced by groups of producers P and P' iff uses of 'NN' in accordance with the first practice and uses of 'NN'' in accordance with the second are informationally transparent to members of P and P'. It follows that if we take the relevant producers to come from those bilinguals who are aware of both 'London' and 'Londres' as names for London, and so for whom the names are informationally transparent, then the names belong to the same name-using practice. (We might refer to the practice as one of calling London both 'London' and 'Londres'.) What I wish to suggest is that in the circumstances envisaged, Pierre fails to understand 'London' and 'Londres', since he is unaware that he is participating in this bilingual practice when he uses the names. For that he must know that 'London' and 'Londres' are part of the practice; and if that were so, they would be informationally transparent to him. But they are not.

14. It will doubtless be objected to this proposal that it has the consequence that monoglot native Londoners will not understand the name of their own city. But it seems to me that this is either not a consequence or one we can perfectly well live with, depending on the facts relating to the producers of the name-using practice that the monoglot Londoners are participating in. For if we take the Londoners to be sufficiently isolated from the producers of the bilingual practice for them to be producers of their own practice, then they would understand the name. (This would evidently be so, if the bilinguals were not as envisaged, but members of a society that introduced a new name for London but wished its own city names to be kept secret.) But if, as is perhaps more likely here, they are in sufficient contact with the more knowledgeable producers of the bilingual practice (through word of mouth, the media, etc.), then they will in effect defer to the bilingual producers. In that case, although strictly they will not fully understand the name 'London', they will certainly understand it well enough for their monoglot practices—and well enough for it to be acceptable, according to the register in which they would normally speak, to attribute to them beliefs to the effect that London is such-and-such in the course of ordinary conversations.

And this carries over to Pierre. Suppose first that the circumstances had been different from those envisaged. Perhaps when Pierre arrived in London, the members of the secret society mentioned above had taken him under their wing; and instead of learning the name 'London', he had learnt their name for the city (say, 'NN'). Then all we would be able to deduce is that he would not be thinking contradictory thoughts when he thought what he would then express by 'Londres est jolie' and 'NN is not pretty'. (This was why I allowed in section 12 that there might be circumstances in which the puzzle could be assimilated to the 'Hesperus'/'Phosphorus' puzzle.) In the circumstances envisaged, however, we may take it as read that he will not be so isolated from producers of the fully bilingual practice that the practices he is participating in when he uses 'London' and 'Londres' do not coincide. Consequently, what he is thinking is not properly expressed either by 'Londres est jolie' or by 'London is not pretty', since he doesn't understand 'Londres' or 'London' fully. Rather he is thinking very similar thoughts, thoughts expressible by orthographically identical sentences, the names in which belong to (what would be) corresponding monolingual practices. But either way—and so even if the implausible scenario obtains—there is no contradiction. Pierre's thoughts are perfectly consistent with one another.[45]

15. Of course this can only be acceptable in the modified Fregean framework we are working within, if it does not have the consequence that in the circumstances normally envisaged, the names 'Hesperus' and 'Phosphorus' are not understood. But I do not think it does. For in those circumstances 'Hesperus' and 'Phosphorus' clearly do not belong to the same name-using practice, since they

[45] At this point, someone might suggest that we try to solve the sheep puzzle in a similar way, by taking the sense of both occurrences of 'that sheep' to comprise the visual presentation of the sheep and the salient 'perceptual-demonstrative-using practice' (and thereby dispensing with its egocentric location). However, although there may be other expressions— natural kind terms and technical terms are the obvious ones that come to mind—for which the strategy of introducing expression-using practices may be appropriate, there is an important difference regarding one-off referential devices such as perceptual demonstratives. For in general it will be the fact that the visual presentation of the referent of the demonstrative displays the referent's (egocentric) location to someone that will enable him to know which demonstrative-using practice he is participating in. But there is no such feature for names. There is no single non-linguistic feature coordinate with the ways of thinking of the referent of a name which will enable someone to know which name-using practice a user is participating in. The name-using practice is fundamental.

are not informationally transparent to *any* producer, nor have they ever been. Hence they do not mean the same thing. We do not have grounds, therefore, for thinking that they are not understood.

That said, however, it is important to recognize that we cannot draw exactly the same conclusion as Frege himself does from his puzzle. For in the light of Kripke's example, it remains a possibility that the non-linguistic information associated with both names is accidentally (so to speak) the same. Hence, it does not follow *of necessity* that the non-linguistic ways of thinking about Venus associated with 'Hesperus' and 'Phosphorus' are different. However, the failure of transparency means that any such congruence is unlikely to continue. Almost certainly, such ways of thinking associated with them will eventually come apart. So although Frege's argument does not show that the names must have different non-linguistic ways of thinking associated with them, it does indicate that it is highly likely that at some stage they will.

16. In the discussion so far, I have argued that the sense of (a use of) a proper name comprises certain ways of thinking of its referent together with the name-using practice that (the use of) the name belongs to. But I have said little about what the specific ways of thinking that partially constitute the sense of (a use of) a name might be. Let me conclude with one or two sketchy remarks about this question.

It is clear that if anyone has a complete understanding of the names belonging to a particular name-using practice, it is the producers—at least while they continue to control the practice. What the consumers understand is at best an approximation to what the producers understand.[46] And since what differentiates the producers from the consumers is recognitional information, it seems plausible to take the partially sense-constituting ways of thinking associated with a name to be correct recognitional information that producers associate with the name in uses of it they know to belong to the salient name-using practice.[47] To ensure the communality of its sense, however, it also seems plausible to insist that this information should be such that producers can reasonably expect other producers to associate it with the name.[48]

---

[46] Just as the thoughts they have concerning the referents of the names will be approximations to what the producers would think.

[47] Though with the caveat mentioned in fn. 38 concerning the corresponding recognitional capacities.

[48] The communality of sense also highlights the importance of the previous footnote. A producer may sometimes know when another producer encountered the referent of a given name; but this will hardly be typical.

Complications will have to be introduced to deal not only with the self-oriented ways of thinking that we may associate with our own names, but also with ways of thinking of public objects employed by informationally restricted groups such as those who encountered what is now a dead dog only as a puppy, and those who encountered it only when mature. For in both cases there will be a lack of communality in information. My characteristic way of thinking of myself is arguably not available to anyone else. And those who encountered the dog only as a puppy will not be able to associate later recognitional information with the dog's name and those who encountered it only when it was mature will be unable to associate puppy-based recognitional information.

Continued insistence on the communality of the sense of an expression—something I am inclined to subscribe to[49]—would exclude self-oriented ways of thinking from the sense of a proper name.[50] But matters are more difficult in respect of name use by the other two groups, since each may involve a group communality of its own.[51] Here, however, we may be able to steer a middle course by appealing once again to name-using practices. For it will be remembered that the underlying feature of such practices that allows us to treat such names as 'London' and 'Londres' as belonging to the same practice is their informational transparency. And although (uses of) names may be informationally transparent for a range of individuals, it does not follow that those individuals each have to associate the *same* information with the names. Hence, although two groups may associate wholly distinct wedges of recognitional information with certain names, the names can still belong to the same name-using practice. And so in such circumstances, the names—as employed by the two groups—would not just be chance homonyms. Indeed, given that an ability to identify the name-using practice which (a use of) a name belongs to is a prerequisite of understanding (the use of) the name—as I have been arguing—such a name could be regarded as a focal homonym, with the name-using prac-

[49] Except when the point of the expression would otherwise be undermined; cp. the first person pronoun.

[50] Though it would also have the consequence that those who cannot see themselves as others see them would not have a proper grasp of their own names.

[51] To emphasize the separation between the two groups, let us suppose that the mature dog was not recognizable as being same dog as the puppy—perhaps it was only identified by a nametag—and that no one was aware of the dog as it matured so that no appeal can be made to 'expert' producers, who associate both wedges of information with the name.

tice as a focus,[52] and uses of the name that are associated with the different wedges of recognitional information as satellites.[53]

These remarks concern the phases of a name-using practice in which the producers still hold sway, and consumers in effect defer to them. But when in the late phase of a practice the producers have ceased to exert an influence, it is hard to stomach the idea that consumers must remain in a state of permanent deference to them. In such cases, we could perhaps allow—*faute de mieux*—the possibility of a more or less radical shift in the ways of thinking that count. For eventually there will be no point in insisting on the hegemony of the ways of thinking adopted by the producers, and hence no obstacle to allowing non-recognitional information of consumers in some way to constitute the sense of the name. Such information will have to be rigid to avoid Kripkean modal puzzles. And it must also be true of the referent of the name (identified indirectly via the name-using practice) if it is to be sense-constituting. (Otherwise what is synthetically false would become analytically true.) It is possible of course that the descriptive information that many consumers in the late phase are apt to associate with uses of a name is false of the referent of the name. But again, all that follows is that understanding can lag behind more or less competent use.[54]

Worcester College, Oxford

[52] I treat 'being called "NN"' as being cognate with 'NN'; cp. sect. 3.

[53] Whether or not such terms are ambiguous is something I remain unsure about. To say, 'X believes that a is F and so does Y', where X is a member of the first group, and Y a member of the second, does not sound odd. But to avoid condemning each group to a necessary ignorance of the senses of the names they use, it might still seem proper to view the names as ambiguous. The above sentence would then have to be understood in more or less the way we eventually interpreted (3). That is to say, when precision matters, it would have to be rewritten as 'X believes something approximating to the thought that a is F and so does Y', where the sense of 'a' is (say) that of the producers in the group to which the utterer belongs. In cases where the overlap in recognitional information is greater, however, we would probably have to allow that the name is univocal but not fully understood by either group.

[54] Notice that some consumers may have greater expertise than others—scholars, for example. So deference, this time amongst consumers, may even be appropriate in the late phase of a name-using practice. It is also worth reiterating that in the late phase a specification of the practice can figure as a way of thinking of the referent of the name on a par with other ways of thinking of it; cp. fn. 41.

Basic Logical Knowledge

BOB HALE

At least some of us, at least some of the time—when not in the grip of radical sceptical doubt—are inclined to believe that we know, for example, that if we infer a conclusion from two true premises, one a conditional whose consequent is that conclusion and the other the antecedent of that conditional, then our conclusion must be true, or that we know similar things about other simple patterns of inference. If we do indeed have knowledge of this sort, it is what I mean by *logical* knowledge. Logical knowledge is, roughly speaking, knowledge *about* logic—such as knowledge that a certain principle of inference necessarily preserves truth, or that every proposition of a certain form must be true—and so is not the same thing as knowledge that is gained by *using* logic, i.e. *inferential* knowledge. That is not to say, of course, that logical knowledge can't be inferential. On the contrary, it is barely open to question that—if there is any logical knowledge at all—there is a lot of inferential logical knowledge. For example, if we know that the introduction and elimination principles for the conditional are truth-preserving, we can surely get to know, by inference, that the principle of hypothetical syllogism (i.e. transitivity of the conditional) is so too, not to mention other, less obvious and more recondite, examples of putative logical knowledge.

One might be tempted—if one believes there is any logical knowledge at all—to think that while a great deal of it (most of it, by a long way) *is* inferential, it isn't, and can't be, *all* inferential, i.e. that there has to be *some non*-inferential logical knowledge if any is to be got by inference. If this is your view, you will find it very natural to say that basic logical knowledge is logical knowledge that is non-inferential. However, I don't want to *define* basic logical knowledge in this way, because I don't think we should rule out in advance the view that *all* logical knowledge is inferential. I think there are obvious and serious difficulties with this view, but we shouldn't foreclose, at this stage, on the possibility that they are answerable—I shall return to this issue later. So I shall characterize basic logical knowledge in a different way. Let us consider just principles of inference and knowledge of their *soundness*, where by this I mean their possession of whatever fundamental properties are essential to being good principles of inference, such as being necessarily truth-

279

preserving, but perhaps also including other properties.[1] Knowledge of the soundness of a principle of inference is logical knowledge in my sense. I shall say that it is *basic* logical knowledge if the explanation of how we have it makes no appeal to the soundness of any principle of inference. This leaves theoretical space for basic logical knowledge to be inferential—a space that may be occupied if, but only if, one can infer the conclusion that some rule of inference is sound without using any premise to the effect that some (possibly other) rule of inference is sound, or otherwise relying upon the assumption of its soundness. Whilst it would beg an important question to assert—without further argument—that there can be no logical knowledge unless there is some non-inferential logical knowledge, it begs no question and is, I think, incontrovertible that there can be no logical knowledge unless there is some basic logical knowledge.

My central question, then, is whether there is any basic logical knowledge and if there is, how this is possible. Before I set about trying to answer it, I want to bring out into the open some other assumptions I'm making, and say something about why it seems so difficult to justify an affirmative answer.

1. The nature of logical knowledge

My characterization of logical knowledge isn't, and isn't intended to be, uncontroversial. As I have characterized it, the object of a piece of logical knowledge is some proposition to the effect that any inference in accordance with a certain specified rule must have a true conclusion if its premises are true, i.e. it is knowledge that a certain

[1] I am concerned exclusively with principles of deductive inference. Other properties which might be taken to be essential to good principles of deduction include, most obviously, conservativeness and harmony. On a broadly constructivist approach to logic, soundness would be understood in terms of proof-theoretic virtues such as these, rather than in terms of necessary truth preservation. In the interests of generality, it is clearly desirable to avoid essential reliance on any assumption about what is required for soundness which divides advocates of classical logic from their constructivist—or, for that matter, relevantist—opponents. I shall not always strive, in presenting the argument that follows, to maintain complete neutrality as between these opposed conceptions of soundness—in particular, I shall often take soundness to require necessary truth preservation; but I believe that wherever I do so, it would be possible to reconstruct my argument to suit any of the principal non-classical conceptions.

rule is (not merely always, but) *necessarily* truth-preserving. So it is modal knowledge. Obviously, then, someone—Quine, for example—who perhaps agrees that some rules of inference *always* preserve truth, but denies that there is any such thing as (logical) *necessity*, will deny that there is any logical knowledge at all, in my sense. I shall not now argue against scepticism of this kind.[2] Here I should like to assume the correctness of that conclusion in order to pursue the question whether and how basic logical knowledge, in my sense, is possible. Anyone who is prepared to make this assumption should have no objection to my characterizing basic logical knowledge as knowledge, concerning certain rules of inference, that they are *necessarily* truth-preserving. If there is such a thing as logical necessity at all, this is surely the fundamental case of it.[3]

It is useful to distinguish between what I shall call absolute and merely relative kinds of necessity, or senses of the necessity operator. The necessity involved in logical knowledge, if there is any, must, I think, be a kind of *absolute* necessity. When we say that some proposition is physically necessary, for example, we may be and probably will be claiming only that the proposition is necessary in a relative way. As a first step towards bringing out the relativity of the necessity involved, we might gloss 'It is physically necessary that p' as 'The laws of physics entail that p' or 'It is a logical consequence of the laws of physics that p'. But this is not quite enough to hit off the idea of merely relative necessity, for two reasons.[4] Firstly, if—generalizing our gloss on the idea that physical necessity is relative—we say that ϕ-necessity is relative if there is some collection of true propositions Φ (the ϕ-laws) such that it is ϕ-ly necessary that p if and only if it is a logical consequence of Φ that p, then every kind of necessity will, quite trivially, count as relative. In particular, since the truths of logic are logical consequences of the empty set of premises, they will be logical consequences of any collection of any set of true propositions whatever. So to capture the more interesting notion, i.e. of a kind of necessity being merely relative, we need to say a bit more. The obvious way to do this is to

---

[2] For attempts to show, contra Quine, that we must believe in logical necessity, see Crispin Wright 'Inventing Logical Necessity' in J. Butterfield, (ed.) *Language, Mind and Logic* (Cambridge: Cambridge University Press, 1986), pp. 187–209; Ian McFetridge 'Logical Necessity: Some Issues' in his posthumously published papers, *Logical Necessity & other essays*, edited by John Haldane & Roger Scruton, Aristotelian Society Series Volume II, pp. 135–54; and Bob Hale 'On Some Arguments for the Necessity of Necessity' *Mind* **108** (1999), pp. 23–52.

[3] Cf McFetridge, op. cit. p. 136.

say that a kind of necessity, φ-necessity, is *merely relative* if there is a kind of possibility, ψ-possibility, such that for some proposition p, it is φ-ly necessary that p but ψ-ly possible that $\neg p$. Correspondingly, we should say that φ-necessity is absolute iff it is not merely relative, i.e. iff there is no kind of possibility, ψ-possibility, such that some proposition is φ-ly necessary but its negation ψ-ly possible. However—and this is the second point—this will still not quite capture the idea we are after. For there is a use of 'possible' in which to say that it is possible that p is, more or less, just to express our ignorance as to whether it is true that p or not. This is often called epistemic possibility. If this (very weak) kind of epistemic possibility is allowed to count as a kind of possibility for the purposes of our criteria (i.e. as a possible value of 'ψ-possibility'), then many propositions which ought, intuitively, to qualify as absolutely necessary will fail to do so. For example, we may think that whichever of Goldbach's Conjecture and its negation is true is not just necessarily true, but absolutely necessary. But since we don't know which is true, the negation of whichever of them is true is epistemically possible, so that whichever is true cannot be absolutely necessary. It is therefore necessary to amend our criterion for a kind of necessity to be absolute, so as to require that, for φ-necessity to be absolute, there must be no *non-epistemic* kind of possibility, ψ-possibility, such that some proposition is φ-ly necessary while its negation is ψ-ly possible.[5]

Since it is widely supposed that there are necessities which are absolute but are knowable only *a posteriori*, it would be unwise simply to assume that logical knowledge must be *a priori* knowledge. But it seems to me that the necessities which are the objects of logical knowledge, if there is any, are quite different from those—metaphysical necessities, as they are often called—commonly taken

[4] It is also open to objection, as it stands, unless a certain qualification is understood. This is because the vast majority of propositions which might plausibly be claimed to be physically necessary are not strictly speaking logical consequences of the laws of physics alone—some laws of mathematics will be required. So the glosses in the text will be acceptable as they stand only if the laws of mathematics are themselves logical consequences of the laws of logic. Whilst I believe that is a defensible view, at least as far as the laws of mathematics that are needed for physics are concerned, it is certainly not widely accepted, and it is therefore desirable to avoid presupposing it here. We can do so by simply stipulating that laws of physics are to be taken as including the the requisite laws of mathematics.

[5] There is obviously a question about how epistemically modal notions may be demarcated. One simple thought would be that ψ-possibility is a species of epistemic possibility if the truth-value of statements of the form 'It is ψ-ly possible that p' can vary, relative to different states of information

to be known or knowable only *a posteriori*, such as that Hesperus is Phosphorus, that the Queen is a child of Elizabeth Bowes-Lyon and George VI, that water is H_2O, that gold is an element (the one with atomic number 79), and the like. In these latter cases[6], the specific necessity—say that water is H_2O—is an instance of a general principle of necessity—in this case, to the effect that a substance necessarily has whatever chemical composition it has, so that if water has a certain chemical composition, it is necessarily so composed or constituted. This much is, at least on the usual view, something we *can* know *a priori*. But empirical investigation is required to discover the actual chemical composition, so that knowledge that water is necessarily H_2O can only be a *posteriori*. But this kind of account, on which acquiring knowledge of the necessity unavoidably involves an empirical discovery of some particular fact—for example, about something's nature or constitution—has little plausibility in the present case. It might, to be sure, be maintained that coming to know, for example, that *modus ponens* is necessarily truth-preserving involves coming to know something about the nature of a certain concept (i.e. of a certain logical constant)—but the acquisition of that knowledge is not plausibly viewed as an empirical discovery.[7] Thus once it is granted that the objects of logical knowledge are modal truths of the kind I've suggested, there is virtually no option but to think that if there is any knowledge of this sort at all, it is *a priori* knowledge of a *conceptual* necessity.

2. The problem of basic logical knowledge

As soon as we start to think about how we might have basic logical knowledge, we can scarcely avoid confronting a problem which is apt not only to make us think that it is very hard, if not impossible, to see how we could explain how we might have such knowledge, but to make us doubt that there can be such a thing as logical knowledge at all (basic or otherwise).

The problem takes the form of a dilemma. Knowledge in general—and so basic logical knowledge in particular—is *either* inferential *or* non-inferential. As I've said, there is no doubt that, if there is any logical knowledge at all, there is a lot of inferential logical knowledge. But it is difficult to see how *basic* logical knowledge could be inferential. For one thing, any inference to the conclusion that

---

[6] Assuming the correctness of the widely accepted view that they are indeed necessities.

[7] It may, of course, be an empirical discovery that a particular word is used to express that concept.

283

Bob Hale

modus ponens, say, is necessarily truth-preserving would, one supposes, have to proceed from some known premise or premises, and it is not at all clear what could serve here—remember that we're looking for an account of how we can *know a priori* that the rule *necessarily* preserves truth, so any premises will have themselves to be necessary and *a priori*. But second, and perhaps even more problematically, any inference must proceed in accordance some rule(s) whose reliability, it would seem, can be taken for granted. But which rule(s) could be used? Not rules other than *modus ponens*—since if we could establish that *modus ponens* is truth-preserving by arguing from suitable premises using (only) other rules, *modus ponens* would not, after all, be basic. But to use *modus ponens* itself would—or so it is apt to seem—be viciously circular. On the other hand, it is equally difficult to see how basic logical knowledge could be *non-inferential*. The difficulty here is not that we cannot come up with (what are plausibly taken to be) kinds of non-inferential knowledge. Sense-perception and instrospection are plausibly taken to be both non-inferential and sources of knowledge, of the world about us and our inner lives respectively. The difficulty is rather to come up with anything—any faculty or mechanism—which could deliver non-inferential knowledge *of the kind we are trying to explain*. Sense-perception and introspection deliver knowledge of *particular contingent* facts. Knowledge that *modus ponens* can never take one from true premises to a false conclusion is, however, is knowledge that is both *general* and of a *necessity*. Nothing like perception, by itself, can yield knowledge of *general* truths; and as for the modality, it appears that Kant was right when he observed[8] that experience can teach us that things *are* thus and so, but cannot inform us that they *must* be thus and so. In short, the only even tolerably clear kinds of non-inferential knowledge we can cite provide a hopeless model for logical knowledge. Appeals at this point to self-evidence or to rational insight—to a supposed capacity to discern things by the light of reason—are subject to familiar difficulties, and in any case seem to amount to relabelling our problem rather than making a significant contribution towards its solution.[9]

---

[8] Kant *Critique of Pure Reason*, B3.

[9] This is not to claim that nothing like self evidence or rational insight can have any part to play in explaining logical knowledge. My claim is only that, pending clarification of its precise rôle and of how it is supposed to work, such an appeal is no advance. In fact, and as I shall try later to explain, I think that there must be an essentially non-inferential component, which might reasonably be viewed as a species of rational insight, in such an explanation.

This dilemma obviously isn't conclusive—rather, it sets the agenda for anyone who wants to make out a serious case for thinking that we can have basic logical knowledge. Minimally, one must either explain how one can use a basic rule of inference in arriving at the conclusion that that very rule of inference is necessarily truth-preserving without being involved in some vicious circularity, or provide an alternative, credible, model for non-inferential knowledge which avoids the shortcomings of any perceptual or inner-perceptual model.

3. Basic Logical Knowledge as Inferential

On the answer I shall propose to our leading question, basic logical knowledge is a kind of non-inferential knowledge. I shall not have time to discuss inferential accounts as fully as they deserve, but I want briefly to indicate why I am somewhat pessimistic about their prospects. As indicated by what I have already said, I think the main difficulty with them is to see how they can avoid vicious circularity. But it will be useful for my purposes later to go into a bit more detail of the difficulty here.

Any attempt to exhibit basic logical knowledge as inferential is likely to start from some premise concerning the meaning of the logical operator involved in the rule(s) of inference knowledge of which it is designed to explain. This premise might take various forms, but we shall lose no generality by supposing—as is perhaps anyway most plausible—that this premise will presuppose that the meaning of the relevant operator can be given in terms of some basic inference rules governing it. For example, it is often suggested that the conditional may be implicitly defined by stipulating that it stands for that function (assuming there is one) which validates the usual introduction and elimination rules for the conditional, i.e. conditional proof and *modus ponens*. It may then be proposed that we can come to know that these rules are valid (i.e. necessarily preserve truth in all applications) by means of a very simple argument:

(1) If 'if' has the meaning assigned to it by the implicit definition, *modus ponens* and conditional proof are valid
(2) 'If' does have that meaning

so

(3) *Modus ponens* and conditional proof are valid

Bob Hale

As I have formulated it, this argument obviously uses *modus ponens*. Since the argument is supposed to explain how we can come to know that this very rule is valid, it appears viciously circular. A proponent of the inferential view can hardly deny that the argument is circular, but he may try to mitigate its circularity by appealing to an idea of Michael Dummett.[10] In the most usual kind of circular argument, the conclusion we are trying to establish appears as a premise, so that the argument assumes what it is supposed to prove, and is therefore useless. The present argument is not circular in this way—it involves not *premise*-circularity but *rule*-circularity[11]: the conclusion that *modus ponens* is valid is drawn by an application of that very rule of inference. Is rule-circularity always vicious? Dummett argues that it need not be. If an argument is intended to *persuade* someone who doubts the soundness of a rule that that rule is sound, and the argument uses that rule, then it will be just as useless as an argument that involves premise-circularity. But if instead the argument is an 'explanatory' (as opposed to 'suasive') argument[12]—if it is aimed at *explaining* why its conclusion is true, as opposed to *proving* that it is true—then rule-circularity, Dummett claims, may not be harmful, since in giving an explanation, we may quite properly take for granted the fact we are trying to explain.

It seems undeniable that the project of explaining why something is—or how it can be—the case differs in important ways from the project of convincing someone (ourselves, or others) that it is so, and that in the former project, one quite properly takes for granted the fact to be explained. But there are at least three reasons why it may be doubted that this is enough to see off concern about rule-circularity, at least in the present case. For one thing, allowing that in an explanatory argument the truth of the conclusion may properly be taken for granted is not to allow that that conclusion may actually be *used* in giving the explanation. It is true that the conclusion that *modus ponens* is sound is not explicitly used in the most direct way possible, i.e. by being taken as a premise in the explanatory argument. But it does still rely on the soundness of *modus*

[10] The idea makes its first appearance, as far as I know, in Dummett's British Academy Lecture 'The justification of deduction', reprinted in his *Truth and other enigmas* (London: Duckworth 1978), pp. 290–318. It reappears in *The Logical Basis of Metaphysics* (London: Duckworth 1991), see especially Ch. 9.

[11] Dummett calls this 'pragmatic' circularity, but I shall follow Paul Boghossian in referring to it as rule-circularity, as this label is the more informative.

[12] These are Dummett's terms.

286

ponens. Second, there is a special difficulty in the present case. Although the argument is to be viewed as an explanatory rather than a suasive one, what we are trying to find is an explanation *how we may come to know* that *modus ponens* is truth-preserving. It seems, in general, that a good explanation of how we may come to know something ought to indicate a route by which someone could come to know it—so that, in the present case, the argument must after all be capable of being used by someone who is unsure about the rule as a means of gaining assurance that it is safe to use it. But it seems that a rule-circular argument could not serve as such a means. Thirdly, there is the worry that, if rule-circular arguments are allowed, they may be used to 'explain' how we can 'know' that patently bad rules of inference—such as Arthur Prior's tonk rules[13]—are guaranteed to preserve truth. Why should we not implicitly define 'tonk' by stipulating that it is to stand for that function which validates the rules Tonk-Introduction: Given A, infer A tonk B, and Tonk-Elimination: Given A tonk B, infer B; and then argue

(1) 'tonk' has the meaning assigned to it by our implicit definition

so

(2) 'tonk' has that meaning tonk Tonk-Intro and Tonk-Elim are valid

so

(3) Tonk-Intro and Tonk-Elim are valid

I should stress that I do not claim any of these worries amounts to a decisive objection to the inferential approach.[14] I claim only that

---

[13] Cf A. N. Prior 'The Runabout Inference Ticket', *Analysis* **21** (1960), pp. 38–9.

[14] I could hardly do so, given the very sophisticated defence of that approach mounted by Paul Boghossian in some recent papers, including 'Analyticity' in Bob Hale & Crispin Wright, (eds) *The Blackwell Companion to the Philosophy of Language* (Oxford: Blackwell, 1997), pp. 331–68; 'Analyticity Reconsidered', *Nous* (1996) pp. 360–91; 'Knowledge of Logic' in Paul Boghossian & Christopher Peacocke, (eds) *New Essays on the A Priori* (Oxford: Oxford University Press, 2000), pp. 229–54. There is also a further paper, 'How are Objective Epistemic Reasons Possible?', originally presented to a recent APA meeting at Albuquerque, which is not as yet, as far as I know, published. A proper assessment of Boghossian's defence of rule-circularity lies well beyond the scope of this paper—here I can only record my opinion that, for all its ingenuity, it does not adequately answer the objections adumbrated here. In addition, Boghossian's defence ultimately requires him—as he clearly perceives ('Knowledge of Logic', p.

Bob Hale

they are serious enough to motivate exploring the prospects for a non-inferential answer, and, in particular, an approach which seeks to avoid the kind of rule-circularity which I've suggested is especially problematic.[15]

4. An alternative strategy

Although, for the reasons I've briefly indicated, I am unpersuaded that basic logical knowledge can be obtained by a rule-circular derivation from implicit definitions of the relevant logical operators, I agree with proponents of this view in thinking that an adequate explanation of logical knowledge, if one is to be had, must draw on, or be grounded in, the conditions for understanding the logical constants. In what follows, I shall try to develop and defend an alternative explanation, starting from this same underlying idea.

In line with this basic idea, it may be claimed—plausibly, and I think correctly—that acceptance of (at least sufficiently simple instances of) basic patterns of inference featuring the operator in

[15] In the papers to which I've alluded, Boghossian claims to show that a non-inferential answer cannot work. However, his argument is an argument by elimination, and since he does not—so far as I have been able to see—consider the kind of non-inferential answer I'm going to propose, I do not need to discuss it here.

253)—to reject what he terms 'the principle of the universal accessibility of reasons', which claims, roughly, that if something is a genuine reason for believing that p, 'its rationalizing force ought to be accessible from any epistemic standpoint'—in particular, reasons for believing that p ought to be, in principle, appreciable as such by someone who doubts or questions whether p. I am not completely certain that this principle is true, and cannot see how to argue for it from premises more likely to command assent but like Thomas Nagel (*The Last Word* (Oxford: Oxford University Press 1997), p. 5—quoted by Boghossian), I do not see how one can give it up without giving way to relativism or subjectivism about reasons Boghossian acknowledges the pull of the principle, but concludes that it must nevertheless be false. Certainly if his account of logical knowledge is correct, it is false. But one man's *modus ponens* ... ! Boghossian's position is subjected to a searching critical examination by Crispin Wright in his response to the last of the papers cited above ('On Basic Logical Knowledge: Reflections on Paul Boghossian's "How are Objective Epistemic Reasons Possible?"', forthcoming, along with Boghossian's paper, in *Philosophical* Studies). I am in agreement with the main critical points he makes there.

question is at least criterial for—and indeed, actually constitutive of—understanding that operator. For example, if someone is unwilling to accept as valid simple inferences by *modus ponens* or simple applications of conditional proof, then—unless there is some saving special explanation—she thereby convicts herself of failure to understand the conditional. One immediate difficulty with the suggestion that this may somehow give rise to knowledge of the validity of those rules has, in effect, been emphasized by Paul Horwich.[16] Acceptance of a proposition or rule of inference is one thing, and its truth or correctness is another. Acceptance doesn't entail truth or correctness—someone's accepting (sufficiently simple instances of) *modus ponens* and conditional-proof as valid [(necessarily) truth-preserving] doesn't mean that they are so.

This objection would be fatal, if the idea were that we could somehow derive the conclusion that *modus ponens*, say, is truth-preserving from the premise that acceptance of this rule is what (partly) fixes the meaning of the conditional. But there is another project for which Horwich's point poses no special problem. We can usefully draw a distinction, between:

A Explaining *how we can come to know* that basic rules such as *modus ponens* are sound

and

B Explaining *why it is not possible intelligently* (i.e. clear-headedly and coherently) *to doubt* the soundness of basic rules such as this one

[16] See his *Meaning* (Oxford: Oxford University Press, 1998), p. 8 and ch. 6 *passim*, but especially sect. 2, and his paper 'Implicit Definition, Analytic Truth, and A Priori Knowledge', *Nous* 31 (1997), pp. 423–40. Horwich is mainly concerned to argue against what he calls the 'standard model of implicit definition', according to which implicit definition proceeds through *stipulation* of the *truth* of some sentence(s) containing the definiendum, and in favour of a 'use-theoretic' conception, according to which the meaning of the definiendum is fixed, rather, by our *accepting*, or *taking as true*, some such sentence(s). And his thought—to put it somewhat crudely—is that once we shift away from the standard model to his preferred account, we can see that implicit definition cannot ground significant *a priori* knowledge, simply because acceptance doesn't entail truth. I am not myself persuaded by Horwich's arguments against the standard model—for some of my reasons, see Bob Hale & Crispin Wright 'Implicit Definition and the A Priori' in Paul Boghossian & Christopher Peacocke, (eds) *New Essays on the A Priori* (Oxford: Oxford University Press, 2000), pp. 286–319, especially 290–95 and 309, fn. 40—but his point about acceptance is ungainsayable, and is all that matters here.

Bob Hale

Project A—the leading project of this paper—is, or at least appears to be, the more ambitious of the two. It is for this project that Horwich's point appears to pose a serious difficulty, at least if we seek to carry it through starting from the claim that acceptance of certain patterns of inference is constitutive of understanding the logical operator they principally feature. My strategy will be to shelve project A for the time being, in favour of the ostensibly more modest project B. My hope will be that, if we can carry through project B to a successful conclusion, it will be possible to advance from there to an explanation of basic logical knowledge.[17]

Granted that acceptance doesn't entail truth, the fact that acceptance of (at least sufficiently simple instances of) basic patterns of inference featuring a logical operator is (at least partly) constitutive of understanding that operator has an important consequence—it means that one cannot regard anything which is recognizably an instance of the relevant inference pattern as unsound without convicting oneself of misunderstanding.[18] Further, if one realizes that

[17] Even if there should prove to be serious, or even insuperable, obstacles in the way of building upon a satisfying explanation why the correctness of basic inference rules is beyond coherent doubt to get an explanation of how we can *know* them to be correct, it seems to me that successful completion of project B would be a significant advance.

[18] But how can this possibly be so, it may be objected, given that clever people who know what they are talking about have seriously proposed counter-examples? (See, for example, Vann McGee 'A Counterexample to Modus Ponens' *Journal of Philosophy*, Vol. 82, Issue 9 (1985), pp. 462–71). Several points need to be made here. First, it is obviously immaterial whether the alleged counter-examples are genuine—it is enough for the objection that someone could intelligibly think them to be so. Second, and equally obviously, the fact—if it is one—that one can intelligibly take something to be a counterexample to *modus ponens* does not go against the conditional claim that, if one's understanding of the conditional is (partially) constituted by one's acceptance of *modus ponens*, then one cannot intelligibly take something to be a counter-example to that rule; what it would show, rather, is that one's understanding cannot be so constituted. If someone *can* intelligibly take something to be a counter-example, it cannot be that understanding of the conditional is (partially) constituted by acceptance of (unrestricted) *modus ponens*. So the supposition that a thinker may, after all, intelligibly view something as a counter-example evidently begs the question: In what *does* understanding of the conditional consist? How is its meaning constituted, if *not* through the entrenchment of the usual inference rules? Well, either through the entrenchment of some *other* rules (perhaps restricted versions of the usual rules), or in some other way (i.e. not through the entrenchment of any inference rules at all but, say, through the assignment of certain truth-conditions to condition-

acceptance of that pattern is in this way constitutive of understanding its principal operator, one cannot rationally entertain the possibility of counter-examples to it. To elaborate, let us suppose that acceptance of the usual introduction and elimination rules for the conditional is required for understanding 'if'. Then there is no coherent practice in which one operates with the conditional construction, so understood, and yet supposes that there may be cases in which both a conditional and its antecedent are true but its consequent not, or in which one can give a sound argument for the consequent of a conditional from its antecedent as premise, and yet in which the conditional is not true.

This takes us a step forward with project B; but there is still a good way to travel, as we shall now see.

5. An apparently lethal dose of tonkitis

If the claim that accepting certain rules of inference is constitutive of understanding the logical operator they concern means that acceptance of those rules *suffices* for understanding, it is plainly unacceptable. Since an expression cannot be understood unless it has a meaning, it would follow that the mere acceptance of certain rules for a logical operator must be enough to ensure that it has a meaning. But it is at least possible that we should accept rules which are inconsistent, or otherwise defective or incoherent. Perhaps only

---

al sentences). Either way, it seems to me, something sufficiently close to my claim can be sustained. Alleged counter-examples of the kind proposed by McGee essentially involve as major premises conditionals whose consequents are themselves conditional (e.g. 'If a Republican wins, then if Reagan loses, Anderson will win'). As McGee himself remarks, such examples have no tendency to suggest that *modus ponens* may be unsound in simple cases where the consequent of the conditional major premise is itself non-conditional. So one might continue to take the meaning of the conditional as (partially) constituted by acceptance of *modus ponens*—but in a suitably restricted version. The argument I develop in the remainder of this paper could be straightforwardly recast to suit such a restricted version of the rule. One may instead take the meaning of the conditional to be fixed by its association with certain truth-conditions, or perhaps conditions of correct or justified assertion. But however these are specified, they will surely validate at least a restricted form of *modus ponens*, even if they do not validate the rule in full generality. And once again, these will be such as to preclude the possibility of intelligibly regarding something as a counter-example to whatever (possibly restricted) version of *modus ponens* they underwrite.

a complete moron could be brought to accept a pair of rules as obviously defective as the Tonk rules—but even that is conceivable, if only barely so; and in any case, the logical defectiveness of rules (whether it resides in their inconsistency or in some other failing) need not be so apparent.[19] The overwhelmingly natural—and I think correct—thing to say in such a case would be that we had failed to endow the would-be logical operator with a meaning. It follows that the mere acceptance of, say, the conditional rules cannot suffice for understanding the conditional. The most that can be claimed is that their acceptance is—constitutively—*necessary* for understanding. And the further claim, consequently, must be that because this is so, one cannot coherently think that one has found, or could find, a counter-example to, say, *modus ponens*.

But this may seem to open the way to a simple counter-thought. If it is insisted that acceptance of the usual rules is required for understanding the conditional, why can't a sceptic retort that the same could be said of the tonk rules, i.e. that accepting them is required for understanding 'tonk'—so that one may just as well argue that there can be no coherently doubting them either! If one can argue: acceptance of *modus ponens* is required for understanding the conditional, so if a thinker supposes she can envisage a counter-example to it (i.e. a case in which it is true that A and that *if A then B* but not true that B), she must be confused, then one can just as well argue: acceptance of tonk-elimination is required[20] for understanding 'tonk', so if a thinker supposes she can envisage a case in which it would be true that A *tonk* B but not true that B, she (too) must be confused. But the tonk rules are clearly duff. It must, therefore, be possible to entertain doubts—indeed, well-founded doubts—about them. So there has to be something wrong with the argument in their case. Since the argument for the conditional rules runs entirely parallel, it must likewise be defective.

This counter is partly right and partly wrong. It is right, of course, in its claim that the tonk rules are defective, and so right in

[19] To borrow an example from the paper by Wright cited in note 14, suppose Frege, instead of formulating his notorious Basic Law V as an axiom, had proposed a pair of introduction and elimination rules governing the course of values operator permitting us, respectively, to infer $\alpha'F(\alpha) = \alpha'G(\alpha)$ from $\forall\alpha(F(\alpha)\leftrightarrow G(\alpha))$ and $\forall\alpha(F(\alpha)\leftrightarrow G(\alpha))$ from $\alpha'F(\alpha) = \alpha'G(\alpha)$. The inconsistency of such a stipulation would have been no less unobvious than was the inconsistency of Frege's actual proposal—it took the genius of Russell realize that not all was well.

[20] It would not, of course, be sufficient, for the reason given above.

its further claim that it must be possible to coherently to entertain (well-founded) doubt about them. It is right, too, that if the meaning-constitutive role of acceptance of the conditional rules precludes coherently thinking one has a counter-example to conditional proof or *modus ponens*, the same will go for tonk-introduction and tonk-elimination. But it is wrong in concluding from this that there must be a mistake in the argument for the conditional rules— that we must reject the claim that one cannot coherently think that one has found, or could find, a counterexample to, say, *modus ponens*. This conclusion would be soundly drawn if, but only if, our rejection of the tonk rules had to be based upon recognition of counter-examples to them, or at least the possibility of such. But it is not, and could not be, so grounded. For that would require us to find, or at least conceive, a case in which, say, some statement A would be true, but A *tonk* B not true, or in which A *tonk* B would be true, while B is not true. And that—or so I claim—is something we cannot do. To be sure, nothing is easier than to come up with examples in which application of the tonk rules *together* would lead us from a true premise, say '7 + 5 = 12', to a false conclusion, say 'Hilary Putnam is a brain-in-a-vat', via the obvious intermediate contonktion. And one might be tempted to think that this shows that one or other of the tonk rules cannot be truth-preserving. But this thought is addled. There is, and can be, no ground for claiming that one rule rather than the other fails to preserve truth, and such examples do not entitle us to claim that neither does. It is no good saying that the tonk rules only fail to preserve truth when used in tandem, and that each of them is fine on its own, since this clashes with the well-entrenched, and surely correct, thought that we can't pass from true premises to a false conclusion by chaining together steps of reasoning each of which is truth-preserving. The immediate morals to be drawn are two. The first (which I am not, of course, the first to draw) is that whilst there is undoubtedly something wrong with the tonk rules, their fault is not most happily or illuminatingly characterized in terms of failure to preserve truth—neither can properly be convicted separately of this failing, and their failure collectively to preserve truth must surely be owed to some shortcoming of sets of inference rules which admits of a better, more informative characterization. One plausible suggestion is that the tonk rules fail a *conservativeness* constraint on rules of deduction, requiring (roughly) that acceptable rules for a logical operator, #, should not enable us to pass from #-free premises to a #-free conclusion in any case where that conclusion cannot be derived from those premises using only rules for logical operators figuring in them.[21] The second is that examples like that of 'tonk' do nothing to dislodge the thought that where acceptance of certain rules is necessary for understanding the logical operator they concern, a doubt about the soundness of those rules cannot take the shape of a belief that one can envisage circumstances in which one or other of those rules would fail to preserve truth.

On reflection, it is clear that a sceptic could accept this much, but insist that enough has been conceded the the counter-thought to block our attempt to carry through project B. Granted that a doubt about the tonk rules cannot be based upon the supposed possibility of envisaging a counter-example to one or other of the rules, it remains the case that a doubt about their soundness is possible, and indeed well-founded. And in just the same way, while a doubt about the rules for the conditional cannot, given their meaning-constitutive character, be based upon the supposed possibility of envisaging a counter-example to one of them, a doubt about their soundness must likewise be possible. And that is enough to show that we have no progress.

6. A Remedy for tonkitis

This sceptic's point is good, as far as it goes. But it would be a mistake to think that it locates an impassable obstacle to the project of explaining why it is not possible intelligently or coherently to doubt the soundness of basic inference rules such as *modus ponens* and conditional proof. To see why not, we need to consider how a doubt about the soundness of certain proposed rules, such as the tonk rules, might be vindicated.[22] We may take it, without loss of generality, that our doubt concerns whether the rules are conservative, in the sense roughly characterized previously. That some pair or, more generally, set of rules have this failing is not something which we

[21] First made, I believe, by Nuel Belnap in 'Tonk, Plonk and Plink', *Analysis* **22** (1962), pp. 130–4. Another, closely related, idea is that acceptable introduction and elimination rules should be harmonious in the sense—to put it roughly and intuitively—that the elimination rule is just as strong as it can be, given the introduction rule, or, putting it the other way around, the introduction rule is just as weak as it can be, given the elimination rule. For a more careful explanation and discussion, see Dummett *The Logical Basis of Metaphysics* chs. 9,11.

[22] I am assuming here that a doubt which admits of no conceivable vindication would be a merely idle doubt, and that we may take ourselves to be concerned with doubts that are real doubts, not merely idle ones.

may simply and literally *see*. It must, crucially, be the conclusion of a piece of *reasoning*, and that reasoning must proceed in accordance with some rules of inference. The obvious next question is: which rules? I claim that the rules one *uses* to demonstrate that certain rules are not conservative must be *other* than the rules whose conservativeness is in question. This claim may seem obviously correct—if so, well and good. But in case not, I had better explain why I think it should be accepted.

Charged with the task of showing that the tonk rules are non-conservative, it would be entirely natural to proceed as follows:

'Take any pair of tonkless $7 + 5 = 12$ and *Hilary Putnam is a*
propositions, say   *brain-in-a-vat*. Suppose

      (1) $7 + 5 - 12$

Then by tonk-   (2) $7 + 5 = 12$ tonk Hilary Putnam is a
introduction   brain-in-a-vat

whence by tonk- (3)   Hilary Putnam is a brain-in-a-va$_t$
elimination

Since the undischarged premise and final conclusion are tonkless, and the latter cannot be inferred from the former without using the tonk rules, those rules are non-conservative.'

There need be nothing amiss in this piece of reasoning, properly construed. But whatever appearance to the contrary it may present, it would be a mistake to construe it as involving a use of the tonk rules. For so construed, the argument would suffer from a fatal instability. One's acceptance of the final conclusion would then rest upon an undischarged reliance upon the tonk rules, but acceptance of the conclusion requires that one not rely upon inferences mediated by those rules, so that one has no business accepting it.

Someone might object that this overlooks the possibility that the quoted reasoning is intended to function as a *reductio ad absurdum*: 'Why *couldn't* one reason, using a rule R, to the conclusion that R is unsound? Wouldn't this just show that if the rule were sound, it would be unsound, so that it must be unsound?'

But it is just a confusion to think that the fact that one is attempting a *reductio* somehow makes it allowable to use an unsound rule in the course of it. It is crucial to any successful *reductio* that the reasoning by which one gets to the contradictory or otherwise absurd intermediate conclusion is *sound* reasoning. In the usual case, where what is discharged with the final step of the *reductio* is one of the premises from which an absurdity has been derived, it is essential that that derivation be correct. It is, obviously, no argument against the premise that one can *fallaciously* infer an absurdity from it. An objector may concede the point for ordinary *reductio* arguments, in which one shows that a *proposition* is false by deducing a contradiction from it, but claim that the present case is different, precisely because the target of the *reductio* is *not* a proposition but a *rule*—given that, why shouldn't proceed by *using* the rule to get to an absurd conclusion?

I think someone who feels disposed to make this counter probably isn't distinguishing carefully enough between reasoning *about* some rule(s) R and reasoning *using* rule(s) R. One could indeed reason, by *reductio*, in this way:

> 'Suppose the tonk rules were sound. Then by applying them, one could establish that .... But in that case, the tonk rules would be unsound. So they are unsound'.

But *this* reasoning doesn't *use* the tonk rules. It has the overall form: S→¬S, so ¬S. So neither of the tonk rules is used for the main step. Nor are they *used* in establishing the conditional premise. The reasoning in support of that will essentially consist of reasoning about what steps one *could* take, were one to use the tonk rules, and so would be reasoning *about* those rules. It won't—and certainly won't have to—involve any use of them. The structure of the quoted reasoning above can, accordingly, be more perspicuously displayed as follows:

> Suppose the tonk rules were sound. Then one could argue as follows, starting from any proposition p as premise:
> | (1) | p | |
> |-----|-----|---|
> | (2) | p tonk q | tonk-introduction, 1 |
> | (3) | q | tonk-elimination, 2 |
>
> where q is any proposition you like. But a rule that enables you to get from any p to any q is unsound. So if the tonk rules were sound, they wouldn't be. So they aren't.

And this patently doesn't involve any *use* of the tonk rules, only a claim about what use of the tonk rules would enable one to do.[23]

If what I've said is right, *any* vindication of a doubt about the

---

[23] A determined objector may retort: 'But suppose I do, by using rule R, reach the conclusion that rule R is unsound. I accept this conclusion, and surely I am right to do so. For either R is unsound or it isn't. If it is, then

conservativeness (or, more generally, the soundness) of *any* rules of inference must involve reasoning which doesn't use those rules, but uses *some* other rules instead—rules whose reliability is assumed in that reasoning. It does not, of course, follow from this that there must be *some* rules whose reliability must, and may properly, be assumed in *any* demonstration we can give of the conservativeness or non-conservativeness (more generally, soundness or unsoundness) of *any* (other) rules. It does not *follow*, but it is—or so I believe—*true*.

To see how it might be true, and what rules might be included in the privileged set, it will be useful to state more explicitly the reasoning given above to bring out the non-conservativeness of the tonk rules. If the reasoning were made more explicit, it would go somewhat as follows:

	(1) Tonk-intro allows you to make any inference of the form '*A*, so *A* tonk *B*'.
So:	(2) If the inference: '*p*, so p tonk *q*' is of the form '*A*, so *A* tonk *B*', then tonk-intro allows you to make it.
	(3) The inference: '*p*, so *p* tonk *q*' *is* of the form '*A*, so *A* tonk *B*'
Hence:	(4) Tonk-intro allows you to infer '*p* tonk *q*' from '*p*'.
Further:	(5) Tonk-elim allows you to make any inference of the form '*A* tonk *B*, so *B*'.
So:	(6) If the inference: '*p* tonk *q*, so *q*' is of the form '*A* tonk *B*, so *B*', then tonk-elim allows you to make it.
	(7) The inference: '*p* tonk *q*, so *q*' *is* of the form '*A* tonk *B*, so *B*'
Hence:	(8) Tonk-elim allows you to infer '*q*' from '*p* tonk *q*'.

clearly I'm right. And we suppose instead that it's sound, then my reasoning to the conclusion that it's unsound stands, and I'm right again. So either way, I'm right.'

But this just repeats the confusion in a new form—this time through not distinguishing what's *true* from what the envisaged proponent of reasoning using R is *entitled to think*. It entirely right that if the objector reasons by an unsound rule R to the conclusion that rule R is unsound, he will wind up with a *true* belief. But he won't be entitled to it. He would be entitled to it, if, having reasoned using R to some intermediate conclusion C (a contradiction, perhaps) on the basis of which he further infers that R is unsound, he stood back (as it were) and argued 'By using R, I was able to reach conclusion C. But any rule that enables one to reach that conclusion must be unsound. So R is unsound.' Once again, it is essential to keep clear the distinction between reasoning with R and reasoning about R (without using it). It is the second piece of reasoning, without R—the meta-reasoning—which entitles one to the conclusion that R isn't sound, not the (unsound) reasoning using R.

297

Bob Hale

Hence   (9) Tonk-intro and tonk-elim allow you to infer '*q*' from '*p*'.

Hence   (10) The tonk rules together allow you to derive any conclusion from any premise

Several points about this derivation merit attention. Lines (1) and (5) are, of course, simply general statements of the tonk rules. Their generality is important. It is because they are general that steps of *universal quantifier elimination* are required to obtain lines (2) and (6). And since those statements are conditional, steps of *modus ponens* are needed to obtain lines (4) and (8), given the relevant minor premises at lines (3) and (7)[24]. The conclusion at line (10) is

[24] The obvious truth of the minor premisses—(3) and (7) should not prevent us from enquiring into their justification. Since what is in question is, in effect, our recognition that a particular inference exemplifies the general pattern sanctioned by a rule of inference, it would be not merely implausible but potentially disastrous to suggest that our knowledge of these and similar such statements is got by inference—quite apart from the difficulty of coming up with any even remotely plausible premises from which such statements might be drawn as conclusions, it seems clear that any such inferential answer would set going a vicious infinite regress, of a piece with that into which Carroll's wily Tortoise enveigles the unwary Achilles Our recognition of their correctness must, it seems, be a non-inferential matter. That is, the right answer is just the one we should naturally give viz. that we can just *see* that the particular inference is of the displayed general form. *Seeing* here is not—or at least not simply—a matter of visual perception. For even if visual perception is involved—as it will be, if we are confronted with an inscription of the particular inference and perhaps also of the general pattern—the recognition that the one exemplifies the other is not a purely visual matter. Nor is seeing in this case, as it no doubt is in others, a matter of there being a more or less simple piece of reasoning which we could, if called upon, articulate. I can see no alternative to acknowledging that what is involved here is a species of non-inferential intellectual recognition—which we may as well call rational insight, and which has an indispensable rôle to play whenever we operate with rules of inference. No doubt there is much more to be said about this. For now, two caveats must suffice. First, I should perhaps emphasize the very limited rôle I am assigning to rational insight—in particular, I am not claiming that extends to recognition of the *validity* of inferences, only that it is mediates recognition of particular inferences as exemplifying general rules. Second, I am not suggesting that whenever we correctly apply general rules of inference, our application must be seen as a matter of inferring that a particular transition accords with the rule. That would be disastrously regressive. Here it is, once again, crucial to remember that explicit derivation of (4) and (8), in the argument in the text, is needed because we are *reasoning about* the tonk rules, *not using* them.

298

justified by the fact that p and q are arbitrary propositions and is, in effect, a step of *universal quantifier introduction*. Further, whilst the step to line (9) is not overtly an application *of conditional proof*, it is at least arguable that it is best understood as tacitly involving a use of that rule.

In short, it is arguable that the standard rules for the conditional and universal quantifier play an indispensable rôle in our argument for the unsoundness of the tonk rules. It does not, of course, follow—at least, not without further argument—that these rules must be involved in any reasoning about the soundness or otherwise of any inference rules. But it seems to me that that is so. Any rule(s) of inference whose soundness we may wish to consider will—or so I think we may assume—be both *general* and *conditional*—general, in the sense that their explicit formulation tells us that a conclusion of some specified general form may be drawn from premises of some specified general form, and conditional, in the sense that they tell us that *given* premises of the specified form, a conclusion of the specified form may be drawn. Any reasoning *about* what inferences they permit—as distinct from reasoning that simply uses those rules—will, at least if fully articulated, involve reasoning from explicit formulations of the rules. In virtue of the general and conditional character of their explicit formulations, any such reasoning must involve at least some steps of universal quantifier elimination and, in conjunction with suitable minor premises, steps of *modus ponens;* and if any general conclusions about the kinds of inference the rules permit are to be drawn, it will involve steps of universal quantifier introduction and, arguably, steps of conditional introduction.

If this is right, then there is what might be called a *minimal kit* of inference rules—including at least rules for the conditional and universal quantifier—required for any reasoning about the soundness of any rules of inference. Clearly there is more to be said in elaboration and defence of this idea[25], but rather than pursue it further here, I want now to explain its bearing on my main issue.

[25] In particular, it is desirable to formulate my claim about the essential involvement of conditionality and generality, and the consequent need for principles governing them, in a way that renders it independent of any assumption about which particular linguistic devices subserve the expression of those notions. Obviously it is inessential that we express conditional propositions using the word 'if', for example, rather than as disjunctions or negated conjunctions. The only essential point is that we have some means of expressing a binary sentential compound with the distinctive inferential properties of the conditional; likewise, *mutatis mutandis*, for generality. A fuller discussion would also investigate what other principles

Let us, first, briefly take stock. We have been concerned with two kinds of doubt about the soundness of rules of inference. We may come to think that some rule of inference is unsound because we think we can envisage direct counter-examples to it, i.e. cases in which its application would lead us from true premises to a false conclusion. I have claimed that whilst a doubt of this kind may lead us to reject, or at least withhold assent to, some suggested rules of inference, there is no space for a coherent doubt of this first kind in any case in which our acceptance of the rule is partly constitutive of, and so required for, understanding the logical operator that rule concerns. However, accepting a rule or pair of rules for a logical operator is insufficient to guarantee a coherent use for it, or to ensure that those rules are sound. In particular, against the claim that there can be no intelligible doubt of this first kind about the standard rules for the conditional, it may be objected that an exactly parallel claim could be made on behalf of rules which are clearly unsound, such as the tonk rules. It may then be claimed that since it must be possible to entertain a coherent doubt about the tonk rules, there must after all be space for such a doubt about the usual rules for the conditional. So we appear to be no further forward with project B—the project of explaining why there can be no intelligible doubt about them. In response to this objection, I have argued that the point about doubt of the first kind is good, as far as it goes—there must indeed be space for doubt about the tonk rules—but that such doubt cannot, any more than in the case of the rules for the conditional, be grounded in the alleged possibility of envisaging direct counter-examples to them. It must rather take the form of a doubt about their possession of other properties required for soundness in a general sense, such as conservativeness. Any vindication of a doubt of this second kind—reason to think the rules are non-conservative, say—must, I have argued, involve reasoning, and this reasoning must, on pain of destabilizing, proceed in accordance with rules *other than* the tonk rules themselves (or whatever rules they may be, whose soundness is in question). It must, I have claimed, rely upon a minimal kit of inference rules which will include at least the usual conditional and quantifier rules.

If a doubt of this second kind were possible in regard to any rules of inference whatever, then we would, of course, be no further forward with project B. Indeed, it would follow that that project is

of inference, in addition to principles concerning conditionality and generality, might be needed in the minimal kit. It is plausible that the kit should provide for reasoning by reductio ad absurdum, and hence that some (weak, non-classical) rules for handling negation will be needed.

hopeless. But if what I have argued thus far is correct—and, in particular, if I am right in my claim that there is a minimal set of inference rules which must be available for use in prosecuting doubts about soundness of the second kind—then we are in position to see that this is not so. For if there is such a minimal kit, its ingredient inference rules cannot be subjected to a genuine doubt of this kind. Any attempt to vindicate the suspicion that they are unsound (e.g. non-conservative) would involve an undischarged reliance upon those very rules, and so would inevitably abort. Nothing I've argued shows that the supposition that the usual conditional rules, for example, might be unsound (because non-conservative, say) is directly incoherent in the way that the supposition that one has found, or could find, a counter-example to *modus ponens* is—or so I've claimed—incoherent. But we can see that it is impossible that we should have a reason to think that supposition true, so that the doubt cannot but be an empty, idle, doubt. My intermediate conclusion, in sum, is that the minimal rules are immune to doubt in a very strong sense. Given their meaning-constitutive character, they are not open to doubt of the first kind; and given their indispensable rôle in reasoning about soundness in general, they cannot be subjected to a genuine doubt on that score. Thus unless there is some way in which they might relevantly be questioned, we have—at least in outline—an explanation why there can be no intelligible doubt about them.[26]

7. Basic logical knowledge

I want now to return to the ostensibly more ambitious of the two projects distinguished in Section 4—the project of explaining *how we can come to know* that basic rules such as *modus ponens* are sound. Assuming my proposed explanation why we cannot rationally and intelligibly doubt the soundness of certain basic rules of inference is, at least in essentials, correct, can we build on it to achieve an explanation of how basic logical knowledge is possible? I think it may be possible to do so, but I must confess that I feel far less sure about this than I feel about what I have argued to this point.

It may seem that any attempt to take this further step is bound to

[26] It may be suggested that, at least when fully articulated, the proposed explanation will be found to involve applications of at least some of the minimal rules, and will therefore be rule-circular. That is probably so—but it will be an objection only if, contrary to what I have claimed, rule-circularity must be vicious even in the context of an explanation why something is the case, just as it arguably is in an explanation how it can be known to be the case or in a suasive argument.

Bob Hale

fall foul of a simple objection. Suppose it is granted that we have an explanation why our basic rules are immune to relevant doubt. To advance from this to the conclusion that claims about their soundness are true, and known to be so, will surely require some reasoning. And it is hard, if not impossible, to see how any reasoning to the purpose could avoid using at least some of those very rules, so that any attempt to close the gap between our intermediate and our final conclusion must be rule-circular. Further, the rule-circularity involved would be of precisely the kind I have claimed to be especially problematic, because it would occur in the context of an attempted explanation of how we can come to know something.[27] So, unless it can be argued that that kind of rule-circularity is, after all, tolerable, we seem to be stymied.

There would, perhaps, be an impassable obstacle here, if—as the objection assumes—moving from an explanation why the soundness of the minimal rules is not open to rational doubt to an explanation how they can be known to be sound must involve representing that knowledge as inferential. But must we, if we are to negotiate this transition, take the impossibility of doubt as a *premise*, and reason from that to a further conclusion, to the effect that the rules are indeed sound? Perhaps it can be maintained that there is, simply, no inferential gap to be traversed—that is, that knowledge can, much as Descartes thought, consist in believing truly something which it is impossible rationally to doubt. If so, then it seems to me that it may be possible to hold that basic logical knowledge is, after all, a species of non-inferential knowledge—but one which diverges sharply from the models of non-inferential knowledge, supplied by sense-perception and introspection, which I dismissed (in section 2) as unhelpful. Part of the trouble with those models lies in their involvement of the idea that we are affected by, and distinctively sensitive to, independently constituted facts, or states of affairs, of the kind to which they give access. This is why they are, at best, models for knowledge of particular and contingent truths. And this in turn is why nothing very like them looks to be a promising model for basic logical knowledge. Such knowledge is knowledge of truths that are both general and necessary, and we can make little or nothing useful of the suggestion that we are affected by and sensitive to general necessities. But what cannot rationally be doubted can perfectly well be a truth that is both general and necessary.

A general model of knowledge—of inferential as well as non-inferential knowledge—which would accommodate my suggestion might run roughly as follows. To know that p is to have a true belief

[27] See section 3 above, and the previous footnote.

that p and to be *entitled* to that belief. There are various much discussed ways in which a thinker may be so entitled. She may have a
warrant to believe that p, in the sense that she has reasons or grounds
to believe that p which she can articulate. Or she may have acquired
her belief that p by a reliable method which does not involve her having independently ratifiable grounds or reasons for her belief.
Perhaps she can just see or hear or otherwise sensorily detect that p,
or be introspectively aware that p—that is, it may be enough that she
be sensorily or introspectively affected in ways that induce in her a
belief that p, provided that there no special grounds to suspect that
she is victim to some perceptual or introspective illusion or mal-
function. Alternatively—and to a first, crude, approximation—she
may satisfy the entitlement condition by believing something which
it is impossible—and so impossible for her—rationally to doubt.[28]

This suggestion gives rise to a host of questions—some concerning the acceptability of this general model of knowledge, others
concerning the possibility of accommodating my specific suggestion within it. And there are also, perhaps, questions about how we
should conceive the facts which are the objects of logical knowledge,
if my suggestion is to be accepted[29]. I must—and thankfully can—

---

[28] This is, fairly obviously, too weak as it stands, since it would have it
that all that is required of me, if I am to qualify as knowing some true and
rationally indubitable proposition p, is that I believe p. But that can hardly
suffice for knowledge—since it imposes no constraint whatever on the reasons why I so believe, or the route by which I come to believe, and so leaves
it open that I may believe p for bad or even quite crazy reasons. I cannot,
for example, get to know that p by fallaciously inferring it from q and *if p
then q* (which I also believe), even if it is true and indubitable that p. It
would not help to require that I believe p precisely because I believe it to
be indubitable, since the same difficulty would arise over my belief that p
is indubitable—if I hold that belief for irrelevant or crazy reasons, I should
(still) not count as knowing. It seems clear that what is required, if my true
belief in what is in fact rationally indubitable is to amount to knowledge,
is that my belief should arise in the right way, or be appropriately caused:
I should believe that p, not as a result of my holding any *other* beliefs, but
simply because I cannot see how it might intelligibly be doubted that p—
where, to stress the crucial point, this does *not* mean that I believe that p
because I believe that there is no room for doubt that p, much less that I
infer that p from my inability to see how one might doubt it.

[29] What I mainly have in mind here is the question whether—to express
the matter in terms of the Euthyphro contrast prominent in much of
Crispin Wright's work on truth and objectivity—the facts which are the
objects of logical knowledge are appropriately conceived as obtaining
independently of, and at most 'tracked' by, our best opinions or judgements under optimal conditions, or whether they ought instead to be

duck out of taking the larger and more difficult among them here. I shall conclude with a couple of fairly obvious points, both of them linked to larger questions or potential difficulties for my view.

First, if my suggestion is to be upheld, it seems to me necessary to distinguish sharply between incorrigibility and infallibility. My proposal is, in effect, that basic logical beliefs are immune to rational doubt, and as such, are incorrigible. But I do not think that this commits me to holding that they are infallible—or, more accurately, that we are equipped with an infallible method of arriving at true logical beliefs. On the matter of what can and what cannot be rationally subjected to doubt, we are no less liable to error than elsewhere. And it is, of course, only if the soundness of a rule really is beyond rational doubt that we can know it to be sound.

Second, what I am taking to be sufficient to entitle us to a basic logical belief is its *being* immune to rational doubt not our *knowing* or *justifiably believing* it to be so. This is obviously crucial, if the worries I have expressed about rule-circular arguments are well-founded. If one tries to view my explanation why we cannot entertain a genuine doubt about the soundness of *modus ponens*, say, as showing how we can know, or justifiably believe, that there can be no such doubt, then, since it undoubtedly involves at least one use of that rule, it would involve a rule-circularity of the kind I have taken to be problematic. If this is to be avoided, I must deny that knowledge, or warranted belief, that the rule is immune to rational doubt is required for entitlement. I think this is defensible, at least if it is defensible—as I think it is—to hold that we may acquire knowledge through sense-perception, say, without having a warranted belief that the relevant conditions for the operation of the sense in question are normal. But I realize that this, along with much else in this closing section, calls for a much fuller defence than I have been able to provide here.[30]

University of Glasgow

[30] This paper grew out of several discussions with Crispin Wright, to whom I am much indebted. Earlier versions had airings at seminars in the universities of Aarhus, Durham, Glasgow, Western Ontario and Waterloo, as well as in the Royal Institute lecture series itself. I am grateful to my audiences on all these occasions, and especially to Bill Demopoulos, Jim Edwards, Laurence Goldstein, Lars Gunderson, Bill Harper, Robin Hendry, Gary Kemp, Max Kölbel, Jimmy Lenman, Jonathan Lowe, David Papineau, Philip Percival, John Benson and Adam Rieger.

viewed as in some manner constituted or determined by such opinions or judgements. For discussion of the Euthyphro contrast, see Wright's *Truth & Objectivity* (Cambridge, MA: Harvard University Press, 1992), especially pp. 108–39.

Frege's Target

CHARLES TRAVIS

'Hostility to psychologism', John McDowell writes, 'is not hostility to the psychological.[1] 'Psychologism' is an accusation. But it may be either of several.

The psychologism McDowell is master of detecting is, as he sometimes puts it, a form of scientism. It is *a priori* psychology where, at best, only substantive empirical psychology would do. It often represents itself as describing the way any thinker (or any empirical, or language-using one) *must* be; as describing requirements on being a thinker at all. But it misses viable alternatives. It is just speculation as to how we are.

McDowell sees Frege as his anti-psychologistic ally. Frege attacked misguided applications of psychology. What he attacked might certainly be called psychologism. But his target was rather different from McDowell's, which is better seen as the mis-derivation of substantive psychological results. Frege objected to mistaking the psychological for the logical. That would involve appealing to perhaps quite genuine psychological facts as deciding questions on which they did not (thus) bear. It would be to suppose our design as thinkers of a special sort to shape, not just our particular ways of thinking of things, or our capacities to see in the world what we can, but also that which we thus think about—to make some realm of non-psychological fact what it is. That worry about reading the wrong significance into a special psychological design runs in roughly the opposite direction to McDowell's worry: failing to see where something *is* a question of special design; trying to derive from some supposed way any thinker *must* be what can only be a matter of how certain thinkers in fact are.

McDowell himself makes frequent appeal to ways in which we, or relevant thinkers, are thinkers of a special sort. Our special design opens our eyes, as he puts it, to particular tracts of reality. That our eyes may be thus opened shows where, and how, there may be facts that it takes special capacities, not enjoyed by just any thinker, to see. It also has metaphysical significance. For it identifies places

[1] John McDowell, 'On the Sense and Reference of a Proper Name', in his *Meaning, Knowledge and Reality*, (Cambridge, Massachusetts: Harvard University Press, 1998), p. 181.

305

where there are domains of facts which are not, or need not be, derivable from facts of other sorts—facts available to any thinker equipped only with somehow more basic, or more widely shared, cognitive capacities. It shows how facts, and domains of them, may have more varied and intricate shapes than such a reductionist demand would permit. As that idea plays out, our special capacities inform—decide in part—the shapes of the facts to which they open our eyes. We hope to read that: they decide, in part, to what shape of fact our eyes are open. But there is a risk that we will have to read it: they decide, in part, the shapes of those facts to which, anyway, our eyes are open. Or there may seem to be that risk. That idea would be the psychologism which is Frege's target. I do not think McDowell guilty of that. But to banish vertigo, one must see just where there is at least apparent risk, and how it may be disarmed. That is the main task of the present essay.

In some sense laws of logic are laws all thinkers must conform to. In whatever sense that is, they describe conditions on being a thinker at all. Depending on the sense, that may leave room for the idea that we have special capacities—features of our design as thinkers of a special sort—which allow us to appreciate the particular logical laws we do. A secondary aim here is to sketch what that room is. Failure to see it may lead one to slide (as Frege may have) from a legitimate view of laws of logic as holding for, and binding, any thinker at all to a view of what any thinker must be like that would be psychologism in McDowell's sense.

1. Logic

For the most part Frege's anti-psychologism is highly domain-specific. It is psychologism about *logic,* specifically its laws, that is, for him, the devil. On occasion he takes a somewhat broad view of the logical, so that what is at stake is not just laws of logic. On at least one occasion he broadens his target beyond the logical to include what he calls the source of logic's brand of unconditioned necessity. Frege's views on laws of logic are encapsulated in the following:

> The question why and with what right we acknowledge a law of logic to be true, logic can answer only by reducing it to another law of logic. Where that is not possible, logic can give no answer. If we step away from logic, we may say: we are compelled to make judgments by our own nature and by external circumstances; and if we do so, we cannot reject this law ... I shall merely remark that

... what is given is not a reason for something's being true, but for our taking it to be true. ... Anyone who has once acknowledged a law of truth has by the same token acknowledged a law that prescribes the way in which one ought to judge, no matter where or when, or by whom the judgment is *made*.[2]

Here Frege assigns two properties to laws of logic. The first might be called *absoluteness*. The truth of a law of logic depends on nothing, or nothing extra-logical. This means that a law of logic would be true (or would be a fact) no matter how things stood extra-logically; so no matter what experience might have to teach us. If we wanted to explain the truth of a law of logic by appealing to *our* nature—say to what, or how, we cannot help thinking—our attempt would misfire. And, though this may be reading things into Frege, if we tried to explain the truth of a law of logic by appealing to facts of geology, say, or chemistry, we would, presumably, equally be barking up the wrong tree (if not just plain barking). One possible source of this idea of absoluteness is the idea that laws of logic are (just) the most *general* facts of meaning.[3] But there is another source for the idea which will emerge presently. The second feature Frege ascribes to laws of logic might be called *universality*. Whatever it is a law of logic says, it is something true of, or binding on, all thought whatsoever. It thus describes a feature of all possible thinkers, not just thinkers who share our special (human) design. (One might usefully take this mark of the logical as helping to identify what it is that a law of logic could possibly say.) That laws of logic are the most general truths, or most general facts of meaning, is an idea often identified in Frege. So, it seems, laws of logic have, on Frege's view, at least three identifying features: absoluteness, universality and (maximum) generality.

Frege sometimes takes a broad view of the logical. Thus, in the introduction to *Grundlagen* he announces his determination 'always to separate sharply the psychological from the logical, the subjective from the objective' and never to ask for the meaning of a word in

[2] Gottlob Frege, *Grundgesetze der Aritmetik,* introduction, reprinted as *The Basic Laws of Arithmetic,* translated and edited by Montgomery Furth, University of California Press, Berkeley and Los Angeles, 1967, p. 15 in this translation.

[3] Of factive meaning, as I prefer to conceive it, or of representation, depending on how one conceives logical relations. Frege speaks of the most general facts of *truth* ('Guiding principles for thought in the attainment of truth' (*Grundgesetze*, p. 101)), which suggests that he thought of logic as about representation.

isolation, but only in the context of a sentence.[4] If one violates the second rule, Frege thinks, one will inevitably try to find the meaning by staring at the word and seeing what comes to mind. What comes to mind will be one or another association one makes with the word—Frege supposes it will be what he calls an 'idea'—where the association in question is a psychological phenomenon. That will be to mistake the psychological for the logical. Whereas if one asks for the meaning of the word in context, one will be apt to answer the question by specifying the (or a) role the word plays in that context. If the context one chooses is a sentence, the role one finds is apt to be the contribution of the word to the conditions for truth of (or for being as represented by) the whole of which the word is a part. To answer in terms of role, or, at any rate, in terms of that role, is to answer by speaking of the logical, and to mistake nothing else for that. Roughly, the logical, on this conception, seems to be whatever it is (including relations to other representations) that fixes, or is fixed by, when a representation would be true.

Laws of logic, Frege insists, depend for their holding on nothing (extra-logical). There is a way in which this autonomy is shared by all logical facts, on the above broad conception of the logical. Suppose one asks why the 'Frege' in a given 'Frege was bearded', is such that if that whole is true, then that 'Frege' referred to someone. The answer might be, 'Because, in that context, that 'Frege' functioned as a name.' Suppose one asked why that 'Frege' then functioned as a name. That might elicit an answer in psychological terms, perhaps on roughly these lines: 'Because that is how a competent speaker would understand it.' And indeed, that the 'Frege' in a given 'Frege was bearded' is a name does seem to depend on psychology in some way. But suppose one asked why a name is such that when it so functions in a true statement it refers to something. The question would seem to reflect some sort of misunderstanding. All one could say by way of answer is, 'That is just (part of) what being a name (or what referring) is.' That *names* have that property depends on no extra-logical fact (on our broad conception of the logical). If all competent speakers understood a given utterance, 'Frege', differently, then perhaps it would not be a name. But a *name* would have the mentioned feature no matter what. Just as with a law of logic, that *names* are thus depends on nothing.

The point extends throughout the logical in the present sense. So, for example, one might consider the English predicate, 'is a chair'.

---

[4] G. Frege, *The Foundations of Arithmetic,* J. L. Austin, translator, Oxford: Basil Blackwell, 1978, p. x.

One might ask what makes that predicate such that it is true of (precisely) chairs. An answer might be that it is that by virtue of its meaning what it does. And there is presumably some psychological, or historical, story as to why it means what it does (perhaps the history of Indo-european languages). A way of capturing the fact of 'is a chair' meaning what it does is to say that it expresses the concept of being a chair. Now suppose we ask why the concept of being a chair is true of (or fits, or is satisfied by) precisely chairs. That question, too, seems to reflect a misunderstanding. For the answer that suggests itself is, roughly, 'For a concept to be the concept of a chair is just for that to be so of it.' Again, nothing extra-logical—in this case, nothing external to its being the concept of a chair that is in question—has any role in determining whether or not that concept has that feature.

At least in the cases at hand, the kind of autonomy which, in the case of laws of logic, is their absoluteness—independence of facts of any other sort—reflects the intrinsicness of relevant features of relevant items. It is intrinsic to a name that (where there is truth or falsity at all) it identifies that item on whose being thus and so the truth of its whole depends. Nothing that lacks that feature would be a name. It is intrinsic to a certain concept that it fits whatever is thus and so. That feature is (part of) what makes a given concept *that* one. Without it, a concept simply would not be that one. So there is no way of picking out something there might be anyway—something determinately what it is independent of its having the relevant feature—and then asking why it should be a concept with that feature. If it *is* so identifiable, then, trivially, it is not that concept. Generalising, facts hold absolutely in Frege's sense where their holding is intrinsic to the things they involve.

Absolute logical facts thus reflect intrinsic features of things they concern—conjunction and negation, say (and truth). A fact about those things depends on nothing just where that is just part of what conjunction and negation are (what it did not hold of *ipso facto* would not be those things). Such absoluteness is possible only for what is austerely enough conceived—what is sparse enough in intrinsic features. If there are too many things conjunction is *per se*—too many ways it is identifiable as the thing it is (say, both by a truth table and by some design which, *per se,* expresses it), then it becomes possible to ask intelligibly how it is that what, *per se,* has some of these features also has the others—that conjunction, say, fixed by a certain distribution in our thought, also has a certain truth table. A substantive answer to such questions, where there is room for one, is liable to make crucial (putatively) intrinsic features

Charles Travis

depend on something. (There may be absolute facts about the concept *chair* which could not hold *absolutely* of the English 'is a chair' precisely because there is something that English looks like; and the point holds even if we think of words as partly individuated by their content.) That laws of logic are to be absolute in Frege's sense puts, I think, severe constraints on what such a law could say—constraints ignored in much discussion of laws of logic.[5] It is easily forgotten that austerity is part of what absoluteness is.

On at least one occasion, Frege broadens the target of his anti-psychologism to include challenges to what he tells us is the source of logic's absoluteness: the objectivity of truth. He says,

> If it is true that I am writing this in my chamber on the 13th of July, 1893, while the wind howls outside, then it remains true if all men should subsequently take it to be false. If being true is thus independent of being acknowledged by somebody or other, then the laws of truth are not psychological laws ... They do not bear the relation to thought that the laws of grammar bear to language; they do not make explicit the nature of our human thinking and change as it changes.[6]

For whatever the notion of truth actually fits,—whatever is, world willing, true, or, at worst, false—there is a substantive distinction between being true and being thought true (by whatever thinkers). If we think truly that such-and-such, then what we thus think so is so, and would be so no matter what, how, or whether, we, or any thinkers, thought. Whether what we think so is so is thus not a matter of psychology. So, Frege tells us, neither are laws of truth (or of logic). To deny the objectivity of truth in this sense would just be to hold that what the facts are in those areas of reality we think about (or some of them) depends on what, or how we, or certain thinkers, think. That doubtfully coherent conception of areas in which, as it has it, facts hold is just idealism. It is just that that McDowell (and with him Wittgenstein) must, but may seem unable to, avoid.

2. Grammar

As has emerged, Frege views grammar as, in some sense, a psychological phenomenon. He says, for example,

[5] See My 'What Laws of Logic Say', *Pragmatics and Realism: Hilary Putnam*, U. Zeglen amd J. Conant, eds., London: Routledge, 2002, pp. 188–208.

[6] Frege, *Grundgesetze der Arithmetik*, p. 13.

Grammar, which has a significance for language analogous to that which logic has for judgment, is a mixture of the logical and the psychological.[7]

If we think of the laws of logic as psychological, we shall be inclined to raise the question whether they are somehow subject to change. Are they like the grammar of a language which may, of course, change with the passage of time? This is a possibility we really have to face up to if we hold that the laws of logic derive their authority from a source similar to that of the laws of grammar ... [8]

What the laws of, say, English grammar are really does depend, in some way, on psychological fact. Frege emphasises this in part with didactic purpose. He contrasts grammar with logic in order to separate off a range of notions, such as those of subject and predicate, which, he insists, have no role to play in logic. Whenever we detect that a notion has psychological content in the way grammatical notions do, we thereby detect, in his view, that it is no part of logic. In any event, whatever objection there is to making logic out as dependent on psychology, there is no objection to making grammar out as so dependent.

Grammar, Frege tells us, is a *mixture* of the psychological and the logical. If so, in what sense is it a psychological phenomenon, and in what sense is it a logical one? For the answer to that we should look to Noam Chomsky (though not all philosophers, nor linguists, agree that grammar is psychological in the way Chomsky has pointed to). I will set out his view in terms suggested by his earliest exposition of it. But, though the terminology has changed with time, I think that, modulo one small detail, the view has remained much the same.

We might use the term 'grammar' either to refer to an explicit theory of some natural language, or to refer to the organisation, or properties, that such a theory might truly ascribe to it. Thinking in the first way, we might think of a grammar as a theory which, with finite means, generates a set of sentence-descriptions, or, equivalently, a set of assignments of properties, to (what according to it) are sentences of its target language. What goals might such a theory aim to meet?

One reasonable goal would be to identify the sentences of the

[7] G. Frege, 'Logic' (1897), in *Posthumous Writings*, Basil Blackwell, Oxford, 1979, p. 129.

[8] Frege, 'Logic' (1897) in *Posthumous Writings*, Oxford: Basil Blackwell, 1979, p. 147.

target language—to distinguish correctly between sentences of that language and strings of words or pseudo-words that were not sentences. To do that, a grammar should at least make some assignment of properties to each sentence of the language, and, for every assignment of properties it generates, there should be some sentence of the language that has those properties. In other terms, for every sentence of the language, the theory should generate some description that fits it, and for every description it generates, that description should fit some sentence of the language. Further, for certain designated descriptions the theory generates (think of them as full, or maximal, ones), those descriptions should fit no non-sentence of the language. One might further demand that, for descriptions of a designated sort, for every two such descriptions the theory generates, there should be two sentences of the language, each of which fits precisely one of these; and that, wherever there are two different sentences, no generated description of this sort fits both of them. (These desiderata leave it open precisely what a sentence is. For all said so far, it might just be a string of words.)

Meeting the above goal is less than one might reasonably hope for. For there seem to be clear grammatical facts a grammar need not capture in order to meet it. To take a hackneyed example, consider the sentences 'Zoë expected Des to spill his beer' and 'Zoë persuaded Des to spill his beer.' A grammar might meet the above goal without marking any structural difference between these sentences. Yet we (any reasonably fluent English speaker) can, on brief reflection, see that there is a difference. To tell the story quickly and sketchily, one expects events (or people, or objects, to arrive) whereas one persuades people (or other thinkers). If sentences may have such things as direct objects, and if direct objects are constituents, then the two sentences just mentioned must have significantly different structures. Any grammar that did not assign them such would miss a syntactic fact.

What goal could we impose on grammars that would require them to capture such facts? I have just pointed to a fact we competent English speakers are prepared to recognise; to a way we, the competent, see, or are prepared to see, such sentences as the above to be structured. One goal for a grammar might be that, in addition to meeting the above goal, it should assign sentences (just) those structures that the fluent are thus prepared to see in them. Or, more liberally, we might require a grammar to assign properties to the sentences of its target language in that way which best reflected what the fluent are thus prepared to recognise (at least so far as it is determinate which way this would be).

There are ways we see the sentences of our languages to be structured. A grammar which said which ways these were would, to that extent, at least, be saying what structure these sentences had, and, more generally, just how the language was organised syntactically. (A remark on the factivity of 'see'.) That there are such structures to describe has implications for the notion of a sentence, and thus for what it would be even to meet the lower goal set above. For it follows that a sentence is not just a string of words, but rather a string of words structured in a particular way. It follows that there might be two sentences made up of the same words in the same order, but differing in their syntactic structure. That idea corresponds to our ordinary way of thinking of a sentence. For we think of a sentence as having such things as a subject, a direct object and a main verb. Strings such as 'Flying planes can be dangerous' are, we can see, structurally ambiguous. What the subject of that string is depends on the structure it is read as having. Which means that, so thinking, that ordering of words is a common feature of two different sentences.

A grammar which met our higher goal would be capturing facts a grammar might miss in meeting the lower one. When we now shift to the other understanding of 'grammar' as those properties of a language which a grammar, in the first sense, might truly ascribe, we get a certain picture of what a language is. If a language is identified by its sentences, then a natural language is identified, not by some set of strings of words, but rather by some definite range of syntactic structures—those structures that its sentences might have. A language thus is, or incorporates, a particular system for forming such constructions.[9]

[9] In *Knowledge of Language* (New York: Praeger, 1986, especially chapter 2), Chomsky puts much the same view in different terms. There he distinguishes between what he calls an E(external)-language and an I(internal)-language. An E-language simply is, by definition, whatever any two grammars would agree on in meeting our first, lower, goal. An I-language is (at least) what a grammar that met our second, higher goal, would say it is. So, for example, an E-language sentence is a string of words (contrary to our ordinary notion of a sentence), whereas an I-language sentence is a particular syntactic structure, not identifiable with a string of words. An I-language is thus, for example, English, as we are able to see it. The only change in view here is that Chomsky no longer regards such notions as *English*, or *German*, as scientifically respectable. None of the reasons he adduces, though, seem good reason not to take 'English' or 'German' as indicating sufficiently (though not perfectly) determinate I-languages—as, I think, a proper appreciation of our mental lives requires.

This view of syntax brings out in just what way grammar is a psychological phenomenon: the syntactic facts of a given natural language are, or include, what its fluent speakers are prepared to see in it. One might view that as a form of idealism: if English speakers thought differently about their language, there might not be the syntactic facts of English that there are. But that is innocent idealism. It only makes what is plausibly the psychological, and not some domain of non-psychological fact, depend on given psychologies.

In what way, then, is grammar a logical phenomenon? 'Des', as it occurs in 'Zoë persuaded Des to spill his beer', plays a particular syntactic role. It has a particular place in a particular syntactic structure. There are two things one can say about that. In one sense (on the present view), for 'Des' to have the syntax it there does is for fluent speakers to see that syntax in it. It has that syntax because of what it is to fluent speakers, and would not have it were it something else to them. In another sense, for 'Des' to have that syntax is for it to have a certain syntactic role in that sentence,—a role that a correct grammar of English (by our higher standard of correctness) would spell out. That is what it is to have the syntax 'Des' there has. That role, and not speakers of the language, is what a grammar would speak of. To speak of it is to speak of the logical in the sense of *Grundlagen*. On the view set out here, the psychologies of fluent speakers decide, at least in part, what the grammatical facts are. But to say that need not be to mistake the psychological for the logical. Nor is there any other reason to refuse to say it. So to refuse would be, it seems, to deny manifest facts.

Chomsky's work on syntax began in a climate in which a certain sort of empiricism was taken very seriously. It would not be genuine work if that empiricism were correct. His view of syntax as a psychological phenomenon is essential to his rejection of that empiricism. Next I will describe that empiricism, and then how that rejection works.

3. Empiricism

What follows is meant, not as stipulation, but as, recognisably, a description of a family of actual positions. Empiricism is, first of all, a position arrived at *a priori*. It's guiding notion, put one way, is that we are universal thinkers: we enjoy no cognitive capacities, so see nothing of the world, that would not be shared by any thinker with our sensory sensitivity to the stimuli that impinge on us (such things as light, sound, pressure). That idea is doubtfully coherent, presupposing as it does that there are enough capacities one *must* have (when equipped with sight, hearing, and so on) to qualify one as a thinker at all.[10] But it is a useful way of thinking of what would move an empiricist to allow, or disallow, us the particular avenues of knowledge that he does.

The principal *a priori* rationale for the empiricist's view of our capacities, and our access to the world, is, I will suggest, epistemological.[11] The epistemology at work there is sceptical. It is this epistemology that can make the empiricist's contentions that we lack cognitive capacities which would be features merely of a special psychological design seem, at least at first blush, something other than blatant psychologism. For it will be stressed that cognitive capacities are, by definition, *knowledge* yielding; and the doubt is whether any features of special design could merit that status. Since Hume, empiricists have typically allowed that we may have all sorts of special tendencies to think or feel things, or otherwise to react to sensory impingements. To that extent there are few *a priori* limits to the ways human beings may be creatures of a special sort. The question is whether such tendencies could ever, strictly speaking, amount to an ability to see, or to discover, how things are. The worry is that only in certain circumstances would such tendencies get things right; the design which confers them is not one for telling whether we are in such circumstances, so the design that confers them on us could never (thereby) confer on us a special route to knowledge.

That qualm is in view, for example, in empiricist attitudes towards 'ordinary language'. There are, the empiricist admits, things a fluent speaker is inclined to say. Part of being fluent may be having such inclinations. In certain cases we just would say that Pia had seen the pig loose in the turnips, or that Zoë had hurt Sid's feelings. Being so inclined is, in some sense, part of the way an unreflective fluent speaker ought to be. What the empiricist does not

[10] The idea that there might *be* a universal seeing, hearing, ..., thinker is reinforced by the rationalist view of our cognitive capacities (as exemplified by Leibniz) in traditional 17th and 18th century debates. One distinct strand in 17th century rationalism is the felt need to posit unmissable, cognitive capacities, though more specific and complex than what the empiricist typically would countenance. There is, presumably, an interesting point of agreement here, worth exploring if one aims for a general picture of psychologism in all its manifestations.

[11] Descartes, in his animal automatism, suggests a non-epistemic rationale. This turns on his way of drawing the distinction between intelligence and brute instinct. I doubt, though, that this line of thought held much sway with, say, Locke, or Hume or Quine.

grant, though, is that what the fluent speaker thus exhibits is an ability to see when things are those ways the relevant bits of his language speak of being—when someone saw a pig, or caused anguish. What is in question is whether the special design that makes for relevant fluent speaking is the sort of thing that could confer the ability to gain such *knowledge,* to enjoy positions in which such questions are really settled.

When empiricism comes to a particular domain of fact, it is marked by three, or, often, four, features flowing out of the general train of thought just sketched. First, it will hold that, relative to that domain, there is a particular, specified domain of privileged fact. Privileged facts are, typically, what, for relevant purposes, is, strictly speaking, *observable*—that is, observable by any thinker with our sensitivity to the relevant sensory media. One might also think of them as what would *always* count as observable by us, no matter what doubts there may be as to how things really are. Empiricism, cast in this form, thus invokes a proprietary notion of the observable. Where there might be a thinker with adequate sensory equipment, but unable to see how things stood in the relevant domain (e.g., because he lacked relevant concepts), the privileged facts will be ones he could, in principle, be aware of, or ascertain, anyway. In such a case, the privileged facts would be distinct from those (supposedly) holding in the relevant domain.

Second, for a given domain, the empiricist will claim to identify those procedures, or abilities, which are the knowledge-yielding ones with respect to that domain. What these are is, from the empiricist perspective, something to be arrived at *a priori.* They will be just those capacities enjoyed by any thinker at all with relevant sensory sensitivities. Again, the guiding idea may be that for any purported capacity conferred by special design, there would be a substantial question as to the right one had to be confident in its deliverances. If we just happen to be designed to take things to be thus and so, perhaps, for all that, they are not that way—perhaps our design happens not to be a design so as to get things right. If we could, in principle, have proof that our design does not thus let us down, that proof would, the thought is, be by exercise of some capacity *not* conferred by special design. But then it will do to suppose that we have natural *tendencies* plus universal knowledge-yielding capacities.

Third, the empiricist will hold that we can know a fact in the relevant domain only where that fact is provable, or ascertainable (with sufficient certainty) from privileged facts by application of the specified knowledge-yielding procedures. Fourth, an empiricist *may* claim that there are facts in the relevant domain only insofar as these are derivable from privileged facts according to the principles defining the correct operation of those knowledge-yielding procedures. Typically, such an empiricist will hold that the facts in the chosen domain are far fewer, and less interesting, than we would have supposed.

The relevant domain for present purposes is grammar—that is, the grammars of particular natural languages. Here the empiricist *par excellence* is Quine. For Quine the privileged facts are what he calls 'behaviour' (of relevant language users). Of course, Quine uses 'behaviour' in a proprietary sense. Sid tells all the women he meets he loves them. That is his wayward behaviour. But it is not behaviour in Quine's sense. The behaviour of English speakers, for Quine, is that which is observable equally by an English speaker and a monolingual speaker of Tagalog.[12] Or, better, what is observable both by a Tagalog speaker and a Martian. Quine's knowledge-yielding procedures are what might be called unconstrained hypothesis formation and confirmation. By those procedures, a given hypothesis about the grammar of the target language is confirmed just where, or insofar as, every conceivable rival hypothesis is (shown) incompatible with the privileged facts.

In the case of grammar, Quine holds not just the third, but also the fourth, tenet on the above list. So, for Quine, the facts of grammar are, in principle, much less rich than Chomsky supposes them to be. Specifically, Quine argues that for any two grammars, both of which meet the lower goal of the last section—that is, both of which distinguish correctly between sentences and non-sentences of the target language—neither is incompatible with any set of privileged facts. So at any point at which two such grammars disagree, it is not the case that one states a *fact* of grammar which the other misses. As we have seen, there is much that that excludes from the domain of grammar. The syntactic difference between 'expect' and 'persuade' is one small example.

There is a level at which Chomsky agrees with Quine's result. So long as the only standard of correctness we have for a grammar is the lower one of the last section—the one that does not require syntax to be a psychological phenomenon—there is no sense in which it can be a fact that 'persuade' behaves differently from 'expect' in the way described above. If privileged facts and knowledge-yielding procedures were as Quine claims, we would have only that lower standard of adequacy. Since Chomsky thinks that such things

[12] That there *is* such a thing is, of course, questionable.

clearly are facts, it is necessary for him to contrapose. He must deny that we are confined to the lower standard of correctness. To do that, he must deny Quine's empiricism. The next section describes how that is done.

4. Anti-empiricism (I)

If empiricism about syntax is mistaken, it is either because it is mistaken about what the relevant privileged facts are, or because it is mistaken about knowledge-yielding techniques. Chomsky holds it mistaken on both counts. The more important count for his programme, hence, perhaps, the most prominent, is the second. The first, though, plays a crucial role in Chomsky's initial case against Quine.

Chomsky's case against Quine begins with a Moorean technique. If we abstract from Moore's execution of it, he had a core idea that went like this. Suppose we wanted to know what we were speaking of in speaking of chairs (or of something's being a chair). We would have, to begin with, two sources of information. There are, first, facts as to what we are prepared to say about particular cases: *this,* anyway, is a chair, or, more subtly, here is a case where something was correctly called a chair. Then, second, there are, or may be, facts as to what we would suppose something must do to count as a chair—be an artefact, say. Given the way human beings are, it would be reasonable to suppose there to be a defensible presumption in favour of the first sort of data against the second, should the two come into conflict (and provided people were not mistaken about the natures of the things they were calling, or refusing to call, chairs). Moore's idea was then simply that, if we want to see what we are speaking of when we speak of someone knowing something, and hence, what would be cases of someone doing that, we should suppose the same rules of the game to be in force. To see what it is we speak of when we speak of knowledge, we must, accordingly, give a due role to what we would say as to when someone knew such-and-such.

Chomsky uses essentially that Moorean idea to turn empiricism upside down. As noted above, empiricist principles are arrived at *a priori*. That goes for Quine's ideas about knowledge-yielding procedures. The empiricist would be in a far different position if we could make his principles empirically testable. Relying on the Moorean idea, that is what Chomsky does. For, he observes, if we are to give particular cases and intuitions about principles their due,

318

it should be non-controversial, by any reasonable standard, that we (tolerably competent English speakers) do know about 'expect' and 'persuade' roughly what has been said about them above. It is not as if there is any serious risk of our being mistaken about such things. What we know are facts. So it is a fact that 'persuade' behaves differently from 'expect' in roughly the indicated way. Such could not be *knowable* fact if Quine were right about knowledge-yielding procedures. It could not be a fact at all given Quine's plausible view about the knowability of syntactic facts. Thus is it empirically demonstrable that Quine is not right.

This case against Quine highlights Chomsky's rejection of Quine's conception of privileged, or (strictly speaking) observable facts. To begin with, if we reflect on what we know about our own language(s), we can see that it is a good bit more than we could know if Quine were right. We thus see ourselves to see our own language as a complex system of syntactic structures. But what we thus see are not *just* facts about ourselves. Solipsism can get no beachhead here. For we see that we can see what others patently can see as well. The above view of 'expect' and 'persuade' is no idiosyncratic one. It is just what any English speaker can readily see. Nor is there any serious question that other speakers do see it, or that we can, if necessary, confirm that they do. Second, 'expect' and 'persuade' are the first small step along a route to seeing the kind of syntactic complexity that English has. But that general sort of complexity is manifestly no idiosyncrasy of English. We can appreciate it as something distinctly human. We thus reasonably come to see (if we did not already) the languages of others as things of similar complexity. If we approach other languages in that way, there is no reason in principle why their speakers' views as to their syntactic structure, and ways of forming such structures, should not be open to view.

If Quine is wrong about the class of privileged facts—facts from which syntactic facts must be derivable—he is also wrong, on Chomsky's view, in his ideas about knowledge-yielding procedures. His fundamental mistake, given our present change of focus, is to suppose it to be discoverable *a priori* what these procedures are. If the procedures are to be ones for arriving at what we in fact know about our languages, then it must be an empirical matter just what avenues are, in fact, at our disposal. That will depend on our special psychological design. (To say that empiricism is demonstrably mistaken, as argued above, is, *inter alia,* to say, against Quine, that our special psychological design—the ways we are *contingently* the sorts of thinkers that we are—may confer special knowledge-yielding capacities on us. I will say more presently in defence of that idea.) Here, though, is a very abstract sketch of how it is possible for Quine to be wrong.

I will speak of H-languages, without defining that notion precisely. An H-language is, by definition, a language whose grammar satisfies a number of severe constraints—which has a highly specific, richly determinate, form. Precision here would be specifying exactly what these constraints are. Now we may compare two problems: first, working out from given data what the grammar of a certain encountered language is, supposing that the language may be any conceivable one; second, working out from given data which H-language a certain encountered language is, given that the language in question is an H-language. In both cases we will suppose the data confined to facts as to what speakers of the language do, and do not, produce in speaking it (and perhaps some facts as to utterances they reject as incorrect). If the constraints on an H-language are tight enough, the second problem may be considerably more tractable than the first (if the first is even soluble at all).

Suppose, now, that we (humans) are so designed as to see ourselves in certain situations as confronting H-languages, approaching the languages we thus confront accordingly.[13] Such insight would consist in being liable to form certain hypotheses as to what speaking correctly from a grammatical point of view would be, but simply failing ever to entertain other hypotheses. What we had seen of the language might lead us to go on to novel uses in certain ways, but not in others. If such special design conferred a knowledge-yielding capacity, then we could describe things as follows. In certain situations, we see ourselves to confront human beings (using language). Part of what it is for us to see it to be human language users we confront is to see in them a certain frame of mind, that of an H-language user. We see them to be engaged in H-language speaking, just as we may see one of them to be expressing pique, or joy. Of course, if what the design conferred was not a *capacity* to discover how things are, then we should describe things differently: we are inclined to treat these people in certain ways; it is another matter whether that is treating them, and their language, as what they are.

Operating in the sort of environment we are designed for, and *de facto* are always in, a human being doing what we are thus designed to do would, peripheral deficiencies aside, arrive at correct views of

---

[13] I abstract here from questions as to whether it is the child learning its first language, or mature humans approaching a strange language, who does this.

the syntax of the encountered language. For the design is one for interacting with other humans. And, *de facto*, when we encounter language users, that is what we have to deal with. Someone doing what we are thus designed to do would thus arrive at just those syntactic perceptions of the target language which a human being, functioning as humans do, would have, so at perceptions his fellow speakers, if human, by and large share. Given the sense in which grammar is a psychological phenomenon, such perceptions are, in the nature of the case, correct, provided only that the target language is indeed the natural language of some community of human beings.

In normal situations, then, we are, to say the least, non-accidentally right in treating the languages we confront as H-languages. One might still resist the idea that what special design thus confers is a *knowledge*-yielding capacity. One thought would be that if the special design does, in fact, lead us to grammatical fact, then there should be a proof we could have, without relying on it, that the grammatical facts are, indeed, what, by the design, we would take them to be. But then the design is dispensable: the grammatical facts are just what they could be shown to be without it. We thus revert to our original empiricism. Another thought is that the design in question is fallible. In environments hospitable to it, perhaps, it leads us to take to be so what is so—it is a sort of access to *fact*. But in inhospitable environments it might lead us to take to be so what is not so. That might happen, for example, if we came upon a community of very human-seeming Martians. Fallibility, the thought is, makes vivid what would be so anyway: we can *know* to be so what, by the design, we would take to be so only where we had a proof that the design was not leading us astray. In that case, the design cannot be, in itself, a design of a knowledge-yielding capacity. By this line of thought, special design could confer no such special capacities, available only to thinkers of a special sort.

The first of these lines of thought is simply a mistake. The proof, in a given case, that the grammatical facts are what the design would lead us to take them to be is just that the language of which they are facts is a natural human language, so that what the special design would lead one to see in it is just what a human being (being so designed) would see in it. We may then appeal to the sense in which grammar is a psychological phenomenon. None of that suggests that the grammatical facts are only what they could be seen to be without appeal to the design, or that someone, neither so designed, nor with adequate access to the facts of what those so designed would see would be able to see what the grammar of the relevant language was.

The second line, though I think it is a significant part of what moves empiricists, is just bad epistemology. It is typical of the abilities we rely on to gain knowledge that they would *be* abilities only in hospitable environments. I can learn whether there is a cat on the mat by looking. In doing so, I rely on my ability to tell a cat when I see one. But that ability, like most, is an ability at all only where the world co-operates. If, unbeknownst to me, I am surrounded by extremely feline Martians, or marsupials, then, perhaps, I cannot tell a cat when I see one, and have not found out whether there is a *cat* on the mat just by looking. If I know there is a cat on the mat, then I have (even if I cannot give) proof that there is. Such proof as I may get, relying on my ability to tell a cat when I see one, contains no proper sub-proof that there are not Martians or marsupials about. But it is a mistake to suppose that only what contained such sub-proof could ever count as proving there is a cat on the mat, and a mistake about knowledge to suppose that without such sub-proof I cannot really know whether there is a cat on the mat. Similarly, one might suppose that to *learn* what an expression's syntax is, I must have proof that that *is* the syntax. If reliance on my special design supplies proof, that proof will have no proper sub-proof that it is human beings, and not Martians, who surround me. But it is equally a mistake to think that I could have such proof only in having such a sub-proof. Whether *such* proof is called for depends on how things are. (Where circumstances mandate relying on more than my design, or my ability to tell a cat on sight—where there *might* be Martians—nothing in that design, or that ability, prohibits my doing so.)[14]

The case of grammar shows the form an anti-empiricism takes. The core idea is rejection of the empiricist's conception of our relation to the universal thinker. The anti-empiricist insists that what we can see about the world is not limited (certainly not *a priori*) to what universally shared capacities would allow. We have, or may have, knowledge-yielding capacities of special designs, with special shape and scope; part of our design as thinkers of a special sort—capacities each of which it is quite conceivable that a thinker should lack. These extend the range of facts that we might know. That leaves it at best unclear whether those capacities, if any, a thinker *must* have would be enough by themselves to qualify anything as a thinker at all.

If special psychological design may bestow such capacities, it is

[14] For further discussion of knowledge-gaining capacities see my 'The Face of Perception', in Hilary Putnam, *The Philosopher Responds to His Critics*, J. Conant, ed., Vanderbilt University Press, forthcoming.

contrary to empiricism, an empirical issue just what our cognitive capacities are. Empiricism, against that background, is at best the sort of psychologism McDowell targets: the supposed *a priori* deduction of how things must be in an area where it can only be a question of how things are.

On Chomsky's view we are so designed as to see certain sorts of phenomena in what we experience, or particular compartments of it. Specifically, we are so designed as, in confronting a human language, to think of it in a given way. There is, by that design, a way we (that is, a human) would come to think of the language in mastering it (given adequate exposure to all about it to which we might, by that design, be sensitive). To think in that way is to see certain syntactic structures in the language and its expressions. That they are so structured is, on that way of viewing things, what one is to think. The anti-empiricist point in the case of syntax is that, where such is so, the language *is* so to be thought of. In so seeing things we are seeing how things are. The relevant design, operating in normal circumstances, is no less than a design for seeing that. So operating, it is thus the design of a genuine cognitive capacity.

Language being the psychological phenomenon it is, that we think of our languages as we do—so that we are designed so to think of them—is part of what makes the facts about them what they are. Such helps to make anti-empiricism about syntax seem innocuous, and, to Frege, not psychologism. The question to be raised now is how far anti-empiricism can be extended beyond the realm of grammar while remaining innocuous, and, specifically, immune to Frege's anti-psychologism.

5. Anti-empiricism II

Anti-empiricism, as exemplified by Chomsky, begins with the idea that special knowledge-yielding capacities, not shared by every possible thinker, may be part of, or conferred by, our design, or certain thinkers' design, as thinkers of a particular sort. Such capacities may gain us access to some range of facts refractory to one equipped only with the capacities an empiricist allows us. The facts to which we thus gain access may fail to connect with any empiricist's 'privileged' facts in the way the empiricist demands. Anti-empiricism so construed represents a clear area of common cause between Chomsky and McDowell. It is evident in McDowell's consistent and wide-ranging anti-reductionism, every instance of which turns essentially on crediting us with knowledge-yielding capacities of domain-specific and design-specific sorts capacities which come in view when we take at face value the facts as to what we are prepared to recognise. The most conspicuous difference between McDowell and Chomsky is that while Chomsky is mainly interested in species-specific design, McDowell tends to suggest that he is thinking of the designs of people with certain upbringings, or initiations into certain perhaps non-obligatory human practices. But that difference, so far as it exists, is over what ought to be a purely empirical question.

Another difference between Chomsky and McDowell is the domains at which anti-empiricism is directed. Chomsky, of course directs it at the domain of grammar which is, as indicated by Frege's attitude towards it, a somewhat special case; one in which a certain degree of idealism may be harmless, and exempt from any Fregean accusation of psychologism. McDowell directs it at a wide variety of domains where its application may be somewhat more contentious. For example, he directs it at facts about the good, and Aristotle's conception of that; and he directs it at facts about human attitudes such as thinking that such-and-such, or intending to do such-and-such. To show what McDowellian anti-empirism is like I will consider those examples in turn. Then in the next section I will consider the scope and what I take to be the source of the general position these examples instance.

There is an idea of the good, or of what is good for us, on which the good is fixed by how a human being ought to live, or aim to; by what a worthwhile or desirable life is. On that conception, something is good just insofar as it is, or may be, part of, or may contribute to, such a life. One might also think that there are facts of human nature. On one conception, at least, of human nature, we may think of such facts as simply a matter of what human beings are, independent of what is desirable for them—facts purely within the domain of ethology, or psychology. As a matter of fact, people tend to—perhaps invariably—seek certain things. Certain things promote, others frustrate, the projects people in fact set themselves. It is natural for human beings to behave in certain ways. One might ask how, and how on Aristotle's view, these two sets of facts relate. For example, should the facts about the good so conceived, if any, be derivable from, or reducible to, facts about human nature so conceived? Here is McDowell's answer:

> It is because a certain life ... is a life of doing what it is the business of a human being to do, that that life is in the relevant sense the most satisfying life possible for its subject ... How one might

argue that this or that is what it is the business of a human being to do is left open. It does not have to be by showing that a life of such doings maximizes the satisfaction of some set of 'normal' or 'natural' desires, whose role in the argument would need to be justified by a prior theory of human nature.

We may still find an intelligible place, in the different position I am considering, for some such idea as this: the life of excellence is the life that most fully actualizes the potentialities that constitute human nature. But the point will be that the thesis ... that this or that is what it is the business of a human being to do can be reformulated, with an intelligibly 'value-loaded' use of human nature; not that the justification of the thesis about the business of a human being is to be found in an independent, 'value-free' investigation of human nature.[15]

This irreducibility of facts about 'the business of a human being' in no way impugns, on McDowell's view, the idea that there are such facts, or that we can know them. Such knowledge requires special knowledge-yielding capacities, part of a special, not inevitable, way of thinking of the world. But, on his view, at least if properly brought up, we may have such capacities.

Special knowledge-yielding capacities may be insusceptible to cognitive prosthetics. That is, what, with them, one is equipped to see need not be what would be derivable from some statable set of principles by a thinker lacking those capacities. Thinking otherwise, McDowell suggests, reflects a

misconception of the deductive paradigm [which] leads us to suppose that the operations of any specific conception of rationality in a particular area—any specific conception of what counts as doing the same thing—must be deductively explicable; that is, that there must be a formulable universal principle suited to serve as major premise in syllogistic explanations of the sort I considered above.[16]

To see what our special capacities allow us to see, one may need nothing short of human sensibility, or the sensibility of human beings properly initiated into a given way of thinking of the world. No principle graspable by a thinker devoid of the right sensibility need entail all that is open to the view of a thinker with that sensi-

[15] John McDowell, 'The Role of *Eudaimonia* in Aristotle's Ethics', *Mind, Value and Reality,* Harvard University Press, Cambridge, Massachusetts, 1998, pp. 18–19.

[16] McDowell, 'Virtue and Reason', *Mind, Value and Reality,* p. 62.

bility. That is to say that the facts such a capacity makes accessible to us need not be equivalent to any construction out of facts of some other sort, notably not out of facts which, by some empiricist's lights, might have privileged status.

The position, then, is this. Human beings, or humans of a certain sort, have a special knowledge-yielding capacity, conferred by a special psychological design, not necessarily shared by just any thinker whatever. That capacity enables such humans to see facts of a certain sort—facts about the proper business of a human being, or the good for a human being. Such a capacity involves an irreducible sensitivity to facts of the relevant sort. It is not constructible out of other capacities a rational being just would have anyway, together with facts such capacities might anyway make accessible. Correspondingly, the facts this capacity makes accessible are, in general, ones it takes this particular sort of sensitivity to see. They are not derivable from facts of some other sort which might be accessible anyway to one who knew nothing of the good. They are not privileged facts in the empiricist's sense, since they are not accessible to one without a knowledge-yielding capacity of a special sort. Nor do they relate to any range of privileged facts in the way an empiricist demands. The irreducibility of the facts of this sort is shown (in one way) by the ineliminable role of a special knowledge-yielding capacity in seeing them.

I turn to the second example: McDowell's attitude towards attitudes such as thinking something to be so. That attitude emerges among other places, in a debate between McDowell and Michael Dummett over the shape a theory of meaning might take. Here acknowledging a point of Dummett's McDowell says,

> If communication is to be possible, that in which our understanding of the language we speak consists must 'lie open to view ... '[17]

From an empiricist standpoint, the idea that our understanding expressions of the language, or particular uses of them, as we do is open to view is likely to suggest, for example, that for someone to understand some utterance as he does is for such-and-such other fact to hold, where that other fact is observable in some sense in which that fact about understanding is not. For example, depending on his conception of privilege, an empiricist might suppose that the requirement McDowell endorses means that facts about how people understand utterances are reducible to facts about behaviour, again in some proprietary sense of that term.

[17] McDowell, 'In Defence of Modesty', *Meaning, Knowledge and Reality*, Harvard University Press, 1998, p. 94.

But, McDowell suggests, we need not think that way. We may, instead, see relevant facts of understanding as themselves open to view, at least for someone with a suitable special knowledge-yielding capacity. With a proper appreciation of the capacities of fluent speakers, we can allow that

> to be a speaker of a language is to be capable of putting one's thoughts into one's words, where others can hear or see them.[18]

The others who can thus see or hear them are, of course, others competent in the relevant language. Someone so equipped can see, often enough, both that such-and-such is the expression of such-and-such thought, and that such-and-such is someone expressing what he thinks. That is a way of just seeing, or hearing, the speaker to think such-and-such. On McDowell's view the capacity that allows us to see such things is a particular kind of sensitivity to a particular range of facts, acquired in that exposure to the language and its use through which one becomes fluent. That is not a sort of sensitivity that could, in principle, be acquired otherwise, through learning such facts as that for someone to say such-and-such is for such-and-such other facts to hold, to which one might have access without such sensitivity—facts, say, as to how that person would 'behave'.

So there are both facts about what people think and facts about what given utterances said which are accessible to one with the right kind of knowledge-yielding capacity. That idea brings facts about the attitudes of others into the realm of the observable. But the relevant capacities here do not admit of prosthetics. They are not constructible out of capacities which any thinker, or even any language user, must share. Correspondingly, the facts to which they gain us access remain resistant to empiricist strictures. Again, we have an instance of anti-empiricism of just the form that Chomsky deploys against Quine, though deployed in a different domain. We must still face the question whether difference in domain makes a difference in the acceptability of such anti-empiricism. First, though, I will consider just how this anti-empiricism might generalise.

6. Generalised Anti-empiricism

Generalised anti-empiricism can be developed from a simple idea. Suppose that some indefinitely expendable group of thinkers take

---

[18] Ibid., p. 99.

themselves to discern some way for things to be, 'F', and agree, or would do, non-collusively, and productively (that is, in an indefinitely expendable range of cases) as to what is, and what is not, 'F'. Then they are marking a genuine distinction. There is at least a genuine distinction between that which is such that they would classify it the one way (as 'F'), and that such that they would classify it as not 'F'. Those, at least, are two genuine ways for things, or a thing, to be. So there is, at least, some genuine way, G, which some things are, and/or some things are not, such that these thinkers, in thinking as they thus do, are distinguishing between things which are that way, and things which are not. That idea is not an explanatory hypothesis, not a piece of psychology. It is rather an idea about what it is for there to be a distinction in nature. Given such productive agreement (as I will term it) in how to treat things, what more could one want for a genuine distinction (at least of some sort)?

The point so far, though not quite what we want, does gain at least some purchase against empiricist strictures. For the point is that there is a sort of productive agreement among thinkers which guarantees that there is a genuine way for things to be—really such a thing as things being that way—without thereby guaranteeing that any particular set of empiricist strictures is satisfied. If people agree in this way as to what they would, and would not, call a novel, or a teaspoon, or elation, then, for at least some way things, in fact, are or are not, their treatment of the world distinguishes between what is, and what is not, that way. It remains, for all that, an open question whether what they are thus distinguishing is capturable so as to satisfy empiricist strictures. Perhaps it is. But we are not entitled to the idea that it must be. To insist that these people could only do what they do in responding to what does satisfy such strictures would be that psychologism which is McDowell's target.

On this core idea, there is a sort of agreement among us, or among whatever creatures, that guarantees that there is something—a genuine way for things to be—to which they are responsive. That core point does not quite yet bear on *thinking* things to be such-and-such way. The anti-empiricist's concern is, not with mere responsiveness to some way for things to be or not, but a responsiveness that consists, in part, in thinking in terms of things being that way or not, and in part in an ability to recognise the, or at least some, facts as to things being that way or not. So we must elaborate the core idea so as to accommodate some features we know the phenomenon of thinking in terms of being such-and-such to have.

First, thinking in terms of such-and-such is, as a rule, an imperfect way of responding to (things being) that. Relevant thinkers (those for whom productive agreement is in question) sometimes disagree, sometimes, in practice, irresolvably. They are sometimes deceived as to how things are, or just ignorant, sometimes irremediably so. Some relevant thinkers are recognised, and recognisable, as better at telling how things are in relevant respects. (Think of telling fine shades of colour, for example.) Such shows where agreement is wanted: not in what people in fact say or judge, all their limitations operating, but in what they would be prepared to recognise as to what is to be judged (what judgments are correct) as to how things are in relevant respects. That is an idealisation. By it we may ignore an actual performance if reasonably ascribed to some disturbance in the responsiveness for which these thinkers are equipped. And, as with the simple core point, there need only be enough productive agreement here to show that there is something to which they are thus equipped to respond.

Second, we typically think in occasion-sensitive ways. Where we think in terms of such-and-such way for things to be, we recognise room for different understandings of what something's being that way might be, on different of which there would be different truths to tell as to what was, and what was not, that way. We further recognise the possibility of speaking, or judging, of things being that way on different such understandings. So we recognise that there may be different truths to tell as to how things are in that respect on different occasions for saying how things thus are. Productive agreement that allowed for that would be, not simply agreement in responses to given situations in the world—to given items being as they then are—but in responses under particular conditions for producing them. Since it is thinking that is in question, that would be (sufficient) productive agreement in what it is, or would be true to say *when* as to how things are in the relevant respect, agreements as to the truths there are to tell (or judge) in speaking (or judging) of how things thus are.

Finally, in thinking of such-and-such we (must) operate with a conception of that of which we think. We are thinking of some given way to be only where our conception is near enough to a right one. We are thinking of a feature of things to which we are thus responsive only where our conception is near enough to a right one of that. Where we think of things as being F or not, there is something we take being F to be, and a way we take questions as to what is F to be treatable. We are thinking in terms of being F only where the conception thus embodied in our way of treating things is near enough to a right way of thinking of what being F is.

It is thus possible to be responsive to some feature of things while thinking, neither of it, nor of any way for things to be. Given thinkers may take themselves to think in terms of women being, or not, witches. They might agree productively as to who is, and who is not, a witch. Perhaps they are responding to a certain hormonal condition present in a minority of women. As they conceive things, witches are malevolent women with supernatural powers. But they are not responding to anything of which that is true. One might still say that there is such a thing as being a witch, and it is that they are responding to—they are just radically wrong about what is involved in being that. But, for most purposes, it is manifestly fairer to the facts to say that there is no such thing as being a witch (or what they thus purport to think of), so that, though responding to a genuine enough feature of the world, they were in fact thereby thinking of nothing at all. Note that if this is right, then whether a conception is good enough for thinkers to be thinking of something to which they are responsive is a question of what is reasonable. That is to say: we correctly count thinkers as thinking in terms of F only where their way of conceiving what they thus think of is reasonably seen as close enough to a right way of conceiving F.

A good enough conception may be significantly wrong. We take ourselves to think of paths in space as straight or not. Perhaps thinking of such things as we do, one could never, travelling in a straight path, return to where one started. Perhaps there are no paths in space of which such is true, or even of which such makes sense. There may still be something we are thus responsive to, whose nature we are most reasonably seen as in error about; so that it is true, for all that, that we think in terms of paths in space as straight. Our conception of such paths may be near enough to a right one for us so to count, without its actually being right.

Such features of *our* thinking show that where productive agreement is to be the mark of thinking in terms of a feature of things to which one thus responds, it must be productive agreement of a certain quality. Thinking of things as a certain way involves thinking in a certain way of what one does in reaching verdicts as to how things are in that respect—of what one thus judges so, and of how questions of that being so are treatable. Thinking of things as a certain way means thinking *in* a certain way of the sort of thing being that way is. Agreement among a given range of thinkers has the right quality when the way they thus think of what it is they think of meshes (well enough) with the verdicts in which their productive agreement consists. Those thinkers will see their verdicts as mandated by the sort of thing the way in question is, or at least by their way of thinking of that. Meshing means that doing so is consistent with the verdicts: their conception must not, *per se,* dictate different ones. And the conception, together with the verdicts, make sense as a rational way of treating the world. Other thinkers (ourselves, perhaps) need not be able to join in this way of thinking. (The relevant thinkers' eyes may be open to features of the world to which ours are shut.) One must grant that in allowing special psychological design the role that anti-empiricism does. But there must be enough coherence in that way of dealing with the world for it to be sufficiently determinate (or reasonable to suppose so) what, on that way of thinking, it would be correct to think and judge. (We correctly count thought as with this quality where such coherence is visible to us.) The anti-empiricist idea is that agreement has the right quality if there is close enough mesh. In that case, these thinkers, in thinking in the way they do, think in terms of the way for things to be they take themselves to think of, and to which they are thus responsive. There is, the idea is, no further room for failure on their part to do that.

Productive agreement, with or without near enough mesh, is responsiveness to a feature things may have or lack. That was the simple core point. Now the idea is: if a way of thinking of what that agreement is about, suitably engaged in, would lead (nearly enough) to that agreement, then it is a way of thinking of something to which, in so agreeing, relevant thinkers are responsive—thus, a way of thinking of a genuine feature things may have or lack. Thinkers whose thinking is close enough to such a way thus think of something to which, in their agreement, they are responsive.

Insisting that productive agreement have this quality does not lose the anti-empiricist force of the core idea. We agree productively as to the colours of things. We think in certain ways about objects being coloured: colour is a visible property of objects, so, in certain standard ways, one can tell the colour of a thing by looking. For most purposes, we suppose the colour of an object to be stable— something it takes chemical processes to change. Supposing that to be the sort of thing an object's being coloured is, and thinking of things as we thus would, one would, intelligibly, reach roughly the verdicts we do. Thinking as we do we thus think of ways for things to be—being coloured blue, and so on—to which we are thus responsive, and which are correctly thought of as we thus do. That is so independent of any relation an object's being coloured thus and so may bear to facts of some other sort (privileged ones, per- haps, by some empiricist's lights).

Suppose, then, that given thinkers take themselves to think in terms of things being some given (putative) way, F. They agree productively in verdicts as to how things stand with respect to

Charles Travis

things being F—the truths there are to tell, on occasion, as to, or
involving, things so being. They think in a certain way of what it is
they thus agree about. Suppose we assume that they are doing what
they thus take themselves to do: there is such a thing as being F, to
(things being) which they are responsive, which they think of in a
way near enough to a way in which it is correctly thought of.
Suppose that, on that assumption, it is determinate enough what
truths (and falsehoods) there would be to tell as to how things are
with respect to things being F—clear enough what such truths
would be if these thinkers really were thus thinking of a genuine
way things may or may not be. Then, the current point is, these
thinkers *are* nearly enough right. There is such a thing as being F,
and a way things stand with respect to things being that. And these
thinkers, at least in what they are prepared to recognise, are roughly
right as to what way that is. There is no further room for them to
fail of that. In being designed, or equipped, to react as they do, they
enjoy a knowledge-yielding capacity. Where that equipment is special psychological design, it is a special such capacity, enjoyed by
some thinkers, but one that need not be enjoyed by all.

Such is the main burden of generalised anti-empiricism. Where
thinkers take themselves to be thinking in terms of a genuine way
things may or may not be, they can be wrong about that only if they
are behaving stupidly, randomly, inconsistently, or something of the
sort—if they fail to produce genuine productive agreement, or their
way of thinking of what they agree about is too far from a coherent
way of viewing that. That is the point of Wittgenstein's remark that
to say that given discourse did not fit the concept truth would be
like saying that pawns did not fit the concept check. But

> to say that check did not *fit* our concept of the pawns, would
> mean that a game in which pawns were checked, in which, say, the
> players who lost their pawns lost, would be uninteresting or
> stupid or too complicated or something of the kind.
> (*Investigations* §136)

It is also the idea, I think, that Wittgenstein worried, 'seems to abol-
ish logic' (*Investigations* §242), but insisted does not. We will next
consider how anti-empiricism may give the impression that it does.

7. Idealism

Chomsky's anti-empiricism contains the idea that how things are in
the domain that concerns him depends on how relevant thinkers
think: grammatical facts just are what we are designed to think

them. It is harmless for our mental equipment thus to shape *grammatical* facts. As Frege noted, grammar *is* a psychological phenomenon. But generalised anti-empiricism, as evidenced in McDowell, for example, does not restrict itself to domains of any particular sort—certainly not to the psychological in the sense that grammar is psychological. The idea the anti-empiricist wants is that one's mind's special design may, in McDowell's terms, 'open one's eyes to some tract of reality'—as a rule, facts there anyway, with our without our capacity to see them. In that case, though special design may select which tract we see, and *perhaps* select in such a way that we are thus designed to think so just what is so, it had better not be that what we are designed to think shapes the facts in that tract—that how *it* is shaped depends on how we think. On the core idea, suitable agreement is engagement with the world: to agree (suitably) is, *per se,* to respond to *something.* But is that idea sustainable? Can mind-design *select* which tract of reality we deal with, on the anti-empiricist plan, without also deciding, of the selected tract, how things there are—without shaping the *world* along with our responsiveness to it?

Suppose given thinkers take themselves, in thinking in a certain way, to be thinking in terms of things being, or not, some given way, and thereby to be thinking, and judging, what is so or not. Suppose it is determinate enough what, on that way of viewing how things are, it would be true to say or judge. Then, the anti-empiricist insists, in thinking as they thus do, these thinkers are responsive to a genuine feature of things, of which they thus think. In that respect, at least, they in fact do what they take themselves to do. What it would be true to think and judge given that so thinking with the verdicts that involves) is genuine responsiveness is what it would be true to think and judge *tout court.* Thus it is that special design may confer special knowledge-yielding capacities.

The main point of this idea is to defuse empiricist critiques, on which genuine matters of what is so or not are not what we intuitively think—Quine's critique of meaning, for example. But there is an immediate worry, easily expressible, at least crudely. Coherence may take many forms. We share a rough conception of being a chair, and, nearly enough, a sense for when something is the right sort of thing to count as one. That makes it clear enough when one would be speaking truly, and when not, thinking of such matters as we in fact do. But if our sense for what a chair is is a feature of special psychological design, then, it seems, we might have had a different one—even while retaining much of our general conception of what is involved in *something's* being a chair. That might have

Charles Travis

made for differences in what, on our way of thinking of such things, it would be true to say as to things being chairs, the presence and absence of chairs, and so on. Or so it seems. Our thinking would still cohere enough to be genuine responsiveness. But what it would be true to say so thinking, so true to say *tout court* of that of which we thus thought, would be different. So it seems that had we been differently designed, that would have mattered to what could have been said truly about chairs: some of what it would now be true to say would not have been; similarly for some of what would now be false. In speaking truth we do nothing less than saying what is so; and in speaking falsehood, nothing less than saying what is not so. So, it seems, had we been differently designed, in ways we might have been, different things would have been so about chairs. If anti-empiricism means that, then it is precisely Frege's target. That, I think, would make McDowell Frege's target rather than his ally.

This worry, we hope, rests on a mistaken view of things. But before trying to say how it does, let us make it slightly less crude. For the anti-empiricist, a way of thinking is identified, in part, by the thinkers who engage in it. It is their responsiveness to things that fixes what it is that is being responded to (and responded to in thinking of it). Nor is that responsiveness eliminable in favour of some set of principles, available to those without it, which would generate precisely those same results—an algorithm, as it were, for determining how things are thus to be responded to. That is the point of speaking of sensibilities—a sense of what responses are called for, on novel occasions, by novel things, or situations, which one confronts. Two points about such sensibilities bear emphasis.

First, where it matters in confronting some empiricism, such a sensibility is a feature of a special psychological design. It is a feature a competent empirical thinker need not have had. The knowledge-yielding capacity it confers is one a competent thinker might have lacked. (*Vide* Chomsky.) There is such a sensibility only where there are alternative ones. We have our sense of when something is to be called a chair. Other thinkers might have had a different one, or at least a different sense of how to respond to the things we thus respond to.

Second, where it matters to empiricism, such a sensibility is, in an important sense, irreducible. What someone equipped with it could see (where it constitutes a genuine knowledge-yielding capacity) is not identical to the deductive consequences of any statable set of principles, or at least any such set graspable by thinkers without the

334

relevant sensibility.[19] If sensibilities could not be like that, empiricist demands for accountings in terms of privileged facts would be in order. (And we would have to be able to make sense of the idea of facts available to any empirical thinker, the availability of which depends on no special psychological design.) This says something about the relation between sensibilities and conceptions. Insofar as a conception of being a chair is identifiable in terms of the sort of thing *something's* being a chair is, and is fixed independent of what it would be right to say, on novel occasions, of novel cases, our sensibility regarding the truths about chairs is not derivable merely from that conception. This means we could have had an alternative sensibility while still retaining that conception of what, in general terms, a chair is. Or, again, other thinkers might have had a different sensibility while sharing that conception with us. We think of chairs as certain sorts of seats for one. With such a different sensibility, we would still so think of them. Our sense for the right *sort* of seat, though, would yield different results as to when some novel item was correctly counted as of the right sort. By the general anti-empiricist idea, a different sensibility might have changed when one would, or at least when we would, be speaking truly in speaking in terms of things being what we thus thought of—being chairs or not, if a general conception may identify it as that which we (or other thinkers) thus think of. If that could mean that something it is in fact true to say might not have been, thus that something so (what would thus be stated) might not have been, then it is enough to make anti-empiricism Frege's target.

We can now broach a ready response to this worry: any sensibility as different as what is now envisioned would, *ipso facto,* change the subject. Had we had a different sensibility, we might still have used such words as 'chair'; and we might still have conceived of what we thus spoke of as a certain sort of seat for one. But we would no

[19] To assign sensibilities this role is not to deny that we may always have principled reasons for classifying as we do. 'The back's too low for it to be a chair. Anything with that low a back is a *stool,* not a chair.' A perfectly acceptable principle, perhaps, and one that decides cases, including the one at hand. Nor is it to deny that our particular exercises of sensibility are subject to rational criticism, and may be shown wrong, in the light of recognisably acceptable principles. But such statable principles, which elaborate, perhaps correctly (in given circumstances), our conception of a chair, are ones we are prepared to abandon if confronted with the right cases. Our commitment to them always leaves room for the possibility that the right object, in the right situation, may show us how, indeed, a chair's back may sometimes be so low. We thus exercise our sensibility in seeing when, and when not, a given principle is to be adhered to.

longer have been speaking (or thinking) of being a *chair*. That, at least, must be so wherever a sensibility is different enough to make for differences in when one, or those with it, would be speaking truly in speaking of that in terms of which they thus thought. For, the thought is, a way for things to be is identified precisely by the truths there are to tell about it. And that, correctly understood, rules out as mere fantasy any instance of the above worry.

But this ready response is suspect. It is so because, for the ways for things to be we name, we are prepared to recognise different ways of thinking of things as being *those* ways or not, where, on these different ways of thinking there are different truths to tell, and where these different truths are all *truths*. Sid buys a DIY chair kit. On bringing it home he discovers that it is much more difficult to assemble than he had imagined. It remains a neatly stacked pile of chair parts in his spare room. One day, someone, pointing at the pile, asks, 'What's that?' 'It's a chair', Sid replies, 'I just haven't got around to assembling it yet.' On a later occasion, Sid and Pia, with guests, find themselves a chair short for dinner. 'There's a chair in the spare room', Sid says helpfully. But there is still only the pile. Recognisably, Sid spoke truly the first time, falsely the second. It just takes a different way of thinking of being a chair to see the truth of that first thing from the way it takes to see the falsehood of the second. Such contrasting ways of thinking are a common everyday part of our way of dealing with the world.

Different ways of thinking of things can even be systematic without changing the fact of thinkers thinking of things as being such-and-such way. Suppose some people—Northumbrians, perhaps—regularly call slippers shoes, while others—Mancunians, perhaps—regularly refuse to do so. Northumbrians think of slippers as house shoes, and count them as shoes when saying, for example, how many pairs of shoes they own. Mancunians regard that as comical. It would be natural, in such a case, to count both the Northumbrians and the Mancunians as thinking of the world in terms of things being shoes. It is just that they think of that in slightly different ways. A Northumbrian would often speak of shoes on the Northumbrian way of thinking of such things. There would thus be truths for Northumbrians to tell, among themselves, at least, the truth of which requires counting slippers as shoes. There would, similarly, be truths for Mancunians to tell, the truth of which requires refusing to count slippers as shoes. Perhaps there are different truths for Northumbrians and Mancunians to tell about shoes. Perhaps thinkers of the one persuasion could never get themselves into a position for telling some of the truths tellable by those of the other. The truth of those distinctively Mancunian truths does not mean that what Northumbrians say to be so in telling distinctively Northumbrian truths is not so. There is no such threat. (Which is a clue to a better way to avoid Fregean psychologism than what the ready answer offers.)

Suppose, now, that Mancunians and Northumbrians and all the rest of us agreed on the right way to talk about slippers. That would exhibit an alternative sensibility, and an alternative way of thinking in terms of things being shoes. There might then not be some of the truths for us to tell about shoes that, on the original supposition, there would be for at least some of us to tell. That simple example shows one thing it might be like for alternative sensibilities to be alternative ways of thinking in terms of things being such-and-such—some given way for things to be. There should be no psychologistic threat in such possibilities. The next section will attempt to spell out precisely why there is not.

8. Platonism

The ready response is unconvincing. It is implausible that thinkers would never count as thinking of the same thing—of being such-and-such—where, on their different ways of thinking of *that*, different things would count as something's being that way. In fact, the ways for things to be that we have names for, or could name, admit of understandings. We speak truth as to things being those ways in speaking of them on some such understanding. There is thus, or so it seems, the possibility that different understandings of being such-and-such might be available to differently designed thinkers, or different ones the ones on which they would speak, or judge, in given circumstances, of things being that way. What we need is, not to rule that possibility out, but rather to see how, while that might make for different truths for such thinkers to tell (than there are for us to tell), nothing we truly state, or take, to be so might thus be thought, truly, not to be so: whatever we think so that is so, would be so no matter how any thinker thought.

To see how psychological design might work that way, we need to dispel the very idea that suggests the ready answer. Trivially, a statement is true just when things are the way they are according to it. That suggests, innocently enough, that a statement's truth depends on precisely two factors: first, how things are according to it; and, second, how things are. Innocence ends if one supposes that one can specify how things are according to a statement—which way it speaks of things as being—in such a way that the truth of any statement which speaks of things as that way can depend only on whether that is, in fact, a way things are. Let P be a way a statement might thus represent things. Then, accepting that idea, we may still innocently allow that the way given thinkers think decides whether some one of their statements stated that P, or, say, that Q, where that is another such way for a statement to represent things.

But one cannot, accepting this idea, allow that, where a statement spoke of things as being P, whether it thus stated truth depends on how a particular (sort of) thinker thinks. For what thinkers could thus decide, in thinking as they do could only be, within this framework, how things were: whether that which is so according to any statement which states P *is* so. That would be mind-dependence of the worst sort. Yet, with the end of innocence in place, anti-empiricism is under pressure to say just that. For, given the role it assigns to sensibilities, it seems, where thinkers think in terms of, say, things being chairs or not, still, for all that, whether things are as they say (on some occasion) in saying such-and-such to be a chair depends in further ways on how they are designed, or equipped, to think. If that dependence must be a dependence of how things *are* on how they think, then, except, perhaps, in special domains such as grammar, anti-empiricism is precisely Frege's target.

We must, then, reverse this end of innocence. But we *have* reversed it with rejection of the ready answer. Sid spoke of an object in the next room as a chair. Rejection in that case means allowing that differently designed thinkers, each thinking of objects as being chairs or not, might think so differently as to make for differences in when what each thought, in thinking a given object to be a chair, would be true. Generalised rejection is insistence that the point holds for any specifiable way Sid may have said the object to be. It would still hold, for example, if he spoke of chairs, where we are to understand such-and-such by being a chair. The generalised point is just Wittgenstein's insistence that there is no such thing as a 'pure intermediary' between a statement and the world—something which still represents the world as thus and so, but which, unlike 'mere' words, is immune in principle to different possible ways of understanding what being as thus represented might be. So for any way of specifying the 'thus and so', there remains room for a way of thinking to contribute to fixing *what* was thus thought (judged) so by fixing the understanding of things being *that* way on which that was what was thought. The influence of thinkers on what it would be true for *them* to think or judge thus never need be—as at some specifiable point it would have to be if the platonist end of innocence were right—an influence on how the world judged about was shaped. Nor need it change what it would be true for *us* (or other thinkers) to say or judge in thinking of things as being, or not, that very same specified way.

In the special case, for some ways an item may be, whether that item is what Sid spoke of in speaking of being a chair may all depend on what one understands (or means) by being a chair. Where such different understandings are open, one may speak, or think, in terms of something's being a chair in thinking of it as being one on any of these. Our differently designed thinkers are equipped with different senses for when something is the right sort of thing—the sort of thing in question when one speaks of chairs. By hypothesis, each sense is compatible with thus thinking in terms of things being *chairs* or not. These different senses, or sensibilities, form, in part, the understandings on which these thinkers think, or speak, of things as chairs or not. Those different understandings make for differences in when what they thus think, or say, would be true. The generalised point is that differently designed thinkers might stand differently, in this way, towards any way we can specify that things may or may not be, so any way we can represent them as being or not. For differently designed thinkers, different understandings would be available of being such-and-such way (for any way that is thus specifiable); and different understandings may be right for given situations in which to speak or judge. Those different understandings would matter to the ways they represented things as being—the ways things were according to their statements—but not the ways the things they thus represented as one way or another were. The anti-empiricist needs this point at least to whatever extent the ready answer is not available. The point is available when we reject the above end of innocence.

Sid said, 'The grass is wet.' I tell Pia, 'Sid said the grass is wet.' If the world is nearly enough what he and I suppose, then the way it is will leave no doubt as to whether he thus said what is so. I said him to have said certain grass to be a given way—wet, on the relevant understanding of grass' being so—and so to have said the world to be a certain way—the way it is when certain grass, on a relevant understanding of what that is, is, on the relevant understanding, wet. If all went well, then whether things are as he said they were will not depend on further issues as to what one understands by being those ways of which I said him to speak. But it is not as if things *must* go well. Whether a strange enough world was the way I said Sid to speak of would have depended on what one understood by its being so. That might make room for different understandings as to what it was Sid said so, and would make room for different understandings on which to speak of that which Sid spoke of as so. That such things are possible is no hindrance to seeing whether, in fact, Sid was right, given that he said what I said he did. Nor do we aim to speak, or to say what others said, so as to eliminate such possibilities. Yet, where they exist, there are different things to be said in speaking of the ways for things to be we speak of, or specify in saying what others said. The idea that ended innocence thus supposes, as we now do not, that there are ways for things to be, and ways for us to say, or think, them to be for which no such possibility exists.

Pia said Sid to have red hair; Zoë said him not to. Each spoke of Sid's having red hair. But dye would make what Pia thus said true, while it would not make what Zoë thus said false. For each spoke of having red hair on a different understanding of what it would be to have it. What the one said thus does not contradict what the other did. If Zoë spoke truth, that does not mean that what Pia said is not so. For thinkers with a different sense of the sort of thing one might call a chair, who, for all that, still thought in terms of things being chairs or not, there might be different truths to tell about chairs than there are for us to tell. Where we spoke truth in calling such-and-such a chair, they might speak truth in denying that it was that. They would do so in speaking of being a chair on an understanding of being one which their sensibilities made available, and right in given circumstances. Perhaps we could not have that understanding, or speak on it, as, perhaps, they could not have some of ours. Such thinkers, insofar as possible, would stand to us as Zoë does to Pia. In speaking of things being chairs or not, they would, to the extent that they so differed from us, say, and deny, different things to be so than what we state in so speaking. The truth of what they thus stated would do nothing to show that what *we* think, and say, truly, in thinking in those terms, was not so.

To see our mind's involvement in shaping what we think we must, so to speak, catch ourselves thinking. In the first instance that is a perfectly mundane thing to do. From the perspective of one occasion on which we find ourselves, we examine how we would stand towards the world on another. It would be correct, in certain circumstances but not in others, to describe Sid as having red hair. That is how, in those circumstances, one would naturally think of things. So we see how ways of thinking, interests, purposes, and so forth, may work to shape truth. It is not as if to do that we need to look at thought without actually doing any or being governed by the specific ways of thinking we are thus involved in. Mind dependence is visible from the inside. Where knowledge-yielding faculties depend on *special* psychological design, different psychological designs must be conceivable. Anti-empiricists, such as Chomsky or McDowell, need the idea of special design. So they must allow the legitimacy of thinking of ourselves as having been otherwise in relevant respects. Where an anti-empiricist needs the idea of special sensibilities—as, I think, McDowell often does—he also needs to make sense of them in terms of the above role for understandings in fixing what is said in speaking of a given way for things to be. But if we are to think of what we might have been, we must do it, just as in the mundane case, by *thinking*, from our actual perspective on the world, with full involvement of our actual sensibities. That may limit what we *can* think—what we can sensibly suppose. It also means that how things *might* thus be is what they might be by those ideas of what is sensible, rational and right which govern, and are fixed by, the way *we,* in fact, thus think.

9. Domains

We have now seen how anti-empiricism steers clear of idealism where it needs to. Where we think so what would be so no matter how one thought, thinkers who thought otherwise would either be thinking of different ways for things to be, or would be thinking of the ways we thus think of, but on different understandings of things being those ways. The coherence of a form of responsiveness to the world, in ensuring something independent of us to which we are thus responsive, ensures no less than that. At this point, though, a question arises. For, for all their common ground, there seemed to be a distinction between Chomsky and McDowell. That distinction turns on Frege's idea that there is something special about grammar. It is (he thought) harmless to suppose that English grammar would have been different than it is had English speakers thought differently enough about their language—or, in a still more Fregean vein, may someday be different than it now is, if English speakers change—in a way that it is not harmless to suppose that the ink in Frege's inkwell might not have been black, or the wind not blowing at gale force, if only people thought differently enough. (For all of which, the facts about what English grammar *is* would be what they are no matter how one thought: differently designed linguists would not change the nature of the object of their study.) What is the difference between these two sorts of cases?

The answer is simple. It is part of our way of thinking of the colours of things, or the forces of winds, that such things are what they are no matter how one thinks; whereas it is (if Frege is right) part of our way of thinking about grammar that grammar is but a reflection of how fluent speakers are prepared to think of what they do in speaking. In each case, that is just part of how we conceive things. In each case, that conception meshes, in the way the anti-empiricist demands, with the rest of relevant practice, as a coherent form of responsiveness to how things are. So in each case, what is thus so on that way of thinking of things is so. There is, on Frege's plausible idea, a significant way in which grammatical facts are a matter of what relevant speakers are *prepared to* recognise—Dutch 'erkennen' (acknowledge), whereas facts about colours or wind velocity are what suitable thinkers are *equipped* to recognise—Dutch 'herkennen' (tell, identify). In each case, that that is so is internal to a particular form of coherent responsiveness to the world.

Objectivity was, for Frege, the root source of (what he called) the laws of truth. Genuine objectivity may be internal to a special-design, non-universal, way of thinking, so as to reign provided that way coheres as described above. That suggests a certain possibility for logic. Perhaps we, for example, enjoy a logical competence conferred by a special psychological design, not necessarily shared by any thinker whatsoever. We are designed, say, to see ourselves (and, perhaps, others) as thinking in terms of certain particular notions of conjunction and disjunction, and to see our thought as organised accordingly. That we think in those specific terms would be part of a special design. For all that, it might be part of the way we thus conceive things that there are facts about those special notions that hold absolutely, that is, depend on nothing, neither on how anyone thinks, nor on how things stand extra-logically. That might be a coherent way of thinking provided it is directed at sufficiently sparse, austere, notions of conjunction, disjunction, or whatever it is of which such facts are to hold absolutely. For, as *per* section 1, absoluteness and austerity must go hand in hand. (And we, at least, do not know how to specify so austerely as to exclude, in principle, any say from the world as to what coherent responsiveness to it might be.) But, if such a way of thinking is responsiveness, then what is so so conceiving things is no less than what is so. So there are absolute facts about those notions of conjunction and disjunction.

That possibility separates several ideas in Frege's thought. One thing Frege wanted for logic was absoluteness. Absoluteness is compatible with special psychological design—though Frege might have regarded it as a cheapened form of absoluteness (given that there is always room for a word from the world as to whether a way of thinking coheres). Another thing Frege wanted was universality: in some sense, the laws of logic should hold for all thinkers. There are several things universality might come to. It might be a matter of how all thinkers must be viewable by us. Or it might be a matter of what all thinkers must be prepared to recognise. In this second case, one might have absoluteness without universality. Frege also had the idea that the laws of truth are the most general laws of thought. The idea of special logical competences threatens to rob that idea of sense. All this, though, just gestures at issues needing much more detailed examination. That task is a separate project.[20]

[20] I have benefited greatly from discussion of these issues with Peter Sullivan and Michael Martin, who have shaped this tract of philosophical reality (without thinking its contents so) perhaps more than they are aware. I would also like to thank the Arts and Humanities Research Board of the United Kingdom for their generous support of this research.

Index

Index